D1327315

WORKPLACE INDUSTRIAL RELATIONS IN TRANSITION

The ED/ESRC/PSI/ACAS Surveys

WORKPLACE INDUSTRIAL RELATIONS IN TRANSITION

The ED/ESRC/PSI/ACAS Surveys

Neil Millward Mark Stevens David Smart W R Hawes

Dartmouth

Aldershot • Brookfield USA • Hong Kong • Singapore • Sydney

321.0942
W92-6

Published by
Dartmouth Publishing Company Limited
Gower House
Croft Road
Aldershot
Hants GU11 3HR
England

Dartmouth Publishing Company
Old Post Road
Brookfield
Vermont 05036
USA

A CIP catalogue record for this book is available from the British Library and the US Library of Congress

ISBN 1 85521 321 4

Printed by Bookcraft Ltd., Bath, England.

Contents

TECHNICAL APPENDIX   367

Foreword

Throughout the 1980s the reform of British industrial relations was high on the agenda of politicians, managers, workers and their trade unions. Vigorous debate took place over what could and should be done, about how best to achieve change and, not least, about the nature, extent and consequences of the developments which were already under way. The Workplace Industrial Relations Survey (WIRS) series was designed to contribute to these continuing debates – and to the better understanding of the processes which underlie employment relationships – by making available for the first time large-scale, systematic and dispassionate evidence about a broad range of industrial relations and employment practices across almost every sector of the economy. The reports on the first two surveys, conducted in 1980 and 1984, were widely welcomed as providing the most comprehensive bank of material on such matters yet available for any developed economy. Not only were the findings much discussed by policy-makers and practitioners within and outside government, but the data were subject to secondary analysis by academic and other researchers in a range of disciplines. The success of the surveys encouraged governments and researchers in other countries to consider the creation of equivalent inquiries. That the venture proved worthwhile cannot be doubted.

This book provides a first report on the third survey in the series. As previously, the 1990 survey was sponsored jointly by the Employment Department, the Economic and Social Research Council, the Policy Studies Institute (with funds from the Leverhulme Trust) and the Advisory, Conciliation and Arbitration Service. As before, each organization brought its particular interests and concerns in the exercise to a joint steering committee which oversaw the project. That committee first met in 1988 under the chairmanship of Peter Brannen, then Chief Research Officer at the Employment Department. He had been closely involved with the development, design and management of the series since its original conception in the late 1970s, and in the intervening years he made a major contribution to its success. In 1989 he moved elsewhere in the Department and the chair of the committee was then taken, first by Vince Keddie and later by me. All four sponsors record their warm appreciation of the imagination, skill and cheerful determination to overcome difficulties which Peter brought to discussions, and which played no small part in developing the spirit of positive cooperation between the sponsors which has characterized their meetings.

The lengthy period needed for the planning and execution of a survey as substantial as WIRS meant that many people took part in the work of the steering committee. For the Employment Department they included Mark Stevens, Neil Millward, David Smart, Mike Lott and Andrew Hardman. For the Policy Studies Institute W. W. Daniel took the lead. For the ESRC responsibilities were taken primarily by Adrian Alsop with A. W. J. Thomson and, later, by Christine McCulloch and Graham Winfield. The ACAS member was W. R. Hawes, who was helped for part of the period by Andrew Scott. I am grateful to them all, both for the important substantive contributions they made to the design and conduct of the survey and for their readiness to see each others' points of view in aid of the greater good.

A key aim of the WIRS series has been to provide evidence on the way industrial relations and employment relations change over time. Initially it was envisaged that this would be done by undertaking a series of cross-sectional surveys based on a central core of questions which would be asked of similar respondents on each occasion. That approach remains a key element in the project design. Following successful experimental work in 1984, however, it was decided to include in the 1990 design an additional large-scale panel element which would provide a substantial body of longitudinal data. It was also decided that interviews should be attempted in an additional sample of very new establishments which were not caught by the basic sampling frame. All this meant that the survey design, always challenging, took on a new and burdensome complexity in 1990. The detailed and difficult work necessary to bring such a design to fruition was undertaken for the steering committee by a research team which included Neil Millward at PSI (on secondment from the Employment Department), Mark Stevens and David Smart at the Employment Department, W. R. Hawes at ACAS and Colin Airey, Nigel Tremlett, Rosemary Hamilton and other colleagues at Social and Community Planning Research. SCPR have been involved as fieldwork contractors for the WIRS series from its beginning. They once again made the fullest contribution to the design, fieldwork and preliminary analysis stages of the survey. The 1990 dataset contains a number of measures of local unemployment levels that were kindly supplied by Mike Coombes and Simon Raybould of the North East Regional Research Laboratory, in association with the Centre for Urban and Regional Development Studies at the University of Newcastle Upon Tyne.

An important feature of the WIRS series has been the determination of the sponsors to provide full and rapid access to its results. The book which follows is a first step in this process. In it four members of the research team offer a preliminary description and analysis of material drawn from the interviews with managers and employee representatives. They write in a personal capacity. What they say on any particular point should not be taken as necessarily representing the views of any of the sponsoring organizations, which publish the volume in the hope and expectation of informing public discussion. This book is to be followed by a second, prepared by W. W. Daniel and Neil Millward, which concentrates on the extent and nature of new developments in the field.

As on previous occasions these books are intended to provide a first word on the results rather than a last. To facilitate more detailed exploration of the survey, the data and accompanying documentation have been made freely available to academic and other researchers through the ESRC's Data Archive at the University of Essex. To assist future analysts a full technical report, by Colin Airey, Nigel Tremlett and Rosemary Hamilton, is available from SCPR. The Employment Department is also publishing on behalf of the sponsors a guide to the questions used in all three surveys, to assist researchers keen to explore changes over time. With the addition of the third survey the WIRS series offers unparalleled opportunities for secondary analysis across a wide range of social science disciplines. The sponsors unite in hoping that they will be taken.

The WIRS venture is undoubtedly costly, but I strongly believe that it is also highly cost-effective. There is every reason to expect this periodic survey to continue and to provide a broad analysis of developments in an area which is forever evolving and changing to meet the requirements and aspirations of both employers and employees.

Zmira Hornstein
Chair, Steering Committee for the Workplace
Industrial Relations Surveys

Acknowledgement

The success of the WIRS series depends very much on the cooperation and support of the managers and worker representatives who participate. The sponsors and research team record their thanks and appreciation to the 4725 individuals who gave freely of their time to be interviewed as part of the 1990 survey.

Notes on Tables Used in the Text

General conventions adopted in tables

§   Unweighted base too low for percentages (see Note A).

( )   Percentages should be treated with caution (see Note B).

..   Data not available (see Note J).

*   Fewer than 0.5 per cent.

—   Zero.

Notes on tables

(A) Unweighted base is fewer than 20 and therefore too low for percentages.

(B) Unweighted base is 20 or more but fewer than 50; percentages should be treated with caution.

(C) Column and row percentages do not always add to 100 owing to the rounding of decimal points.

(D) The proportions in subsidiary categories do not always add to the proportion in a composite category owing to the rounding of decimal points. For example, in 12 per cent of private sector workplaces in 1990 the pay of full-time employees was less than half average earnings; in 6 per cent it was more than twice average earnings; and in 19 per cent it was either below half or twice average earnings.

(E) Column and row percentages sometimes add to more than 100 because more than one answer was possible.

(F) The proportions in subsidiary categories do not always add to the proportion in a composite category because more than one answer was possible. For example, in 73 per cent of cases in 1990 lay union representatives of the same employer, but from various workplaces organized primary picketing; in 67 per cent of cases lay representatives at the picketed workplace organized it; and in 20 per cent of cases it was organized by lay representatives based at other establishments of the same employer.

(G) The base numbers for the individual categories in a variable do not add to the total base number because the necessary information was not provided in a number of cases.

(H) The weighted base numbers for the individual categories in a variable may not add to the total weighted base number owing to the rounding of decimal points.

(J) The data are not available because either the question was not asked, or it was asked of a different respondent, or the question was asked in a sufficiently different form to make strict comparisons difficult.

(K) The base numbers for the individual categories in a variable do not add to the total base number because only an illustrative range of categories was included. For example, in our analysis of trade union organization we use a variable which shows the union to which our worker representative respondents belonged. It includes a column for all representatives but provides more detailed information for only the three or four unions with sufficient numbers of observations among our sample.

The different sources of information
As is the case with the text, where data are presented in tables without the source of the information being identified it will have been provided by the management respondent. Where 1980 data are used and the source is identified as the manual or the non-manual worker representative without any further qualification, it will be the primary worker representative.

Unless otherwise specified the information used for breakdown variables, such as number employed at establishment, size of total organization, industrial sector, ownership and trade union membership density, will be that provided by managers.

1 The Surveys and their Context

Few can doubt that industrial relations in Britain changed during the course of Mrs Thatcher's term as Prime Minister. Brought to power on a wave of public antipathy to the 'winter of discontent' of 1979, industrial relations reform was high on her party's political agenda throughout the 1980s. Most of that programme of reform was highly controversial at the time and some of it remains so. A series of Acts of Parliament through the course of the 1980s, as well as many other actions by the Government, turned that political agenda into a host of changes to the context of the relationships between employers, employees and trade unions. Many other factors influenced those relationships during the course of the decade: changes in the structure of the economy both in Britain and abroad; demographic changes in the British working population; changes in the style and methods of management and in the habits and preferences of employees at work and as consumers. Yet the changes that took place over the period in British industrial relations would be hard to trace in a systematic fashion if it were not for the series of surveys which provide the foundations for this book.

In our report on the Workplace Industrial Relations Survey of 1984[1] we highlighted – and, we hope, demonstrated – the enormous advantages of being able to compare the results of that survey with its predecessor in 1980. Then, for the first time in Britain, we had comprehensive, nationally representative survey data on industrial relations at the place of work at two points in time. Now, with results from a third survey conducted in 1990, we have an unparalleled opportunity to describe and analyse the changes that have taken place over a decade.

However, although the conduct of a third survey in the series may have seemed to some to be an entirely unsurprising event, it was never an inevitable one. The earlier collaboration between the four sponsoring bodies had to be revived to produce the joint commitment and funding for a third survey. It is a measure of the success of the two previous surveys from the point of view of each of the four organizations that the new commitment and funding were forthcoming from all four of them. So it was that the Employment Department, the Economic and Social Research Council, the Policy Studies Institute (with funds from the Leverhulme Trust) and the Advisory, Conciliation and Arbitration Service came to commission Social and Community Planning Research to conduct the 1990 Workplace Industrial Relations Survey (WIRS).

The design of the 1990 survey

Like its predecessors, the 1990 WIRS was a representative national survey of establishments with the respondents being key role-holders in those establishments. Like its predecessors, it contained predominantly factual questions about the formal structures and practices of industrial relations at the sampled workplace. To maximize the potential for comparisons it had to have the same comprehensive coverage of sizes and types of establishment as the earlier surveys. And it had to involve interviews with at least one of the same type of respondent as before. With these fundamental characteristics kept constant there were still many possibilities for variation and choice in the design of the third survey, choices which would impact on the comparability of the results. Below we outline the most important of these to give the reader a basis on which to evaluate the material presented in the chapters that follow. Further details on the design and conduct of the survey are contained in the Technical Appendix.

The sample   ·

With the workplace or establishment firmly fixed as our unit of interest, our sampling frame needed to be as similar as possible to that used for the 1980 and 1984 surveys. On previous occasions the most comprehensive and up-to-date sampling frame of workplaces had been the most recent *Census of Employment* – those for 1977 and 1981 respectively; similarly in late 1989, when we needed to approach employers for interviews for the third survey, the results of the September 1987 *Census of Employment* had just become available. With interviews beginning in late January 1990 this provided us with a frame that was of the same age – roughly two and a half years – as the one used in 1984.

No major changes were made in the scope or design of the sample. As before it was limited to workplaces with 25 or more employees, the decision to include establishments down to this relatively small size having been well justified by previous experience. In fact, the possibility of lowering the threshold to cover even smaller workplaces was seriously discussed, but finally rejected as requiring too many additional resources if other parameters were to be maintained.[2] As before the survey covered England, Wales and Scotland.[3] Its industrial coverage was again all manufacturing and services (Divisions 1 to 9 of the *Standard Industrial Classification*, Revised 1980), in both public and private sectors. The only exclusion from these industries remained the deep coal-mining industry, which had been omitted from the sample issued to interviewers in 1984 because of the widespread stoppage of work in that industry at the time and hence a lack of potentially available respondents. The industrial coverage of the three surveys is thus identical.

The sample was again an unclustered, stratified one with size (number of employees) being the basis of stratification. To enable comparisons between large and small establishments to be made, and to increase the accuracy of estimates of employees covered by particular practices or arrangements, we oversampled large establishments, as before. The sampling fractions used varied from 1 in 90 for the smallest establishments (with 25 to 49 employees) to 1 in 1.8 for the largest (with 1000 or more employees).[4] The essential principle of weighting the data to compensate for the oversampling of larger establishments has been maintained.

Fortuitously, the achieved sample in 1990 was very similar in size to the previous two samples: 2061 cases compared with 2019 in 1984 and 2040 in 1980. The 2061 establishments in the 1990 survey employed a total of 1,143,019 employees, a slightly larger figure than the previous ones. The intention for the 1990 survey had been to achieve about 1870 cases from the sample taken from the 1987 *Census of Employment*, a little lower than on previous occasions. But as in 1984 this target was overshot considerably, again largely because of a higher than anticipated response rate. In fact the response rate in 1990 was 83 per cent, a fine achievement by those concerned and a very solid underpinning to the quality of the survey dataset.

The respondents
The 1990 survey design specified between one and four respondents to be interviewed in each selected workplace: either one or two representatives of management and up to two employee representatives. This was similar to the 1984 survey, the only change being in the role specified for the second management representative.

The senior person at the establishment dealing with industrial relations, employee relations or personnel matters remained our primary management respondent. A completed interview with such a person was, as before, an essential requirement of the survey. However, at some workplaces belonging to larger organizations, especially in the public sector, the role specified to interviewers did not exist or could not be identified. In such cases, the information was sought from people at other levels of the organization, usually an area or headquarters office; in these cases the focus of the interview was still the sampled establishment, not the unit at which the interview was being conducted. The great bulk of interviews, 86 per cent, were with a manager at the sampled address.

The additional management respondent interviewed in 1990 was a financial manager, again a manager with responsibilities for the sampled establishment. This role replaced the production manager used in the 1984 survey to obtain additional information on the introduction of new technology. The 1990 financial manager interviews were added to supplement information obtained from the primary respondent where the primary respondent was clearly in the industrial relations or personnel function, rather than being a general manager. They expanded the range of information obtained on the economic circumstances and performance of larger establishments in industry and commerce. Some 454 such interviews were completed.

Interviews with worker representatives have been an important part of the design of the series since its inception, providing information that added to or complemented the data obtained from management. For the third survey we confined the number of possible worker representative interviews to two, as we had also done in 1984. As before, the circumstances where such interviews were required were based upon data collected during the course of management interviews. In establishments with recognized trade unions for manual workers an interview was sought with the senior shop steward (or similar lay representative) of the negotiating group which represented the largest number of manual workers. Similarly, where non-manual unions or staff associations were recognized, the senior lay representative of the largest non-manual negotiating group was sought for interviews. Such were the bulk of cases where we required and obtained an interview with worker representatives, always with the knowledge and often the help of management. They are directly comparable with those obtained in 1984 and with the great majority of those obtained in 1980. The response rates achieved in 1990 were 78 per cent for manual representatives and 79 per cent for non-manuals – a fraction lower than the comparable figures in the 1984 survey.

An additional set of worker representatives was specified in 1990 in circumstances where there were no recognized trade unions but there was a joint committee of managers and employees' representatives with a broad remit. These circumstances were relatively rare and generated only a few additional interviews (26 manual representatives and 44 non-manual ones), as indeed happened in 1980 when there was also a requirement for interviews with additional worker representatives.[5] The response rates for these interviews in 1990 were 63 per cent for manual and 67 per cent for non-manual representatives.

In total the main sample generated 2550 completed questionnaires for management respondents, including financial manager questionnaires not counted above as they were cases where they were not strictly required, and 1466 worker representatives (752 manual, 714 non-manual). Interviews took place between late January and September 1990, with nearly four fifths concentrated in the four months February to May. The

median interview date in late March was earlier than the median interview date for the 1984 survey by a month and that for the 1980 survey
by two months. Interviews in 1990 typically took about the same amount
of time as they did before, that is about an hour and a half for the main
management interview, three quarters of an hour for worker representatives and half an hour for financial managers.

Interview content and structure
The content of the 1990 questionnaires followed quite closely the lines
of the first two surveys, with one exception. The section of the 1984
questionnaires dealing with the introduction and impact of technical and
organizational change – always envisaged as a special addition to that
survey alone – was omitted except for a very small number of items of
enduring interest. Instead, questioning was added or expanded on two
topics. One was the outcomes and performance of the establishment and
its employee relations practices: questions on absence, labour turnover
and accidents are examples; and the financial manager interview provided the opportunity to expand questions of a financial or economic
nature. The second topic for additional questioning was concerned with
recent innovations in the field of employee relations. Initial findings
from both of these sets of new questions are briefly mentioned in this
book, and a fuller analysis of those concerning new practices is to be
found in our companion volume.[6]

A general impression of the degree of change in questionnaire content between the second and third surveys is given by the fact that about
two thirds of the questions in the 1990 survey were repeated from the
1984 questionnaires. Most of the repeated ones were also used in 1980.
These 'core' questions form the basis for most of the analysis of change
in this book.

For the most part the structure of the questionnaires remained the
same. But in one fundamental area we made an important alteration,
described in detail in Chapter 3. In essence, we abandoned our assumption in the previous two surveys that trade unions at an individual
workplace had either manual or non-manual employees as members, but
not both. This meant a wholesale revision of the sections of the main
management questionnaire dealing with union membership, union recognition and negotiating structures. In most respects the new structure
allows direct comparisons with the earlier surveys, but more elaborate
terminology is sometimes required.

A second structural change was made in order to contain the length
and cost of the main management interview. The longest interviews in
the previous surveys were almost invariably with personnel or industrial
relations specialists in the industrial and commercial sectors. These
were also the circumstances in which we sought the additional financial

manager interview in 1990. Background questions where we felt that either respondent could give a reliable answer were therefore duplicated across the two questionnaires but omitted from the main management interview where a financial manager interview was required. The objectives of the change were achieved in the main, but at some cost in terms of the quality and increased complexity of the data.[7]

Although the establishment or workplace has remained the focus of data collection throughout the series, the design has always catered for variation in many industrial relations practices within establishments. The key distinction between manual and non-manual workers was maintained, although problematic for some respondents, along with the occasional subdivisions of the workforce into male and female and full-time and part-time employees. We also kept to the original notion of negotiating groups or bargaining units, that is, groups of employees with common representational arrangements involving a trade union or group of unions recognized by management for collective bargaining over pay.

Weighting

We mentioned earlier that the design of the 1990 sample, as with earlier surveys, involved the selection of workplaces with different sampling fractions, with larger workplaces having higher probabilities of selection than smaller workplaces. Weighting is required to compensate for this. In broad terms, the weights applied in this report to the raw survey data were those necessary to restore the numbers of cases in each size band to their proper proportions in the population. For convenience the results have again been weighted back to a base of 2000 establishments. A modification to this basic principle, detailed in the Technical Appendix, was also used for the earlier surveys. However, it was only made to the 1980 survey after our report on that survey was published.[8] In consequence, figures for the 1980 survey given in this report (which always uses the modified weighting scheme) may differ slightly from those given in that report. The critical point when using the results from the three surveys to monitor change is to use weighting schemes that are strictly comparable. This we have done.

Accuracy of the results

The results of the 1990 survey, as with all surveys, are subject to sampling errors, reflecting the possibility that the various measures such as proportions and averages computed from the sample may not correspond to those of the population from which the sample was drawn. Because of the disproportionate sampling of large establishments, the sampling errors in all three surveys were generally greater than would have been the case if simple random sampling had been used. We

Table 1.1 Sample errors for estimates derived from each of the three surveys and for differences between the three surveys

	Percentage found by survey			
	10 or 90	20 or 80	30 or 70	50
Confidence limit for single estimate (per cent)	1.6	2.3	2.5	2.8
	Difference in percentages between the three surveys (for whichever percentage is the more extreme)			
	10 or 90	20 or 80	30 or 70	50
Confidence limit for the difference (per cent)	2.3	3.0	3.5	3.8

estimate that the design had the effect of increasing sampling errors by about 25 per cent in each survey. Given the virtually identical sample sizes, the sampling errors for the three surveys are for practical purposes the same. Sampling errors can be converted into confidence limits. In Table 1.1 we give the approximate 95 per cent confidence limits attached to a selection of proportions for each survey. These are the confidence limits attached to a single estimate for any of the three surveys taken on their own. The sampling errors attached to measures of change between two surveys have to encompass the sampling error attached to both surveys and are therefore computed differently. These are shown in the second half of the table.

The interpretation of sampling error for these two alternative conditions can be illustrated as follows. If a particular characteristic was found among 30 per cent of the sample in the 1990 survey sample (or, indeed, the 1980 or 1984 sample) the confidence limit would be, from the table, 2.5 per cent. We could therefore be 95 per cent certain that the true proportion in the whole population was within the range 27.5 per cent to 32.5 per cent. Suppose this characteristic showed a change from 24 per cent in 1984 to 29 per cent in 1990. Using the more extreme of the two figures, the 24 per cent, and taking the nearest column in the table we would have a confidence limit for the difference of 3.0 per cent. Thus we could be 95 per cent confident that our change between the two surveys of some 5 per cent was not due to sampling error but represented a real change in the population over the period between the two surveys of somewhere between 2 per cent and 8 per cent. Naturally, measures of characteristics of subsamples – and of change from a subsample in 1984 to the same subsample in 1990 – are subject to greater sampling errors. We have taken this into account when reporting changes in the body of this report. Sampling error is, however, only one of the possible sources of error in survey research. Measurement error can arise from imprecision in the questions asked, misinterpretation of instructions by interviewers and of the questions by respondents, coding errors by interviewers or coders and many other sources. Fortunately, these largely unquantifiable sources of error can be discounted when the interest is in aggregate change between two surveys of nearly identical design and with standardized administration in the field. The use of the same research organization, Social and Community Planning Research, to carry out the three surveys, as well as continuity within the research team, undoubtedly helped to minimize the introduction of new and unquantifiable sources of error at the fieldwork and data processing stages of the work.

The choice of respondents for the analysis
Multiple-respondent surveys, as all the Workplace Industrial Relations Surveys have been, widen the possibilities for analysis because they allow a wider range of questioning and because some of the questions may be asked of more than one respondent. In the 1984 survey something less than two fifths of the questions were put to both our main management respondent and to worker representatives. In 1990 this proportion was a little lower. A few questions were also asked of both the main management respondent and the financial manager. In such cases the answers from the two sets of respondents can be compared as a check on the reliability of the information obtained, provided the question is a factual one, as most of them were. Our practice in this book, as in the earlier ones, has been to confine ourselves to a single account of the topic in question, usually that of the management respondent. This is largely because we have a primary management respondent for every case in the survey, whereas we only have worker representatives or financial managers for a sub-sample. Generally we have satisfied ourselves that the two sets of responses have a similar distribution (among establishments where additional respondents were interviewed) before doing this. Where the distributions were different we have generally pointed them out, especially if the patterns in relation to other variables were different. Exceptionally, as in Chapter 8, we have combined information from the two sets of respondents to give what we consider to be a more reliable measure of the phenomenon in question.[9]

The 1984–1990 trading sector panel sample
All that we have said so far about the design and conduct of the 1990 survey has been concerned with the main, cross-sectional sample. In fact, an additional feature of the project in 1990 was the inclusion of a separate 'panel' sample, drawn from establishments where interviews had been carried out in 1984. A similar feature was tried out in 1984 on a small scale and felt to have been generally successful. However, the small number of observations had greatly limited its use.

The scope of the 1984–1990 panel sample was restricted to industrial and commercial establishments, the 'trading sector', because it was here that most of the interest among potential analysts of the data was concentrated. The target sample size was 375 to 400 cases. As with the main sample, this was exceeded, largely because of a higher than anticipated response rate. The number of productive cases was 537; the response rate was 87 per cent.

In most respects panel cases were treated in exactly the same way as those that formed part of the main, cross-sectional sample. The questionnaires were identical and so were most of the interviewers' instructions. However, no interviews with worker representatives were conducted for the panel sample because the bargaining unit selected under the 1990 rules for identifying respondents could well have been different from the one similarly selected and interviewed about in 1984.[10] Another variation was that interviewers were given a very brief summary of the 1984 survey data for the sampled address to help them identify the correct establishment. This also helped achieve a good response.

As with the main sample, data from the panel sample have to be weighted to make them representative of the population from which they were drawn. Details of how this was done are contained in the Technical Appendix. All panel results given in this volume use weighted data.

In common with most panel studies, the WIRS panel results generally show a degree of volatility which is sometimes surprising when compared with the apparent stability shown by comparing the cross-sectional results from the same two points in time. It would be a mistake to conclude from this that the panel results necessarily contain more measurement error than the cross-sectional results. The amount of movement over time is hidden in the cross-sectional comparisons, which only show the net result of changes in both directions; but the amount of change is explicit in the panel results. Using the two types of analysis to examine changes in key variables can lead to difficulties in interpretation, but it more usually reduces the number of plausible explanations for a given change.

The 1990 sample of 'new workplaces'

Our final elaboration of the survey design in 1990 was to add a sample of 'new workplaces'. The purpose of this was to remedy the inevitable age of the main, cross-sectional sample, which was drawn from a sampling frame which was about two and a half years out of date at the time of interviewing. The supplementary sample of 'new workplaces' aimed to identify establishments that came into being, or grew from below our threshold of 25 employees to at least that size, between September 1987 and early 1990. A total of 84 establishments formed the achieved sample, considerably fewer than had been intended. The results of the 'new workplaces' sample and results based upon it are reported in our companion volume,[11] where they add a further dimension to the picture of change described in this book.

The context of change

The context of British industrial relations altered radically over the decade covered by our surveys and many contextual changes are relevant to interpreting our survey results. The continuous period of Conservative government from 1979 to the present brought numerous important alterations to the legislative framework surrounding workplace industrial relations. Our first survey was carried out prior to the first move in the Government's 'step-by-step approach' to industrial relations reform, the Employment Act 1980; our second survey was conducted after the second step, the Employment Act 1982, had been in place for some time. The third step, the Trade Union Act 1984, was enacted towards the end of our 1984 interview programme, but most of its provisions came into force well after completion of the survey. The Employment Act 1988 fell clearly between our second and third surveys, while the Employment Act 1990 came into force after the end of our 1990 survey interviewing. In essence, then, the 1980 and 1982 Acts were the ones of relevance to our study of industrial relations change over the period mid-1980 to mid-1984; the 1984 and 1988 Acts are most immediately relevant to changes between our second and third surveys. The Acts covered a wide range of matters, including: trade union recognition; trade union membership and non-membership rights; unfair dismissal; liability for organizing industrial action; and methods for electing trade union leaders.[12] Other matters were also the subject of statutory codes of practice, including: the closed shop; picketing; and union industrial action ballots. On all of these (except the methods of electing union leaders) our surveys have directly relevant information. On some of them the connection between our evidence and the legal changes that were made is fairly direct; on others the connection is a tenuous one. In any event, the legal changes were amongst many other influences that bore upon the matters in question and the attribution of a direct causal connection between the legislation and any specific change in industrial relations behaviour, practices or structures is difficult. We mention the possibility of such connections, where appropriate, in the substantive chapters that follow.

While the 1980s were a period of political continuity in Britain the decade also saw the emergence of the European Community as a political force on the employment and industrial relations front. The potential of the Community as a champion of workers' rights was highlighted for British trade unions at the Trades Union Congress in 1988 in a speech by the EC President. Subsequently, in December 1989, all member states of the Community except the UK signed the *Community Charter of Fundamental Social Rights of Workers*. The European Commission's associated Action Programme contained a broad range of initiatives to implement the principles of the Charter. Some of these soon became incorporated into statute law – such as further underpinning to the right to belong to a trade union. Others were the subject of longstanding opposition by the UK Government, culminating in the deletion of the draft Social Chapter from the Treaty of Maastricht in December 1991. Lively public debate on the issues of employment and related rights continues. Again, our survey findings have a bearing on many of the issues in that debate, notably on provisions for informing and consulting employees, which are the focus of Chapter 5.

The economic context
A second critical part of the context for our analysis of industrial relations change is the developing economic situation. In broad terms the 1980s started off with a severe recession, particularly in manufacturing, and then witnessed a period of continuous growth, rapid in 1987 to 1989, until another downturn began in 1990. Between 1980 and 1984 real gross domestic product (GDP) rose by 5 per cent and real manufacturing output fell by 2 per cent. Subsequently, between 1984 and 1990 real GDP rose by 23 per cent and manufacturing output grew by 25 per cent.[13]

The short-term trends at the time of our three surveys were thus at different points in the economic cycle, although the 1980 and 1990 surveys were somewhat alike in this respect. At the time of our 1980 survey GDP had fallen in the previous year by nearly 3 per cent and manufacturing output had fallen by 9 per cent. In 1984 GDP was rising at the rate of 2 per cent per annum and manufacturing output at 4 per cent. In 1990 the recent trend in GDP was still upwards by around 2 per cent, while manufacturing output was only 1 per cent higher than a year earlier and subsequently the trend was downward.

Other important aspects of the changing nature of the British economy are not captured by official statistics, but can be illuminated by back-

Table 1.2   The economic environment of trading establishments, 1984 and
1990

| | Manufacturing | | Services | |
	1984	1990	1984	1990
Market for main product			*Column percentages*	
Local	6	10	45	54
Regional	18	10	18	19
National	47	53	26	20
International	29	27	12	7
Number of competitors			*Column percentages*	
None	5	6	14	10
1–5	46	41	30	26
More than 5	49	54	56	64
Price sensitivity			*Column percentages*	
Insensitive	39	43	57	61
Moderate	12	5	9	6
Sensitive	49	53	34	34

Base: industrial and commercial establishments producing products or services
and reporting on the respective questions

| *Unweighted* | *421* | *445* | *482* | *611* |
| *Weighted* | *298* | *338* | *648* | *820* |

ground questions in our 1984 and 1990 surveys. (Comparable questions
were generally not included in 1980.) The findings from these questions
show considerable stability but some detectable changes in the nature of
product markets and the degree of competition, as seen by our management respondents. Table 1.2 gives the results.

In broad terms the markets served by our national sample of industrial and commercial establishments remained much as they were.
Manufacturing plants continued to supply products mostly to national or
international markets, with a slight shift away from the latter. There was
certainly no detectable movement towards international markets, as might
have been anticipated. Service sector establishments continued to supply mostly local and regional markets, with the former clearly predominant. Here there was a clear shift towards a more localized economy:
the proportion of service sector establishments supplying local or regional
markets increased from 63 per cent in 1984 to 73 per cent in 1990.
Again, the move away from national and particularly international markets in services is perhaps surprising.

More establishments faced highly competitive markets in 1990 than
did so in 1984. In manufacturing the change was slight: the proportion

whose sole or main product market had more than five competitors rose from 49 to 54 per cent. But in the service sector there was a clear increase, from 56 to 64 per cent. Despite this, our other indicator of competitive pressure, the sensitivity of demand to price increases, moved (if at all) in the opposite direction. In both manufacturing and services rather more managers reported that their products would not suffer a decline in demand if the price were unilaterally increased.

Perhaps the most dramatic change in British workplaces over the ten years covered by our surveys was in the use of computers and other micro-electronics technology. The rapid diffusion of micro-electronics in manufacturing industry in the early part of the decade was documented by a series of surveys carried out at two-yearly intervals until 1987.[14] But manufacturing hardly had a monopoly of micro-electronics applications and their extent in 1984 across the whole of the economy was revealed from analysis of our module of questions in the second survey on the implications of adopting the new technology.[15] By repeating some of those questions in the 1990 survey, a clear measure of the continuing diffusion of the technology across all sectors of the British economy became available. Table 1.3 gives 1984 and 1990 results for different sizes of workplace, since the earlier work on manufacturing industry had demonstrated that the adoption of micro-electronics technology tended to begin with the largest plants and percolate down to smaller ones as time progressed. A similar process appears to have been at work in the economy as a whole.

Taking all types of computing facilities together, three quarters of workplaces had on-site facilities in 1990 compared with less than half of workplaces (47 per cent) in 1984. The smallest workplaces had the fastest rate of adoption (the proportion rising from 40 per cent to 70 per cent), whereas almost all of the largest workplaces already had on-site facilities in 1984 and by 1990 achieved virtual saturation. Almost all sectors of industry and types of workplace were affected by the diffusion of on-site computing facilities: public and private sectors; manufacturing and services; and each of the broad divisions of industry. The one type that proved an exception was the nationalized industries where the proportion of establishments with on-site facilities remained low and close to its 1984 level of about one third. The incidence of computing facilities in 1990 in 11 separate sectors of manufacturing and 15 service sectors is shown in Table 1A at the end of the chapter.[16]

Besides the increasing use of any on-site computing facilities, Table 1.3 also makes clear that each of the types of facility was subject to substantial increase. Micro or personal computers were particularly likely to have been introduced between 1984 and 1990. In the largest workplaces they were clearly in addition to other more substantial computers, so the diffusion of the technology was continuing within establishments to

Table 1.3   Computing facilities by size of establishment, 1984 and 1990

Percentages

	All establishments		Number of employees at establishments							
			25–99		100–499		500–999		1000 or more	
	1984	1990	1984	1990	1984	1990	1984	1990	1984	1990
Types of computing facilities in use:										
On-site facilities:										
Main-frame computer	9	18	5	13	18	34	36	37	54	62
Mini computer	23	39	19	33	34	60	54	69	72	80
Isolated micro-computer(s)	27	59	22	54	40	76	61	83	74	95
Networked micro-computers		29		22		49		62		73
Computer linked to employee working at home	..	4	..	3	..	8	..	12	..	20
Any on-site facilities	**47**	**75**	**40**	**70**	**64**	**90**	**82**	**90**	**93**	**98**
Off-site facilities:										
Link to computer elsewhere in same organization[1]	26	50	20	44	40	67	54	77	69	87
Link to computer in another organization	6	15	5	12	9	22	20	27	22	42
Any computing facilities	**61**	**84**	**54**	**81**	**82**	**95**	**93**	**93**	**98**	**99**
Base: establishments employing non-manual employees										
Unweighted	*2010*	*2058*	*709*	*701*	*721*	*717*	*295*	*262*	*285*	*378*
Weighted	*1985*	*1992*	*1520*	*1552*	*403*	*388*	*40*	*34*	*23*	*17*

[1] Base excludes single independent establishments.

new applications and new groups of employees. Local networks of micro-computers – virtually unheard of at the start of the decade – had become commonplace in larger workplaces by 1990. Taking on-site and off-site facilities together, 84 per cent of all workplaces had some computing facilities in 1990 compared with only 61 per cent in 1984.

An obvious implication of this rapid adoption of micro-electronics technology is that very many managers, employees and their representatives must have been affected by, if not involved in, the introduction of changes. This applies not only to products incorporating the technology, but more particularly to processes, work practices and job content. The technical changes involving micro-electronics technology were much more common in relation to white-collar workers than to manual workers in 1984 and this difference persisted in 1990 (see Table 1.4). Such changes formed the vast majority of technical changes affecting white-collar workers and accounted for over a half of technical changes affecting manual workers. The rate of change – measured by the proportion of establishments that had experienced any change of that type in the previous three years – was at least as high in 1990 as in 1984. In relation to white-collar employees it may even have increased. [17]

Other substantial changes – not involving new equipment or machinery – were also common and probably more so in 1990 than in 1984. The proportion of workplaces experiencing substantial changes in work organization or working practices affecting manual workers during the

Table 1.4   Technical and organizational change affecting a) manual workers and b) non-manual workers, 1984 and 1990

Percentages

	Manual employees		Non-manual employees	
	1984	1990	1984[1]	1990
Proportion of workplaces experiencing in the previous three years:				
Technical change	37	40	57	55
Technical change involving micro-electronics	22	23	49	52
Organizational change	23	29	20	41
Technical or organizational change	**47**	**53**	**63**	**67**

Base: establishments with 25 or more of the specified type of employee

Unweighted	*1423*	*1401*	*1547*	*1581*
Weighted	*985*	*954*	*1012*	*1004*

[1] In 1984 the questions were about changes affecting 'office workers'; in 1990 they covered any non-manual employees.

previous three years increased from 23 per cent in 1984 to 29 per cent in 1990. Regarding non-manual workers our question was broadened from covering only 'office workers' in 1984 to all non-manual employees in 1990. Some of the increase from 20 to 41 per cent shown in the table must be attributable to this, but it is unlikely that all of it was. And as we know from a subsequent question that technical changes almost invariably affected office workers (defined as clerical, administrative, secretarial and typing staff), it seems unlikely that this was generally not the case with other types of change. Thus while the size of the increase in the extent of organizational change is uncertain, there can be little doubt that both organizational and technical change were at least as common in the period 1987 to 1990 as they had been in the period up to 1984. The opportunities for cooperation and the potential for conflict between managers and employees arising from technological and organizational change remained substantial.

The labour market context

There were also major changes in employment. In the economy as a whole, the number of employees in Great Britain fell from 22.5 million to 20.7 million between June 1980 and June 1984, a drop of some 8 per cent. By June 1990 the total, 22.3 million, was virtually back to its 1980 level. Some of the change in numbers of employees reflected a shift to self-employment. Those in self-employment rose steadily from 2 million in June 1980 to 3.2 million in June 1990. Unemployment levels varied markedly over the period, rising from 1980 to 1986 and falling to a low point in early 1990. In fact our first survey was conducted as unemployment was beginning to increase rapidly, although the fastest rate of increase was experienced later in 1980. In 1984 our survey was carried out during a time of unusually high unemployment, but the rate of increase was modest by then. Subsequently, unemployment fell rapidly throughout 1987 and 1988 and had levelled off by the end of 1989. Our third survey was conducted at the low point of the curve, with the return to increasing unemployment only becoming apparent as our fieldwork was being completed.[18]

Despite the fact that our surveys do not cover the whole of the economy, the numbers of employees to which our samples relate broadly reflect the movements in overall employment levels. The population of workers covered by the WIRS series fell from 16.3 million in 1980 to 14.9 million in 1984 and increased to 15.6 million by 1990.[19] The drop between 1980 and 1990 is largely due to the decline in the proportion of employees working in the larger establishments (25 or more employees) covered by WIRS. But there was also a move towards smaller establishments within the WIRS population. The mean size of workplaces in our sample was 118 employees in 1980, 109 in 1984 and 102 in 1990.

The decade saw a substantial shift in employment away from manufacturing industry, as indeed was also apparent in other advanced economies. For Great Britain as a whole, manufacturing's share of employment fell from 31 per cent in mid-1980 to 26 per cent in mid-1984 and to 23 per cent in mid-1990. The WIRS sample figures were 40 per cent, 29 per cent and 27 per cent respectively. Between 1980 and 1984 the proportion of workplaces in the WIRS sample that were in manufacturing industry fell from 25 to 21 per cent; in 1990 it was still 21 per cent. The period between the first two surveys saw a substantial net loss of manufacturing facilities – the 'shake-out' of the early 1980s recession; the 1984 to 1990 period saw no such loss, but a continuation of the trend towards smaller workplaces. The mean size of manufacturing establishments in WIRS was 185 employees in 1980, 147 in 1984 and 128 in 1990. Table 1A shows the variation in the mean size of establishments by industry in 1990.

In contrast, service industries, by which we mean all non-manufacturing except Agriculture, Forestry and Fishing, grew between 1984 and 1990 by 12 per cent in terms of employees, after a small contraction between 1980 and 1984. Again the WIRS sample figures mirror these changes closely, although some of the growth in the late 1980s was in small establishments below the WIRS threshold of 25 employees.

The decade saw a marked move away from public ownership,[20] largely through privatisation but also latterly through the contracting out of services by public bodies. Employment in state-owned industrial and commercial enterprises (nationalized industries and public corporations) in the WIRS sample fell from 1.3 million in 1980 to 0.8 million in 1990, most of this decline being since 1984. Indeed, nationalized industries had shrunk sufficiently by 1990 to preclude their separate analysis for most purposes because there were so few establishments left in the category. The effects of privatization upon our analysis do not end there. The private sector in 1990 had been expanded substantially by the addition of formerly state-owned enterprises, a fact that must be borne in mind when we compare the private sector in 1990 with the same sector in previous surveys.

Within the industrial and commercial sector the increasing degree of foreign ownership was also apparent. Foreign-owned workplaces grew from 7 per cent of our sample in 1980 to 9 per cent in 1990; their share of employment also grew, but less markedly. The growth of small firms over the decade was not, however, reflected in our sample. Independent workplaces in the trading sector – a close approximation to small firms – remained at 28 per cent of our trading sector sample. Presumably the growth of small firms was concentrated in the smallest ones below our sample threshold of 25 employees.

General trends in the composition of the employed workforce through the 1980s were clearly reflected in our data. Manual employees constituted a smaller proportion of the workforce in 1990 than they did in 1980 (46 per cent, compared with 53 per cent previously). There was, however, no detectable movement in the proportion of manual workers that were regarded as skilled. This was 28 per cent in both 1980 and 1990. (The 1984 figure was 29 per cent, but this difference was not statistically significant.) Sociologists who have argued that there has been substantial 'de-skilling' in the 1980s and those who have maintained that there has been substantial 'up-skilling' (due to technical and other changes) have both been half right, it seems.[21] No doubt this overall picture of stability hides significant changes (in either direction) within individual workplaces.

The shift towards white-collar occupations was greatest in manufacturing, but was not confined to that sector. And part of the shift was attributable to the relative growth within the services sector of industries employing almost entirely white-collar workers – financial and business services are the exemplar of this. Among white-collar occupations it is hard to measure an equivalent to the manual skilled/unskilled mix, given the rather broad categories that we asked about. But if we take senior professional or technical staff, together with middle or senior managers, as a proportion of all non-manual employees we have a rough equivalent. This proportion rose slightly from 30 per cent in 1980 to 32 per cent in 1990, suggesting a modest increase in the employment of higher non-manual occupations.[22]

There was in the 1980s a further substantial growth in part-time employment, mainly among women. Overall, 14 per cent of employees in our 1980 survey were part-time, whereas 18 per cent were in this category in our 1990 survey. This growth occurred through two distinct routes. One was the use of increasing proportions of part-time workers and was most apparent in the public sector. The other was through growth in the numbers of workplaces in the private services sector, while the proportion of employees working part-time remained at the same, relatively high, level. The growth of part-time employment – and indeed the other changes in workforce composition mentioned above – are often implicated in our analysis in the chapters that follow.

More generally we hope that the above discussion has demonstrated two points. First, the data from our surveys that bear upon the economic and labour market context of British workplaces tally well with those from familiar statistical sources. Secondly, our survey questions on these contextual matters have worked well. They provide a rich source of explanatory variables for analysis of the industrial relations structures and practices – and changes in them – that are the focus of interest in this volume.

The nature and contents of the book

Readers of our earlier volumes will be familiar with the largely descriptive analysis that we have reported in our initial overviews of the WIRS data. The desirability of being able to compare the most recent results with those from the two previous surveys has imposed a consistency of treatment for which we make no apology. Comparisons over time have been our primary concern and these can be simply presented in tabular form. We have undertaken a certain amount of analysis of what lies behind the overall changes and continuities that we have reported, but the extent of such analysis has been severely constrained by the time available, the length of this volume and the objective of reporting as comprehensively as possible on the enormous quantity of information that the three surveys contain. We know we have only dipped our toes into the large pool of potential findings about British industrial relations that the surveys make possible and, for lack of time and space, our references to other research and relevant literature are necessarily sparse. Nevertheless, we hope the findings reported here will not only provide a context and an incentive for further investigation by others, but also provide a valuable overview of the changes and continuities in industrial relations over the ten years covered by the series so far.

In structure as well as style this book is similar to its predecessors. In Chapter 2 we examine data from the three surveys on how management at establishment and higher organizational levels organized themselves for industrial relations purposes and on the qualifications and experience of those most closely involved. Chapter 3 covers the formal structures through which employees were represented in their dealings with management: it describes various features of trade union membership and representation, particularly where trade unions were recognized by management, with a final section on the closed shop. Chapter 4 goes into more detail on trade union representatives and their own organization at workplace and branch level. Chapter 5 deals with formal methods of communication and consultation irrespective of the presence of trade unions. Industrial relations procedures form the focus of Chapter 6. Chapter 7 deals with the structures, processes and outcomes of pay determination and payment systems as well as the scope of collective bargaining with trade unions. Chapter 8 deals with industrial action. Finally, in Chapter 9 we analyse data from a number of questions, including several new ones, on employment practices. Each of the substantive chapters, Chapter 2 to Chapter 9, ends with a general synopsis. Our concluding chapter takes a different approach, drawing together material from the earlier chapters to address more general themes.

As in the previous book, tables and text use information supplied by our primary management respondents unless otherwise specified. We have introduced the presentation of our results from questions used in the interview schedules either by direct quotation of the question or by incorporation of the gist of the question in the text, usually the latter. We have not, however, reproduced the interview schedules either in their entirety or in part. This is due to lack of space: the interview schedules from the 1990 survey alone amounted to some 141 pages. Instead, a fully referenced guide to all the data items in the three surveys is being published separately.[23] Copies of the three sets of questionnaires, as well as the data from the three surveys, are available at cost from the ESRC Data Archive at the University of Essex.[24]

Notes and references

1.   N. Millward and M. Stevens (1986) *British Workplace Industrial Relations 1980– 1984: The DE/ESRC/PSI/ACAS Surveys*, Gower, Aldershot.

2.   A supplementary telephone survey of very small establishments (down to five employees) was used successfully in the Australian Workplace Industrial Relations Survey of 1989–90 and could well be reconsidered for the next survey in the British series. (See R. Callus A. Moorehead M. Cully and J. Buchanan, *Industrial Relations at Work: the Australian Workplace Industrial Relations Survey*, Australian Government Publishing Service, Canberra.)

3.   A separate survey with some similarities to WIRS was conducted in Northern Ireland in 1987 and is reported in B. Tipping and P. McCorry (1988) *Industrial Relations in Northern Ireland: The LRA Survey*, Labour Relations Agency: Belfast.

4.   These are the effective sampling fractions for the bulk of the main sample. Certain industries, specified in the Technical Appendix, were undersampled by a factor of a quarter.

5.   The secondary worker representatives in the 1980 survey were selected on a different basis from those selected in 1990. See W. W. Daniel and N. Millward (1983) *Workplace Industrial Relations in Britain: The DE/PSI/ESRC Survey*, Gower, Aldershot, pp. 6–9.

6.   W. W. Daniel, and N. Millward (forthcoming 1993) *The New Industrial Relations?*, Policy Studies Institute, London.

7.   This change was made between the pilot and main stage surveys and so the revised questionnaires were not themselves piloted. In designing the final questionnaires three questions that should have been duplicated across both management questionnaires were omitted from the financial manager questionnaire in error. The three questions concerned the organization or enterprise's total UK employment, any changes in ownership during the previous three years and the ratio of labour costs to total costs. The first of these was considered the most serious and was partially remedied by imputing data from published directories or from other establishments in the same organization. Despite this there remains a regrettably high number of missing values for the question.

8.   W. W. Daniel and N. Millward (1983) op. cit.

9.   A new complication arose from our duplicated questioning across the main management and financial manager questionnaires, plus the decision to retain financial manager interviews even if they were not strictly required. In such cases, of which there were 35, we had to ignore one set of respondents when producing a combined variable for all establishments. This we did after considerable analysis of the patterns of response and non-response and forming a judgement about which type of respondent gave the better data. Sometimes it was the main respondent, sometimes the financial manager, depending on the type of question.

10. There was a small amount of overlap between the panel sample and the cross-sectional sample. Duplicate cases, of which 48 were productive, were treated as main sample cases for the purposes of interviewing so that appropriate worker representative interviews would be included.

11. W. W. Daniel and N. Millward (1993) op. cit.

12. The legal changes are summarized in R. Lewis (1991) 'Reforming industrial relations: law, politics and power', *Oxford Review of Economic Policy*, **17**, 1, pp. 60–75.

13. Economic statistics given in this and subsequent paragraphs are taken from *Economic Trends*, HMSO, London. Figures for 1980, 1984 and 1990 are for the second quarter of each year; figures for recent trends are for the change over the twelve months preceding June of each year. All are adjusted for inflation.

14. J. Northcott with A. Walling (1988) *The Impact of Microelectronics*, Policy Studies Institute, London.

15. W. W. Daniel (1987) *Workplace Industrial Relations and Technical Change*, Frances Pinter (Publishers) and the Policy Studies Institute, London.

16. Summary tables of this sort also appear at the end of most chapters. In addition, further tables of the main 1990 survey variables, classified by a number of standard breakdowns, will be included in the companion volume.

17. The implications of this are to be investigated as part of a separate analysis of the 1990 questions on technical change in a chapter in J. Clark (ed.) (forthcoming 1993) *Personnel Management and Technical Change*.

18. The 1990 dataset contains a number of measures of local unemployment levels, derived from NOMIS (at the University of Durham) by Mike Coombes and Simon Raybould of the North East Regional Research Laboratory (NERRL), in association with the Programme on Information and Communication Technologies (PICT) project sponsored by ESRC, at the Centre for Urban and Regional Development Studies (CURDS) in the University of Newcastle Upon Tyne.

19. The figure for 1990 is a projection based on the 1987 *Census of Employment*. (See Technical Appendix for further details.)

20. The proportion of establishments that were in the public sector and the proportion that were independent (not part of a larger organization) in 1990 are shown for 26 industrial sectors in Table 1A.

21. See, for example, S. Wood (ed.) (1989) *The Transformation of Work? Skill, Flexibility and the Labour Process*, Allen and Unwin, London; R. D. Penn (1990) *Class, Power and Ideology: Skilled Workers in Britain and America*, Polity Press, Oxford.

22. Comparisons between the 1981 and 1990 Labour Force Surveys show an increase of similar magnitude in the proportion of non-manual workers classified as 'managerial and professional'.

23. D. Smart and M. Stevens (1992) *A Guide to Questions in the Workplace Industrial Relations Surveys*, Employment Department, London.

24. Enquiries should be made to The Director, ESRC Data Archive, University of Essex, Wivenhoe Park, Colchester, Essex CO4 3SQ quoting Study Nos. 1575 for the 1980 survey, 2060 for the 1984 survey and 2858 for the 1990 survey.

Table 1A   **Mean establishment size and proportion of establishments a) independent, b) in the public sector and c) with any computing facilities, by industry, 1990**

	Mean size (employees)	Percentages			Unweighted base	Weighted base
		Inde-pendent	Public Sector	Any computing facilities		
All industries	**102**	**21**	**30**	**84**	*2061*	*2000*
All manufacturing	**128**	**37**	*	**91**	*637*	*427*
Metals & Mineral Products (21–24)[1]	115	20	—	96	*52*	*36*
Chemicals & Manufactured Fibres (25–26)	(192)[2]	(38)	(—)	(100)	*48*	*20*
Metal Goods (31)	(94)	(55)	(—)	(94)	*30*	*30*
Mechanical Engineering (32)	111	41	—	95	*83*	*64*
Electrical & Instrument Engineering (33–34,37)	156	22	—	100	*106*	*50*
Vehicles & Transport Equipment (35–36)	237	35	4	70	*65*	*23*
Food, Drink & Tobacco (41–42)	180	39	*	94	*72*	*31*
Textiles (43)	(113)	(46)	(—)	(92)	*21*	*16*
Leather, Footwear & Clothing (44–45)	(104)	(46)	(—)	(75)	*38*	*38*
Timber & Furniture, Paper & Printing (46–47)	102	42	*	94	*85*	*84*
Rubber, Plastics & Other Manufacturing (48–49)	(106)	(31)	(*)	(90)	*37*	*34*

Table 1A continued

All services	95	16	38	83	1424	1573
Energy & Water (11–17)	192	3	14	100	53	21
Construction (50)	89	51	16	79	72	90
Wholesale Distribution (61–63)	70	18	—	96	79	115
Retail Distribution (64–65)	84	14	—	90	160	183
Hotels, Catering, Repairs (66–67)	59	21	*	71	71	122
Transport (71–77)	99	32	20	80	84	75
Posts and Telecommunications (79)	123	—	58	59	71	52
Banking, Finance, Insurance (81–82)	81	1	*	100	100	115
Business Services (83–85)	78	29	6	91	104	144
Central Government (9111, 915)	140	1	100	83	62	51
Local Government (9112, 912–914,919)	152	1	100	93	104	96
Higher Education (931)	(444)	(40)	(62)	(100)	27	9
Other Education (932–936)	61	8	87	92	121	251
Medical Services (95)	237	27	52	68	149	64
Other Services (92,94,96–99)	88	17	64	55	167	186

Base: all establishments

[1] Industry codes from the *Standard Industrial Classification* (SIC).
[2] See Note B.

2 Management Organization for Industrial Relations

We begin our account by looking at the way managers organized themselves to deal with industrial relations. It has long been established that management structures play an important role in determining the presence and form which trade unions and other worker representative bodies and structures take. If there had been changes in patterns of trade union recognition, the internal organization of trade unions and in the coverage and functions of collective bargaining we expected these to have arisen in part because of changes in management organization.

The second half of the 1980s saw a growing debate in Britain about the role and functions of specialist personnel and industrial relations managers and specialist personnel departments. Two competing strands were to be observed as we designed our survey.[1] One suggested that new demands on employers might be encouraging them to rely less on generalist managers who dealt with employee relations as only one of a wide range of responsibilities, and more on specialist, highly trained personnel managers. A corollary was that within personnel management itself a greater degree of specialization might be becoming evident. It was argued, for example, that the growing complexity of statutory employment law was placing new burdens on employers, particularly those with large workforces, and was bringing with it demands for greater consistency in personnel procedures and practice. The consequence was said to be a growing demand for personnel managers with expert knowledge of the law. It was also said that new competitive pressures were leading employers to take greater care in recruitment and selection procedures, bringing demands for specialists in these areas. Growing debate about the design and reform of payment systems, with moves in many sectors away from centralized to more local arrangements for pay determination, was thought to be leading to a greater demand for specialist managers skilled in the arts of negotiation and consultation about pay. Further emphasis was being placed on training, again leading to new demands for specialists in this area. All these changes, it was suggested, were leading organizations to demand more sophisticated personnel and record-keeping systems, with consequences for the employment of yet further specialists. If these developments were real they could be expected to encourage a greater specialization in the personnel and industrial relations function leading, perhaps, to a growth in the numbers of professional personnel managers and, possibly, an increase in the influence they could wield.

At the same time other factors were suggesting that a contrary process might be at work. We noted in our introductory chapter the tendency across much of the economy during the second half of the 1980s for establishment size, measured in terms of the number of people employed, to fall. Smaller establishments might be expected to need smaller and different management teams from larger ones, including fewer specialist personnel staff. There were suggestions too that the focus of personnel work might be changing, away from a concentration on collective bargaining and the control and containment of adversarial relationships between managers and managed, towards the generation of greater employee commitment to the broader commercial and other aims of businesses. Much of this discussion about a new human resource management suggested the desirability of unifying management structures and processes rather than emphasizing and extending their fragmentation; personnel management was, on some views at least, no longer an activity to be undertaken by departments of specialists, but an activity to be incorporated in the tasks of all employees with management and supervisory responsibilities.[2] If this view were being acted on we might expect to see not an increase but a fall in the numbers and functions of specialist personnel staff across the economy as a whole.

The establishment and complex organizations

As in previous surveys, we aimed to achieve our principal management interview with the senior person at each establishment who was responsible for industrial relations, employee relations or personnel matters. Where that role was undertaken by a specialist we aimed to talk to that person rather than someone whose responsibilities were more diffused or ranged wider. It was from this informant that we sought information about employment and industrial relations practices at the establishment. In multi-establishment organizations the same person was asked about any higher-level management structures and policies which might affect behaviour at local level. Although the great majority of our interviews, even in the most complex organizations, were successfully completed at establishment level, practical considerations in some larger organizations meant that a proportion of our interviews in multi-establishment organizations took place at a level above the establishment. In 1990 that proportion was 14 per cent,[3] a rather higher figure than in 1980 and 1984 reflecting, we think, changes in industrial distribution and concentration rather than changes in the willingness of local respondents to be interviewed. In the greater part of this book responses from managers interviewed at a higher level are treated as equivalents to those gained at the establishment. Given that the extent and nature of centralization of personnel and industrial relations management was one of the key features of the enquiries carried out for this chapter, however, we did not feel that we could adopt this course when discussing this special area. Following the approach of our earlier reports we therefore concentrate much of our attention in this chapter on responses gained at the establishment, referring to the accounts given by higher-level managers only when they modify results for our total sample in a substantial way. To assist analysts who might wish to take a different approach, selected results for the whole sample are set out in Table 2A at the end of this chapter.

Personnel and other managers
As in our earlier surveys, we began our interviews by asking managers about their role and responsibilities in the organization. We explored these matters first in general terms and secondly by asking whether the terms 'personnel, human or manpower resources' or 'industrial, employee or staff relations' explicitly figured in their job titles.

All but 5 per cent of our respondents in 1990 regarded their establishment as either having or having access to a personnel department, office or function of some kind.[4] As in 1980 and 1984, however, the great bulk of our respondents (83 per cent) said they had a broad range of responsibilities which included, but was not limited to, personnel and related matters. Overall a quarter (24 per cent) described themselves as general managers, nearly as many (22 per cent) as branch, depot or establishment managers and a further 6 per cent as production, works, factory or plant managers. Technical and professional titles outside the personnel area were held by about one in 6 (17 per cent), accountants and financial managers made up a further eighth (12 per cent) of the total and sales and marketing managers an additional 2 per cent.

This meant that some 17 per cent of respondents had a job title which included an explicit reference to personnel, industrial relations or human resource management. Our earlier surveys had shown that the overall proportion of establishments with 'specialist' personnel managers defined in this way remained unchanged in the economy as a whole between 1980 and 1984.[5] Table 2.1 suggests that this broadly stable picture was maintained during the second half of the decade, although if there was a change it was towards an increase, concentrated in middle-sized establishments with between 200 and 999 employees. That increase was particularly evident in establishments with between 500 and 999 employees where four fifths (81 per cent) had designated personnel managers in 1990 compared with only two thirds (68 per cent) in 1984.

Table 2.1   The presence of designated personnel managers by size of establishment, 1980, 1984 and 1990

Percentages

| | All establishments | Size of establishment | | | | | |
		25–49	50–99	100–199	200–499	500–999	1000 or more
Whether personnel in job title							
1980	15	5	12	25	52	74	88
Unweighted base[1]	*1868*	*340*	*339*	*353*	*343*	*233*	*260*
Weighted base	*1831*	*936*	*456*	*239*	*138*	*38*	*26*
1984	15	4	12	29	54	68	88
Unweighted base	*1794*	*311*	*315*	*313*	*321*	*267*	*267*
Weighted base	*1779*	*933*	*432*	*229*	*130*	*36*	*21*
1990	17	6	12	34	64	81	87
Unweighted base	*1697*	*286*	*292*	*296*	*272*	*219*	*332*
Weighted base	*1644[1]*	*866*	*423*	*203*	*108*	*29*	*16*

Bases: managers interviewed at sampled establishment.

[1] See Note H.

Data from private sector trading establishments in our panel at which interviews were conducted in both 1984 and 1990 lent weight to these findings, with significantly more establishments gaining designated managers between the two years than losing them.[6]

When we looked at the particular titles used by designated specialists we found nearly all reporting that 'personnel' figured in their titles. Only one in a hundred, rather fewer than in 1984, said that their title concentrated on 'industrial', 'staff' or 'employee' relations. And an even smaller minority, of less than 1 per cent, said that they were called 'human resource' managers. Interestingly, these last were not confined to larger establishments and multi-establishment organizations, but were to be found in small numbers across all parts of the private and public sectors and establishments of all kinds.

Job titles are, of course, only one indicator of what managers actually do. With a view to establishing the extent to which designated personnel managers actually specialized we went on to ask them what proportion of their time was spent in practice on personnel and industrial relations matters. The results show that designated managers did indeed specialize to a high degree, but not necessarily to the exclusion of other activities. Details are shown in Table 2.2. In fact only two fifths (42 per cent) of them said that they spent the whole of their time on personnel work

Table 2.2 Proportion of time spent on employee relations matters by designated personnel managers by broad sector, 1990

Percentages

	All designated personnel managers	Private manufacturing	Private services	Public sector
Percentage of time				
1–9%	*	*	1	—
10–24%	4	5	5	2
25–49%	9	9	13	2
50–74%	19	21	21	10
75–89%	13	14	10	15
90–99%	8	8	3	17
100%	42	36	40	54
Not known	*	1	—	—
Not answered	5	6	7	1
Base: managers interviewed at sampled establishments				
Unweighted	*657*	*290*	*171*	*196*
Weighted	*198*	*64*	*90*	*44*

Table 2.3   Time spent on personnel matters by managers responsible for personnel and industrial relations, by size of establishment, 1984 and 1990

Percentages

	All establishments	25–49	50–99	Size of establishment 100–199	200–499	500–999	1000 or more
A quarter or more time spent on personnel and industrial relation matters							
1984	42	31	42	55	79	81	95
Unweighted base	*1794*	*311*	*315*	*313*	*321*	*267*	*267*
Weighted base	*1779*	*933*	*432*	*229*	*130*	*36*	*21*
1990	46	37	47	59	78	87	94
Unweighted base	*1697*	*286*	*292*	*296*	*272*	*219*	*332*
Weighted base	*1644*	*866*	*423*	*203*	*108*	*29*	*16*

Bases: managers interviewed at sampled establishments.

and four fifths (82 per cent) that they spent more than half. Four per cent said they spent less than a quarter of their time in this way.

If not all designated personnel managers actually specialized fully in personnel and related work, what of managers with other titles? We asked them too about the amount of time they expended in this area compared with other activities. Broad results appear in Table 2.3, showing that in 1990 more than two fifths of respondents with indications of being personnel specialists in their job title spent more than a quarter of their time on personnel work, the proportion rising steeply as size of establishment increased. Indeed as many as 16 per cent of such non-specialists reported spending a half or more of their time on personnel work, with 3 per cent claiming that all of their time was spent in this way. It is clear that between 1984 and 1990 there was a small but noticeable increase in the proportion of non-specialist respondents reporting that they spent a significant part of their time on personnel matters, again concentrated in medium-sized establishments, with between 200 and 999 employees.

Two preliminary conclusions emerge from these findings. The first is consistent with the broad suggestion that, over the second half of the 1980s, personnel and related matters were being given somewhat greater attention within organizations. There was clearly no drop in the proportion of establishments with designated personnel specialists across the economy and indeed there may have been a small increase. Managers with other titles were also apparently giving more of their time to personnel and related activities than they had in earlier years. The second, perhaps unsurprising, conclusion is that any picture of personnel management in Britain in 1990 would be seriously incomplete if it were to concentrate on designated personnel managers alone. In much of the remainder of this chapter we therefore divide our establishment-level interviewees into three groups. The first, those who had personnel or a related matter in their job title, we call 'designated' personnel managers. The second, managers with other titles, who spent a substantial amount of time on personnel and industrial relations issues, we call 'non-designated' personnel staff. To provide continuity with our earlier volumes we defined these as people spending a quarter or more of their time in this way. As we show later, when designated and non-designated personnel specialists were considered together, over half (52 per cent) of establishments in 1990 had at least one manager who spent a substantial part of his or her time on personnel work. The third group we distinguish as other non-specialist managers, all of whom were formally responsible for personnel and industrial relations activities but who spent little time on them.

When we looked in detail at where personnel managers were located we found, not surprisingly, that the larger the establishment the more

Table 2.4   Incidence of designated and non-designated personnel managers, by broad sector, 1990

Percentages

	All establishments	Private manufacturing	Private services	Public sector
Designated personnel manager	17	22	15	14
Non-designated personnel manager	35	15	35	54
Base: managers interviewed at sampled establishments				
Unweighted	*1697*	*583*	*617*	*497*
Weighted	*1644*	*404*	*800*	*440*

likely it was that at least one designated personnel specialist would be present. As in 1984, establishments with fewer than 200 employees overall were relatively unlikely to employ designated personnel staff while above this level three fifths or more did so. At the same time, establishments with high concentrations of white-collar employees were rather more likely to have designated personnel staff on site than were others.

As with our earlier surveys, respondents in the private sector were much more often designated personnel specialists than those elsewhere. Eighteen per cent were in this role, compared with only 14 per cent in the public sector. As in 1984, however, these overall figures concealed a good deal. As Table 2.4 shows, private manufacturing remained considerably more likely to have designated managers than private services. Twenty-two per cent of the former had them compared with only 15 per cent of the latter. Table 2A shows that designated managers were most common, being found in more than a third of establishments, in the following sectors: chemicals; food and drink; vehicle manufacture; banking; and energy. By contrast, they appeared in no more than one in eight establishments in the following: Construction; catering; Transport; and Metal Goods. In the public sector there were also wide variations, ranging from 85 per cent in nationalized industries to only 21 per cent in local government and even lower levels in central government. In 1984 we noted that in respect of this last group our questions may not have picked up titles such as 'establishment officer' which were then in common use to describe a number of functions falling within the personnel field and it may be that, despite recent attempts by central government to enhance the professionalization of civil service personnel managers, the older terminology remained in place in many areas at the time of our survey.

We found in 1984 that two other factors were associated with the presence of clearly titled personnel managers in the private trading sector. These remained important in 1990. The first was ownership, whether the establishment was owned in the UK or whether it was part of a foreign-owned organization. The contrast between these two groups remained striking. Twice the proportion of foreign-owned establishments as indigenous employed designated personnel specialists: as many as a third (32 per cent) of the former did so compared with only 15 per cent of UK-owned establishments. As in 1984 the differences remained substantial when we compared establishments of similar size and they provided a first indicator of the continuing differences between UK and foreign-owned establishments which we describe at a number of points in this report and in our companion volume.

The second was the presence of advanced technology. In the two publications describing our 1984 survey we noted a clear relationship between the use of advanced technology in both manufacturing processes and office applications and the presence of a specialized personnel function.[7] The rapid extension of computerized office equipment over the second half of the 1980s meant that the second of these factors discriminated less well in 1990. Nonetheless, in both cases the associations with foreign ownership and advanced technology were maintained and held good when proportion of time spent on personnel matters was considered.

A third factor which might be expected to be associated with increased professionalism among personnel managers is the presence of trade unions. For the decision to recognize a trade union and to treat its officials as representatives of all or part of a workforce has, of course, important consequences for the whole conduct of employment relationships within organizations. We describe our approach to the identification and measurement of trade union recognition fully in the next chapter: as we explain there, our definition relates principally to recognition for the purposes of collective bargaining over pay, a more restrictive approach than some may have taken. In the event, while some one in eight establishments (12 per cent) where trade union recognition was absent had a designated specialist, as many as one in five (21 per cent) which recognized at least one union had such a manager. The number of trade unions recognized was also important in this area: establishments which recognized more than four unions, for example, were twice as likely to have a designated manager than those which recognized only one. Again these relationships held good when we compared establishments of similar sizes.

When we looked at the whereabouts of non-designated personnel managers we found a broadly similar picture. Size of establishment was again a key factor. While even in the smallest establishments, with between 25 and 49 employees, 13 per cent of non-designated respondents reported spending more than a quarter of their time on these matters, this was true of about three fifths (62 per cent) in medium-sized establishments, with between 200 and 499 employees. And nearly nine out of ten in the largest establishments, with more than 1000 employees, did so. Ownership and trade union organization again proved significant. Fully half (51 per cent) of non-specialist respondents in foreign-owned establishments reported that they spent a quarter or more of their time in this way, while among indigenous establishments the proportion was only two fifths.

But independently of size and these other factors there was a marked difference when we explored the picture by industry. Our suggestion that the terminology of personnel management might still differ between the private and public sectors was strongly reinforced. Non-designated respondents in the public sector were very much more likely to say that they spent a quarter or more of their time on personnel matters than those elsewhere: over a half of all those interviewed at establishment-level did so, bringing the combined proportion of establishments with designated and non-designated personnel managers to two thirds (68 per cent) of the total in that sector.

A smaller, but still substantial proportion of workplaces in the private service sector had non-designated managers. There, designated personnel managers were reported half as frequently as non-designated specialists, bringing the proportion of establishments where substantial personnel activity was said to be undertaken to half of the total. Non-designated managers were most common in Hotels and Catering, Banking, Finance and Insurance and Retail Distribution, least common in Wholesale Distribution and Construction. In private manufacturing, by contrast, where we found the highest proportion of designated managers, non-designated managers were much rarer, so that the figure for combined coverage was no more than two fifths (37 per cent) of the total.

It appears from these findings that personnel management activity, whether carried out by designated managers or others, continued to figure most heavily in the operations of foreign-owned establishments, those which recognized trade unions and those which employed substantial concentrations of white-collar workers. But, not surprisingly, the key factor associated with personnel operations remained the total number of employees. Because of this link the proportion of employees covered by our survey who were in establishments where personnel specialists operated was substantially higher than the proportion of such establishments itself. Overall we estimate that some 5.9 million employees, or 38 per cent of the total covered by our survey, were in establishments with designated personnel staff in 1990. Forty one per cent of manual employees were in this position, much the same as in 1984, but there was perhaps a small increase in the coverage of non-manual employees, from 47 to 50 per cent of the total. The small proportion of establishment managers with 'human resource' in their titles covered no more than a total of 130 thousand employees. A further 4 million employees were covered by non-designated personnel managers, again a small increase over 1984, bringing the total in 1990 covered by both forms of specialist managers to nearly 10 million.

The experience and qualifications of personnel managers
Our earlier surveys indicated that between 1980 and 1984 there had been a substantial increase in the extent to which designated personnel managers had formal qualifications directly related to their tasks. In 1980 about half (49 per cent) were in this position; in 1984 the figure was nearly three fifths (58 per cent). Part of the explanation for the change was no doubt the impact of the recession in 1979–1980 which led to the disappearance of substantial areas of manufacturing industry where personnel practices were of long standing and reliance may have

Table 2.5   Qualifications, experience and support of managers, 1980, 1984 and 1990

Percentages

	Designated personnel managers			Non-designated managers spending a quarter or more of their time on personnel or industrial relations matters		
	1980	1984	1990	1980	1984	1990
Professional, educational qualifications	49	58	54	16	19	28
Support staff	48	54	50	57	50	54
Two or more years' experience in the work	89	95	95	82	95	98

Base: managers interviewed at sampled establishments spending a major part of their time on personnel in 1980, a quarter or more of their time in 1984 and 1990

Unweighted	*711*	*786*	*657*	*344*	*493*	*515*
Weighted	*244*	*259*	*198*	*364*	*635*	*574*

Table 2.6   Qualifications of managers responsible for personnel and industrial relations matters, by broad sector, 1990

Percentages

	All establishments		Private manufacturing		Private services		Public sector	
	Designated	Non-designated	Designated	Non-designated	Designated	Non-designated	Designated	Non-designated
Professional qualification with personnel/IR content	72	22	69	22	73	33	73	14
Professional qualification with no personnel/IR content	13	12	4	8	14	5	20	19
Degree/postgraduate diploma in personnel/IR/trade union studies	7	1	13	7	5	*	5	*
Degree/postgraduate diploma in general management/ administration	5	2	6	3	5	3	3	1
Other diploma, etc. personnel/ IR/trade union studies	14	10	15	15	16	11	11	9
Other diploma, etc. general management/administration	7	32	10	34	5	18	7	42
Other degree/diploma/ certificate in social studies	1	6	2	5	1	2	1	9
Other degree/diploma/certificate	10	17	10	*	9	26	13	14
Base: managers with qualifications interviewed at sampled establishments								
Unweighted	*427*	*206*	*184*	*47*	*105*	*76*	*138*	*83*
Weighted	*107*	*163*	*31*	*17*	*44*	*65*	*31*	*81*

been placed principally on experience rather than qualifications. Part, however, is likely to have been a result of the general increase in formal qualifications then beginning to be observable across Britain in a wide range of management functions: in 1984 more of our respondents had degrees and more had professional qualifications than before.

We expected to see evidence of a further increase in the incidence of qualifications across the board. In fact, the picture proved complex, as the results in Table 2.5 show. If anything, there was a slight fall in the proportion of designated personnel managers who reported relevant qualifications, down from 58 to 54 per cent of the total. If designated managers seemed less well qualified however, the reverse was true of others. There was a substantial increase in qualifications among non-designated staff, up from a fifth (19 per cent) in 1984 to over a quarter (28 per cent) in 1990. When we looked at all non-specialists together we found that between a quarter and a fifth had qualifications either fully related to personnel and industrial relations work or containing a substantial element of these subjects. Details of the kinds of qualifications held are shown in Table 2.6.

In 1984 we found, as we expected, that managers with formal qualifications were more likely to be responsible for the personnel function in larger workplaces than small. Nonetheless, even in the smallest establishments we covered, with between 25 and 49 employees, just over a fifth of respondents claimed a relevant qualification. This remained the case in 1990. In larger establishments, with between 500 and 999 employees, some two thirds (66 per cent) of designated specialists and just under half (45 per cent) of non-designated specialists were in this position. In the largest establishments (over 1000 employees), where the proportion of qualified designated staff had always been high, the numbers of qualified non-designated managers also increased further.

In our second survey we found that personnel specialists in private service establishments were much less likely to have formal qualifications than those in either private manufacturing or the public sector. In 1990 the private services sector had shown no difference from private manufacturing: in both instances half of personnel specialists had professional qualifications.

We noted above that personnel specialists were more likely to be found in the private sector in establishments that were part of organizations with overseas ownership. Not surprisingly, we found a similar pattern for qualifications: three fifths (58 per cent) of personnel staff in foreign-owned establishments had formal qualifications compared with half (49 per cent) of those in indigenous ownership. The complexity of organizations was also related to the presence of qualifications: branches of multi-establishment companies, whether foreign-owned or UK-owned, were more likely to have professionally qualified staff than others.

Professionally qualified personnel managers were also more likely to be found in 1990 in establishments where trade unions were recognized: some two fifths (39 per cent) of designated personnel managers in establishments without recognized trade unions were formally qualified, compared with nearly two thirds (64 per cent) where at least one trade union was recognized. And broadly speaking, too, the larger the number of unions which were recognized the more likely it was that designated staff would be professionally qualified. Similar relationships held for non-designated staff: only 13 per cent of all non-specialists were professionally qualified in establishments where no recognition had been granted while the figure was double this (24 per cent) where at least one union was recognized.

Size of establishment remained the principal determinant of the presence of professionally qualified personnel staff in 1990. The consequence was again that a substantially higher proportion of employees in our survey were in situations with professionally qualified staff responsible for personnel than would be suggested from the number of establishments they were in: we estimate that in all 4.9 million employees were in this position out of the total of 15.6 million covered by the survey. Of these, nearly 3 million were covered by managers with personnel or a related matter in their title and some 2 million by other managers.

Support staff

Table 2.5 also shows a simple measure of the amount of support available to our main management respondents. We asked, as we had in 1980 and 1984, whether in addition to clerical and secretarial staff, they had someone to assist them with personnel and employee relations in the establishment. The results showed a curious similarity to those for qualifications: managers with personnel or industrial relations in their titles reported having support staff in slightly fewer cases than before. Only 50 per cent of them did so in 1990, down from the 54 per cent recorded in 1984 to much the same figure as in 1980. Non-designated specialists, however, reported a change of similar proportions in the opposite direction, up from 50 per cent to 54 per cent. Consistent with our earlier results suggesting a growth in personnel activities in private services, specialists there were no less likely to report they had staff support than those in private manufacturing. Public sector managers continued to suggest a still higher degree of support: no fewer than three quarters of personnel specialists and 60 per cent of non-specialist public sector respondents said they enjoyed staff support in personnel matters.

As in 1984, support staff were also more likely to be available to managers in establishments where trade unions were recognized: only three in ten designated managers reported having support staff in situations where no unions were recognized, while fully three in five (63 per cent) of those in unionized establishments did so. The relationship once more held firm even when we compared establishments of similar sizes. Personnel management continued, it seemed, to be conducted on a larger scale, with a greater degree of professional specialization, in situations where trade unions were recognized than elsewhere.

The activities and responsibilities of personnel managers

As in previous surveys, we examined what personnel functions our respondents actually undertook by asking them to consider a list of possible issues for which they might be responsible. In 1984 we had seen evidence of some widening of managers' responsibilities, with a substantial increase in the proportion of respondents indicating that they dealt with procedures for grievances, discipline and disputes, with settling and negotiating terms of employment and with job evaluation. When we took all of our main manager respondents in our 1990 survey together these patterns of activity appear to have hardly changed over the second half of the decade. If anything, however, recruitment and settling and negotiating terms and conditions received more prominence than before, dealing with disciplinary cases perhaps rather less. The one major exception was an indication that a larger proportion of managers were becoming directly responsible for systems of pay, a matter we consider in more detail in Chapter 7.

At the same time growing differences were becoming apparent between the responsibilities exercised by designated and other managers. In 1990 four fifths (82 per cent) of non-specialists regarded themselves as responsible for training, much the same as in previous years; but there was a substantial fall in the proportion of designated specialists in this position, down from 78 per cent in 1984 to 67 per cent in 1990. Similarly, designated specialists were less often involved in job evaluation arrangements and less often had responsibility for systems of pay than their non-specialist counterparts, who in the latter case reported a noticeable increase in coverage. The suggestion must be that, in establishments where the personnel and employee relations function was separately identified, a greater division of labour between designated managers, training managers and others concerned with sub-sets of the broad employee relations area arose over the second half of the 1980s.

More detailed analysis suggests that, as in 1984, the range of managers' responsibilities was much the same in private manufacturing and services. As in earlier years the only major difference between the public and private sectors lay in the extent of involvement in the negotiation of pay and conditions. This was much lower in the public sector, reflecting the heavy concentration of centralized pay bargaining still to

Table 2.7   Managers' two main personnel and industrial relations activities, 1990

Percentages

	All managers	Designated personnel managers	Other managers spending a quarter or more of their time on personnel matters
Disciplinary cases	4	9	3
Recruitment	39	55	41
Training	38	24	45
Settling/negotiating terms of employment	27	44	20
Job evaluation/grading	12	8	14
Industrial relations procedures	8	18	8
Responsibility for systems of pay	10	7	6
Staffing/manpower planning	41	20	46
Base: managers interviewed at sampled establishments			
Unweighted	*1697*	*657*	*515*
Weighted	*1644*	*198*	*574*

be found there at the end of the decade and the removal of pay determination to Review Bodies and the like. Responsibilities varied little with patterns of trade union recognition and were much the same for indigenous and foreign-owned establishments.

In 1990 we went further than in previous surveys by asking not only about the range of responsibilities undertaken by our respondents, but also about which two of them occupied most of their time. Responses are set out in Table 2.7. While it was not to be expected that there would be a simple relationship between amounts of time spent on particular issues and their importance to managers and employees, the table does perhaps indicate something of the relative significance of different issues in managers' working lives in 1990. On this measure, recruitment was by far the most substantial preoccupation of designated personnel managers and one of the three most time-consuming for all others. In line with the findings noted above, non-designated and other managers mentioned training as a major pre-occupation much more often than did designated specialists and the same was true of staffing and manpower planning. Settling and negotiating terms of employment figured largely for all private sector respondents though not, as expected, for those in the public sector. Perhaps just as interesting, foreshadowing results on the operation of disciplinary and other procedures which we describe in detail in Chapter 6, were our findings on how few managers saw dealing with disciplinary cases and the operation of industrial relations procedures as major preoccupations. Again these patterns varied little with industry, size of establishment and trade union recognition.

Personnel management in multi-establishment organizations

So far in this chapter we have looked at the activities of managers responsible for personnel and industrial relations issues who were within the establishment we visited. As in 1980 and 1984, however, four fifths of the establishments in which we conducted interviews were parts of larger organizations, and in some of these it was clear that personnel and industrial relations specialists would be concentrated at a higher level in the management structure. Even in situations where professional personnel expertise was available at local level and responsibilities were devolved to a high degree, we expected that responsibility for certain functions, including the provision of legal advice, might be based at a higher level.

To gain a view of the involvement of higher-level managers in local personnel activities we asked establishment managers whether they had contact with a manager or director at a higher level, and in a separate establishment in the organization in the UK, who spent a major part of his or her time on personnel and industrial relations matters. Where the answer was yes we went on to ask where that superior manager was

Table 2.8   Extent to which designated personnel specialists had a line relationship with a personnel manager at another establishment, by broad sector, 1984 and 1990

Percentages

	All establishments		Private manufacturing		Private services		Public sector	
	1984	1990	1984	1990	1984	1990	1984	1990
Existence of superordinate								
Reports to personnel manager outside establishment	60	60	46	42	65	51	54	44
Not answered	7	11	11	14	—	3	—	23
Base: designated personnel managers at establishments, other than head offices, belonging to larger organizations.								
Unweighted	*610*	*613*	*304*	*268*	*117*	*157*	*189*	*188*
Weighted	*195*	*182*	*69*	*56*	*72*	*83*	*54*	*43*
Frequency of contact								
Once a week or more	59	62	51	63	61	60	70	66
Level of superordinate								
Head Office	61	63	61	72	53	62	73	65
Intermediate level	37	35	38	26	46	26	22	18
Both	..	2	..	2	..	2	..	18
Base: designated personnel managers who reported to a superordinate								
Unweighted	*423*	*328*	*206*	*145*	*79*	*86*	*138*	*97*
Weighted	*118*	*85*	*42*	*24*	*47*	*42*	*29*	*19*

located, how frequently the two were in contact and about the subjects which they discussed.

Results are shown in Table 2.8 for designated personnel specialists. They suggest little change in the position and role of this group. In 1984 three fifths (60 per cent) of all such managers reported that they had contacts with a senior personnel manager elsewhere. In 1990 the picture remained much as before. In most industries it seemed that contact with superordinates was more likely where at least one trade union was recognized.

There were, however, changes in other respects. In 1984 we observed that a majority of contacts with superior levels were at head office level rather than at any intermediate level. In 1990 in the private sector, that majority was substantially increased: nearly three quarters (72 per cent) of such contacts in private manufacturing were with a head office manager compared with 61 per cent in 1984 and in private services the increase was of a similar magnitude, up from 53 to 62 per cent. There was also an increase in the frequency of contact, of a marked kind in private manufacturing where nearly two thirds (63 per cent) of designated personnel manager respondents had contact with the higher level at least once each week compared with only 51 per cent six years earlier. In private services there was less change, with some three fifths continuing in this position.

When we extended this analysis by comparing the position of designated and non-designated personnel managers in 1990, we found, as might be expected, that, taking all sectors together, non-designated managers in multi-establishment situations were a good deal more likely that their designated counterparts to consult above. As before, however, on further examination the picture proved complex, for the difference was confined to the private services sector and the public sector. It was notable, too, that while non-designated managers and other non-specialists were more likely to report the possibility of higher consultations, these tended to happen less frequently than among their specialist colleagues.

When we asked about the matters on which consultation took place there were also changes. Our question here asked about matters on which our respondent 'ever' consulted a higher-level manager; space did not on this occasion allow us to ask about frequency of contact by subject. Nonetheless the results are of some interest. Table 2.9 gives details. As in 1984 changes in industrial relations procedures were seen by a substantial majority of respondents as subjects for consultation with higher levels: three quarters or more said they were in this position. Much the same was true of the treatment of disciplinary cases: overall two thirds, including a rather larger proportion of designated managers, sometimes referred these upwards for discussion. Perhaps the most sig-

Table 2.9 Matters for consultation at a higher level in the organization, 1990

Percentages

	Designated personnel managers	Non-designated managers spending a quarter or more of their time on personnel or industrial relations matters	All non-designated managers
Pay/conditions of employment	77	66	63
Procedures for grievances, discipline, disputes	78	78	74
Recruitment and selection	47	63	58
Training	53	49	47
Systems of payment	45	31	30
Job evaluation/job grading	57	48	42
Disciplinary cases	69	78	70
Staffing/manpower planning	58	58	55

Base: managers who reported to a superordinate outside the establishment

Unweighted	328	281	474
Weighted	85	334	650

nificant changes, however, were again to do with pay: whereas in 1984 only two thirds (68 per cent) of designated managers reported discussing pay negotiations with superiors, in 1990 nearly four fifths (77 per cent) did so.[8]

There was some tendency for more issues to be discussed upwards in private services than elsewhere, but other differences between sectors and types of establishment proved few. Managers in establishments which recognized trade unions were no more and no less likely than others, for example, to consult upwards on pay systems or on pay and conditions. And this was one area where behaviour was similar in foreign-owned and indigenous establishments.

Sources of external advice about personnel and industrial relations matters

Finally, in exploring how personnel and other managers responsible for industrial relations went about their tasks, we asked about any sources of advice they used from outside their organization. We had asked questions about this matter in 1980 and reported fully on them in our first book. We found then that external advice was much more likely to be sought by establishments where in-house professional personnel managers were present than by those where personnel responsibilities were exercised by other managers. In exploring the issue in 1990 we expected to see a continuation of this pattern and had in mind two additional possibilities. The first was that over the latter part of the 1980s a devolution of responsibilities on personnel matters might have led to a greater reliance on in-house expertise. The second was that in a number of specialist areas, at least, managers might now be relying more on external help.

A first and obvious source for many organizations at the start of the decade had been an employers' association. Many of these had, of course, been closely involved in pay negotiation processes at industry and sometimes regional level. As we explain in Chapter 7, we expected that the move away from industry-wide bargaining over the second half of the 1980s would have led to a further reduction in their membership.

In fact that proved to be the case. Table 2.10 shows that, while in 1980 as many as a quarter of establishments in our overall sample had been members of employers' associations, by 1990 the figure had fallen by half to just 13 per cent. Membership remained highest in three sectors: engineering, where 32 per cent of establishments reported affiliation; Textiles, where 32 per cent were also in this position, in each case reflecting the continuing influence of industry-wide procedures; and in Construction where three quarters (75 per cent) were in membership. Interestingly, membership was by no means confined to the smallest establishments and nor were there differences in the incidence of mem-

Table 2.10 Membership of employers' associations, 1990

Percentages

	All establishments			Private manufacturing			Private services		
	All managers	Designated personnel managers	Non-designated personnel managers	All managers	Designated personnel managers	Non-designated personnel managers	All managers	Designated personnel managers	Non-designated personnel managers
Members	13	14	9	20	22	23	10	9	7
Non-members	82	81	83	74	71	72	82	89	84
Don't know/not answered	4	5	4	6	7	5	5	2	10
Base: all establishments in the trading sector[1]									
Unweighted	*1510*	*480*	*331*	*630*	*290*	*104*	*799*	*171*	*215*
Weighted	*1452*	*156*	*345*	*426*	*64*	*60*	*980*	*90*	*280*

[1] For designated personnel managers the base is all such managers interviewed at establishment level.

bership between foreign-owned and indigenous establishments. Membership in the service sector, never substantial, remained highest in Retail Distribution where one in eight managers reported it. Establishments with designated personnel managers were no more and no less likely to be in membership than others. Panel data confirmed this picture: four times as many establishments abandoned employers' association membership between 1984 and 1990 than the number which took it up.

In addition to employers' associations a wide variety of other sources of help and advice were available to managers. We show results on their use in Table 2.11. Our questions here were not asked in 1984 and took a somewhat different form in 1980 so some caution is needed in considering changes in managers' responses. Nonetheless they suggest a more striking change in behaviour than any so far described in this chapter. In 1980 almost two fifths of all establishments reported that an issue had arisen in the past year over which they had consulted an external body of some kind, suggesting a heavy and perhaps routine recourse to external advisers. In 1990 that proportion fell to a third, suggesting a greater

Table 2.11   Managers' sources of advice, 1980 and 1990

Percentages

	Body ever consulted		Body consulted most often (1980) or on most important occasion (1990)	
	1980	1990	1980	1990
Any outside body consulted	38	33	—	—
ACAS/other government agency	9	15	5	5
Management consultant	4	8	3	2
Employers' association	12	7	10	2
Full-time officer of trade union	12	8	6	1
Outside lawyer	10	19	5	8
Outside accountant	3	2	1	*
Personnel manager outside establishment/organization	10	8	10	1
Base: all establishments				
Unweighted	*2040*	*2061*	*2040*	*2061*
Weighted	*2000*	*2000*	*2000*	*2000*

degree of managerial self-confidence within establishments. Nor was that all, for there were substantial changes in the use of particular kinds of advisory body. Not surprisingly, in view of the fall in their membership, employers' associations were consulted much less frequently than before. Full-time trade union officers, who had figured prominently in 1980 as sources of management advice, were also mentioned much less frequently. In 1990 they were consulted two thirds as often as they had been earlier, providing a first indication of the general decline in the influence of trade unions which is a feature of many of the results we present in later chapters.

At the same time other sources of advice were in much higher demand than before. The most striking increase was in relation to outside lawyers, whose use almost doubled over the decade, and there was also increasing recourse to the Advisory, Conciliation and Arbitration Service (ACAS) and other government agencies, and to management consultants. In 1980 we had gone on to ask managers about which of these bodies they had consulted most frequently over the past year. In 1990 we changed our question to cover the 'most important' occasion. The change means again that caution is needed in making comparisons. Nonetheless the results, also set out in Table 2.11, are clearly consistent with the view that there was a substantial fall over the decade in the relative importance of employers' associations and trade union officials and an increased reliance on lawyers.

We have already noted that in 1980 designated managers were a good deal more likely to seek external advice than their less specialized counterparts. That remained very much the case in 1990, not only in general but in relation to each kind of potential adviser. For managers of both kinds external lawyers were the most frequently mentioned source and also the source mentioned most often in relation to the most important occasion on which advice had been sought. ACAS and other government agencies were once again the next most frequently mentioned source.

The influence of the personnel function – personnel and the board
One potentially important indicator of the way in which personnel and industrial relations issues are managed is the extent to which clear and direct responsibility for them rests on one or more members of an organization's top governing body. The suggestion is that representation at board level may indicate a particularly positive commitment to the management of human resources. An increase in the incidence of board membership might then be evidence of a growth in the influence of the personnel function, while a decline might suggest the reverse. As in our earlier surveys we asked respondents in the private sector and the trading parts of the public sector whether there was someone on the top governing

Table 2.12   Representation of the personnel function on the board, by size
of organization, 1980, 1984 and 1990

Percentages

	All establishments	Size of organization			
		25–499	500–1999	2000–9999	10,000 or more
Any representation on board					
1980	71	59	71	76	79
1984	73	66	68	68	85
1990	69	61	65	70	74
Specialist representation					
1980	42	11	39	46	64
1984	43	8	40	49	70
1990	40	10	21	43	60

Base[1]: trading sector establishments that were part of multi-establishment organisations

Unweighted	*1271[2]*	*140*	*85*	*158*	*474*
Weighted	*1039*	*250*	*83*	*107*	*351*

[1] Only 1990 bases are given, for presentational reasons.
[2] See Note G.

body of the organization in the UK who was responsible for personnel and industrial relations. Where such a person was reported we asked whether this was their main job or just one of a number of responsibilities they carried.

Any expectations we might have had of any dramatic extension of personnel influence at board-room level, as indicated by these measures, were to be disappointed. We had recorded no significant change in the incidence of board-level personnel representation between 1980 and 1984. Our results for 1990, given in Table 2.12, show that 69 per cent of respondents mentioned board-level representation, a slight fall since 1984.[9] In two thirds (64 per cent) of these situations one director took combined responsibility for both industrial relations and personnel matters. The picture for specialist representation was more stable, however, with around two fifths of managers indicating a board-level specialist. As in 1984, specialist representation was affected much less by size of establishment than the total number employed by the enterprise as a whole. Among establishments that were part of the very largest organizations, with over 100,000 employees, nearly four out of five managers reported a specialist director. The proportion was only one in ten for

Table 2.13   Representation of personnel and industrial relations on senior management bodies in single–establishment organizations, by size of establishment, 1990

Column percentages

	All establishments	25–49	50–99	Size of establishment 100–199	200–499	500–999	1000 and over
Yes	49	45	56	60	59	72	77
No	50	55	43	40	32	24	19
Not answered	1	—	—	—	8	3	4
Base: single–establishment organizations in the trading sector							
Unweighted	*239*	*90*	*56*	*41*	*20*	*16*	*16*
Weighted	*412*	*284*	*88*	*30*	*8*	*2*	*1*

establishments that were part of organizations employing less than 500. Professional boardroom representation was much more likely to be reported in private services and, to a lesser degree, where at least one trade union was recognized. Additionally, as before, we found no clear links between the presence of personnel specialists at the establishment and personnel and industrial relations specialists at board level. In multi-establishment organizations 29 per cent of establishments with managers whose titles included the words personnel or industrial relations reported that their specialization had no regular representation at board level.

These questions covered, as they had in our earlier surveys, only multi-establishment organizations in the trading sector. For independent trading establishments that were not part of larger organizations we asked instead whether the most senior management committee present included anyone with specific responsibility for personnel and industrial relations work. Responses for 1990 are shown in Table 2.13. Once again they showed little change compared with 1984. Overall half of respondents reported that there was such a committee member, with the proportion increasing with establishment size and rather higher in private manufacturing than private services. On this issue trade union recognition again made little difference: 48 per cent of non-union single establishments had a person responsible for personnel on their main committee, much the same (52 per cent) as those which recognized at least one trade union.

Other measures of influence

A second measure of the influence exerted by particular management role-holders and their departments can, of course, be derived from more direct questioning. In 1984 we had asked personnel managers whether, in their view, the influence of their department had increased or decreased in the previous three years, and if so by how much. We described in our previous report our reasons for thinking that the responses to these questions, which suggested a significant increase in the influence being wielded by personnel managers, were not simply wishful thinking by those with a vested interest in the matter.[10]

Given this conclusion we repeated some of our questions in 1990. Broad results are given in Table 2.14, distinguishing between the answers given by designated and non-designated managers. Perhaps not surprisingly, the former were clearest that their influence had increased: fully seven out of ten claimed that the influence of their department had grown, while only one in 20 said that it had decreased. Among non-designated specialists, responses were somewhat less forceful but even so two in five took a similar view. Managers in private manufacturing and in Construction were rather less likely than others to say their

Table 2.14   Changes in influence of the personnel department over the three years to 1990

Percentages

	All managers responsible for personnel or industrial relations	Designated personnel managers	Financial managers
Increased a lot	20[1]	46	34[2]
Increased a little	19	24	26
Much the same	43	22	30
Decreased a little	3	3	7
Decreased a lot	1	2	1
In post less than three years	4	2	—
No personnel department	5	—	—
Don't know/not answered	7	1	2

Base: [1] managers interviewed at sampled establishments; [2] all financial managers interviewed.

Unweighted	*1697*	*657*	*489*
Weighted	*1644*	*198*	*231*

influence was unchanged, while those in foreign-owned, smaller and non-unionized establishments and with substantial concentrations of white-collar employees were more likely to suggest that their influence had increased.

In 1984 we were able for many establishments to compare these responses with those from a range of supplementary questions asked of works managers. In 1990, when circumstances allowed, we took a manager responsible for financial matters as our second management respondent. We asked that person, too, about changes in the influence of the personnel department over the past three years. As Table 2.14 shows the drift of financial managers views was strikingly similar to those of designated and non-designated personnel specialists. Nearly three out of five of them agreed that the personnel function had increased in influence compared with only eight per cent saying it had fallen.

Synopsis
If anything, the influence of the personnel function rose rather than fell in the population of British workplaces during the second half of the 1980s. But this change was complex and certainly not based exclusively

on the activities of designated personnel managers. Designated managers were perhaps slightly more frequently reported in 1990 than they had been in 1984, but they were no better qualified and enjoyed no greater staff support than before. In many cases, too, they seemed to be concentrating on a narrower range of activities, leaving training in particular to other, even more specialized colleagues. Nor were they more often represented on the boards of companies than they had been in the early years of the decade. It was rather non-designated personnel managers, those who carried out the function for a quarter or more of their time but without using the title, who were more frequently to be found than before, who were better qualified and who were, if anything, undertaking a wider range of functions.

There were other conflicting changes. In multi-establishment organizations fewer designated managers reported that they consulted personnel specialists at higher levels within the organization, suggesting perhaps that they were enjoying a greater degree of autonomy from above. At the same time those who did consult above reported that they were doing so more often, perhaps on more issues. By contrast while a larger proportion than before of non-designated managers said they reported upwards, they did so only relatively infrequently.

Our results on the use of external advice also suggest that complex changes were under way during the second half of the decade. Fewer managers responsible for personnel matters were apparently seeking advice from outside their organization. But those who did seek advice were very much more likely to approach lawyers, and to a lesser degree ACAS and other state agencies, than before. By contrast references to employers' associations were much less frequent and so were those to full-time trade union officers. The role of law, it seems, was indeed assuming much greater salience for personnel managers than before, while the role of trade unions, to which we turn in our next two chapters, was apparently on the wane.

Notes and references

1. See generally K. Sisson (1989) 'Personnel management in transition?' in K. Sisson (ed.), *Personnel Management in Britain*, Blackwell, Oxford; G. Thomason (1987) *A Textbook of Industrial Relations Management*, Institute of Personnel Management, London.

2. See for example D. E. Guest (1990) 'Human Resource Management and the American Dream', *Journal of Management Studies*, July; J. Storey (ed.) (1989) *New Perspectives in Human Resource Management*, Routledge, London.

3. Based on unweighted data. The figure is increased to 18 per cent if cases are included in which part of the interview was conducted at the establishment and part at a higher level. Unless otherwise indicated multi-site interviews are treated as establishment-level interviews in the analysis conducted for this book.

4. Our evidence here derived from questioning, considered later in this chapter, about the influence wielded by personnel managers.

5. We did not explore how far establishments had more than one specialist manager in 1990, so we cannot estimate the total number of such role-holders over the economy as a whole. Membership of the Institute of Personnel Management, however, more than doubled in the 1980s to 47,000, suggesting a substantial increase in their number over the period.

6. These results provide a first indication of the degree of volatility in arrangements within panel establishments on which we remark at several points in this book and which receive fuller attention in our companion volume. Fully one quarter of panel respondents reported a change: 19 per cent of establishments which had no designated manager in 1984 had acquired at least one in 1990; and balancing this to some degree were 7 per cent of establishments which had a designated manager in 1984 but not in 1990. Only three fifths (60 per cent) had no designated manager at either date; and only 14 per cent had one in both years.

7. N. Millward and M. Stevens (1986) *British Workplace Industrial Relations 1980–1984: The DE/ESRC/PSI/ACAS Surveys*, Gower, Aldershot; W. W. Daniel (1987) *Workplace Industrial Relations and Technical Change*, Frances Pinter (Publishers) and the Policy Studies Institute, London.

8. In 1980 the question had asked about 'determining or negotiating terms of employment'. In 1984 and 1990 it changed to 'negotiating pay and conditions'.

9. Data from the panel of private sector trading establishments suggests more firmly that there may have been a fall in the use of personnel directors. Nearly a third (29 per cent) of panel respondents said there had been a change in personnel representation on their board, but with a significantly greater movement away from personnel specialist representation than towards it.

10. N. Millward and M. Stevens (1986) op. cit., pp. 36–41.

Table 2A   Presence of personnel managers and proportion of time spent on personnel and industrial relations matters, by industry, 1990

Percentages

	Designated personnel manager	Mean proportion of time spent by managers responsible for personnel and industrial relations on these matters
All industries	**17**	**32**
All manufacturing	**22**	**26**
Metals & Mineral Products	(18)	(35)
Chemicals & Manufactured Fibres	(35)[1]	(34)
Metal Goods	(9)	(20)
Mechanical Engineering	16	26
Electrical & Instrument Engineering	28	29
Vehicles & Transport Equipment	32	22
Food, Drink & Tobacco	46	38
Textiles	(23)	(22)
Leather, Footwear & Clothing	(22)	(28)
Timber & Furniture, Paper & Printing	14	22
Rubber, Plastics & Other Manufacturing	(25)	(18)
All services	**15**	**34**
Energy & Water	(40)	(48)
Construction	10	21
Wholesale Distribution	13	25
Retail Distribution	14	30
Hotels, Catering, Repairs	18	34
Transport	11	31
Posts and Telecommunications	(84)	(70)
Banking, Finance, Insurance	(38)	(38)
Business Services	22	37
Central Government	13	45
Local Government	22	36
Higher Education	(28)	(42)
Other Education	2	32
Medical Services	23	43
Other Services	12	36

Base: all establishments (see Table 1A for SIC codes) but bases are generally a little smaller than those given.

[1] See Note B.

3 The Structure of Management–Trade Union Relations

The representation of employees by trade unions and staff associations was seen as a key feature of institutional industrial relations in Britain when we began our survey series in 1980. Our 1980 survey results showed how trade unions represented employees in the clear majority of workplaces and through a number of different channels, ranging from direct collective bargaining over pay and conditions of employment through to participation in grievance handling and disputes procedures and a wide variety of communication and consultation functions. In many cases trade unions provided the only formal channel of communication between management and the workforce.

In 1984 this picture remained largely true. Although widespread closures of mature, highly unionized parts of manufacturing industry during the recession of the early 1980s had reduced union presence, and despite substantial losses of membership by the trade unions, the traditional institutions of industrial relations were largely intact. Our findings showed that although the scope of union bargaining activity had been severely reduced, trade unions were still a core element of the system of industrial relations in Britain. By 1990 much of this had changed. Key elements of the system of collective representation had faded or been transformed. Others had survived relatively unscathed. We begin our account of these changes by examining trade union membership, widely understood as one of the foundations of the system of collective representation in Britain as elsewhere.

Naturally enough, our basic survey questions about trade union membership and the role of the unions in the institutional structure of employee relations had to be repeated in our 1990 survey to establish how far they had retained their central position. We could indeed have repeated these core questions *verbatim* in an effort to minimize the difficulties of comparing the results between the three surveys. But there were two considerations which argued against this. First, the distinction between manual and non-manual employees that we had found useful in 1980 for describing broad groups of the workforce with distinct institutional arrangements for bargaining, representation and so on was becoming a less useful and clearly understood distinction. Secondly, whereas in 1980 it was relatively easy and useful to classify trade unions as organizing either manual workers or white-collar workers, by 1990 this admitted over-simplification was less tenable. We decided to continue using the crude categories of manual and non-manual employee where appropriate; but we did make some changes to acknowledge more fully that some unions might represent both manual and non-manual employees. Given that our previous questionnaires had had separate sections of questioning about manual unions and non-manual unions, this decision necessitated a radical redesign of major parts of the 1990 main management questionnaire. The result is that in many respects the 1990 data are more straightforward to present when referring to the workforce as a whole. The complexities arise when talking about the different types of union, particularly when comparing the results with the earlier surveys. This we do later in the chapter.

Trade union membership (including, hereafter, staff association membership) is the first and most basic indicator of union presence that we examine. The second, and more critical indicator, is the recognition of unions by management for collective bargaining over pay. Widespread change on both of these measures was evident over the second half of the decade.

Trade union membership

The most rudimentary question regarding union membership is whether an establishment has any union members. At this fundamental level, our earlier surveys showed virtually no change between 1980 and 1984. Overall, 73 per cent of workplaces in both years had union members, as

Table 3.1 **Presence of trade union and staff association members, 1980, 1984 and 1990**

			Percentages
	1980	1984	1990
Proportion of establishments with members among:			
Manual employees	64	68	58
Non-manual employees	55	58	51
Manual or non-manual employees	73	73	64

Base: all establishments employing type of employees specified.
Note: In the 1980 and 1984 results, other answers, don't know and not answered were treated as 'no'. In the 1990 survey the data were coded directly by interviewers from the previous question about numbers of union or staff association members; these data have no missing values.

Table 3.1 shows. However, by 1990 this proportion had dropped to 64 per cent. Regarding manual workers only, the drop during the period 1984–1990 was from 68 to 58 per cent; for non-manual workers it was at a very similar rate, from 58 to 51 per cent. Irrespective of any slight

Table 3.2 Aggregate union membership density in 1984 and 1990 within industries and broad sectors

Percentages

	All employees		Manual employees		Non-manual employees	
	1984	1990	1984	1990	1984	1990
All industries	**58**	**48**	**66**	**53**	**51**	**43**
SIC Divisions						
Energy and water supply industries	87	75	91	80	82	69
Extraction of minerals and ores other than fuels; manufacture of metals, mineral products and chemicals	64	56	79	77	41	23
Metal goods, engineering and vehicles industries	59	46	74	59	37	23
Other manufacturing industries	52	47	65	58	29	22
Construction	36	46	41	58	25	17
Distribution, hotels and catering; repairs	31	19	42	24	20	13
Transport and communication	89	73	97	82	73	56
Banking, finance, insurance, business services and leasing	29	29	57	21	27	29
Other services	67	61	60	50	72	65
Broad sector						
Private manufacturing	56	48	70	60	32	22
Private services	30	27	40	32	23	24
Public sector	80	72	82	72	79	72

Base: all establishments with specified employees giving answers on the number of union members.

effect of changes in question wording between our 1984 and 1990 surveys,[1] the clear picture is of a sizeable decline in the number of workplaces with trade union members between the early 1980s and the end of the decade. All of this decline was in the private sector of the economy: it remained the case that virtually all (99 per cent) of public sector workplaces had trade union members.

Union membership density
When we come to look at the more general and widely used measure of union membership, the proportion of employees who were members, our figures show a substantial decline in density from 58 per cent in 1984 to 48 per cent in 1990.[2] Table 3.2 gives the results. The decline was apparent among both manual and non-manual employees, but somewhat more marked for manuals, the traditionally more highly unionized. For them the fall was from 66 to 53 per cent; for non-manual employees, the growing sector of employment, the fall was from 51 per cent to 43 per cent. Table 3.2 also shows the comparisons within the main sectors of the economy (Divisions of the *Standard Industrial Classification*) and within the three broad sectors of employment: private manufacturing, private services and the public sector.[3]

Looking first at the analysis by industry, falls in membership density were recorded in seven of the nine industry Divisions for employees in general. Amongst manual workers there were falls in eight out of nine Divisions; amongst non-manual workers the pattern was similar. In private manufacturing and the public sector, the declines in membership density were substantial, among manual and non-manual workers alike. However, in private services, the decline in density was only slight and was confined to manual workers. Union membership density among the more numerous white-collar employees in private services remained constant at just under a quarter. The decade ended, then, with the public sector still having the highest union membership density at nearly three quarters, private manufacturing having dropped to below a half and private services falling slightly to around a quarter.

This picture of widespread decline in union membership density can be further illuminated by examining the distribution of density across establishments in the two surveys. Table 3.3 classifies each establishment into one of a number of ranges of union density, with separate categories for those with no members and those with 100 per cent membership. Thus in the 1990 survey, 9 per cent of establishments had between 1 and 24 per cent membership density among all employees, 8 per cent had between 25 and 49 per cent, and so on up to the 7 per cent with all employees belonging to a union.

The most striking feature of the table is the increase in the proportion of establishments with no members at all, a corollary of the changes that

Table 3.3 The distribution of union density in 1984 and 1990 for a) all employees, b) manual employees and c) non-manual employees

Column percentages

	All employees		Manual employees		Non-manual employees	
	1984	1990	1984	1990	1984	1990
Proportion of establishments with union density of:						
0	27	36	32	42	42	49
1–24%	8	9	8	8	4	5
25–49%	9	8	7	7	6	5
50–89%	23	26	14	15	17	17
90–99%	9	7	6	6	7	5
100%	11	7	26	14	15	12
Not answered	11	8	7	7	7	6
Base: all establishments with specified employees						
Unweighted	*2019*	*2061*	*1853*	*1831*	*2010*	*2058*
Weighted	*2000*	*2000*	*1749*	*1697*	*1985*	*1992*

we have already shown in Table 3.1. It is likely that some of this increase arose from compositional changes, but there are indicators elsewhere in the survey data that some of it was where workplaces with low levels of density changed to having none. Recent research using the data from our 1984 survey has suggested that there is a ratchet effect on union membership which makes a change from low to zero density more probable than a change in the reverse direction.[4]

Table 3.3 shows clearly that the overall shape of the distribution of union membership density changed little over the period. Among establishments with any union members, density was concentrated towards the higher end of the continuum. This was so in both 1984 and 1990. Indeed, of those establishments with members, 72 per cent had densities of a half or more in 1984; the comparable figure in 1990 was 70 per cent.

The third notable feature of Table 3.3 is the decline in the proportion of workplaces with 100 per cent density. Considering only those with any members, this proportion dropped from 18 per cent to 13 per cent. However, among manual employees the likelihood of an establishment having 100 per cent membership dropped by half, from 26 per cent to 14 per cent (or from 43 per cent to 28 per cent of those establishments with any manual union members). Clearly, 100 per cent union membership became far less common, but it would be wrong to draw the conclusion that this merely reflected a disappearance of compulsory union membership arrangements, as we show later in the chapter when we discuss the changed extent and nature of closed shop arrangements. But it is worth noting here that a relaxation of closed shops alone would be unlikely to have produced the changes apparent in Table 3.3. If workplaces had lost their closed shops, but otherwise remained unchanged we would have expected increased proportions of workplaces in the density ranges just below 100 per cent. This is not the case. The decline in density between 1984 and 1990 is certainly partly explicable by the drop in the number of workplaces with 100 per cent membership and the increase in the number of workplaces with no members. But there were also drops in density in industries and types of workplace in which 100 per cent density was a rarity in 1984.

More detailed analysis suggests that the decline in union membership over the period 1984 to 1990 affected the great bulk of industrial sectors and types of workplace. The main exceptions that we noted were in certain parts of the public sector (notably in medical and social services) and in the Banking, Finance and Insurance sector, where non-manual union membership had stayed at similar levels over the six-year period. Table 3A gives a more detailed picture of the variation in union density by industry in 1990.

Given the widespread decline in union membership, it is pertinent to ask whether the main determinants of membership changed between 1984 and 1990. We do not have information on individual reasons for joining or not joining a trade union, but our survey data are highly suitable for examining the characteristics of workplaces and organizations that are associated with high union membership. Our earlier books reporting the WIRS data included some detailed discussion of these relationships and our findings have been largely confirmed and considerably extended by secondary analysis.[5] We therefore comment only briefly below on the chief sources of variation in union density that appear in the survey data and are illustrated in Table 3.4. As before, the table is confined to private sector workplaces since the variation is greatest in this sector.

In the first three sections of the table we show the variation in union density by three measures of size. In the first of these, union density continues to show the strong relationship with size of establishment in 1990 as it did in 1984. In the second, the change in establishment size over the previous three years also continues to be strongly correlated with density, but the relationship appears to have weakened. A small part of this is an artifact of measuring change over a four-year period in 1984, compared with three years in 1990. But another part of the explanation may be that there was not such a severe contraction in employment in large, highly-unionized manufacturing plants in the period 1987–

1990 as there was in the period 1980–1984. The size of enterprises continued to show a strong positive correlation with union density.

A second characteristic of workplaces, associated with their size, is their age. In broad terms older workplaces have higher densities, partly because they are bigger. But age has an effect independent of size. There is also an interesting feature of the 1990 survey results which was not present in the earlier survey, namely that the youngest workplaces in the survey had slightly higher density levels than those in the five to nine year age range. This seems to indicate something distinctive about workplaces that were established in the early part of the 1980s, a matter we consider further in our companion volume.

The next two sections in Table 3.4 show how density varied with two aspects of the composition of the workforce: the proportion who were manual and the proportion who were part-time workers. Again both these characteristics were related to density in a similar fashion in 1990 as in 1984, but with an indication that the associations were weaker.

In the next four sections the table shows how union density in the private sector varied with a number of characteristics which secondary analysts of the 1984 data found to be significant in their multivariate analyses.[6] The first of these is the number of competitors in the establishment's product market, a rough measure of the degree of competition, a measure found by secondary analysts to be related to manual union density, after controlling for other factors. It appears to be a weak relationship in 1984 in our tabulation (which covers all employees) but rather stronger in the 1990 figures. Indeed, establishments with no competitors (comprising only around a tenth of the private sector sample) had similar union density in 1990 to that in the previous survey. In part this may be due to the movement into the private sector of highly-unionized workplaces from the former state-owned monopolies.

The suggestion from the 1984 results that more profitable workplaces had lower levels of union membership is shown in crude form in the next section of the table. The equivalent 1990 tabulation appears to show a much weaker relationship, indeed there must be doubts as to whether this association persisted.

No such doubts need be entertained over the next variable shown in the table: the local unemployment rate. The high correlation found in multivariate analyses between the local level of unemployment and the degree of union organization amongst the employed in 1984 appears to have persisted.[7] However, the idea that union membership lessens the risk of dismissal where alternative jobs are fewer is not the only plausible explanation for the relationship. One alternative but related explanation could be that employees are attracted to union membership by the more favourable redundancy terms that unions can negotiate. Another interpretation, that unions predispose unionized workplaces to employ-

Table 3.4   Aggregate union density in the private sector in relation to the characteristics of workplaces, 1984 and 1990

Percentages

	1984	1990	1990 Unweighted base	1990 Weighted base
All private sector	**42**	**35**	*1319*	*1332*
Size of establishment				
25–49 employees	26	19	*238*	*705*
50–99 employees	30	25	*247*	*352*
100–199 employees	39	33	*250*	*167*
200–499 employees	47	49	*236*	*86*
500–999 employees	60	54	*161*	*16*
1000 or more employees	72	53	*187*	*7*
Change in establishment size[1]				
Decrease of 20% or more	60	43	*128*	*94*
Decrease of less than 20%	48	45	*216*	*198*
Stable	45	40	*208*	*202*
Increase of less than 20%	36	36	*191*	*233*
Increase of 20% or more	21	25	*248*	*297*
Not known/not applicable	37	36	*328*	*308*
Age of establishment				
Less than 3 years	27	25	*79*	*97*
3–4 years	32	19	*95*	*126*
5–9 years	37	20	*147*	*208*
10–20 years	37	32	*267*	*305*
21 or more years	47	44	*701*	*566*
Size of enterprise				
25–99 employees	20	15	*170*	*432*
100–199 employees	22	17	*88*	*111*
200–999 employees	35	28	*130*	*142*
1000–4999 employees	48	39	*133*	*83*
5000–49999 employees	55	45	*224*	*174*
50000 employees or more	58	49	*209*	*161*
Not known	57	43	*365*	*227*
Proportion of employees who were manual				
More than 70%	53	43	*558*	*580*
Between 31% and 70%	45	35	*370*	*355*
Between 0 and 30%	25	26	*391*	*397*
Proportion of employees who were part-time				
More than 40%	24	21	*184*	*229*
Between 6% and 40%	35	30	*329*	*439*
Between 0 and 5%	51	42	*788*	*648*

Table 3.4 continued

Percentages

	1984	1990	1990 Unweighted base	Weighted base
Product market competitors				
None	48	48	*113*	*78*
Up to 5	48	39	*356*	*345*
More than 5	42	33	*599*	*727*
Financial performance compared with others in same industry				
Lots better	29	33	*219*	*254*
A little better	44	37	*285*	*300*
About average	45	35	*348*	*357*
A little below average	52	40	*63*	*59*
Lots below average	(74)	(63)	*27*	*16*
Local labour market unemployment rate				
Less than 3%	..	23	*280*	*322*
3–5%	..	32	*467*	*442*
5–7%	..	41	*277*	*277*
7–9%	..	48	*159*	*164*
9–11%	..	49	*96*	*87*
11% or more	..	(58)	*35*	*34*
Unions recognized by management				
Yes	67	66	*736*	*496*
No	5	4	*583*	*836*

Base: private sector establishments where number of trade union members was known
[1] In 1984, over last 4 years; in 1990, over last 3 years.

ment decline (and hence increase local unemployment) has also been put forward.[8] The first interpretation is a matter that we will return to in Chapter 6 when we look at dismissal rates.

The final section of Table 3.4 illustrates the unsurprising but crucial relationship between union membership and recognition. The contrast in membership levels between establishments in the private sector where management recognized trade unions and those where they did not is particularly striking. In 1984 the density figures were 67 per cent and 5 per cent respectively. In 1990 they were virtually unchanged at 66 per cent and 4 per cent respectively. This can be reconciled with the sub-

Table 3.5   Union membership density in 1984 and 1990 in the panel of trading sector workplaces

Number of cases (weighted)

		Union density in 1984						
		No members	1–24%	25–49%	50–79%	80–89%	90–99%	100%
Union density in 1990	No members	*148*	17	5	2	—	—	—
	1–24%	3	*19*	19	3	—	—	—
	25–49%	4	1	7	5	1	3	—
	50–79%	—	3	3	*18*	11	3	2
	80–89%	3	—	—	7	7	7	2
	90–99%	*	—	—	1	1	5	11
	100%	3	—	—	1	—	1	9

Base: panel cases with 25 or more employees in 1984 and 1990, providing overall union density estimates in both years and having no queries about consistency or establishment definition
Unweighted base: 382
Weighted base: 353

stantial decline in density across the private sector as a whole and the declines across virtually all types of establishment only by looking at changes in the pattern of union recognition by management. But before we begin that analysis we have further information about union membership which will illuminate the changing pattern of union density.

Union membership in the trading sector – panel analysis
In our panel of establishments that were interviewed in both 1984 and 1990 we have the opportunity to examine more closely what lies behind the overall decline in union density in the industrial and commercial sector of the economy, that is all the private sector plus the trading public sector as it existed in 1984. We can see how many workplaces experienced substantial changes in union density and how the overall level of density changed for these workplaces.[9] Their union densities in 1984 and 1990 are cross-tabulated in Table 3.5.

In over half of these cases there had been no change of any great magnitude (within the bands of density defined in Table 3.5). But among the remainder there was a strong preponderance of workplaces where union density had fallen over workplaces where it had risen. In fact, cases where density had fallen outnumbered cases where it had risen by a factor of three to one.

Few of the cases where density had fallen or risen had had dramatic changes in density. Of those experiencing a fall, three quarters were to the next lower band of density as we have specified them in Table 3.5; but a quarter of them lost all their members. Of those experiencing an increase in density, a half moved to the next higher band; and nearly a half of them had previously had no members at all. However, workplaces where all members were lost between 1984 and 1990 outnumbered cases where membership moved from zero to something positive by a factor of nearly two to one. However, it is the preponderance of changes to the next lower band of density that is the most striking feature of Table 3.5. So the panel results suggest a substantial drift away from union membership amongst workplaces that continued in existence from 1984 to 1990. It affected workplaces with very high density as well as those with moderate or low density. But those with low density seemed particularly likely to have lost members.

This picture of declining union density within continuing workplaces is reinforced when we look at average figures. The overall mean density in the panel cases considered above was 51 per cent in 1984. In 1990 these identical workplaces had a mean density of 42 per cent.[10] Falls were registered by every category of workplace we looked at: nationalized industries (whether privatized after 1984 or not); private manufacturing; private services; large or small workplaces; and so on. Moreover, the fall in density was very similar to that shown by our cross-sectional samples for 1984 and 1990. In the trading sector subsamples of these, density fell from 50 per cent in 1984 to 39 per cent in 1990. Thus changes in density within continuing workplaces appear to have been more important than compositional changes in the population of trading sector establishments in the overall decline in union membership.

Union recruitment and management attitudes
In examining the issue of union presence so far we have relied on information from management respondents about the current situation at their workplace regarding membership. This information has been supplemented in the second and third surveys by a few additional questions. In both the later surveys we asked managers in workplaces without union members whether unions had attempted to recruit members there. Naturally the question only gives us information about unsuccessful attempts, since it was asked only in workplaces without union members. Successful recruitment attempts are registered in the panel sample as changes from having no members to having some members – these were briefly referred to earlier. In the 1990 survey we added a further question to managers in non-union establishments about management's general attitude to trade union membership at their workplace. We expected that, taken together, these two questions would illuminate the circumstances in which workplaces were 'union free'.

Although our questions about past, unsuccessful, union recruitment attempts were asked separately about manual and non-manual workers, it is simpler for present purposes to ignore the distinction and look at the 36 per cent of our sample where there were no union members present, either manual or non-manual. As we noted earlier, these were virtually all in the private sector.

Table 3.6 shows how extensively establishments of different types had been subject to an unsuccessful attempt to recruit union members in the six years prior to our 1990 survey, so far as our management respondents were able to recall.[11] Over the private sector as a whole 12 per cent were subject to such efforts. As the table indicates, they were more likely to have occurred in larger workplaces, in manufacturing than the service sector and in independent establishments than in one belonging to a larger organization. The table also shows these same characteristics as being associated with unfavourable attitudes towards unions among management. And indeed there was an association over the sample as a whole between unfavourable management attitudes and union failures to recruit new members.

It is also noteworthy how extensive the negative attitudes to trade unions were in the private sector. In nearly a third of workplaces without union members management attitudes to unions were hostile. What is more, in only 2 per cent of the remainder did managers claim to

Table 3.6 **Recent union recruitment attempts and management attitude to unions in private sector non-union workplaces, 1990**

Percentages

	Unsuccessful union recruitment attempt in last six years	Management not in favour of trade unions	Unweighted base	Weighted base
All private sector non-union				
establishments	**12**	**31**	*488*	*713*
Establishment size				
25–99 employees	10	30	*275*	*613*
100–499 employees	21	33	*159*	*95*
500 or more	19	43	*54*	*4*
Sector				
Manufacturing	21	46	*138*	*181*
Services	9	26	*350*	*532*
Ownership				
Independent	14	39	*128*	*250*
Part of larger organization	10	25	*360*	*463*

Base: private sector establishments with no current union members

favour trade union membership. So, as two thirds of managers reported an attitude of neutrality, management antipathy cannot be the major reason for over a third of private sector workplaces having no union members.

While unfavourable attitudes on the part of management may explain part of the extent to which workplaces have no union members, a rather stronger influence might be actual behaviour on the part of management to discourage union membership. When designing the questionnaires for the 1990 survey we were aware of the ongoing debate about the rights to belong or not to belong to a trade union that culminated in the provisions of the Employment Act 1990 that gave legal force to both of these individual rights. Our final question about union membership in non-unionized workplaces thus asked management respondents if any steps were taken to find out whether potential recruits to their workforce were union members. In 10 per cent of cases (all of them in the private sector) respondents said that such steps were taken. In the great majority of cases this amounted to asking job applicants if they were union members; very few used other methods, which we may assume included reference to information agencies supplying lists of union members to employers.

Surprisingly, managements that enquired about union membership from job applicants were no more likely to report hostile attitudes to trade unions than other managements in non-union workplaces. Hostile attitudes were much more prevalent among workplaces with a predominantly male workforce and somewhat more prevalent among branches of larger organizations than among independent workplaces. This latter relationship is suggestive of a general management policy of union avoidance in some larger organizations rather than a widespread anti-union stance among smaller firms.

Trade union recognition

The recognition by management of trade unions for negotiating pay and conditions of employment remained the key expression of management's willingness to allow trade unions to represent employees in our survey. Having ascertained that there were some union members present and recorded the names of the unions (or staff associations) concerned, interviewers asked our main management respondents, 'Are any of these unions recognized for negotiating pay and conditions for any section of the workforce in this establishment?' As in previous surveys, if agreements were negotiated at a higher level in an organization than the establishment, but applied to members or other employees in the establishment, the unions were counted as being recognized. Table 3.7 shows the results overall and for the three broad sectors of the economy.

The extent of recognition, 1980, 1984 and 1990

The clear picture is one of substantial decline in the extent of recognition since 1984. The figure for all workplaces and all employees fell from 66 per cent in 1984 to 53 per cent in 1990. Thus by 1990 only just over half of workplaces were ones where the employer recognized one or more unions for collective bargaining over basic pay for some of the employees present. This is a striking change compared with the 1980 to 1984 period, when there was stability in the overall figures. Moreover, whereas in the earlier period there was a mixture of sectors with increasing and decreasing recognition, the later period shows substantial falls in each of the three broad sectors. We discuss the three sectors in turn below.

In private manufacturing, the fall in the proportion of workplaces with recognized unions, from 56 to 44 per cent, continued a trend that was already apparent at the beginning of the 1980s. Recognition of manual trade unions fell from 65 per cent to 44 per cent of workplaces over the decade, representing a major weakening of union presence in a sector of traditional strength. Regarding non-manual employees in pri-

Table 3.7 Trade union recognition, by broad sector, 1980, 1984 and 1990

Percentages

	All establishments			Private manufacturing			Private services			Public sector		
	1980	1984	1990	1980	1984	1990	1980	1984	1990	1980	1984	1990
Establishments with recognized trade unions for manual workers:												
as a proportion of all establishments	55	62	48	65	55	44	33	38	31	76	91	78
as a proportion of establishments with manual union members	86	91	83	85	85	77	80	81	76	92	99	91
Base: establishments with manual workers												
Unweighted	*1899*	*1853*	*1831*	*734*	*580*	*616*	*521*	*515*	*654*	*644*	*758*	*561*
Weighted	*1823*	*1749*	*1697*	*498*	*412*	*417*	*755*	*689*	*780*	*570*	*648*	*500*
Establishments with recognized trade unions for non-manual workers:												
as a proportion of all establishments	47	54	43	27	26	23	28	30	26	91	98	84
as a proportion of establishments with non-manual union members	87	92	84	74	75	89	82	85	80	93	99	85
Base: establishments with non-manual workers												
Unweighted	*2034*	*2010*	*2058*	*743*	*592*	*630*	*585*	*593*	*798*	*706*	*825*	*630*
Weighted	*1987*	*1985¹*	*1992*	*503*	*424*	*426*	*854*	*836*	*977*	*631*	*726*	*590*
Establishments with recognized trade unions for any workers:												
as a proportion of all establishments	64	66	53	65	56	44	41	44	36	94	99	87
as a proportion of establishments with any union members	88	91	83	84	83	77	81	82	78	95	99	89
Base: all establishments												
Unweighted	*2040*	*2019*	*2061*	*743*	*592*	*630*	*587*	*597*	*799*	*710*	*830*	*632*
Weighted	*2000*	*2000*	*2000*	*503*	*424*	*426*	*859*	*843*	*981*	*638*	*733*	*594*

¹ See Note H.

vate manufacturing there was little change: a modest fall from just over a quarter of workplaces in 1984 to just under a quarter in 1990. It remained the case in manufacturing, almost without exception, that non-manual unions were only recognized where manual unions were recognized at the same workplace.

The decline in union recognition in private manufacturing industry was not widespread, but confined to certain substantial parts of it. We distinguished 11 industrial sectors within manufacturing in our analysis: four of these showed declines in recognition, the other seven showed little, if any, change. Three of the four with a substantial decline covered the engineering and vehicles industries, where the collapse of the industry-wide negotiating machinery in 1989 may well have had an impact.[12] Broadly speaking, recognition covered just over half of engineering workplaces in 1984 but only a third in 1990. The fourth industry sector within manufacturing showed an even sharper drop. This sector included printing and publishing, with the drop in workplaces with recognition being from over three quarters to under half. This reflects the well-known moves by employers in the printing and publishing industries to de-recognize or reduce the influence of the trade unions in other ways. But engineering and printing are exceptional; if we look at the rest of manufacturing the level of recognition stayed constant between 1984 and 1990 at around half of workplaces.

Besides their industrial activity, we examined a number of other characteristics of manufacturing workplaces to explore further the change in the extent of union recognition. The pattern in relation to establishment size was particularly illuminating, for it appeared that the decline in recognition was primarily a feature of smaller establishments. In establishments with fewer than 200 employees the fall was substantial; above this size there was hardly any change, the figures for 1984 and 1990 being 84 and 81 per cent respectively. Moreover, when we turned our attention to establishments that were independent of any larger organization, mostly small firms, the decline in recognition was again particularly marked, from 43 to 26 per cent.

In private services the drop in the extent of union recognition was smaller than in manufacturing: from 44 to 36 per cent between 1984 and 1990 and from 41 to 36 per cent over the ten years covered by our surveys. There are some similarities with the pattern of change in private manufacturing and some notable differences. In terms of industries, three sectors had substantial declines: Hotels and Catering; Transport; and Business Services (excluding banking and insurance). In both Transport and Business Services, substantial parts of the sectors had experienced deregulation, with a shift in the structure of the industry towards new small firms and these, as in manufacturing, were much less likely to recognize unions. On the other hand, two sectors of private service industry showed marked increases in union recognition. These sectors were Energy and Water and the residual 'Other Services'. Both of these had experienced a transfer of organizations or activities from public ownership arising from privatization: our panel data showed that such employers retained their basic recognition arrangements in virtually every case.

As in manufacturing, the drop in the extent of recognition in private services was largely confined to smaller establishments – those with less than 200 employees. Similarly, it was more pronounced in independent establishments than in those that belonged to larger organizations. Of the latter, foreign-owned workplaces were particularly prominent; among them recognition fell from 45 to 27 per cent. There was also a marked drop in the extent of recognition in those establishments employing substantial numbers of ethnic minority workers, a trend that was already apparent in the private sector between 1980 and 1984.

An obvious source of explanation for a drop in the extent of recognition is if new establishments are less likely to have recognition than establishments that have ceased to exist. We will be examining this issue in more detail in our companion volume, where both the sample of new workplaces and the panel sample will be brought to bear. However, we can already see from the main 1990 survey results that newer workplaces in the private sector were considerably less likely to have recognized unions than older workplaces. Workplaces that were less than 10 years old recognized unions in 23 per cent of cases compared with 52 per cent of those that were more than 20 years old. But this relationship with age was not a smooth one; the private sector workplaces that had the lowest level of recognition were those that were seven to ten years old, in other words, those that were set up in the early part of the 1980s. This must largely explain the similar, but less pronounced relationship, regarding membership density that we remarked upon earlier.

In the public sector the fall in the extent of union recognition is almost entirely explained by the withdrawal by the Government in 1987 of negotiating rights for teachers in state schools in England and Wales. Nearly 90 per cent of the publicly-owned workplaces with no recognized unions were in the education sector. They tended to be small schools with small numbers of non-teaching staff. (In larger schools, significant numbers of non-teaching staff covered by negotiated settlements for non-teaching local authority employees meant that these establishments would have some recognized unions.) Schools account for a substantial proportion of public sector workplaces and the effect of this one case of withdrawal of recognition is almost wholly responsible for the overall public sector figure dropping from 99 to 87 per cent between 1984 and 1990.

Changes in recognition 1984–1990

The results we have presented so far have traced the extent of trade union recognition at the time of our three surveys. These three snapshots can be enhanced by additional information derived from two sources in the 1990 survey. One is our panel of trading sector workplaces interviewed in both 1984 and 1990. The other is some brief additional questioning inserted into the 1990 questionnaire to ascertain the extent of new recognition and of de-recognition. In the current context we use the term *de-recognition* to refer to the complete withdrawal of trade union negotiating rights over pay at a workplace; later in the chapter we will mention partial de-recognition, where the number or coverage of negotiating groups is reduced but there remains at least one recognized union at the workplace in question.

Regarding full de-recognition, we asked managers in workplaces with no recognized unions if there had been any recognized unions there during the last six years, a considerable period over which to recall such matters. We anticipated that there would be very few such cases and therefore did not ask a number of other questions about de-recognition which it would have been interesting to ask. In practice we merely asked how long ago the de-recognition had taken place.

As expected, the number of cases of reported de-recognition was small. Three per cent of all workplaces without any recognized unions in 1990 had previously had recognized unions at some stage in the period 1984 to 1990. These amounted to just over 1 per cent of all workplaces in 1990. In the public sector nearly all cases were in the education sector, reflecting the government's abolition of the teachers' negotiating machinery in 1987.

In private sector workplaces, the overall extent of de-recognition was very small. One per cent of managers in workplaces without recognized unions reported having de-recognized their trade unions during the previous six years. The proportions were a little higher in manufacturing, a little lower in the services sector. Taking the whole of the private sector it amounted to less than 1 per cent. More broadly, these results appeared to confirm the judgement of specific research on de-recognition[13] that concluded that it was not widespread. However, our limited data on the timing of de-recognition, with a substantial concentration in 1989, was suggestive of a growing phenomenon.

To examine the extent of new recognition, which we also expected to be rare, we asked managers in workplaces with recognized unions how many recognized unions there were there three years ago.[14] The results on the numbers of unions are discussed in a later section of this chapter, but for the moment we need just consider the responses that reported that the number three years ago was zero. These cases of new recognition amounted to less than 1 per cent of private sector workplaces with recognized unions in 1990 or less than half of 1 per cent of the whole private sector sample over the three-year period. This compares with half of 1 per cent over the most recent three years for de-recognition.[15] On this evidence, then, cases of new recognition and of de-recognition were extremely rare. So much so that the balance between the two directions is not detectable with any reliability from our cross-sectional surveys.

The evidence from our panel of trading sector workplaces, however, shows a considerably greater degree of change and a clear preponderance of de-recognition. Comparing 1984 with 1990 responses to our basic question on the presence of recognized unions, 87 per cent of the panel sample showed no change, 9 per cent indicated that de-recognition had occurred and 4 per cent indicated that unions had become recognized in the last six years. More strikingly, nearly a fifth of panel workplaces that reported recognized unions in 1984 reported no recognized unions in 1990. And nearly a tenth of workplaces with recognized unions in 1990 apparently had none in 1984. There seems therefore to be a conflict of evidence here between our panel data and our retrospective data, but, on methodological grounds, the panel evidence seems preferable to the retrospective evidence.[16]

There are also substantive grounds for taking the panel evidence more seriously. Within the manufacturing sector, nearly all of the cases of de-recognition were in the engineering industry and were quite small establishments. These were plausibly cases where the collapse of the industry's national agreement left management with an opportunity to determine pay on its own. Secondly, in both manufacturing and services the establishments apparently affected by de-recognition were ones where union density in 1984 had been lower than average and had fallen sharply. In over half of the cases there were no union members present in 1990. It seems plausible that in many of these workplaces union negotiating rights simply withered away through lack of support from employees. This would fit with the under-reporting of de-recognition from the retrospective questions and adds further weight to our judgement that the panel data are more dependable.

On this basis it seems likely that the private sector in the late 1980s saw a fall in the proportion of establishments with recognized trade unions that arose in part from a withdrawal, or withering away, of recognition in a substantial minority of workplaces that existed throughout the period. Changes in the composition of the population of workplaces, especially the closure of large, traditional, highly-unionized plants in manufacturing, seem to have played a lesser part in the overall picture of change than was the case in the early 1980s.

Union presence without recognition

The recognition by management of trade unions for the purposes of collective bargaining over rates of pay – the sense in which we use the term 'union recognition' throughout this book – reflects a critical level of acceptance by management of a role for the union or unions in the conduct of industrial relations. Unions may have members in a workplace but fail to achieve this level of acceptance by management. Nevertheless they, through their lay or paid officials, may still have some representational role, possibly negotiating about issues other than pay, perhaps representing employees in disciplinary hearings or being consulted on matters such as health and safety. Such representational activities are discussed at a number of points in later chapters of the book. At this point our aim is to describe the prevalence of such situations and the types of workplace involved. We distinguish two types of situation.

In the first, unrecognized unions exist alongside recognized unions at the same workplace. This was the case in 6 per cent of all establishments in our 1990 survey, much the same as in 1984 when it was 7 per cent. However, there was a distinct change in the types of workplace where these situations occurred. In 1984 private manufacturing had the highest incidence (11 per cent) with the public sector intermediate at 8 per cent and private services the lowest at 3 per cent. In 1990 the sector with the highest incidence was the public sector where 15 per cent of workplaces had both recognized and unrecognized unions. This in large part reflects the loss of pay bargaining rights by the nursing and teaching unions. In private manufacturing there was a substantial drop from 11 per cent to 3 per cent of establishments. From what we have already seen about changes in recognition over the period it is highly unlikely that this change occurred because managements recognized unions which previously they had not recognized. Far more likely is that unions that had members but no recognition failed to keep those members. This would also help to account for the substantial fall in membership in manufacturing industry which we discussed earlier.

The second type of situation that we distinguish is where there are union members at a workplace but no union is recognized by management for pay bargaining. The incidence of such workplaces rose from 7 per cent in 1984 to 11 per cent in 1990. Here again the de-recognition of the nursing and teaching unions seems to account for nearly all of the change. In the public sector the figure rose from 1 per cent in 1984 to 11 per cent in 1990. Elsewhere there was no change, the figures for both manufacturing and services in the private sector being close to 10 per cent in both surveys.

Union density in these latter situations was generally low. In 1984 membership density where no unions were recognized was 22 per cent; in 1990 it was 33 per cent. The increase was largely a reflection of the education and medical sectors where membership remained high despite the loss of union bargaining rights over pay. Elsewhere membership density was usually lower, reflecting perhaps a combination of employer antipathy to unions and a lack of widespread support for union membership among employees. Employer antipathy may indeed be the dominant factor since the incidence of union membership and no recognition was particularly high in independent firms. In fact, in the independent firm sector it was nearly as common for workplaces with union members to have no recognition as it was for them to have recognition (48 per cent were in the former category). It was here too, as we noted earlier, management attitudes were more commonly antagonistic to unions.

Multi-unionism

One of the distinctive features of British industrial relations is the large number of trade unions. Compared with most other European countries the number is enormous and the sheer complexity of negotiating arrangements in Britain is almost incomprehensible to Europeans. Our two previous surveys have been widely used to document this complexity and to explore its consequences for strike incidence.[17] During the 1980s there emerged a considerable body of opinion in favour of moving towards less complex representational and negotiating arrangements; and there were some well-publicized 'single-union deals' and moves to 'single-table bargaining'. The WIRS surveys contain much evidence relevant to these discussions and we added to our core questions from the previous surveys to give us additional information. We begin our analysis of this material by looking at the numbers of recognized unions in a way that permits direct comparisons with the 1980 and 1984 results. Thus Tables 3.8 and 3.9 show the distribution of numbers of recognized unions with manual members and with non-manual members respectively.

The picture, broadly speaking, hardly changed. Regarding manual unions the distribution within workplaces of the number of unions in 1990 was much the same as it was in 1984 and indeed in 1980: close to a third of workplaces with recognized manual unions had two or more recognized manual unions; around 15 per cent in each of the three surveys had three or more. Nor has there been much sign of change within the three broad sectors of the economy identified separately in the table. The only possible exception to this appears to be an increase in private services of establishments with four or more recognized manual unions: the proportion with this number rose from practically nil to 4 per cent. That was largely the by now familiar effect of privatization; the service sector gained a number of large establishments with multi-union representation from the former nationalized industries.

Table 3.8   Number of recognized manual unions, by broad sector, 1980, 1984 and 1990

Column percentages

	All establishments			Private manufacturing			Private services			Public sector		
	1980	1984	1990	1980	1984	1990	1980	1984	1990	1980	1984	1990
Number of recognized unions												
1	65	65	66	63	58	61	86	80	77[1]	55	62	61
2	18	21	19	18	22	23	8	18	17	23	22	19
3	9	8	9	10	14	9	3	2	3	12	8	13
4 or more	8	6	6	9	6	7	3	*	4	10	8	6
Not known	*	*	—	—	—	—	—	—	—	2	*	—
Base: establishments with recognized unions for manual workers												
Unweighted	*1375*	*1405*	*1236*	*596*	*462*	*443*	*231*	*231*	*299*	*548*	*712*	*494*
Weighted	*1021*	*1077*	*815*	*324*	*228*	*186*	*256*	*260*	*242*	*441*	*589*	*388*

[1] See Note C.

Table 3.9 Number of recognized non-manual unions, by broad sector, 1980, 1984 and 1990

Column percentages

	All establishments			Private manufacturing			Private services			Public sector		
	1980	1984	1990	1980	1984	1990	1980	1984	1990	1980	1984	1990
Number of recognized unions												
1	43	39	45[1]	65	69	73	68	63	58	28	25	33
2	29	28	31	20	21	22	29	32	34	32	27	31
3	12	15	9	13	7	3	2	3	5	16	21	13
4 or more	16	18	14	3	3	2	2	2	3	25	26	23
Not known	*	*	—	—	—	—	—	—	—	*	*	—
Base: establishments with recognized unions for non-manual workers												
Unweighted	*1277*	*1397*	*1230*	*407*	*351*	*341*	*208*	*229*	*306*	*662*	*817*	*583*
Weighted	*943²*	*1069*	*848*	*134*	*109*	*100*	*236*	*247*	*255*	*572*	*713*	*493*

[1] See Note C.
[2] See Note H.

There is slightly more change in the equivalent picture for non-manual unions. The proportion of establishments with three or more recognized non-manual unions fell from 33 per cent in 1984 to 23 per cent in 1990; but over the whole decade the drop was only five percentage points. The change between 1984 and 1990 was confined to the public sector and here we must remember the widespread effect of the de-recognition of the nursing and teaching unions.[18] In fact, if we exclude the education and medical services sectors from the comparison there is no change in the public sector between 1984 and 1990: the proportion of workplaces with three or more recognized non-manual unions remained the same at 19 per cent.

Extreme cases of multi-unionism were by 1990 confined to the public sector. In 1980 there were some large manufacturing plants with ten or more manual unions as well as large public sector workplaces, notably hospitals, with ten or more non-manual unions. By 1990 only the latter remained; they constituted only 1 per cent of public sector workplaces but accounted for a much larger proportion of employment.

Multi-unionism in 1990

So far we have examined multi-unionism in the same terms as in previous surveys, classifying trade unions as either having manual members or non-manual members. This was the distinction that we used in the first two surveys in the series but decided not to maintain in the 1990 survey. In fact the results presented so far have had to combine data about the types of union present to make the results comparable over time.[19] Specifically, we have added recognized unions with both manual and non-manual members to those with only manual members to give the number of recognized manual unions; recognized non-manual unions have been defined so far in an analogous way. It is now time to drop that form of redefinition and describe unions in the terms we actually asked about them in the 1990 survey. The results presented are in terms of recognized unions only.

Having established that there were some union members at a workplace, interviewers asked our main management respondents in 1990, 'How many unions are there that have members only among the manual workforce, members only among the non-manual workforce, and members both among the manual and non-manual workforce'. Answers were recorded separately for these three categories, as well as for the total number of unions. The next questions identified the unions (or staff associations) by name and then which of them, if any, were recognized. For convenience we refer here to unions with both manual and non-manual members as 'mixed' unions.

Table 3.10 shows the distribution of the number of unions in each of the three categories for all establishments with recognized unions of any

Table 3.10   Numbers of recognized unions, 1990

	Any unions	Manual only	Non-manual only	Mixed
				Column percentages
None	—	46	37	64
1	36[1]	40	33	29
2	31	9	15	5
3	12	4	5	1
4 or more	20	2	9	*
Mean	2.5	0.8	1.3	0.45
Base: establishments with recognized unions				
Unweighted	*1417*	*1417*	*1417*	*1417*
Weighted	*1058*	*1058*	*1058*	*1058*

[1] See Note C.

type.[20] Mixed unions were present in 36 per cent of such establishments, a clear confirmation that our elaboration of the questionnaire was necessary. However, separate unions for manual and for non-manual employees remained the dominant form of representation in unionized workplaces in Britain; 54 per cent of unionized workplaces had 'manual-only' unions; 63 per cent had 'non-manual-only' unions. Moreover, it was not only that separate unions for manual and for non-manual employees was the more common pattern – separate unions were also more numerous in the workplaces where they were present. Compared with an average of 0.4 for mixed unions, there were 0.8 manual-only unions and 1.3 non-manual-only unions. The overall average of 2.5 unions (of any type) in workplaces with recognized unions is a measure of the high degree of multi-unionism in Britain. In Table 3.11 and the following paragraphs we examine the variation of that measure across different types of workplace. We also highlight the more extreme cases by showing the extent of workplaces with four or more unions.

The most striking feature of Table 3.11 is the much greater degree of multi-unionism in the public sector than the private sector of the economy. The average public sector workplace had 3.3 recognized unions compared with 1.7 in the private sector. Thirty three per cent of public sector workplaces had four or more recognized unions, whereas only 8 per cent of private sector workplaces had this many. Secondly, in both sectors multi-unionism increased markedly with the size of the workplace. No doubt this reflects a greater variety of occupations in larger workplaces and the historical fact that most British trade unions were founded on an

Table 3.11   **Degrees of multi-unionism, 1990**

	Mean number of recognized unions	Percentage of establishments with 4 or more recognized unions	*Unweighted base*	*Weighted base*
All sectors	**2.5**	**20**	*1417*	*1058*
Public sector:	**3.3**	**33**	*594*	*519*
Establishment size:				
25–99	2.9	26	*165*	*385*
100–499	3.7	43	*185*	*109*
500–999	5.9	84	*80*	*16*
1000+	8.4	91	*164*	*10*
Private sector:	**1.7**	**8**	*823*	*538*
Establishment size:				
25–99	1.5	2	*187*	*369*
100–499	2.1	16	*322*	*151*
500–999	3.4	48	*147*	*13*
1000+	4.0	63	*167*	*6*
Age of establishment:				
Less than 5 years	1.5	3	*69*	*70*
5–9 years	(1.7)	(3)	*48*	*37*
10–20 years	1.4	4	*135*	*97*
More than 20 years	1.9	11	*549*	*314*

Base: establishments with recognized unions.

occupational basis. However, if workplaces of a similar size are compared across the two sectors it is clear that public sector workplaces had a much greater degree of multi-unionism than the private sector for workplaces of a given size. And all the extreme cases of multi-unionism were by 1990 in the public sector: the majority of large hospitals had more than ten recognized unions or staff associations with members present; the most extreme case in the sample reported well over 40.

The final section of Table 3.11 shows how multi-unionism varied with the age of establishments in the private sector. The only clear difference here is between establishments that were less than 20 years old and ones that were older than this. The latter had more unions on average. And this difference persisted when we compared establishments of similar sizes in our analysis. Partly this may be because many of the older workplaces had contracted substantially and their union representation reflected their previous, larger size. Looking at the other, younger workplaces, it may be a cause for some surprise that those that were set up during the 1980s, and particularly in the latter part of the decade, showed no tendency to have fewer recognized unions.

Other characteristics of establishments that we examined in relation to multi-unionism showed little systematic variation. Of particular interest is the result that foreign-owned and UK-owned workplaces had similar degrees of multi-unionism when we compared workplaces of similar sizes. But this is not to say that their bargaining arrangements were of similar complexity, as we shall see in a later section.

Changes in multi-unionism at individual workplaces
The above analyses have been concerned with the population of workplaces as it existed at the time of each of our surveys – they compared 'snapshots' using the main cross-sectional samples. We have an additional source of information on the changing extent of multi-unionism from some new, retrospective questions included in the 1990 survey. Besides asking managers the number of recognized unions at their establishment three years ago, we asked them, in cases where there had been a change, what was the reason for the change and whether management had tried to change the bargaining arrangements in ways that, *inter alia*, would affect the number of unions.

The retrospective question on the number of recognized unions three years before the survey showed a modest net decrease in the degree of multi-unionism. Compared with a current mean of 2.5 unions per establishment, the mean for three years previously was 2.7 unions.[21] Overall, 10 per cent of unionized establishments – or 14 per cent of multi-union establishments in 1987 – experienced a decrease in the number of recognized unions; on the other hand, 3 per cent experienced an increase. The overwhelming majority of unionized establishments, 86 per cent, had the same number of unions in 1990 as they had in 1987.

In the private sector, 15 per cent of multi-union workplaces had experienced decreased numbers of unions, while only 1 per cent of unionized workplaces showed increases. The mean number of unions fell from 2.1 to 1.9. The main reason given in this sector for having fewer unions was that membership of particular unions had dwindled away to a point where separate representation was no longer justified. In nearly a half of cases managers said this. The second most common reason given was that unions had amalgamated.

Most of the change in multi-unionism was in the public sector, where it was most widespread anyway. But the proportion of establishments affected was similar to that in the private sector. Here 14 per cent of multi-union workplaces had had decreases while 6 per cent had had increases in the numbers of recognized unions. The mean number of unions in this sector fell from 3.5 to 3.3. The two most common reasons for decreases were union amalgamations and the de-recognition of the teaching unions. Transfers of membership from one union to another also played a small part.

The small numbers of cases with increases in the number of unions preclude any detailed analysis of the reasons given. Taking all sectors together, the two most common reasons were that an additional union gained recognition from management and that new jobs or occupational groups at a workplace led to an increase. Again, most cases were in the public sector. In response to the additional question about recent management moves to alter bargaining arrangements, 4 per cent of managers where unions were recognized reported attempts within the last three years to reduce the number of unions they dealt with. These attempts were equally spread across the main sectors. Moves towards the opposite direction – dealing with more unions – were reported in 1 per cent of cases. In short, this evidence points towards some limited movement in the period up to 1990 concerning the degree of multi-unionism, with the balance clearly towards reducing it.

Our panel data, which cover the whole of the period from 1984 to 1990, not just the last three years, confirm this trend. In workplaces that had only recognized manual unions in 1984, two thirds had the same number in 1990; but where the number changed, decreases were more common than increases by a ratio of three to two.[22] For non-manual unions there was less change but a greater tendency towards fewer unions: over three quarters had the same number in both years, but the ratio of reductions to increases was four to one. Overall, both the cross-sectional and the panel evidence point strongly to a decrease in multi-unionism.

Competition for membership in multi-union situations
One of the implications of the high degree of multi-unionism described above is that the potential for inter-union competition is widespread. Of course, this potential is not limited to multi-union workplaces, but realistically it is much more likely where more than one union already has members. However, actual competition between unions for members at existing workplaces has been constrained for a long time by the Trade Union Congress's 'Bridlington Principles'. Recent suggestions within the trade union movement that the principles are in need of review together with government proposals to provide individuals with the right to join the union of their choice[23] have brought the issue of inter-union competition back into public discussion. It is thus of interest to know the extent to which inter-union competition for membership already exists, prior to any legal changes which might stimulate it.

On such an issue it was most appropriate to include questions in our interviews with worker representatives. We asked those that represented recognized unions and who had already stated that there were other unions at their workplace[24] two questions in the 1990 survey: first, considering groups of employees doing broadly similar jobs, were there any of these groups in which more than one union had members; for those that answered positively we asked whether there was active competition between the unions to recruit members. The first question revealed clear majorities of multi-union workplaces with immediate potential for inter-union competition: 54 per cent of manual worker representatives in multi-union workplaces said there were occupational groups with more than one union having members; 63 per cent of non-manual representatives reported similarly. The circumstances were more commonly reported in the public sector than elsewhere, although for non-manuals it was equally high in private services. And as we might expect, these cases of potential inter-union competition for membership were more common in workplaces with greater numbers of unions and in larger workplaces. But what about the incidence of active competition in such circumstances?

About a quarter of worker representatives who reported that there were groups with members in more than one union said there was active inter-union competition at the time of our survey (25 per cent of manual representatives; 27 per cent of non-manual representatives). It was more commonly reported by manual representatives in the public sector (32 per cent of cases) and only rarely (10 per cent) in private manufacturing. For non-manual workers it was the private services sector where inter-union competition was more commonly reported – a half of cases, compared with a quarter for the other two main sectors.

In broad terms, then, active inter-union competition was not prevalent where multi-unionism was already established. Just over half of worker representatives in multi-union workplaces reported the conditions for its existence and a quarter of these reported that it actually occurred. Its occurrence is thus reported in something over 10 per cent of multi-union workplaces or around 5 per cent of workplaces with recognized unions. However, this was at the time when the institutional restraints on TUC-affiliated unions were in operation. It could be substantially larger in other circumstances.

Bargaining structure

The complexity of the relationships between management and trade unions in Britain is further illustrated by their bargaining structure. In some cases, all the employees at a workplace whose pay is covered by collective bargaining have their pay and conditions of employment agreed in a single negotiating forum, an arrangement that has recently come to be referred to as 'single-table bargaining'. Such an arrangement may involve just a single union or it may involve several unions. In more

Table 3.12   **Numbers of bargaining units, by broad sector, 1990**

	All establishments	Private manufacturing	Private services	Public sector
				Column percentages
Number of bargaining units				
1	43	63	58[1]	26
2	32	22	25	41
3	13	11	13	15
4 or more	12	4	5	19
Mean	2.0	1.6	1.7	2.5
Base: establishments with recognized unions				
Unweighted	*1417*	*450*	*373*	*594*
Weighted	*1058*	*189*	*349*	*519*

[1] See Note C.

complex situations there are two or more negotiating forums, each with one or more unions representing employees. Unions may take part in more than one of these sets of negotiations.

Our summary measure of the complexity of these negotiating arrangements is the number of bargaining units. Table 3.12 shows the distribution of this measure, both for the whole economy and separately for the three broad sectors of employment. Overall, there was an average of 2.0 bargaining units in 1990 for each workplace with recognized unions. Over two fifths of such workplaces had just a single bargaining unit; over a tenth had four or more. The table also shows clearly that the most complex structures were overwhelmingly in the public sector. Only a quarter of public sector workplaces had a single bargaining unit compared with around three fifths in the private sector. A fifth of public sector workplaces had four or more bargaining units compared with just 5 per cent of private sector ones. It is also striking how similar the two parts of the private sector were. Our analysis below therefore examines separately the public sector and the private sector (both manufacturing and services, combined).

The public sector average of 2.5 bargaining units per establishment varied most notably with the size of the establishment. In the smallest public sector workplaces, with 25 to 49 employees, the average was 2.2, but in the largest workplaces it was 4.3. As was the case with the number of unions, this must in part reflect the greater number of occupational groups in larger workplaces. Among the different activities covered by the public sector, medical services had the highest average at

Table 3.13   **Number of bargaining units, by number of recognized unions in the public sector, 1990**

Percentages

	Number of recognized unions			
	1	2	3	4 or more
Number of bargaining units				
1	(12)	8	4	2
2	(1)	29	4	7
3	—	1	7	7
4 or more	—	—	1	17
Base: public sector establishments with recognized unions				
Unweighted	*44*	*124*	*83*	*343*
Weighted	*69*	*198*	*83*	*171*

3.7. And, clearly, this understates the complexity of pay determination structures in this sector because major occupational groups such as doctors and nurses have their pay determined by methods other than collective bargaining. However, even staying with our current concern, bargaining units involving unions and management, the medical services sector had by far the most complex structures, with some cases having over ten bargaining units.

Table 3.13 shows how the number of bargaining units and the number of recognized unions related to each other in the public sector. The numbers given are the percentage of all public sector workplaces with the combination specified by the row and the column in the table. Thus only 12 per cent of public sector workplaces had a single recognized union *and* a single bargaining unit (the cell in the top left-hand corner of the table). All the remainder had complex arrangements. Thus 14 per cent (the remainder of the top row of the table) had a single bargaining unit with more than one constituent union. All the rest had multiple bargaining units, virtually all with multiple unions. Workplaces with four or more bargaining units and four or more unions (the bottom right-hand cell of the table) accounted for 17 per cent of the public sector sample. Such workplaces employed 38 per cent of employees.

The similar table for the private sector (Table 3.14) shows a much greater prevalence of simple bargaining structures. Over half of private sector workplaces with recognized unions had just one bargaining unit comprising a single trade union. A further 5 per cent had 'single-table bargaining' involving two or more unions. The most complex structures with four or more bargaining units and four or more unions accounted

Table 3.14   Number of bargaining units, by number of recognized unions in the private sector, 1990

Percentages

	Number of recognized unions			
	1	2	3	4 or more
Number of bargaining units				
1	54	3	1	1
2	4	17	1	1
3	*	3	6	3
4 or more	*	1	1	3
Base: private sector establishments with recognized unions				
Unweighted	*288*	*169*	*104*	*262*
Weighted	*315*	*133*	*48*	*43*

for only 3 per cent of workplaces with recognized unions (and only 12 per cent of employees).

The private sector average of 1.6 bargaining units also varied markedly with the size of workplaces. For the smallest workplaces it averaged 1.4; in the largest with over 1000 employees it was 3.1. Older workplaces (those more than 20 years old) tended to have rather more bargaining units and this tendency persisted when we compared workplaces of similar size. But there was no clear tendency for sites established in the 1980s to have less complex negotiating structures than those established in the 1970s. Simpler structures were more common in foreign-owned workplaces, a relationship we noted in both the earlier surveys.[25] As before this was particularly apparent when we compared results among workplaces of similar size. In an analogous way there was a tendency in the 1990 survey for workplaces belonging to UK-based multinational companies to have more bargaining units than those belonging to purely domestic companies.

Changes in bargaining structure at individual workplaces

In our report comparing the first two surveys in the series we noted a slight movement from more complex to simpler bargaining structures. Unfortunately our modifications to the survey questioning on the union composition of negotiating groups prevent us from making precise comparisons between 1990 and the earlier dates. In the earlier surveys we maintained a strict distinction between manual and non-manual workers in asking about their unions and bargaining groups. In the 1990 survey we allowed for the possibility that unions with predominantly manual workers might negotiate as part of a bargaining unit that covered mostly non-manual workers. In fact, this arrangement was the sole form of pay bargaining arrangement for manual workers in 8 per cent of establishments where a predominantly manual union was recognized. Nearly all of these cases were in the services sector, with private and public ownership having a similar incidence of such cases. However, the reverse case was even more common. A full 15 per cent of establishments that recognized predominantly non-manual unions had no separate bargaining unit for these employees. Their pay was determined in a negotiating group consisting mostly of unions representing manual workers. In private manufacturing industry this was in fact the most common arrangement, being present in 53 per cent of plants with recognized non-manual unions. In private services, where non-manual workers are usually the majority of the workforce, it was far less common, affecting 16 per cent of workplaces with recognized non-manual unions. It seems clear, then, that in the private sector, at least, negotiating arrangements often involved a mixture of unions with manual employees and unions with non-manual employees as well as unions with both manual and non-manual employees. It is highly likely that this situation was more common in 1990 than when we started the survey series in 1980, but there is no simple and precise set of results that we can present to demonstrate this. We do, however, have some further evidence from retrospective questions asked in the 1990 survey that enables us to examine changes in bargaining structure over the more recent past.

The first of these retrospective questions asked managers the number of bargaining groups three years prior to the interview.[26] Compared with a current mean of 2.0 bargaining groups per establishment the mean for three years previously was 2.2 groups. Eight per cent of establishments with recognized unions had fewer bargaining groups than before, but this amounted to 14 per cent of those that had multiple bargaining groups in 1987. Four per cent of unionized establishments had a greater number of bargaining groups in 1990 than in 1987. The overwhelming majority (88 per cent) had the same number as three years before. Service sector establishments, particularly in the private sector, showed a greater tendency to change than manufacturing, but the differences were not great.

As with the shifts in the number of unions, the number of establishments affected by changes in the number of bargaining groups were too few to sustain detailed analysis of the follow-up question asking for the reasons for the change.[27] The most common reason for an increase in the number of bargaining units was that the establishment had created new jobs involving occupations not previously employed there. A smaller proportion mentioned the break-up of joint negotiating arrangements. Of the more numerous cases involving fewer bargaining groups than three years previously, the most common were public sector establishments where recognition had been withdrawn for some but not all employees – notably for schoolteachers. There were few similar cases in the private sector and these were mostly in services, not manufacturing. More common, again mostly in private services, were moves from separate to joint negotiations; such moves affected over a half of the private sector workplaces that had reduced their number of bargaining units over the three-year period, amounting to 8 per cent of private sector workplaces with two or more negotiating groups. On this evidence some employers appear to have succeeded in simplifying their negotiating structures in recent years, although not all those who tried to succeeded.

This was revealed when we looked at responses to another retrospective question concerning *attempts* at changing their arrangements. A reduction in the number of bargaining groups was the most common of such attempts at simplification. We mentioned earlier that some 4 per cent of management respondents reported an attempt in the last three years to reduce the number of unions they recognized. Compared with this number, 5 per cent reported moves to deal with fewer negotiating groups and a further 5 per cent reported moves towards dealing with a single negotiating group. Altogether, then, some 10 per cent of workplaces with recognized unions – or 15 per cent of those with two or more negotiating groups – attempted to simplify their negotiating structure. Such attempts were particularly common in the private sector where they were reported in 23 per cent of workplaces with two or more negotiating groups in 1987. This is somewhat higher than the proportion who reported that they had achieved a reduction in the number of negotiating groups (15 per cent in the private sector) and underlines the difficulty of changing negotiating structures by agreement. But when we take attempts to simplify negotiating structures *and* achievements in that direction it seems clear that there is a substantial body of opinion among managements that the balance of advantage lies with simpler structures than are often found in larger workplaces. This was the case in our first survey in 1980, where we asked both managers and worker representatives their reasons for preferring joint or separate negotiations. The differences in view between the parties that we reported on then[28] seem likely to have persisted. They must surely go some way to explaining the continuing prevalence of complex structures.

The coverage of collective bargaining
Union recognition for collective bargaining does not automatically lead to all employees in a workplace being directly covered by the collective bargaining agreements. Indeed, complete coverage is unusual. Managers and senior professional employees are groups that are commonly omitted from the coverage of collective agreements. Sometimes collective bargaining only covers a few employees in a workplace, perhaps a

Table 3.15   Distribution of coverage of collective bargaining, by broad sector, 1990

	All establish-ments	Establishments with recog-nized unions	Private manufacturing		Private services		Public sector	
	(a)	(b)	(a)	(b)	(a)	(b)	(a)	(b)

Proportion of establishments with percentage of employees covered by collective bargaining in the specified range

							Column percentages	
None	47	—	56	—	64	—	13	—
1–19 %	4	7[1]	3	7	3	9	5	6
20–49 %	7	12	8	18	4	11	10	12
50–79 %	11	20	13	29	7	18	16	18
80–99 %	13	25	14	32	10	27	19	22
100 %	18	35	6	13	13	35	37	42
Overall percentage covered	54	80	51	76	33	78	78	84
Total employees covered in millions	8.4		2.1		2.0		4.3	

Bases: a) all establishments; b) establishments with any recognized unions

Unweighted	*2061*	*1417*	*630*	*450*	*799*	*373*	*632*	*594*
Weighted	*2000*	*1058*	*426*	*189*	*980*	*349*	*594*	*519*

[1] See Note C.

single, highly unionized occupation in some strategic position. The proportion of employees in a workplace that are covered by agreements can therefore vary from zero in workplaces with no union recognition to 100 per cent in workplaces where all employees are covered by agreements.

In our 1984 survey we asked about the coverage of collective bargaining for manual and for non-manual employees separately. While retaining those questions in the 1990 survey we added a further question concerning employees as a whole. Considerable efforts were made to make the responses to this question as complete as possible so that we could present a reliable and complete picture for this important feature of industrial relations practice.[29] That picture is presented in Table 3.15. One half of the table shows coverage for the whole sample of workplaces. The other half shows – because of the crucial influence of recognition for *any* employees – coverage for those workplaces with any recognized unions.

Looking first at all workplaces, 47 per cent of establishments had no employees covered by collective bargaining; 4 per cent had low coverage (1–19 per cent); a further 7 per cent had under a half; 11 per cent had moderate to high coverage (50–79 per cent); 13 per cent had high coverage (80–99 per cent); and 18 per cent of establishments had 100 per cent coverage. The tendency for coverage to be high or complete, once union recognition is achieved, is illustrated by the fact that 60 per cent of workplaces with union recognition had 80 per cent or more employees covered.

Aggregate coverage is shown in the lower part of Table 3.15. Over the whole sample 54 per cent of employees were covered by collective bargaining in 1990.[30] When grossed up to the population of employees covered by the sample this amounted to some 8.4 million out of a total of 15.3 million. As the 6.6 million employees excluded from our survey population – essentially those in small workplaces – are generally much less likely to be covered, it is clear that collective bargaining directly affected only a minority of employees in Britain.

Coverage broadly follows the pattern of recognition. It was highest in the public sector (78 per cent of employees), intermediate in private manufacturing (51 per cent) and lowest in private services (33 per cent). Over half of employees covered were in the public services. This reflects not only the greater likelihood of public sector workplaces having recognition for any employees, but also the greater likelihood of all employees being covered. In the public sector 37 per cent of workplaces had all employees covered, and altogether 56 per cent had coverage of 80 per cent or more. Corresponding figures for the private sector were 20 per cent for manufacturing and 23 per cent for services. However, where there was recognition, it was more common for workplaces in private services to have all employees covered than was the case in private manufacturing (35 per cent compared with 13 per cent). This appears to arise from the lesser diversity of occupations within establishments in private services than within manufacturing workplaces.

In broad terms it is clear that the coverage of collective bargaining reflects the pattern of union membership and recognition to a large extent. Our previous reports have examined these patterns in some detail and the data from the earlier surveys have been used by other researchers for further analysis using multivariate statistical methods.[31] A lengthy examination of the 1990 coverage data would not, therefore, be appropriate here. However, if we confine our attention to workplaces with recognized unions in the private sector, it is worth noting the characteristics of workplaces that are particularly associated with the proportion of employees covered. The most marked association, unsurprisingly, was with overall union density. When we took this source of variation into account in our analysis, it was still the case that workplaces with a single negotiating group had lower than average coverage. Again, taking union density into account, workplaces belonging to larger enterprises had higher levels of coverage, presumably reflecting enterprise-wide policies on union recognition for occupational groups that were present in many of the enterprise's workplaces. Workforce composition also appeared to play a role in the pattern of coverage. For example, it was generally the case that workplaces that either had a predominantly manual or a predominantly non-manual workforce had higher than average coverage, both generally and when we took union density into account; conversely workplaces with the greatest variety of occupations had lower coverage. Establishments with a high proportion of part-time workers had lower than average coverage, but this relationship disappeared when we compared workplaces with similar union densities. It seems reasonable to deduce that part-time workers are less likely to be covered by collective bargaining because they are more difficult for trade unions to organize. Indeed, it is more than likely that the growth of part-time employment (reflected in our samples as a rise from 16 per cent to 18 per cent of employees from 1984 to 1990) explains some of the decline in coverage which we discuss below.

Changes in the coverage of collective bargaining, 1984 and 1990
The fall in aggregate coverage from 71 per cent in 1984 to 54 per cent in 1990 (Table 3.16) is one of the most dramatic changes in the character of British industrial relations that our survey series has measured. The reductions from 64 per cent to 51 per cent in private manufacturing and from 41 per cent to 33 per cent in private services mean that in the

Table 3.16   Proportion of employees covered by collective bargaining, 1984 and 1990

Percentages

	All establishments		Establishments with any recognized unions	
	1984	1990	1984	1990
All establishments	**71**	**54**	**89**	**80**
Sector:				
Private manufacturing	64	51	82	76
Private services'	41	33	82	78
Public sector	95	78	96	84
Union density – all sectors				
None	1	*	§	§
1–24 %	30	15	52	29
25–49 %	63	54	67	62
50–74 %	87	75	88	80
75–89 %	92	84	93	87
90–99 %	97	91	97	93
100 %	98	94	99	99

Base: all establishments

	All establishments		Establishments with any recognized unions	
Union density – private sector only				
None	*	*	§	§
1–24 %	27	12	51	27
25–49 %	58	47	64	55
50–74 %	80	77	82	80
75–89 %	86	84	88	88
90–99 %	94	94	95	94
100 %	93	(100)	97	(100)

Base: all private sector establishments

private sector as a whole coverage dropped from a majority of employees (52 per cent) to a minority of two fifths (41 per cent).

In the public sector the fall has been equally stark: from 95 per cent in 1984 to 78 per cent in 1990. Much of this fall in the public sector must reflect two large groups of workers losing their negotiating rights – the teachers and the nurses. However, the reductions were not confined to these two cases. Reductions also occurred in Central Government and Local Government. Moves to turn parts of the civil service into semi-independent agencies and in local government to contract out or privatize various services have often been accompanied by – if not positively designed to achieve - reductions in the role of trade unions.

The pattern of change in the private sector is illuminated by comparing the change for all workplaces with the change within workplaces with recognized unions. Taking the service sector by way of illustration, the fall in coverage within workplaces with recognized unions is quite slight – from 82 per cent to 78 per cent. By contrast, the overall coverage figure fell from 41 to 33 per cent. It is thus the fall in the proportion of workplaces with recognized unions (from 44 per cent to 36 per cent in Table 3.7) which has been primarily responsible for the fall in coverage. Having fewer employees covered within workplaces with recognized unions seems to have played a lesser role in the change. Much the same story appears true for manufacturing.

A further gloss on this analysis is shown in the lower half of Table 3.16, where we look at the changing pattern of coverage in relation to union density in the private sector. From this we can see that coverage stayed at the same levels where union density was high. However, where density was low the falls in coverage were substantial. For example, in workplaces with recognition and union membership density of less than 25 per cent, coverage was 51 per cent in 1984 but only 27 per cent in 1990. This points to coverage being reduced by management as a result of lack of union support. How much of the total fall in coverage arose from the changing composition of workplaces in this sector or from other causes we cannot say, but it seems unlikely that formal cases of partial de-recognition account for most of it.[32]

Although all employees may be regarded by the trade union movement as potential members, the ease with which unions may recruit new members varies between different types of workplace. In many respects it is easier to recruit members in a workplace where there are already union members, particularly if the specific occupation of a potential member is already covered by collective agreements, than in a totally unorganized workplace. The potential members already covered by collective agreements, sometimes referred to as 'free-riders', constitute a substantial proportion of employees. A crude measure of their extent would be to subtract our overall estimate of union density (48 per cent in 1990) from our overall figure for the coverage of collective bargaining (54 per cent in 1990). This difference of 7 per cent in 1990 is substantially less than the comparable figure of 13 per cent in 1984, when coverage was 71 per cent overall and average density was 58 per cent. It would be wrong, however, to conclude that the number of free-riders had nearly halved. This is because the crude difference between coverage and density oversimplifies the situation.[33] First, there are members in workplaces without recognition; these increased from 4 per cent of employees to 7 per cent in the period 1984 to 1990. Secondly, within workplaces that recognize trade unions, coverage may be less than 100 per cent. The extent of this increased markedly between the two surveys, particularly in the public sector. Thus the number of employees without union representation in collective bargaining increased over the period and may account for most if not all of the decline in the difference between coverage and recognition. Whether or not the number of free-riders decreased – or even increased – remains an open question until further analysis is carried out.[34]

The closed shop
Compulsory trade union membership, the closed shop, has been one of the chief focuses of the changes in labour law during the period covered by our survey series. Successive Acts have made it more and more difficult for employers and trade unions to operate a compulsory union membership arrangement within the law. In the early 1980s it was largely the more common, post-entry closed shop that was the target of legislative action. At the end of the decade, legislation was brought forward to make attempts to enforce pre-entry closed shops unlawful. The provisions of the 1990 Employment Act, providing a right of complaint to an industrial tribunal for anyone refused employment on the ground of non-membership (or membership) of a trade union, were brought into effect in early 1991, well after our 1990 survey interviews. The Act's provisions concerning the closed shop had, however, been widely anticipated since the publication of the Government's Green Paper in March 1989.[35] Our 1990 survey results on the closed shop should, therefore, be viewed in the context of these developments.

In the public and parliamentary debate on the issue of the closed shop the results from our earlier surveys were one of the chief sources of information about the extent of the practice and some of its consequences.[36] Here, as in our earlier reports, our aim is to present the survey findings on the extent of the closed shop and some of the characteristics of the arrangements supporting it. As before, exploration of its consequences must await further analysis. Our results are based on the responses of managers to questions about arrangements for union membership.

The extent of the closed shop, 1984 and 1990
In the 1984 survey we elaborated our original, 1980, question concerning the existence of a closed shop and thereby complicated comparisons with the earlier results. In 1990 we repeated the 1984 questions *verbatim*. Straightforward comparisons between 1984 and 1990 are therefore possible and are given in Table 3.17. The question was posed separately for manual and for non-manual workers and consisted of asking the main management respondent which of the following arrangements, shown on a printed card, applied to union membership at their establishment:

Table 3.17 Union membership arrangements for manual and non-manual workers, by broad sector, 1984 and 1990

Column percentages

	All establishments		Private manufacturing		Private services		Nationalized industries		Public services	
	1984	1990	1984	1990	1984	1990	1984	1990	1984	1990
Manual workers										
All have to be members	17	3	16[1]	5	10	2	68	*	15	3
Some groups have to be members	3	1	2	1	3	1	13	—	2	—
Management strongly recommends all are members	15	14	11	11	6	7	14	48	30	26
Management strongly recommends some groups are members	1	1	2	2	*	1	1	—	1	1
None of the above arrangements[2]	64	80	69	80	80	89	4	52	51	66
Not answered	*	2	—	1	*	1	—	1	1	4
Base: establishments with manual workers										
Unweighted	*1853*	*1831*	*580*	*616*	*515*	*654*	*191*	*76*	*567*	*485*
Weighted	*1749*	*1697*	*412*	*417*	*689*	*780*	*103*	*42*	*545*	*457*
Non-manual workers										
All have to be members	6	1	1	*	5	1	28	—	6	2
Some groups have to be members	3	*	2	*	1	*	37	—	2	1
Management strongly recommends all are members	16	10	5	1	7	4	22	36	35	27
Management strongly recommends some groups are members	1	1	1	*	*	*	1	—	2	2
None of the above arrangements	74	87	91	97	87	94	19	64	54	66
Not answered	*	1	*	*	*	*	1	*	1	2
Base: establishments with non-manual workers										
Unweighted	*2010*	*2058*	*592*	*630*	*593*	*798*	*194*	*81*	*631*	*549*
Weighted	*1985³*	*1992*	*424*	*426*	*836*	*977*	*105*	*46*	*621*	*544*

¹ See Note C.
² Includes establishments where there were no recognized trade unions and the question was therefore not asked.
³ See Note H.

All workers have to be members of unions in order to get or keep their jobs.
Some groups of workers have to be members of unions in order to get or keep their jobs.
Management strongly recommends that *all* workers are members of unions.
Management strongly recommends that *some* workers are members of unions.
No workers have to be members of unions nor is it strongly recommended that they are members.

The first two categories correspond to *comprehensive* and *partial* closed shops; the third and fourth categories we refer to as *employer-endorsed unionism*, as we did with the 1984 survey data. Table 3.17 shows the responses to this question for the four sectors of the economy used in our previous report. In this case, although the number of observations for the nationalized industries is fairly small, we show them separately from the rest of the public sector because of the very high incidence of closed shops in this sector in 1984.

There can be little doubt from our results that formal closed shop arrangements became far less numerous between 1984 and 1990. In the case of manual workers, 20 per cent of establishments had a closed shop arrangement in 1984 compared with only 4 per cent in early 1990. For non-manual workers the respective figures were 9 per cent and 1 per cent. Comprehensive and partial closed shops were both affected. The results for manual workers suggest that it was comprehensive closed shops that declined most severely, but because of the small numbers involved in the 1990 figures this cannot be stated with certainty.

Clearly it was in the public sector that the most dramatic decline in formal closed shop arrangements occurred. In the non-trading part of the public sector the fall in the incidence of manual closed shops was from 17 per cent to 3 per cent of establishments. However, it was the nationalized industries that showed the most dramatic change. Over 80 per cent of nationalized industry workplaces had manual closed shops in 1984; in 1990 the figure was less than 1 per cent.

Our panel data give strong confirmation of this. Among panel establishments that were part of the nationalized industries in 1984, 90 per cent had a manual closed shop in that year, but less than 1 per cent of those same establishments reported a manual closed shop in 1990. Thus formal closed shops had disappeared in both the remaining nationalized industries and in the former nationalized industries that had been privatized since 1984 and were largely replaced by employer-endorsed unionism.

In private services the declining incidence of manual closed shop arrangements, from 13 per cent of establishments in 1984 to 3 per cent of establishments in 1990, reflected the general trend. In private manufacturing the decline was slightly less dramatic, the proportion of establishments with closed shops falling from 18 per cent to 6 per cent. Again our panel sample also showed a dramatic decline: only a sixth of private sector workplaces that had a manual closed shop in 1984 also had one in 1990.

Where had the closed shop survived in early 1990? Of the 26 industries that we distinguished in Table 3A there were 21 that still had at least one observation where our management respondent reported a closed shop for all or some workers in 1990. These included all of the 11 manufacturing sectors. Industries with a higher than average incidence were Metals and Mineral Products; Food, Drink and Tobacco; Textiles; the sector that included Printing and Publishing; Transport; and Banking, Insurance and Finance. Nearly all of these contained traditional areas of the closed shop.

Although changes in the population of workplaces must have played a part (as they did in the declining extent of union recognition in the private sector), the dramatic decline in closed shop arrangements must have arisen largely from the legislative changes of the 1980s and possibly some anticipation of the 1990 Employment Act. However, managements might still find it in their interest to have the great majority of their employees represented by trade unions and indeed to take positive steps to encourage union membership. In 1984 we found such employer-endorsed unionism in something over 15 per cent of cases. In 1990 this was still the case for manual workers, but somewhat less so for non-manuals (see Table 3.17). The highest incidence of such encouragement was in the nationalized industries and, to a lesser extent, in the public services sector, where it related to both manual and non-manual workers. But the extent of such encouragement was very much lower in 1990 than in 1984, especially in Central Government. In the private sector around 10 per cent of managers reported employer-endorsed unionism in 1990, but this almost invariably applied only to manual workers.

What of the numbers of employees covered by closed shop arrangements in early 1990? Our results suggest about 5 per cent of manual employees were covered by closed shop arrangements, putting the figure for all employees for the whole economy somewhere between a third and half a million. This represents a dramatic decline since mid-1984, when our comparable estimate was between 3.5 and 3.7 million.[37]

Do remaining closed shops and employer-endorsed unionism account for most of the cases where union density approaches 100 per cent? The answer is 'only just'. Of the substantial number of workplaces with manual union density of 100 per cent, 16 per cent reported a comprehensive manual closed shop and a further 40 per cent reported employer-endorsed unionism. The remainder – nearly half – thus had 100 per cent membership without substantial support from management. This con-

Table 3.18   **Employers' policies and manual union membership density, 1984 and 1990**

	Union membership density	
	1984	1990
	Mean percentages	
All establishments	66	53
Comprehensive closed shop	99	98
Comprehensive employer-endorsed unionism	88	88
No employer support for union membership	35	35

Base: establishments with manual workers and specified arrangements for union membership

trasts with the picture in 1984 when 57 per cent of workplaces with 100 per cent manual union density had a comprehensive closed shop and 26 per cent had employer-endorsed unionism; a mere 14 per cent had neither. It seems therefore that those workplaces which in 1990 had 100 per cent union membership were much more likely to have maintained this level of support for the union without any active endorsement or encouragement from the employer. However, the fact that there were so many fewer cases of 100 per cent membership must be substantially due to the withdrawal of support for union membership by employers and the increased legal obstacles to maintaining closed shop arrangements.

Another way of looking at the association between employer policies on union membership and the actual level of membership is shown in Table 3.18. This compares union density in 1984 and 1990 in the three main types of workplace according to management policy on union membership. In comprehensive closed shops average density remained very close to 100 per cent. In workplaces with employer-endorsed unionism it remained constant at 88 per cent. And in workplaces with neither of these conditions it also remained constant at 35 per cent. What changed was the incidence of employers who insisted on or strongly endorsed manual union membership. The decline in the extent of employer support must, therefore, account substantially for the fall in manual union density from 66 per cent to 53 per cent over the period; there was no drop in union density where membership received strong encouragement from management, nor did density decline in workplaces with no strong employer support for unionism.[38]

A final piece of evidence concerning the closed shop and union density comes from our panel sample. Workplaces that had a closed shop covering all manual workers in 1984 had an average level of manual union density of 99 per cent. These same establishments in 1990 had an average level of manual density of 93 per cent. This is perhaps the clearest indication that the decline of the closed shop had only a limited part to play in the overall drop in union membership during the latter part of the 1980s.

The characteristics of manual closed shops in 1990
Despite its dramatic decline in prevalence, at least one characteristic of the closed shop remained much as it was in 1984. This was the mix between pre-entry arrangements, where membership is required before starting the job, and post-entry arrangements, where it is required at or shortly after starting. Thus of manual closed shops in 1990, 25 per cent were comprehensive pre-entry arrangements compared with 19 per cent in 1984; 67 per cent were comprehensive post-entry arrangements, compared with 74 per cent in 1984, the remainder in both years being establishments with a mixture of types.[39] The few remaining pre-entry closed shops were virtually confined to the private manufacturing sector; post-entry arrangements were spread across all three broad sectors.

Workplaces with closed shops continued to have a single arrangement covering the practice, reflecting the tendency to have either a comprehensive pre-entry or a comprehensive post-entry arrangement. They also continued, although possibly to a lesser extent, to have written agreements about the arrangement: of those establishments with a manual closed shop in 1990, 77 per cent had a written agreement covering it. In 1984 the comparable figure was 89 per cent. Judging from the types of exemptions they mentioned and the date of the most recent revision (where there was a written closed shop agreement), about half of the closed shop arrangements predated the early 1980s legislation and the other half had been revised to take account of it.[40]

Synopsis
The surveys reveal a marked decline in the extent of trade union representation during the course of the 1980s, particularly in the latter half of it. All of our indicators of trade union presence and strength show this decline, although sometimes the change was confined to particular sectors or types of establishment.

More establishments had no trade union members at all, a change that was confined to the private sector of the economy. But both private and public sectors showed falls in trade union membership density. Workplaces with 100 per cent density among manual workers became much less common, no doubt partly because of changes to the legal status of closed shop arrangements. Our panel data highlighted the loss of membership from workplaces where density had been low. In the first half of the decade it appeared that changes in the population of workplaces – particularly the demise of large, highly-unionized manufacturing plants

– played a key role in the decline in union membership. In the second half, the explanations for the continuing decline are more likely to be weakening support for unionism among employees, various government measures constraining it and antipathy amongst a growing number of employers.

The recognition of trade unions by employers for jointly determining rates of pay – our key indicator of the role of unions in industrial relations – also registered a substantial decline over the decade. This change was concentrated in the period since 1984. It was apparent in the private sector, both manufacturing and services, and the public sector. But within these broad sectors the drop in the extent of recognition was patchy, particularly prevalent among smaller establishments in the private sector and largely confined to two main occupational groups in the public sector. Clear cases of de-recognition were much more apparent in the second half of the decade than in the first.

The decline in the extent of union recognition naturally fed through into a fall in the proportion of employees covered by collective bargaining. This had shrunk to 54 per cent in 1990 from 71 per cent six years earlier. As most employees outside the scope of the WIRS series are almost certainly not covered, it is clear that only a minority of employees in the economy as a whole had their pay jointly determined by management and trade unions.

Changes in the complexity of union representation were far less apparent than changes in recognition and coverage. Indeed, within the unionized sector the degree of multi-union representation for manual workers showed no change. The fall in the degree of multi-unionism for non-manual employees was confined to the public sector and resulted from the de-recognition of the teachers' and nurses' unions for pay bargaining. If there was a reduction in multi-unionism it was that more unions represented both manual and non-manual employees, partly a consequence of union amalgamations. There did appear to be a continuing slight move to joint negotiating structures where several unions were recognized, but in the main multiple bargaining units remained a feature of the public sector and large, unionized private sector workplaces.

The closed shop – perhaps the clearest symbol of union strength at workplace level, and the object of successive legal restrictions over the course of the 1980s – showed the sharpest fall of any of our measures of trade union representation. Arrangements reported by managers covered nearly five million employees in 1980 and only half a million in 1990.

Notes and references

1. As we remarked in our previous book, the slight rise from 1980 to 1984 on both of these separate measures was largely a matter of the changing level of indefinite responses to our question. (See N. Millward and M. Stevens (1986) *British Workplace Industrial Relations 1980–1984: The DE/ESRC/PSI/ACAS Surveys*, Gower, Aldershot, Chapter 3.)

In the 1990 interviews we removed this uncertainty by reformulating the question to our management respondents. Instead of asking an initial question as to whether there were any union members and then asking for their numbers, interviewers initially asked for the numbers and then coded a second question as to whether there were any or none. In cases of doubt, the second question was always coded 'yes' or 'no' after discussion with the respondent. This revised format gives us a more secure set of figures for 1990 than was obtained with the earlier questions.

2. Our revised questions were again more satisfactory. Non-response dropped from 11 per cent in 1984 to 8 per cent in 1990, giving a more secure basis for analysis.

3. Comparisons with 1980 are not possible because the 1980 survey questionnaires did not include questions on union membership for all categories of employee.

4. R. Naylor and M. Cripps (1991) 'An economic theory of the open shop trade union', *Warwick Economic Research Papers* No.372, University of Warwick, Coventry.

5. R. Naylor and P. Gregg (1989) 'An inter-establishment study of union membership in Great Britain', *Warwick Economic Research Papers* No. 322, University of Warwick, Coventry; D. G. Blanchflower, C. Crouchley, S. Estrin and A. Oswald (1990) 'Unemployment and the demand for unions', *National Bureau of Economic Research Working Paper* No. 3251, Cambridge, Mass.

6. Both of the works cited above examined manual and non-manual workers separately, in contrast to our discussion here which looks at all employees together.

7. Blanchflower *et al.* (1990) op. cit. and others used a less precise measure of unemployment than we have on the 1990 survey data.

8. D. G. Blanchflower, N. Millward and A. J. Oswald (1991) 'Unionism and employment behaviour', *Economic Journal*, July, pp. 815–34.

9. Our analysis is subject to three restrictions. We only considered establishments in the panel sample where our editing procedures raised no doubts that we were interviewing at the same establishment in 1990, defined in the same way, as we had been in 1984. We only included cases where we had estimates of union membership density in both 1984 and 1990. And we excluded cases where employment in 1990 was less than 25 employees. This left us with 382 cases.

10. If panel workplaces with less than 25 employees in 1990 are excluded, the 1990 average density figure is 42 per cent.

11. Non-response to this question (don't know or not answered) amounted to a mere 6 per cent in relation to manual workers and 5 per cent regarding non-manual workers.

12. It seems likely that some small employers who followed the previous national agreement did not replace this method of wage fixing with any other type of negotiated settlement, but moved to unilateral determination of pay.

13. T. Claydon (1989) 'Union de-recognition in Britain in the 1980s', *British Journal of Industrial Relations*, July, pp. 214–24.

14. The comparisons with the question on de-recognition would have been easier if we had used the same recall period for both questions, but we felt that recalling the number of unions longer ago than three years would have been too unreliable.

15. This comparison has been made using the additional question on when de-recognition occurred and restricting the result to cases that took place in the three years prior to the survey. On this basis there were 4 (weighted) cases of new recognition and 7 cases of de-recognition in the whole private sector sample of 1406 (weighted) cases.

16. A number of considerations are relevant to that judgement. It is generally accepted in survey research that retrospective questions are less reliable than questions about the current state of affairs, especially when the recall period is long and any implied change

cannot be tied to some significant event in the respondent's history. In fact, a sizeable minority of our respondents in 1990 said that they had not been in their current job for more than five years. So when our rare retrospective questions were being put, this minority were being asked about conditions which existed when they were perhaps not even employed at the workplace they were being asked about. This was particularly so in the cases where our panel data conflicted with the retrospective question about whether there was de-recognition (these were given a special code on the dataset); indeed, in a majority of these cases our 1990 respondent had worked at the establishment for less than six years. This must cast strong doubts on this piece of retrospective data. On the other hand, panel data are also known in survey research circles for straining one's credulity on occasions. But in view of the importance attached in our surveys to the accuracy of answers on the question of union recognition, it is highly unlikely that most or even much of the change shown by our panel sample could have arisen from measurement error.

17. D. Blanchflower and J. Cubbin (1986) 'Strike propensities at the British workplace', *Oxford Bulletin of Economics and Statistics*, February, pp. 19–39.

18. Collective bargaining over pay for nurses and midwives was ended in 1983 when the Nurses and Midwives Pay Review Body was established; the nurses' and midwives' unions make representations to this body, but do not negotiate within it. The Review Body issued its first report in June 1984, when the bulk of interviews for our 1984 survey had been carried out. The 1984 WIRS data therefore mostly reflects the pre-existing arrangements for collective bargaining. With regard to teachers in state schools, the collective bargaining arrangements were terminated by the government in 1987 with the abolition of the Burnham Committee and its replacement by a government-appointed Interim Advisory Committee on Teachers' Pay, to which the teachers' unions make representations.

19. Combining the 1984 data on the numbers of manual and non-manual unions to give a total number of recognized unions is not a feasible alternative. This is because it is not always possible to identify the same union within the two lists of unions in an establishment in order to eliminate double-counting.

20. For convenience, in the remainder of this chapter such establishments are sometimes referred to as 'unionized'. Earlier in the chapter the same term was used to refer to those with any union members.

21. The analysis in this section excludes cases where the number of unions three years ago was nil; these were discussed in an earlier section dealing with changes in recognition. The base for the results given here is therefore establishments interviewed in 1990 with recognized unions in both 1990 and 1987.

22. The analysis here had to be restricted to cases with only manual unions in 1984 because of our different treatment of unions in the two surveys. In essence, our separate treatment of manual and non-manual unions in the earlier surveys gives an exaggerated picture of the total number of unions because some unions represented both manual and non-manual employees.

23. Cm 1602 (1991) *Industrial Relations in the 1990s: Proposals for the further reform of industrial relations and trade union law*, HMSO, London.

24. In fact manual representatives were asked at the beginning of the interview whether there were any other manual unions that had members at their establishment; non-manual representatives were asked a similar question. For simplicity the questions about the potential for inter-union competition and actual competition were asked irrespective of the answers to that question, but our analysis takes as its base only those that said there were other unions.

25. See Millward and Stevens (1986) op. cit., p. 75.

26. As with the earlier analysis of changes in the number of unions, we restrict our results here to cases where there was union recognition at the time of interview and three years earlier; the cases of new recognition and of de-recognition have been discussed in an earlier section.

27. The scope for analysis of the reasons for change is further restricted by the relatively large proportion of 'don't know' and 'not answered' responses.

28. See W. W. Daniel and N. Millward (1983) *Workplace Industrial Relations in Britain: The DE/PSI/ESRC Survey*, Gower, Aldershot, pp. 47–50.

29. Non-response to the question on the overall coverage of collective bargaining was very low at 1 per cent. For ease of presentation these few cases have been recoded to the average for their industry.

30. The aggregate percentages referred to here and later are obtained by calculating the total number covered and dividing by the total number of employees; they are not averages of the percentage covered in each establishment.

31. See, for example, P. B. Beaumont and R. I. D. Harris (1988) 'Sub-systems of industrial relations: the spatial dimension in Britain' *British Journal of Industrial Relations*, November, pp. 397–407; P. B. Beaumont, and R. I. D. Harris (1989) 'The North–South divide in Britain: the case of trade union recognition', *Oxford Bulletin of Economics and Statistics*, February, pp. 413–28.

32. Cases of partial de-recognition, sometimes referred to by management as moves to individual contracts of employment, were included in the study of de-recognition by Claydon (1989) op. cit. Up to 1987, when that study was completed, such cases were rare and did not appear to have affected large numbers of employees.

33. For further discussion of this point in relation to individual survey data see N. Millward (1990) 'The state of the unions' in R. Jowell, S. Witherspoon and L. Brook (eds.), *British Social Attitudes: the 7th report*, Gower, Aldershot.

34. The possibility that free-riders increased in numbers is raised by the fact that workplaces with 100 per cent coverage in 1984 had an average union density of 82 per cent, whereas similar workplaces in 1990 (which were much less numerous) averaged 78 per cent density.

35. Cm 655 (1989) *Removing Barriers to Employment: Proposals for the further reform of industrial relations and trade union law*, HMSO, London.

36. For example, the majority of articles in learned journals cited in the Green Paper initiating the debate were based on analysis of WIRS data.

37. Millward and Stevens (1986) op. cit., pp. 106–7. Those estimates included allowances for very small establishments and for the coal-mining industry, both of which are excluded from WIRS. Neither allowance is thought to be necessary for the 1990 estimate. WIRS results are less likely to include informal closed shop situations that rely on peer-group pressure for their effective operation than overt and formally agreed arrangements. This should be borne in mind when comparing the findings from WIRS with those from surveys of individuals, particularly on the extent of the closed shop (e.g. M. Stevens, N. Millward and D. Smart (1989) 'Trade union membership and the closed shop in 1989', *Employment Gazette*, November, pp. 615–23 and N. Millward (1990) op. cit.

38. This accords with a recent time-series analysis of density up to 1986 which concludes: 'the vast bulk of the observed 1980s decline in union density in the UK is due to the changed legal environment for industrial relations ... particularly those [laws] relating to union organization.' See R. Freeman and J. Pelletier (1990) 'The impact of industrial relations legislation on British union density', *British Journal of Industrial Relations*, July, pp. 141–64.

39. The unweighted bases for these estimates were 522 in 1984 and 83 in 1990; the small base in the latter year means that the change in proportions cannot be regarded as statistically significant.

40. About two fifths of managers reporting a written closed shop agreement were not able to say in which year it had been most recently revised, a similar proportion to that in 1984.

Table 3A   Main indicators of union presence, by industry, 1990

	Percentage of establishments with union members	Percentage of employees in unions (union density)	Percentage of establishments with recognized unions	Percentage of employees covered by recognized unions
All industries	**64**	**48**	**53**	**54**
All manufacturing	**58**	**48**	**45**	**52**
Metals & Mineral Products	77	68	77	75
Chemicals & Manufactured Fibres	(66)[1]	(42)	(42)	(50)
Metal Goods	(61)	(50)	(53)	(51)
Mechanical Engineering	73	42	31	38
Electrical & Instrument Engineering	40	33	37	38
Vehicles & Transport Equipment	52	68	36	73
Food, Drink & Tobacco	51	52	46	62
Textiles	(76)	(41)	(68)	(57)
Leather, Footwear & Clothing	(43)	(45)	(38)	(47)
Timber & Furniture, Paper & Printing	63	48	48	50
Rubber, Plastics & Other Manufacturing	(32)	(44)	(32)	(46)
All services	**66**	**47**	**55**	**55**
Energy & Water	96	75	96	85
Construction	64	46	46	45
Wholesale Distribution	40	23	32	24
Retail Distribution	46	25	36	29
Hotels, Catering, Repairs	13	3	8	7
Transport	76	63	55	67
Posts and Telecommunications	99	86	99	95
Banking, Finance, Insurance	88	53	88	69
Business Services	21	11	9	11
Central Government	100	58	99	78
Local Government	95	70	94	82
Higher Education	(62)	(57)	(60)	(85)
Other Education	92	63	63	44
Medical Services	61	65	56	72
Other Services	81	47	79	65

Base: all establishments (see Table 1A for bases and SIC codes)
[1] See Note B.

4 Trade Union Organization

In the previous chapter we examined the state of the main institutional structures through which employers and trade unions have traditionally related to each other. Our analysis revealed a picture of widespread decline since the mid-1980s in trade union membership, recognition, collective bargaining coverage and the closed shop. Although part of the explanation for these changes was the changing composition of workplaces, declining support for trade unions among employers and employees seemed to be a more relevant factor in the late 1980s.

We examine this proposition of declining support for unions further in the present chapter by assessing the extent to which trade unions' own organizational arrangements were adapted to meet the changing conditions of the late 1980s. The matter has been keenly debated[1] and is one on which our surveys can bring ample evidence to bear. Comparing results from our 1980 and 1984 surveys it was clear that the main features of local union organization – joint shop stewards committees and the like – were as commonly reported in the mid-1980s as they had been at the start. Our analysis of the 1990 survey results in this chapter suggests that although this picture remained largely true at the end of the decade, it was against the backcloth of a large overall decline in union presence during the late 1980s.

Lay union representatives

The actual presence of a trade union representative or 'steward'[2] at a workplace is one of the more visible indicators of trade union organization on the ground and an important adjunct of recognition. A representative provides a primary channel of communication between local membership and management. Representatives also form the basic building block for more complex forms of union organization involving further hierarchical levels, including committees of representatives at the workplace and beyond. Granting representatives facilities and time-off from their normal jobs or providing clerical and other facilities to assist them in undertaking trade union work are indicators of the degree of support that local management give to workplace trade unionism. Enthusiasm for shop steward organization from the local membership is evidenced partly through the willingness of individuals to take on the role and partly through the membership's endorsement of the appointment.

We have results on all these matters, but begin by describing the extent to which trade union representatives were present in establishments in 1990, a key indicator of the extensiveness of local union organization. Our information on the incidence and numbers of trade union representatives comes from interviews with our main management respondents. The subsequent discussion of trade union organization is based on information supplied by worker representatives themselves.

Changes in the incidence of lay union representatives
We expected to find the simplification of bargaining arrangements in the late 1980s, particularly in the private sector, to be reflected in our results concerning the presence of union representatives. This proved to be the case. It is more straightforward to present the results in overall terms – whether representatives of any recognized unions were present – to give a more robust picture of change since our last survey.[3]

In overall terms the proportion of establishments with recognized unions where at least one representative of a recognized union was reported dropped from 82 per cent in 1984 to 71 per cent in 1990, representing a fall from 54 per cent of all establishments to 38 per cent over the period. The fall, however, was concentrated in smaller workplaces, employing fewer than a hundred people. Such workplaces formed a larger proportion of all workplaces with recognized unions in 1990 than in 1984, which partly explains how the overall decline in reporting of representatives might have come about. It was still the case that representatives were more commonly reported in larger workplaces, where other aspects of trade union organization were also more prevalent.

Analysis using the broadest (Divisional) level of the *Standard Industrial Classification* (SIC) revealed falls in the reporting of representatives among workplaces with recognized unions in six of the nine Divisions covered by our survey. In a further two Divisions – Mineral and Chemicals; and Banking and Business Services – there was stability. In the remaining sector, Construction (Division 5), a slight increase over the period was recorded, from 40 to 45 per cent.[4]

There was decline in the presence of representatives among workplaces with recognized unions in all three broad sectors of employment. Table 4.1 gives the overall results. At the time of our last survey union representatives were almost universally reported in private manufacturing plants with recognized unions (98 per cent); in 1990 they were reported in 90 per cent of them. The fall in private services, from 67 per cent to 57 per cent, would probably have been even larger without the influx of the more highly unionized former public utilities into the private sector

Table 4.1   Presence of trade union representatives, by broad sector, 1984 and 1990

Percentages

	All establishments		Private manufacturing		Private services		Public sector	
	1984	1990	1984	1990	1984	1990	1984	1990
Manual or non-manual workers represented by:								
1 or more representatives at own workplace	82	71	98	90	67	57	84	73
Representatives elsewhere in organization	29	26	3	3	20	23	42	37
Full-time union official	8	14	1	7	11	12	10	17
Senior representative of 2 or more present	19	22	46	40	9	12	14	23
Full-time representative present	2	2	5	2	1	2	3	2
Base: establishments with recognized unions for manual or non-manual workers								
Unweighted	*1593*	*1417*	*469*	*450*	*300*	*373*	*824*	*594*
Weighted	*1327*	*1058[1]*	*235*	*189*	*369*	*349*	*723*	*519*

[1] See Note H.

between our 1984 and 1990 surveys. Decline was also evident in the public sector; 73 per cent of workplaces with recognized unions had representatives in 1990, compared with 84 per cent in 1984.[5]

The pattern of change was rather different within these three broad sectors and our results were particularly revealing in relation to union density. Most of the fall in private manufacturing plants, for example, was in workplaces with low union density. Just 28 per cent of workplaces with less than a quarter of employees in membership had representatives in 1990, compared with 84 per cent in 1984. In private services the changes were less straightforward. Among low-density workplaces in the sector there was stability in the reporting of representatives (41 per cent in 1990). There was also stability in the highest density workplaces, with 90 per cent or more in membership, where eight out of ten managers reported them. But in mid-range densities (25 to 89 per cent density) there was decline, with just over half of workplaces with recognized unions reporting them in 1990. Finally, in the public sector our analysis detected little or no change in the presence of representatives when we compared establishments with similar membership density, with over three quarters of managers reporting them in each case.

Results from our panel sample indicate that the broad picture of decline in the private sector was not just compositional. Between 1984 and 1990 almost twice as many private sector workplaces lost union representatives they previously had than had gained them – 36 as against 20.

The disappearance of union representatives from workplaces that formerly had them, coupled with the decline in their incidence at the lower end of the density spectrum, may reflect the local response to dwindling membership. At low membership levels there may be little demand for representation from the local membership so that individual union members may be less willing to put themselves forward for the role of steward. There is some evidence for such reluctance in material presented later in the chapter on the ways in which local representatives were appointed. And the position would be compounded if local management were less willing to provide facilities and support to local lay representatives in circumstances of dwindling membership. We show later that managements were less likely to provide facilities for unions in low density workplaces than in their higher density counterparts. In addition, it may be more economic for unions to attempt to organize several low-density workplaces together, if representatives are failing to emerge in each one.

Our results for other, quite different, forms of representation at workplace level throw further light on these developments. First, in workplaces where more than one lay representative was reported we asked whether management acknowledged any of them as *senior* and whether any spent all or most of their time on union matters. Secondly, in workplaces where trade unions were recognized but there were no representatives on site, we asked how the local membership was represented. Our results on these matters are also shown in Table 4.1.

The lower portion of the table gives the results on the incidence of senior and full-time representatives. The slight problem of double-counting of both these types of representative in 1984 means that, as with ordinary representatives, their incidence was slightly inflated in our previous survey. A simple comparison of figures from the two surveys shows that senior representatives were as frequently reported in 1990 as in 1984; around a fifth of all workplaces with recognized unions which had at least two representatives present had senior representatives in both 1984 and 1990. Senior representatives were still most commonly reported by managers in private manufacturing, where two fifths of managers in workplaces with recognized unions reported them in 1990, compared with 12 per cent in private services and 23 per cent in the public sector. This suggests, perhaps surprisingly, that, despite our possible double-counting of them in 1984, there was a substantial increase in the reporting of senior representatives in the public sector since our last survey. Although privatization has meant that there have been changes to the structure of the public sector between 1984 and 1990, this increase is probably an artifact of our changed question-wording.[6]

The incidence of lay representatives who spent all or most of their time on trade union matters showed no change over the period, but of course they were much less common than senior representatives, being reported in 2 per cent of workplaces with recognized unions in both 1984 and 1990. Full-time convenors or representatives were as commonly reported in all three broad sectors of employment in 1990. So, despite the overall decline in the incidence of lay representatives, full-time representatives, at least, and possibly senior representatives also, appeared to be as common in 1990 as six years earlier. Table 4A gives a more detailed picture of the variation in the incidence of each type of representative by industry in 1990.

If there was some stability in the more highly organized workplaces, how were members being represented in places where there were no representatives on site? Our questioning covered this area also, in workplaces with recognition but no lay representatives. The results are particularly interesting in 1990, given the decline in the proportion of workplaces with any representatives in the period since 1984. Again, the results are given in Table 4.1.

The table shows there was little change in the incidence of representation 'from elsewhere in the same organization' since 1984, with 26 per cent of managers in workplaces with recognized unions reporting it in 1990. The most notable change was the increase in the incidence of representation by paid trade union officials. This almost doubled in the 1984 to 1990 period, from 8 to 14 per cent, with workplaces in both private manufacturing and the public sector being particularly affected. Workplaces with relatively low union density in particular were much more likely to be represented by paid officials than in the past. Such establishments would have been likely candidates for external representation, of course, as the decline in the incidence of ordinary representatives was particularly marked among them.

The distribution of lay union representatives in 1990

Although the revisions to our questionnaires made our assessment of changes in the incidence of representatives less straightforward than they might have been, our new questioning allows us to elaborate the pattern of representation in 1990. In particular, in relation to the incidence of three types of representatives – those representing only manual workers, those representing only non-manual workers and those representing both.

In 1990 representatives of only manual workers were reported in just under a third (32 per cent) of all workplaces with any recognized unions. Those representing only non-manual workers were reported in just over a third (35 per cent) and those covering both types of employee ('mixed' representatives) were reported in a quarter. However, each of the three broad sectors of employment had its own distinctive pattern, reflecting the different types of union present (see Chapter 3). Representatives of only manual employees were most frequently reported in private manufacturing (68 per cent) while their non-manual equivalents were most common in the public sector (51 per cent). In private services a fifth of managers reported each of the three types. Representatives of only manual employees were uncommon in manufacturing plants (15 per cent), whereas mixed representatives were most frequently reported there (36 per cent). In the public sector, 26 per cent of managers reported 'manual-only' representatives and 'mixed' representatives were reported in just under a quarter of cases (23 per cent). In the main, just 4 per cent of workplaces with any recognized unions had all three types of representative and there was little variation in this among the three broad sectors of employment.[7]

Table 4.2 shows the extent to which the specific type of union recognized had representatives on site in 1990. It is notable that unions recognized for representing both sections of the workforce were much more likely to have representatives on site than either of the other two types. This was so in each broad sector of employment. The fact that such unions usually existed as the sole union on site makes this finding all the more interesting, given that the overall incidence of lay representatives was associated with complexity of local organization. Manu-

Table 4.2 Presence of trade union representatives, by broad sector, 1990

Percentages

	All establishments	Private manufacturing	Private services	Public sector
Representatives present for:				
Manual employees only	59	88	52	47
Base: establishments with recognized unions representing manual employees only				
Unweighted	*875*	*361*	*163*	*351*
Weighted	*574*	*147*	*142*	*285*
Representatives present for:				
Non-manual employees only	56	72	46	58
Base: establishments with recognized unions representing non-manual employees only				
Unweighted	*962*	*209*	*198*	*555*
Weighted	*664*	*40*	*173*	*451*
Representatives present for:				
Manual & non-manual employees	71	93	64	67
Base: establishments with recognized unions representing both manual and non-manual employees				
Unweighted	*756*	*224*	*205*	*327*
Weighted	*376*	*72*	*125*	*178*

facturing workplaces with recognized unions representing both manual and non-manual employees were much more likely than workplaces in any other sector to have representatives for such unions on site.

There was little difference, overall, in the extent to which either manual-only unions or non-manual-only unions had representatives on site – approaching three fifths in both cases. Again, representatives for both types of union were much more likely to be reported in manufacturing workplaces than elsewhere. Foreign-owned workplaces were much more likely to have each of the three types of representatives on site than their domestically-owned counterparts.

We have so far defined local trade union organization in terms of the presence of *any* representatives on site or elsewhere. This is clearly only part of the picture. The extent to which union members can be organized also depends on the numbers of representatives available in relation to the size of the local membership.

Numbers of lay union representatives
If fewer workplaces reported representatives in 1990 than in 1984, then, given the direction of the other indicators of union presence reported earlier, we would have been surprised to find that the overall numbers of union representatives in the economy as a whole did not also decline over the period. But we might expect the scale of the decline to be more related to changes in the level of union membership than to changes in the proportion of establishments with stewards. In fact, while changes in the numbers of representatives are difficult to quantify precisely due to changes to our questionnaires, there is little doubt that there was decline across the 1984 to 1990 period and that it was substantial.[8] Perhaps the most straightforward means of assessing change in the numbers of representatives in relation to changes in membership is in terms of the average number of members per representative.

Allowing the technical difficulties of making a precise comparison, our evidence points to either a slight decline or perhaps stability in the numbers of union members per representative between 1984 and 1990.[9] In 1984 the average steward represented 22 union members. The equivalent figure for 1990 was 20. Table 4.3 gives results for the number of members per representative in relation to both workplace size and

Table 4.3   **Numbers of trade union members per representative in relation to characteristics of workplaces, 1984 and 1990**

Means

	Number of members per representative	
	1984	1990
All establishments	**22**	**20**
Size of establishment		
25–99 employees	15	13
100–499 employees	23	22
500–999 employees	30	27
1000+ employees	30	32
Change in establishment size	**since 1980**	**since 1984**
Decrease of 20% or more	21	17
Decrease of less than 20%	21	19
Stable	22	19
Increase of less than 20%	24	20
Increase of 20% or more	25	22

Bases: establishments with recognized unions for manual or non-manual workers where numbers of union members and numbers of representatives were known changes in workplace size. As in 1984, it was still the case that union members in larger workplaces shared their representative with a greater number of other members. If anything that relationship became stronger. The lower portion of the table shows a clear association between member-representative ratios and changes in workplace size.

There was a tendency for numbers of representatives to be relatively sluggish in responding to workforce contraction. In fact, our data suggest that steward numbers as a whole declined by proportionately less than union membership over the period: by 47 per cent and 52 per cent respectively, among workplaces relevant for calculating the number of members per steward.[10]

There was a marked fall in the number of members per representative in private services, from 23 to 17, though there were both increases and decreases within particular sectors. For example, representatives in Distribution had just 11 members in 1990 compared with 26 in 1984. In Banking, Finance and Insurance, one of the few industries with a rise in union density over the period, the average number of members per representative increased from 19 to 25. In private manufacturing the average steward represented 21 union members in 1990 compared with 23 in 1984. There was also little change over the period in the public sector, from 22 to 21 members per representative.

Overall, although there were some movements in the private service industries, member-representative ratios changed little in the late 1980s. Despite the overall decline in the incidence of representatives, on this measure at least, where representatives still existed in 1990 their membership base was still on a par with their own numbers.

Facilities for lay union representatives

In addition to the extensiveness of lay representatives across the economy, other factors that are relevant to assessing the relative strength of local trade union organization from one period to another include the degree of support representatives receive from local management. Facilities provided by management for time off work for trade union duties, the provision of clerical and office back-up and the extent to which representatives received training for trade union work are indicators of this. So too is management's willingness to deduct union dues from members' wages, as it frees local representatives from the potentially time-consuming task of collecting subscriptions personally. The effectiveness of individual representatives is partly dependent on the range and quality of facilities they receive. The best source of information on these and related issues are the worker representatives themselves and it is to the information from these respondents that we now turn.

We explained in Chapter 1 that the main worker representative respondents in the WIRS series are the senior representatives of the largest manual and non-manual negotiating groups, who had to be present on site at our sampled establishment. We noted earlier that the proportion of all establishments where worker representatives were present – rather than just those with recognition – fell from 54 per cent in 1984 to 38 per cent in 1990. However, there was an even more dramatic fall in the proportion of all establishments with a *senior* representative of the largest manual or non-manual negotiating groups on site. They were reported in 38 per cent of workplaces in 1990, compared with 67 per cent in 1984.[11] Senior representatives of white-collar unions, in particular, appeared to be much less prevalent than previously, declining from 58 per cent to just 21 per cent of all establishments. Senior manual representatives were present in 35 per cent of all establishments in 1984 and 24 per cent in 1990. These figures indicate the maximum sub-population of workplaces to which our worker representative samples relate. Even among workplaces with any recognized unions the proportion with either sort of senior lay representative based on site fell from 96 per cent to 72 per cent over the period. So if local union organization remained as strong as before in workplaces where senior representatives remained in existence – a theme running through the results we present below – it was in the context of a much smaller number of such workplaces by 1990.

The training of lay union representatives
The training of union representatives is a key factor determining their effectiveness in performing their role. The extent of training across workplaces also gives an indication of the degree of support given to representatives both by their union and by the management at their place of work. Worker representatives were asked whether, in the twelve months prior to interview, any representatives from their workplace had received courses of training or instruction connected with their role. The results are given in Table 4.4.[12] They show that there was little difference between manual and non-manual representatives in the reporting of such training in 1990, 37 per cent and 38 per cent respectively, and that there was a slight increase since 1984 when the respective figures were 28 per cent and 33 per cent.[13]

There was an increase in the incidence of training for manual stewards in private manufacturing (24 per cent to 38 per cent) and private services (16 per cent to 31 per cent), with stability in the public sector (around two fifths). By contrast, for non-manual representatives it was the public sector that was the source of the increase, rising by a quarter from 36 per cent in 1984 to 45 per cent in 1990. The increase in reported training may in part reflect the need for trade unionists to be kept informed of legal changes surrounding their role and, perhaps, attempts to sustain workplace organization in changed economic circumstances.

Table 4.4 Establishments having worker representatives trained in previous year, by broad sector, 1984 and 1990

Percentages

	All establishments		Private manufacturing		Private services		Public sector	
	1984	1990	1984	1990	1984	1990	1984	1990
Manual								
Representatives trained	28	37	24	38	16	31	38	39
Base: manual worker representatives belonging to recognized trade unions								
Unweighted	*910*	*726*	*349*	*330*	*137*	*142*	*424*	*254*
Weighted	*554*	*367*	*169*	*121*	*133*	*90*	*252*	*156*
Non-manual								
Representatives trained	33	38	21	18	26	27	36	45
Base: non-manual worker representatives belonging to recognized trade unions								
Unweighted	*949*	*670*	*250*	*170*	*122*	*131*	*577*	*369*
Weighted	*560*	*342[1]*	*61*	*28*	*88*	*87*	*412*	*226*

[1] See Note H.

Certainly, there was no change in the organization of trade union education. As before, the majority of all courses for either manual or non-manual representatives were organized by the TUC or union training colleges, though there appears to have been some decline in the reporting of this by non-manual representatives. Even so, a sizeable minority of courses (37 per cent for manual and 41 per cent for non-manual representatives) continued to be held at some other training or education establishment.[14]

Although it was still the case that in the great majority of cases (93 per cent of manual stewards and 98 per cent of non-manual representatives) some of the training was held at the initiative of the trade union, management was much less likely to initiate training for workplace representatives in 1990 than had been the case in 1984. A quarter of manual stewards and 15 per cent of non-manual representatives in 1984 had said that some training was also organized on the initiative of management. By the end of the decade the figures were 17 per cent and 5 per cent respectively.

Despite the declining involvement of management in initiating training for trade union work, where training was undertaken, it was still usually held in work time[15] and, hence, effectively partly funded by management. However, only in a very small proportion of cases for either manual stewards (8 per cent) or non-manual representatives (4 per cent) did management decide the majority of any course content. The greatest variation here occurred among manual stewards. In private manufacturing only 3 per cent of them reported that management decided the majority of the course content compared with 10 per cent in private services and the public sector. It appears that at the end of the decade manual trade unions in private manufacturing exercised greater control over the training of their workplace representatives than their counterparts in other sectors.

The great majority of representatives thought that training helped them in their jobs, as they had done in 1984. But a question new to the 1990 survey asked if there were any ways in which the training could be made more useful. Around half (47 per cent of manuals and 52 per cent of non-manuals) of respondents appeared to be satisfied with the current content of courses. Seven per cent of non-manual representatives reported a concern that existing training should be more widely available and a further 7 per cent simply wanted more training, with the implication that the demand was for more of the same. The most commonly reported suggestion for improvement put forward by manual stewards (8 per cent) concerned making it more 'vocationally specific'.

Office facilities provided by management for lay union representatives
A fairly obvious measure of the degree of support management gives to workplace trade union activities is the range of office facilities made available to local representatives. If there had been some general shift in the approach of management then we would expect it to be reflected, first, in a reduction of such facilities. The relevant questions formed part of the 1980 and 1990 surveys.

Our results show that the overall picture in 1990 was remarkable for its similarity with 1980. Three quarters of manual and non-manual representatives had access to office facilities of one kind or another and access to a telephone was almost universal. It is perhaps worth noting, however, that while the proportion of representatives having the use of a telephone increased, there was a decrease in those having their own telephone. Naturally, office facilities were more commonly reported where there was a concentration of white-collar occupations.

One difference between 1980 and 1990 reflected not so much a change in the range of facilities management made available *per se*, as developments in office technology. We asked in 1980 about access to a typewriter; in 1990 the equivalent question referred to typewriters or wordprocessors. Almost three fifths (57 per cent) of manual stewards and three quarters of non-manual representatives reported access to a typewriter or wordprocessor in 1990. Access to a fax machine was reported in 28 per cent and 42 per cent of cases, respectively.

Overall, manual stewards in establishments with low trade union density (below 25 per cent) were less likely to report access to any facility than counterparts in higher density workplaces, in part, no doubt because management take relatively low density levels as indicators of low commitment to unionism from employees.[16]

Facilities expressly provided to union representatives through written agreements are less directly dependent on day-to-day management consent than more informal arrangements, and provide a further indicator of management support for workplace trade union organization. In fact, in the great majority of cases in 1990, both manual and non-manual representatives' access to facilities was regulated by informal arrangements with management (around three quarters in each case). But this was also the position a decade earlier. Indeed, in private manufacturing, informal arrangements were even more common than before; in private services less so.

It seems, then, that where senior representatives were present at local level, the extent of management support for workplace trade union activities, at least in terms of the range of facilities provided, remained much the same in 1990 as it had been ten years previously. The fact that such support continued to be largely informal reflects a continuance of previous practice, although the increase in informality in private manufacturing and the decline in private services are notable.

Time off work for union duties and activities
The role of the lay union representative inevitably takes up a certain amount of employee time that would otherwise be spent working. Exactly how much time will depend on a variety of factors, such as the number of members and the number of other representatives at the establishment. Some level of activity may well take place without the knowledge of management. However, in most cases we would expect worker representatives to have some form of agreement or understanding with management covering their trade union duties and activities and the earlier surveys showed this to be the case. A further question concerns the nature of the arrangement; its degree of formality.

In fact, around nine out of ten workplace representatives in 1990 (manual and non-manual) reported an arrangement with management covering their trade union duties and activities, about the same as in 1984. There was little variation across private services or the public sector but in private manufacturing, in both surveys, a smaller proportion of manual stewards reported these arrangements (84 per cent in 1984 and 82 per cent in 1990).

As for the nature of these arrangements, however, there was an across-the-board decline in the proportion of manual stewards reporting written agreements, from three fifths (58 per cent) in 1984 to a half in 1990, with a consequent rise in informality. Among non-manual representatives there was little change since 1984, and written agreements were still more frequently reported by non-manual representatives than by their manual counterparts. However, while the situation in private manufacturing remained about the same over the period, written agreements were more frequently reported in 1990 in private services and less frequently reported in the public sector than was the case in 1984, probably reflecting the impact of the relatively highly unionized public utilities joining the private sector.

Use of legal provisions for time off work for union duties and activities
Of course, regardless of the arrangements managers and worker representatives may have arrived at among themselves, representatives of recognized trade unions have a statutory right to reasonable paid time off work for trade union duties and associated training and, as union members, to reasonable unpaid time off for trade union activities.[17] Our previous surveys explored the extent to which trade union representatives made use of the legal provisions for time off.[18] In 1980, around two fifths of representatives (manual and non-manual) reported having used the provisions since the Employment Protection Act, 1975 came into

force. Results from the 1984 survey suggested the level of use had increased substantially in the intervening period with 53 per cent of manual stewards and 44 per cent of non-manual representatives reporting using them in the four years since 1980. Use of the provisions was related to union density and to workplace size, no doubt because the need for time off becomes more pressing when there are more members to serve.

In the 1990 survey the question was changed slightly, to focus more clearly on the use of the statutory provisions as part of the initial request to management for time off. Accordingly, our worker representatives were asked if the Employment Protection Act had 'been *cited* in the last *three* years to try to obtain any time off for (manual or non-manual) representatives or members of (their) union'. A follow-up question asked whether the attempt was successful. Almost a fifth (19 per cent) of manual stewards and 12 per cent of non-manual representatives reported having cited the Act in the 1987–1990 period. Nine out of ten of these (manual and non-manual representatives) reported using it successfully.

The more restrictive wording and the shorter period of recall in the 1990 question would tend to result in lower proportions than those found previously. The most recent statutory changes are unlikely to have been a significant factor in this as they were introduced only at the very end of our respondents' recall period.

Use of legal provisions for disclosure of information
In addition to statutory rights covering time off for union-related matters, representatives of recognized trade unions also have rights under the Employment Protection Act 1975 to request the disclosure of certain kinds of information from management for the purposes of collective bargaining. Questions on the use of these provisions were also asked in our previous surveys.[19] We consider the range of issues over which management and trade unions bargain in Chapter 7, while the broader topic of employee involvement is the subject of Chapter 5.

The 1984 questions were repeated in 1990, though the recall period was changed to the previous three years rather than the previous four. The figures show little change in the proportion of manual stewards who made such a request for information – a fifth did so in both surveys. Manual stewards in private manufacturing were about twice as likely to report such requests as those in private services or the public sector. The proportion of non-manual representatives making use of the disclosure provisions also remained about the same over the period (13 per cent in 1984, 12 per cent in 1990).

As in the 1984 survey, we asked a further question in 1990 about how successful these requests for disclosure were seen to have been. Those who had made such requests were asked, on the last occasion they had

done so, how much of the information management had given them –
all, most, some or none at all.[20] Overall, it appeared that representatives
were about as successful at obtaining information in 1990 as before.
Four fifths of representatives (manual and non-manual) said they received
all, most or some of the information in 1990, about the same proportions
as received all or some of the information in 1984.

Check-off and other methods of collecting union dues
Perhaps one of the most important facilities trade unions can enjoy is
the check-off – the deduction of union members' subscriptions directly
from pay. Surprisingly, our previous surveys showed that there was no
necessary connection between the operation of check-off and trade
union recognition. The practice extended to workplaces which had no
recognized unions but which nevertheless had some union members on
site. Our previous analyses also showed that check-off arrangements
became more widespread between 1980 and 1984. Naturally, we included check-off questions in the 1990 survey to assess change in the
intervening period. The period since fieldwork for the 1990 survey was
completed has seen the publication of proposals which would make it
unlawful for an employer to deduct individual members' subscriptions
from their pay without their periodic, written consent.[21] Our 1990 survey results therefore form a useful benchmark from which to assess
future changes in the operation of the check-off in the context of possible
changes in the law.

For technical reasons it is appropriate to focus our analysis of management questionnaire material on check-off arrangements for manual
and non-manual sections of the workforce together.[22] In fact, our results
show little change overall in the extent of the check-off. In 1984, 74 per
cent of managers in workplaces with union members reported such an
arrangement for either manual or non-manual members. In 1990 the
equivalent figure was 73 per cent. Check-off was still more commonly
reported in workplaces with recognized unions, however, with 83 per
cent of managers in such workplaces reporting it in 1990. The incidence
of the check-off increased in private services workplaces with recognized unions (from 75 per cent to 85 per cent), partly due to the effects
of privatization, but there was virtually no change in the public sector
and in private manufacturing (75 per cent in 1990). Data from our
worker representative respondents show that in 1990 check-off was
more commonly reported by senior manual stewards than their non-
manual counterparts.

Of the nine industry Divisions covered by the survey, five showed
increases, three showed stability and in only one – Construction – was
there a decline in the reporting of check-off, from 68 per cent of establishments to 59 per cent. But it was again in relation to union density

that our results were particularly revealing. Overall, there was an increase in check-off in workplaces with recognized unions where less than half of employees were in membership and stability among workplaces with over half of employees in membership. The increases in check-off arrangements in low density workplaces were predominantly in the private sector, particularly manufacturing. In other words, there was growth among workplaces where check-off had previously been relatively uncommon. In 1990 around three quarters of workplaces with recognized unions which had membership density below half had check-off arrangements compared with three fifths in 1984. Some 83 per cent of workplaces in the 50 to 89 per cent density range reported check-off in 1990, about the same as previously. In recognized workplaces with 90 per cent or more employees in membership, around nine out of ten reported check-off, again about the same as 1984. It appeared, then, that there was some growth in one of the more obvious supports to trade union membership among the types of workplaces which had also seen the disappearance of local lay representatives.

We also asked some additional questions about check-off and other methods of dues payment, but of our worker representative respondents only. These included a slightly amended version of a 1980 question concerning whether unions paid the employer for the check-off and a new question about alternative methods of paying union subscriptions. In 1980, employers charged unions for check-off in a minority of establishments: just 17 per cent of senior manual stewards in workplaces with a check-off *agreement* reported that at least one union paid for the facility and 14 per cent of their non-manual equivalents did so. In 1990, the figures were 13 per cent and 9 per cent respectively.[23]

Clearly, check-off was still by far the most common method of paying union subscriptions, but our expanded questioning about the variety of payment methods revealed some other findings of interest. The full results are shown separately for manual and non-manual members in Tables 4.5 and 4.6. It should be emphasized, of course, that the figures given for check-off in each table are higher than those given above because our worker representative respondents were based at relatively highly unionized workplaces, usually with several unions on site, rather than simply those with any recognition, on which the question to managers was based. In 1990, a quarter of white-collar representatives said that at least some of their members paid their union subscriptions straight from their bank accounts by direct debit or standing order. This was a less common method among manual stewards, however, with just 4 per cent reporting it.[24] Other methods were rare. After check-off and direct debit, the next most frequently mentioned method by non-manual representatives was by *union members themselves, by post*. Six per cent reported it, compared with 1 per cent of manual stewards. In a further 4

Table 4.5   Methods of paying union subscriptions among manual unions, by broad sector, 1990

Percentages

	All establishments	Private manufacturing	Private services	Public sector
Collected personally by representative	8[1]	18	5	1
Paid by members themselves at office/branch meeting	5	5	4	6
Paid by members themselves by post to office	1	3	1	*
Paid straight from members' bank account by direct debit/standing order	4	2	5	5
Deducted by the employer from members' pay and sent to the union	89	80	90	95
Not answered	1	*	—	1

Base: manual worker representatives belonging to recognized trade unions
| *Unweighted* | *726* | *330* | *142* | *254* |
| *Weighted* | *367* | *121* | *90* | *156* |

[1] See Note E.

per cent of cases non-manual representatives collected union subscriptions personally. Among manual unions, personal collection was the second most popular method of collecting members' dues, being reported by 8 per cent of manual stewards, with a further 5 per cent saying collection was at a workplace meeting.

Personal collection methods were more commonly reported in private manufacturing than in other sectors and, as might be expected, in low density than high density workplaces. Direct debit was most common in the service sector, public or private, in workplaces with over half of employees in membership and in smaller workplaces, employing less than a hundred people.

These results show that, although the check-off remained the most common method of collecting union subscriptions in 1990, a variety of other methods were being used. Indeed, some 5 per cent of non-manual

Table 4.6   Methods of paying union subscriptions among non-manual unions, by broad sector, 1990

Percentages

	All establishments	Private manufacturing	Private services	Public sector
Collected personally by representative	4[1]	11	2	4
Paid by members themselves at office/branch meeting	*	*	*	*
Paid by members themselves by post to office	6	7	1	7
Paid straight from members' bank accounts by direct debit/standing order	25	15	29	24
Deducted by the employer from members' pay and sent to the union	79	85	73	80
Not answered	1	*	—	1
Base: non-manual worker representatives belonging to recognized trade unions
Unweighted	*670*	*170*	*131*	*369*
Weighted	*342[2]*	*28*	*87*	*226*

[1] See Note E.
[2] See Note H.

representatives reported that both check-off and direct debit were being used to collect subscriptions from members within the same workplace, while just 1 per cent of manual stewards reported this. A further 2 per cent of non-manual representatives reported both check-off and personal collection methods, with again just 1 per cent of manual stewards reporting the same. However, there is evidence from other sources which suggests that some unions are seeking to increase the proportion of members who pay their subscriptions by direct debit and similar arrangements.[25] This is no doubt linked in part to the growing numbers of employees with personal bank accounts, and perhaps, to a preference on the part of some unions to opt for collection methods that do not require the endorsement of management.[26]

Facilities provided by unions for lay union representatives
For the 1990 survey, we extended our questioning on facilities available
to workplace representatives by asking them about the forms of assistance they received from their own unions. A preponderance of our
representatives were in the larger unions. Overall, a very large majority
of manual and non-manual representatives reported receiving union
support in each of the four areas we asked about – legal advice, research
information, trade union education and the provision of meeting rooms.
The most common input from the union took the form of legal advice,
with 94 per cent of manual stewards and 96 per cent of non-manual
representatives reporting it. In large part this reflects the changing legal
environment in which trade unions and their representatives were operating through the 1980s. It suggests that the unions acted as important
centres of knowledge and expertise on which workplace representatives
could draw.

This applied equally to the provision of research information. Over
three quarters of all representatives (78 per cent of manuals and 77 per
cent of non-manuals) said their union provided them with research
information. This was especially true in private manufacturing, where
86 per cent of manual stewards and 94 per cent of non-manual representatives reported this facility.

Given the extensive role of trade unions in initiating, designing and
conducting training courses, it was not surprising to find that trade
union education was available to nine out of ten representatives (90 per
cent of manuals and 88 per cent of non-manuals). However, both manual
and non-manual representatives in private services and those in smaller
establishments, with less than 100 employees, were much less likely
than others to have this available. Almost seven out of ten manual
stewards (68 per cent) and six out of ten (62 per cent) non-manual
representatives said that their unions provided rooms for meetings.

It would seem, then, that the conclusion to be drawn from the results
given above is that among workplaces with a strong union presence,
such as a senior representative, management support for trade unionism,
as measured by the facilities they provided for trade union work, remained high throughout the latter part of the 1980s and probably across
the decade. Local representatives themselves continued to make use of
statutory provisions for their role and unions outside the workplace
provided a range of services to underpin local organization. But these
are not the only forms of support open to lay representatives.

**Contacts between lay union representatives within the workplace
and outside**
Our previous surveys demonstrated that contacts between stewards and
representatives themselves both within and across workplaces were

common. They involved meetings between representatives of the same and different unions and, on occasion, extended to workplaces belonging to other employers. In addition, stewards and representatives, naturally, met with paid officials of their union, including those at their union's head office. If the incidence of these contacts was at a similar level as previously, we might conclude that it was 'business as usual' in unionized workplaces. Decline, on the other hand, may point to a weakening of local organization. We look first at contacts with the union, at local and national level, before moving on to the various kinds of committees of stewards and representatives.

Contact with paid officials of the union
In fact, our data suggest that the demands made of paid officials by workplace representatives were greater in 1990 than they had been in 1984 and perhaps even in 1980. In 1990, three quarters of senior manual representatives reported meeting a paid official in the 12 months prior to interview, the same proportion as 1984. But, for senior non-manual representatives, there was an increase from 57 per cent in 1984 to 69 per cent in 1990.

In private manufacturing, contact with paid officials by senior manual stewards increased by a fifth, from 69 per cent in 1984 to 88 per cent in 1990. This followed a slight decline between 1980 and 1984, from three quarters to 69 per cent. There was also a small increase for senior non-manual representatives in private manufacturing, from 64 per cent to 70 per cent. This change may reflect the campaign within manufacturing industry for a shorter working week which was active during our study period. In private services, there was a sizable increase in the proportion of non-manual representatives who had meetings with paid officials, from 52 per cent in 1984 to 88 per cent in 1990. At the same time, there was a slight fall recorded among manual stewards in this sector, from 73 per cent to 65 per cent.

The differences in reporting between manual and non-manual representatives in the private sector were apparent also in the public sector, albeit much less pronounced. Meetings between manual stewards and paid officials were still common, but declined slightly from 77 per cent in 1984 to 71 per cent in 1990. Among non-manual representatives there was little or no change (58 per cent in 1984, 61 per cent in 1990).

In addition to these dealings with paid officials, workplace representatives may also have contact with national union officials and the union's Head Office. In fact, our results show that over the 1980s there was a clear increase in the extent of contact by local representatives with their unions at national level. Half of manual stewards reported these contacts compared with 38 per cent in 1980 (46 per cent in 1984). Three fifths of non-manual representatives reported contacting either a national official or the union Head Office in the 12 months preceding the interview, compared with half in 1984 and 43 per cent in 1980.

The pattern of change across the 1980s was different for manual stewards in private manufacturing. Following a decline between 1980 and 1984 from 43 per cent to 34 per cent, the extent of contact with the national level of the union increased to half (53 per cent) in 1990. By contrast, among non-manual representatives in private manufacturing, the incidence of such contact fell, from 53 per cent in 1984 to 46 per cent in 1990. Once again, the campaign for a shorter working week was likely to have been reflected in the results for manual stewards in private manufacturing. In private services, there was an increase in reporting of contacts with the national union by both manual and non-manual representatives, respectively from 51 per cent in 1984 to 59 per cent in 1990 and from half to 62 per cent. In the public sector, the experiences of manual and non-manual representatives differed. The incidence of contacts by manual stewards declined (from half to two fifths), but among non-manual representatives it increased (from half to three fifths).

It appears, then, that trade unions in 1990 were much more heavily involved in workplace-level matters than they were in 1984. All levels of the union were affected, it seems, from the local paid official being more likely to represent members in the absence of lay representatives, or to be in contact with representatives that still existed, up to union national officers being much more commonly consulted directly by establishment-based representatives.

In previous surveys we asked about the extent of joint meetings between workplace representatives, local paid officials and management. In 1990, the question was modified to focus on meetings between workplace representatives and management. We were interested in the extent of meetings which were outside any framework of negotiation or consultation.[27]

Such meetings with managers were mentioned by 81 per cent of manual stewards and 76 per cent of non-manual representatives. They were reported by manual stewards in nine out of ten workplaces in both private manufacturing and private services, but in only seven out of ten workplaces in the public sector. Among non-manual representatives, meetings were most frequently reported in the public sector (84 per cent) and private manufacturing (77 per cent) and least frequently in private services (60 per cent). Meetings by both manual and non-manual representatives were more commonly reported in larger establishments.

We turn now to the contacts between worker representatives themselves, both within and beyond the workplace. As in previous years we asked questions about *intra-union* committees and meetings and *joint shop stewards* committees and meetings at the workplace. Respectively, these covered meetings between representatives of the same union and meetings between representatives of different unions within the same workplace. We also asked about *single-employer combine committees* and *multi-employer combine committees.*

Intra-union stewards' meetings at the workplace
Excluding those establishments with only one manual steward, the proportion of manual stewards reporting meetings with other representatives of the same union at the workplace increased slightly from 36 per cent in 1984 to 43 per cent in 1990.[28] There were increases in each of the three broad sectors of employment. For non-manual representatives, with the same exclusion, there was no change (34 per cent in 1984 and 36 per cent in 1990). In this case there were increases in private manufacturing and the public sector, but stability in private services. Thus, it seems that the overall decline in the reporting of these meetings in the early 1980s seems to have been reversed by the end of the decade. Further, the higher incidence of such committees among manual stewards compared with non-manual representatives, slight in 1984, was more evident in 1990.

Not surprisingly, both manual and non-manual representatives were more likely to report meetings the larger the number of manual and non-manual employees at the establishment. And manual stewards were, overall, more likely to have meetings the higher the union density, which is generally higher in larger establishments. In 1990, as in our previous two surveys, the typical frequency of both manual and non-manual 'intra-union' meetings was once a month or more often.

Joint shop stewards' committees at the workplace
In addition to meetings among representatives of the same union, in workplaces where more than one trade union had members we asked whether there were any committees or meetings of representatives from different unions.[29] While the period between our 1980 and 1984 surveys may have seen some decline in the extent of these joint shop stewards' committees, it is likely that there was an increase between 1984 and 1990. Table 4.7 gives the results.

The table shows that, for manual unions, the incidence of joint shop stewards' committees increased between 1984 and 1990 from 32 per cent to 37 per cent. Although this increase could be due to sampling error, it is certain that there was no decline in activity over the period. However, we can be confident that the incidence of committees did increase in private manufacturing from a third to over half of workplaces with two or more unions. This is a surprising finding to the extent that the decline in multi-unionism within the sector will have reduced the opportunities for such meetings. There was little change elsewhere.

Table 4.7   **Extent of joint shop-stewards' committees or meetings, by broad sector, 1984 and 1990**

Percentages

	All establishments		Private manufacturing		Private services		Public sector	
	1984	1990	1984	1990	1984	1990	1984	1990
Manual								
Committee or meeting reported	32	37	33	52	(21)[1]	31	32	28
Base: manual worker representatives belonging to recognized trade unions at establishments where workforce was represented by two or more unions								
Unweighted	*587*	*468*	*255*	*215*	*41*	*65*	*291*	*188*
Weighted	*230[2]*	*145*	*97*	*54*	*16*	*23*	*116*	*67*
Non-manual								
Committee or meeting reported	20	30	26	24	(8)	16	21	33
Base: non-manual worker representatives belonging to recognized trade unions at establishments where workforce was represented by two or more unions								
Unweighted	*661*	*463*	*143*	*91*	*41*	*70*	*477*	*302*
Weighted	*375*	*233*	*25*	*10*	*23*	*38*	*327*	*185*

[1] See Note B.
[2] See Note H.

The incidence of joint shop stewards' committees involving non-manual representatives increased by half between 1984 and 1990, from 20 per cent to 30 per cent. The increase was most pronounced in the public sector, rising from a fifth to a third over the period, reflecting increased activity in both Local and Central Government.

Although the incidence of manual joint shop stewards' committees increased, they met less frequently than in 1984: once every three months rather than once a month. Non-manual committees met as often in 1990 as they did in 1984, typically at least once every three months. And, as previously, in the great majority of cases both manual and non-manual committees met in work time.

Single-employer combine committees
Contacts between lay representatives often extend beyond the workplace, to other workplaces that are part of the same employer and even to workplaces of other employers. Linkages such as these may be of an *ad hoc* kind, such as when stewards and representatives combine together to organize industrial action. But more often they take on a routine form, involving regular meetings to discuss matters of mutual interest. As we reported in the previous book, such committees are at a level above our unit of analysis and great care must be taken in interpreting the results, because of possible multiple counting of the same committee by respondents in different workplaces.[30] First, we consider committees of stewards and representatives from a number of separate establishments belonging to the same employer, commonly known as 'single-employer combine committees', before moving on to their 'multi employer' equivalents.

Overall, there was little or no change in the reporting of single-employer committees by both manual and non-manual representatives in establishments belonging to multi-establishment organizations. As Table 4.8 shows, they were reported in around two fifths of cases in each of our surveys. There was also little change in each of the three broad sectors of employment and it was still the case that these committees were very much more common among service sector workplaces, regardless of ownership. It is also of interest, however, that by 1990 these committees were as frequently reported by manual as non-manual representatives, whereas previously the latter were more common.

The typical reported frequency of single-employer combine committee meetings was at least once every three months, about the same as 1984, although manual combines were more likely to meet at least once a month than non-manual combines (42 per cent and 28 per cent respectively). Both manual and non-manual combines were much more likely to meet at least once a month in the public sector than elsewhere.

In 1990, we re-introduced some questions from the 1980 survey about the support management may offer to these combine committees. How-

Table 4.8 **Proportion of workplaces where worker representative reported single-employer and multi-employer combine committees, 1984 and 1990**

Percentages

	Manual		Non-manual	
	1984	1990	1984	1990
Single-employer combine committee reported	42	38	41	39
Base: worker representatives belonging to recognized trade unions at establishments that were part of multi-establishment organizations				
Unweighted	*853*	*665*	*912*	*644*
Weighted	*482*	*320*	*534*	*335*
Multi-employer combine committee reported	11	12	11	11
Base: worker representatives belonging to recognized trade unions				
Unweighted	*910*	*726*	*949*	*670*
Weighted	*554*	*367*	*560*	*342*

ever, our new question differed slightly from the 1980 equivalent which means the data from the two surveys are not strictly comparable.[31] We noted earlier that management provision of facilities for senior representatives had remained at least as widespread in 1990 as in 1980. We were also interested to assess the degree of management support for these combines, either at the workplace or at a higher level in the organization, which, to some extent, attempts to reflect the organization of management. As such there may be mutual benefits to both sides in their existence.

Overall in 1990, 35 per cent of manual stewards and 36 per cent of non-manual representatives reported that management within the *organization* had given financial or other assistance to these combine committees. In 1980, 36 per cent of manual stewards and 32 per cent of non-manual representatives said that management at the *workplace* had given them financial help. Had our 1980 respondents who said they did not receive workplace-based management support been given the opportunity to report that they received support from elsewhere in the organization, then it is likely that the total level of management support reported in 1980 would have been higher. Exactly how much higher we cannot tell, so it is difficult to assess the direction of change in the intervening period. However, it is clear that management support for manual combines in 1990 was more frequently reported in the private sector than the public sector, whereas for non-manual combines the reverse was the case. Most commonly for both manual or non-manual representatives, assistance from management took the form of help with meeting rooms, although manual stewards mentioned 'help with travel costs' almost as often.

Multi-employer combine committees

The final committees we asked about were those involving representatives from establishments belonging to different employers. Naturally, the possible multiple reporting discussed previously in relation to single-employer combine committees applies equally to these multi-employer combine committees. The decline in multi-employer bargaining might have been expected to be reflected in our results on the incidence of these combines. In fact, as with single-employer combines, there was little or no change since 1984, as shown in Table 4.8. As before, membership of a multi-employer combine was reported by manual or non-manual representatives in just under an eighth of workplaces, less than a third of those reporting membership of single-employer combines. There was little variation by broad sector, save that they were least often reported by non-manual representatives in private services. The early 1980s had seen a decline in multi-employer combine activity in the private sector and an increase in the public sector. It would appear that the late 1980s saw stability rather than change in this aspect of trade union organization.

But what of management support for these combines? Given the decline in multi-employer bargaining since the mid-1980s, we might have expected to find some decrease in management support for these committees. To assess this we again re-introduced a question from the 1980 survey but this time the question replicated that of 1980, so direct comparisons between these two surveys can be made with confidence. Despite our expectations, our results show that the degree of management support for these combines increased substantially across the decade. Fully a fifth of manual stewards in 1990 reported that management at their establishment had given financial or other support towards the setting up and running of the multi-employer combine committees, up from just 7 per cent in 1980. For non-manual representatives, the increase was less spectacular, but still substantial, from 9 per cent in 1980 to 17 per cent in 1990.

There were differences in the level of management's enthusiasm in different sectors, however. Management support in 1990 was three times as likely in the public sector than in private manufacturing. In private services, there was little or no support for the combine committees reported by manual stewards, but about the same level of support for those reported by non-manual representatives as for their equivalents in private manufacturing.

Overall, then, our results on the incidence of contacts between representatives themselves and between representatives and their area and national officers of their unions held up during the 1980s and in some cases increased. But if managements and trade unions and their representatives continued to provide support to local organization, what of local members themselves?

Lay union representatives and the local membership
Finally, in this chapter, we turn to the constituencies which, over and above management and trade union support, provide representatives with their legitimacy – the local membership. In particular, we focus on the ways in which trade union members appointed their local workplace representatives. Our focus then shifts to the types and size of union branches to which both lay representatives and their constituents themselves belonged.

The methods of appointment of workplace representatives
Following the earlier surveys, we distinguished between *senior* and *ordinary* (non-senior) stewards or representatives in our questionnaires. Where there was only one representative on site, this respondent was treated as 'senior' for the purposes of the questionnaire, but the results are reported separately under *sole* stewards.[32] Tables 4.9 and 4.10 give the results, separately for manual and non-manual representatives.

By far the most common method of appointment of all lay trade union representatives in both 1984 and 1990 was by a show of hands at a meeting. The tables show that over half of all manual stewards were appointed in this way – whether senior, ordinary or sole – and so were around a half of senior and ordinary non-manual representatives. A third of sole non-manual representatives were appointed by a show of hands. There was little change in this since our last survey, with the exception that ordinary non-manual representatives were more likely to report this method than previously.

The second most frequently mentioned method of appointment in both 1984 and 1990 was some form of balloting procedure.[33] For the composite category, 'any type of ballot', the tables show that there was little or no change among either manual or non-manual unions over the 1984 to 1990 period. In general, between a quarter and a third of representatives of each type reported some form of ballot. In most cases these were workplace rather than postal ballots. It would appear, then, that legal requirements on unions to ballot in other spheres of their activity had by 1990 had little effect on areas that were still governed by

Table 4.9   **Methods of appointment of manual union representatives, 1984
and 1990**

Percentages

	Type of representative					
	Senior		Ordinary		Sole	
	1984	1990	1984	1990	1984	1990
Method of appointment						
Appointed or nominated without election	3[1]	5	3	3	6	9
General feeling of a meeting without a vote	13	8	14	8	23	24
Show of hands at meeting	58	60	54	57	51	53
Voting slips/secret ballot at workplace or other meeting place	28	25	25	22	20	10
Postal ballot/secret postal ballot	4	5	3	9	1	5
Other answer	1	2	1	3	*	1
Any type of ballot[2]	**32**	**30**	**28**	**31**	**21**	**15**
Base: manual worker representatives belonging to recognized trade unions						
Unweighted	*721*	*506*	*721*	*506*	*190*	*220*
Weighted	*299*	*185*	*299*	*185*	*256*	*183*

[1] See Note E.
[2] This category includes a few cases where some other form of balloting was mentioned.

union choice. There were some changes at the margin, however. Sole representatives, whether manual or non-manual, were less likely to report workplace ballots than previously, although the use of postal balloting by manual sole stewards seems to have increased slightly. There was also an increase in postal balloting among ordinary manual stewards.

The tables show that a smaller proportion of senior and ordinary manual stewards mentioned 'general feeling of a meeting without a vote' than previously, with just 8 per cent reporting it in 1990. There was no similar change in the responses of non-manual equivalents. Interestingly, perhaps, the use of the general feeling of a meeting was as commonly reported by

Table 4.10   Methods of appointment of non-manual union representatives, 1984 and 1990

Percentages

| | Type of representative | | | | | |
| | Senior | | Ordinary | | Sole | |
	1984	1990	1984	1990	1984	1990
Method of appointment						
Appointed or nominated without election	5[1]	6	5	8	5	8
General feeling of a meeting without a vote	22	23	16	18	25	33
Show of hands at meeting	46	47	38	52	37	32
Voting slips/secret ballot at workplace or other meeting place	27	25	23	21	26	18
Postal ballot/secret postal ballot	6	4	5	1	7	5
Other answer	2	1	3	3	4	3
Any type of ballot[2]	**32**	**29**	**27**	**24**	**29**	**23**

Base: non-manual worker representatives belonging to recognized trade unions
Unweighted	*788*	*466*	*788*	*466*	*161*	*204*
Weighted	*373*	*133*	*373*	*133*	*188*	*208*

[1] See Note E.
[2] This category includes a few cases where some other form of balloting was mentioned.

sole manual stewards in 1990 as in 1984 and, indeed, was mentioned three times more often by sole manual stewards than by their ordinary and senior counterparts. In addition, sole manual stewards were much more likely to be appointed or nominated without an election than other types of manual steward in 1990. In this there was little change since our last survey, but since more of our workplaces had fewer stewards, including more with just one, the overall impact of these informal, non-elective methods will have grown. Allowing that union members have always been reluctant to take on the steward role, the use of non-elective appointment methods at a larger number of workplaces in 1990 suggests that this reluctance may have increased and may partly explain the decline in the numbers of stewards as a whole.

The size and composition of trade union branches
Finally, in this chapter, we turn to the position of our worker representatives as constituents themselves – of the branch or local unit of organization of their union itself. Since its inception the WIRS series has asked questions about the size and composition of the main types of union branch to which our worker representative respondents belonged. The questions were repeated in 1990. Again we examined the composition of trade union branches in terms of three main types: *workplace-based branches*, where all branch members are employed at the same workplace; *single-employer branches*, which draw membership from more than one workplace belonging to the same employer; and *multi-employer branches*. As with the reporting of higher-level committees discussed earlier, care must be taken when interpreting our results on higher-level branches because of possible multiple reporting of such branches. Our results allow us to have confidence about the incidence of workplace-based branches, however, and our analysis concentrates on that particular type.

Our results are presented first in relation to the main manual and non-manual unions to which our worker representative respondents belonged. These are shown, respectively, in Tables 4.11 and 4.12. The lower portions of both tables gives results on the overall incidence of workplace-based branches, which show no real change for manual unions, but an increase for non-manual unions. By 1990, therefore, there was more similarity in the two types of union than previously, with around a quarter of representatives of each type reporting workplace-based union branches (27 per cent manual, 22 per cent non-manual). However, there was no change in the incidence of workplace-based branches among any of the main unions in our sample, manual or non-manual.

Of the other main types of branch that we asked about, only the results for single-employer branches of manual unions showed statistically significant change. These types of branches were less commonly reported in 1990 than in 1984, a pattern reflected in the results for each of the three main manual unions: the TGWU, the GMB and the AEU. There was no change in the reporting of single-employer branches of white-collar unions, either overall or for the main unions in our sample.

Tables 4.11 and 4.12 contain a wealth of information, including the distribution of categories of branch size and the average (median) size of branches, in relation to the main named trade unions. Tables 4.13 and 4.14 present our analysis of branch size in relation to branch composition, from which it is easier to assess the nature of the changes that occurred in the late 1980s, at least for workplace-based branches.[34]

Table 4.11 Size and composition of union branches (manual workers), 1984 and 1990

	All representatives		TGWU		GMB		AEU		NUPE	
	1984	1990	1984	1990	1984	1990	1984	1990	1984	1990
										Numbers
	319	291	193	192	235	354	425	362	488	392
Number of branch members										
										Column percentages
Median[1]	18[2]	21	28	24	13	17	17	5	3	15
1–49	9	9	10	8	18	6	2	4	6	7
50–99	8	7	6	13	11	7	10	*	7	4
100–199	7	6	4	8	10	6	1	10	11	7
200–299	5	6	3	4	6	9	11	25	7	11
300–399	4	5	3	4	2	3	3	6	10	9
400–499	12	9	8	12	9	7	21	12	20	11
500–999	9	7	12	3	6	11	3	5	9	11
1000–1999	15	16	12	13	16	16	16	4	14	12
2000–9997	13	14	15	12	10	17	15	28	12	14
Don't know/not answered										
Branch composition										
Workplace-based	24	27	33	43	22	21	10	9	5	10
Single-employer	32	24	25	11	37	17	22	6	62	64
Multi-employer	42	47	40	45	42	61	68	85	33	23
Don't know/not answered	2	2	2	1	—	1	—	—	—	3
Base: manual worker representatives belonging to recognized trade unions										
Unweighted	*910*	*726*	*189*	*163*	*126*	*109*	*121*	*99*	*140*	*99*
Weighted	*554[3]*	*367*	*129*	*74*	*69*	*65*	*47*	*25*	*93*	*53*

[1] Median linearly interpolated from weighted absolute numbers, excluding don't knows.
[2] See Note C.
[3] See Note K.

Table 4.12 Size and composition of union branches (non-manual workers), 1984 and 1990

| | All representatives | | Union to which representatives belonged | | | | | |
| | | | NALGO | | MSF | | CPSA | |
	1984	1990	1984	1990	1984	1990	1984	1990
								Numbers
Number of branch members								
Median[1]	328	256	634	573	337	290	228	160
								Column percentages
1–49	9[2]	20	3	2	7	22	(17)[3]	(12)
50–99	9	9	6	3	4	2	(11)	(26)
100–199	12	9	7	9	4	14	(10)	(7)
200–299	12	10	11	14	16	6	(41)	(22)
300–399	7	7	8	7	8	13	(6)	(6)
400–499	6	5	10	8	5	7	(7)	(*)
500–999	15	11	14	16	21	9	(4)	(7)
1000–1999	6	6	5	5	7	7	(*)	(3)
2000–9997	13	11	32	28	2	5	(*)	(—)
Don't know/not answered	12	12	6	9	26	14	(4)	(15)
Branch composition								
Workplace-based	15	22	8	10	17	23	(5)	(15)
Single-employer	64	57	78	77	18	17	(94)	(82)
Multi-employer	19	20	11	12	65	57	(1)	(3)
Don't know/not answered	2	1	4	—	—	3	(—)	(—)
Base: non-manual worker representatives belonging to recognized trade unions								
Unweighted	*949*	*670*	*167*	*141*	*176*	*129*	*34*	*36*
Weighted	*560[4]*	*342*	*93*	*67*	*42*	*29*	*32*	*44*

[1] Median linearly interpolated from weighted absolute numbers, excluding don't knows.
[2] See Note C.
[3] See Note B.
[4] See Note K.

Table 4.13   Size of union branches in relation to branch composition (manual workers), 1984 and 1990

	Workplace-based		Single-employer		Multi-employer	
	1984	1990	1984	1990	1984	1990
						Numbers
Number of branch members						
Median[1]	38	46	354	517	908	588
					Column percentages	
1–49	65	53[2]	6	12	3	6
50–99	14	16	16	10	2	4
100–199	9	14	12	4	5	5
200–299	4	4	9	7	9	8
300–399	2	4	6	*	6	11
400–499	1	2	4	9	6	4
500–999	3	2	15	12	14	12
1000–1999	1	1	8	11	14	9
2000–9997	1	3	14	21	24	21
Don't know/not answered	*	2	10	13	18	20

Base: manual worker representatives belonging to recognized trade unions

Unweighted	*240*	*218*	*283*	*167*	*375*	*332*
Weighted	*131*	*101*	*180*	*87*	*235*	*173*

[1] Median linearly interpolated from weighted absolute numbers, excluding don't knows.
[2] See Note C.

The tables clearly show the typical (median) size of workplace-based branches of manual unions to have increased slightly, while the typical size of their non-manual equivalents dropped by a third. The net result is, again, convergence between the two types of union. Workplace-based branches of both types of union contained around the same number of members in 1990 (just over 40), whereas previously, workplace-based branches of white-collar unions were almost twice as large (64 members compared with 38). So there were fewer, but larger workplace-based branches of manual unions in 1990 than previously. By contrast there were a larger number of smaller workplace-based branches of non-manual unions than in the past.

Synopsis
Our earlier surveys showed that the basic institutional structures of industrial relations in general, and local trade union organization in particular, hardly changed between 1980 and 1984. There have been changes since. Our analysis in this chapter showed that the late 1980s

Table 4.14   Size of union branches in relation to branch composition (non-manual workers), 1984 and 1990

	Workplace-based		Single-employer		Multi-employer	
	1984	1990	1984	1990	1984	1990
						Numbers
Number of branch members						
Median[1]	64	41	396	328	466	609
					Column percentages	
1–49	39[2]	57	5	11	3	4
50–99	24	13	7	10	3	3
100–199	15	8	12	9	11	11
200–299	4	7	14	12	12	11
300–399	6	1	8	11	6	1
400–499	2	2	6	6	8	3
500–999	4	4	17	12	17	17
1000–1999	*	1	6	6	9	11
2000–9997	*	3	16	14	12	13
Don't know/not answered	6	4	9	9	19	25

Base: non-manual worker representatives belonging to recognized trade unions

Unweighted	*205*	*166*	*482*	*304*	*248*	*195*
Weighted	*85*	*75*	*358*	*196*	*108*	*69*

[1] Median linearly interpolated from weighted absolute numbers, excluding don't knows.
[2] See Note C.

saw fewer lay union representatives – the most basic building blocks of local trade union organization. The fall was widespread, affecting workplaces of all types, but particularly smaller workplaces and those with low levels of union membership.

But, in the much smaller number of workplaces where lay union representatives still operated, stability rather than change prevailed. On average, there was the same number of union members per lay representative as before. In workplaces where local organization traditionally had been strong, it remained so. The incidence of full-time representatives remained stable, though they were still very rare. Management support for local unionism in such workplaces remained high, as measured by the facilities provided by management for trade union work. Union representatives continued to use the statutory provisions for time off work and for requesting information from management. The incidence of the check-off remained widespread and had grown in workplaces with lower union membership. There was also some experimentation by unions with direct debiting, a method of dues payment not dependent on employer endorsement.

Local committee structures through which lay representives relate to each other, within and between workplaces, remained very much in evidence in more heavily organized workplaces. Committees of lay representatives from the same and different unions within the same workplace were slightly more common in 1990 than before. Committees with representatives from several workplaces – 'combine' committees – were as common and management more often gave financial and other support to multi-employer combines in 1990 than in 1980.

But it also appeared that trade union officials outside the workplace had assumed a larger role in workplace matters than before. Contacts between lay representatives and the union at national level increased. Paid union officials had much more contact with senior white-collar representatives in the late 1980s than before. And unions were an important source of advice on legal, educational and research matters for the great majority of local lay representatives. In workplaces where lay representatives were failing to emerge, paid union officials were more often providing the representative function for the local membership in 1990 than previously.

Notes and references

1. For example, J. Kelly (1990), 'British trade unionism 1979–1989: change, continuity and contradictions', *Work, Employment and Society*, Special issue, May, pp. 29–65. Volume 24, No. 2, pp. 169–179.

2. The term 'steward' is usually reserved for lay union representatives of unions with mainly manual members, with 'representative' for those with mainly non-manual members. We adopt this convention in this chapter, but use the term 'representatives' when generically referring to representatives from either type of union.

3. In 1984 we asked the same sequence of questions separately about representatives of manual unions and of non-manual unions. In the 1990 survey, in addition to these two groups, we asked about representatives of recognized unions that organized both sections of the workforce. One consequence of this change is that it is not possible to present strictly comparable 1984 and 1990 results separately for manual and non-manual unions. Allocating the cases of the third, 'mixed' type of representative in the 1990 survey to the results for both other types of representatives would give a misleading impression of any changes that had taken place. There is no simple, accurate measure available for allocating 'mixed' representatives to either the manual or the non-manual category.

4. The WIRS sample coverage of Construction is uneven due to the fact that our sampling frame – the *Census of Employment* – is over two years out of date by the time of our fieldwork. Many construction sites will have disappeared between the Census and our fieldwork period.

5. Excluding state schools from our analysis of the 1984 survey, to take account of the necessary exclusion of teachers' unions in England and Wales from the recognition sections of the 1990 questionnaire, made very little difference to the results. The revised 1984 figure was 83 per cent rather than 84 per cent.

6. From our 1984 survey results we observed differences between the three broad sectors in the definition of seniority used by our management respondents and our 1990

form of questioning may have partly obscured this. It is possible that had we used our 1984 question-format in 1990, our results would have shown an overall decline in the incidence of representatives that were acknowledged by management as senior and stability, or even a slight drop in the public sector. In our 1984 survey we asked two questions about senior representatives designed to ascertain, first, whether there were any at the establishment and, secondly, whether management acknowledged them as senior. Interestingly, there was a high degree of overlap in the responses to both questions by managers in private manufacturing plants, but in the service sector, among both publicly-owned and privately-owned workplaces, only about half of managers who had initially reported senior representatives went on to say that they were acknowledged by management as such. Combining the two questions into one in the 1990 survey may have meant that the 'acknowledged' part of the question was not sufficiently emphasized and, therefore, disproportionately affected responses in the service sector.

7. An additional question in the section on representatives in the 1990 survey concerned the presence of 'non-union' representatives. Results from this question are given in Chapter 5.

8. The changes in the structure of the main management questionnaire mean that our estimates of the numbers of stewards in each survey are not directly comparable. Although we are able to get a good indicator of the number of stewards representing both manual and non-manual employees in 1990, this is obviously not possible for 1984. It seems likely that such 'mixed' stewards were in existence in 1984, though presumably less common than in 1990. As we asked only about two categories of steward in 1984, those for manual employees and those for non-manual employees, it is likely that some 'mixed' stewards were counted twice in that survey. It is difficult to assess the scale of this. In addition, the exclusion of state schools from the recognition section of the 1990 questionnaire will have deflated the 1990 figure somewhat. Finally, the increased level of non-response to the questions on the numbers of stewards in 1990 will have deflated the 1990 estimate even further. Because the scale of the decline in numbers of stewards is difficult to quantify precisely, we do not present national estimates of the numbers of stewards and representatives in the economy as a whole. There are, of course, implications for the calculation of ratios of union members per steward, as shown below.

9. The number of union members over the number of representatives was calculated in the following way. In order to be included in the respective numerator and denominator, establishments had to have recognized unions for the category of employees (manual, non-manual or mixed) and had to have known both the numbers of representatives and the number of union members for each category of employees. The slight difficulty with the 1990 calculation was that, although it was a straightforward matter to isolate establishments that had recognized unions of both manual and non-manual employees (mixed unions) where the number of representatives of such unions were also known, our union membership data were not collected separately for such mixed unions – simply members of the manual workforce and members of the non-manual workforce. In this case, therefore, the added condition for the 'mixed' part of the 1990 steward density calculation was that the *total* number of union members was known. However, the total number of union members in the numerator of the final density calculation was arrived at in the same way as in 1984 – adding the manual and non-manual equivalents together. The possible double-counting of mixed representatives in 1984 will mean that the number of union members per steward in that year was larger than the figures given, though we cannot quantify it. Although it is certain that, overall, the number of members per steward did not increase over the 1984–1990 period, it could be that numbers either stayed the same or declined slightly.

10. These were workplaces with recognized unions for the relevant section of the workforce where the number of stewards and the numbers of union members were known.

11. The format of the questioning in 1990 was similar to 1984, so the question was asked separately for senior manual representatives and for senior non-manual repre-

sentatives. We did not make provision for senior representatives of 'mixed' unions here because it had been ascertained whether the 'majority' of members covered by such unions were either manual or non-manual and then sent through the appropriate route of the questionnaire. These questions were primarily included to allow us to identify the appropriate worker representative to interview. Using this data as it is here, therefore, will 'double-count' some senior representatives of 'mixed' unions, so the true 1990 figure would actually be lower than the 38 per cent given. However, the changes in reporting since 1984 are real in the sense that the questions were asked in exactly the same way in both surveys.

12. Changes to the structure of the 1984 and 1990 management and worker representative questionnaires mean that it is difficult to present reliable results on the proportion of representatives trained over the period. Hence our analysis focuses on the proportion of establishments where some training was reported by worker representatives.

13. Figures for 1984 published in our previous book differ slightly as they were based on management responses, rather than worker representatives, as given here.

14. In 1984, respondents were asked whether any of the training courses were held at a jointly (i.e. with management) agreed education establishment. In 1990, the 'jointly agreed' condition was dropped. Instead, we asked whether any of the courses were *held at any other training or education establishment.*

15. In 1984 we asked whether any of the courses were held in working hours and whether any were held outside working hours. In 1990 the question asked whether the time to attend courses was paid for by management and the precoded responses were as follows: *none of the courses in work time; yes – all of the time; yes – some of the time; no – none.*

16. There are no comparable data for either of the previous surveys. In 1980, we asked about facilities provided by management but the measure of union density was less complete than in later surveys, in that we only collected union membership data in respect of full-time employees. In 1984, the union density calculation was much more reliable, but we did not ask about facilities provided for trade union representatives.

17. These rights were initiated in the Employment Protection Act 1975, subsequently re-enacted in the Employment Protection (Consolidation) Act 1978. More recently the Employment Act 1989 amended the statutory provisions on time off for trade union duties, primarily by restricting the range of issues for which paid time off can be claimed to those covered by recognition agreements between employers and trade unions. These new provisions came into force in February 1990 (early in our fieldwork period) and a revised Code of Practice was issued by ACAS in May 1991.

18. The statute distinguishes between trade union *duties*, for which the employer must allow representatives paid time off during working hours, and trade union *activities*, for which employers are not required to allow any paid time off. The main question in the WIRS series on time off does not distinguish between these and relates to time off in general.

19. Details of the matters which may fall under these provisions are set out in the *Annual Reports* of the Central Arbitration Committee (CAC) for 1989 and 1990. In 1990, the CAC heard only seven cases concerning these provisions.

20. The *most* category was an innovation in the 1990 survey.

21. Cm 1602 (1991) *Industrial Relations in the 1990s: Proposals for the further reform of industrial relations and trade union law*, HMSO, London; Employment Department (1992) *Press Notice*, 31st January.

22. Following the experiences of the first two surveys, and a further survey of individuals conducted in 1989 (see M. Stevens, N. Millward and D. Smart (1989) 'Trade union membership and the closed shop in 1989', *Employment Gazette*, November, pp. 615–623),

some modifications were made to our questions on arrangements for paying union subscriptions. As in 1984, we asked managers about the existence of the check-off in all workplaces where union members were present, irrespective of whether trade unions were recognized. In line with the restructuring of our main management questionnaire referred to earlier, however, a single question covered arrangements for manual and non-manual members, whereas in 1984 we had sought information for each section of the workforce.

23. In 1990 we asked the question in all workplaces with check-off – the reference to an agreement having been dropped. In 1990, a high proportion of worker representatives did not know whether trade unions paid employers for the check-off facility. The relevant figure for manual stewards was 43 per cent and for non-manual representatives, 36 per cent. While representatives who knew only that their own union paid for check-off were recorded separately, those who knew that their own unions made no such payment but had no knowledge of any other union were coded as 'Don't know'. However, these results may be an indication that payment for check-off often occurs at a level above the establishment, involving the union at national or regional level, and about which workplace representatives (and perhaps local management) have no knowledge. It may also suggest, perhaps, that payment is not a current or continuing issue; if it ever had been, it was probably settled years ago.

24. M. Stevens, N. Millward and D. Smart (1989), op. cit., p. 620, revealed that 14 per cent of individual union members paid their subscriptions by direct debit. WIRS data give some idea of the extent of direct debiting and other arrangements among *workplaces*.

25. For example, the AEU has run full-page adverts in its journal offering discounted subscriptions to members paying by standing order or direct debit.

26. A survey in 1989 reported that four fifths (82 per cent) 'of working people' held a current account with either a bank or a building society (Association for Payment Clearing Services, *Research Brief*, December 1989). This compares with 77 per cent in 1984 (Inter-Bank Research Organization, *Research Brief*, October 1985). The same surveys also revealed that the proportion of people paid in cash fell from over a third (37 per cent) in 1984 to around a quarter (23 per cent) in 1988.

27. The 1990 question was as follows: 'During the last year, apart from meetings of a formal negotiating or consultative committee, have you had contact with management here above supervisor level to discuss matters affecting the workers you represent?'

28. Further work on the 1984 survey revealed that, excluding establishments where there was only one representative of the relevant union, 36 per cent of manual stewards reported these meetings rather than the half we reported erroneously in our second book. This means that there was a decline from about half in 1980.

29. As in the previous book, the convention adopted in these sections is to use the term 'committee' as an abbreviated form of the actual form of words in the questions put to respondents which referred to 'committees or regular meetings'.

30. Our survey gives details of the proportion of establishments where worker representatives reported the existence of single-employer combine committees of which their unions were members. Representatives at different workplaces could be members of the same committee. Without being able to identify specific committees and the establishments in their constituency, it is not possible from our data to give a clear guide to the prevalence of such committees in British industry. The likelihood of multiple-reporting is especially pertinent when presenting data over time because the composition of the committee may have changed in the intervening period. More respondents from the same committee may be reporting membership, which may point erroneously to an increase in the number of single-employer combine committees. However, whatever the position regarding the number of such committees, our data do give a good guide to the level of participation in combine activity among our sampled workplaces.

31. The question asked in 1990 was as follows: 'Has management here, or at a higher level in this organization, given financial or other help towards setting up and running these meetings?' The 1980 question asked: 'Has management (at this establishment) given any financial help towards setting up and running these meetings?'

32. In our previous book we described how experience gained in the 1980 survey led us to make changes to the wording of questions and the way they were asked of respondents in the 1984 survey (N. Millward and M. Stevens (1986) *British Workplace Industrial Relations 1980–1984: The ED/ESRC/PSI/ACAS Surveys*, Gower, Aldershot, pp. 123–4). We made further changes in 1990. In particular, we expanded the range of response categories to include methods of appointment that did not involve elections and made further refinements to the existing response categories.

33. In 1984 we used the term *voting slips* to refer to some form of workplace ballot. In 1990 this was changed to *secret ballot at workplace or other meeting place*. In addition, whereas we asked about a *postal ballot* in 1984, this was changed to *secret postal ballot* in 1990. We have assumed these are broadly comparable and are presented as such in the tables.

34. The same difficulties of multiple reporting of higher-level branches *per se* apply equally to assessing their average size; multiple reporting would tend to inflate average size.

Table 4A Types of union representative at establishments, by industry, 1990

	Percentage of establishments with		
	union represen- tatives	senior lay represen- tatives	full-time represen- tatives
All industries	**38**	**12**	**1**
All manufacturing	**40**	**18**	**1**
Metals & Mineral Products	77	39	2
Chemicals & Manufactured Fibres	(42)[1]	(24)	(1)
Metal Goods	(53)	(24)	(*)
Mechanical Engineering	26	10	1
Electrical & Instrument Engineering	30	19	1
Vehicles & Transport Equipment	37	14	7
Food, Drink & Tobacco	41	28	1
Textiles	(41)	(21)	(*)
Leather, Footwear & Clothing	(37)	(14)	(—)
Timber & Furniture, Paper & Printing	44	12	*
Rubber, Plastics & Other Manufacturing	(24)	(11)	(1)
All services	**37**	**10**	**1**
Energy & Water	77	21	*
Construction	21	5	1
Wholesale Distribution	28	8	1
Retail Distribution	18	4	1
Hotels, Catering, Repairs	5	1	—
Transport	49	13	4
Posts and Telecommunications	64	22	10
Banking, Finance, Insurance	45	6	*
Business Services	9	2	*
Central Government	85	30	3
Local Government	80	33	2
Higher Education	(61)	(23)	(1)
Other Education	41	12	—
Medical Services	27	11	1
Other Services	49	11	2

Base: all establishments (see Table 1A for bases and SIC codes)
[1] See Note B.

5 Consultation and Communication

Involving employees in the activities of their employing organizations is a topic of enduring interest in Britain and elsewhere. Much of the WIRS series focuses on the ways in which managements and trade unions relate to each other through a particular channel: collective bargaining. But, in addition, our surveys have always examined the various other channels through which managers and employees relate to each other, sometimes involving trade unions, sometimes not. Such arrangements have added significance in the 1980s in the light of the decline in trade unions' role in collective bargaining activity reported in previous chapters and broader economic and political developments in Britain which have emphasized the importance of individual employee commitment for organizational effectiveness. As trade unions were less involved in bargaining than before it is pertinent to ask whether there were similar changes in the other channels through which they may relate to management.

Our questions have focused on a variety of mechanisms for involving employees or their representatives, including the structure and operation of formal consultative committees at workplace level and at higher levels in the organization; other less formal consultation methods; committees and other methods for dealing with health and safety matters; the nature of information collected by managements and given to employees; and a variety of other methods of involving employees, such as quality circles and briefing groups. We have also always asked a general question about any new initiatives employers have been taking in the area of employee involvement in the few years prior to each survey. Results on these matters are described in this chapter. We begin with formal committees for consulting employees.

Joint consultative committees at workplace level
We discovered from our first survey that workplace-level joint consultative committees had become a more common feature of British industry between 1975 and 1980. By the time of our fieldwork in 1980 they were reported at around a third of our sampled workplaces. When we compared these results with those from our second survey, in 1984, it appeared that there had been little or no change in the overall extent of

Table 5.1   Proportion of establishments where managers reported a joint consultative committee, by broad sector, 1984 and 1990

Percentages

	All establishments		Private manufacturing		Private services		Public sector	
	1984	1990	1984	1990	1984	1990	1984	1990
Consultative committee currently exists	34	29	30	23	24	19	48	49
Workplace consultative committee or higher-level committee with local representatives	41	35	33	25	28	25	62	59
Base: all establishments								
Unweighted	*2019*	*2061*	*592*	*630*	*597*	*799*	*830*	*632*
Weighted	*2000*	*2000*	*424*	*426*	*843*	*980*	*733*	*594*

workplace-level joint consultative committees in the 1980 to 1984 period (just over a third of workplaces had them in 1984). This lack of change overall had come about as a result of movements in different directions: an increase in the reporting of committees in the public sector but a decline in the private sector, particularly among manufacturing plants. The decline in the incidence of committees in the private manufacturing sector continued to 1990, whereas there was little or no change among workplaces in the service sector, whether publicly or privately owned. Table 5.1 gives the results. Just under a quarter (23 per cent) of establishments in private manufacturing had committees in 1990, representing a fall from 30 per cent six years previously and 36 per cent in 1980. By contrast, around half of managers in public sector workplaces reported committees in 1990 and a fifth of those in private services did so, reflecting little or no change through the 1980s in each case.[1] The net result of the changes since our previous survey was that the overall proportion of workplaces with committees fell between 1984 and 1990, from 34 per cent to 29 per cent.

In private manufacturing some of the decline in the incidence of consultative committees came about as a result of the changing size distribution of workplaces in the sector. Joint consultative committees were still more common in larger workplaces than smaller workplaces: 71 per cent of establishments with 1000 or more employees had them in 1990 compared with 24 per cent of those with between 25 and 99. However, there was a decline among all sizes of workplace and as smaller workplaces made up a larger proportion of our sample in 1990 than in 1984 their lower tendency to have committees is reflected in the lower incidence overall.

Committees were still more frequently reported in unionized than in non-unionized workplaces. Indeed, there was little or no change in this since our previous survey, when 41 per cent of workplaces with recognized unions had committees, compared with 21 per cent of workplaces with no recognized unions. In 1990 the figures were 37 per cent and 19 per cent respectively. The pattern was much the same among workplaces of all sizes. It seems logical to conclude that the overall decline in the incidence of committees must, in part, have arisen from the reduction in the number of larger, more unionized workplaces. Certainly, among the highly unionized workplaces in which senior worker representatives were interviewed, committees were no more likely to have been abandoned in the six years up to 1990 than in the five years up to 1984.[2]

The information from our trading sector panel sample sheds further light on whether, in addition to any compositional changes, there was a tendency for workplaces to abandon committees between our 1984 and 1990 surveys. The results suggest there was no such tendency – just as many (49) trading sector workplaces had acquired joint consultative committees since 1984 as had lost the consultative committee they had in 1984 (48).[3] And when we restricted the analysis to manufacturing plants the result was much the same – 15 plants had acquired them and 17 had abandoned them during the period. From these results we can conclude that the changing composition of workplaces was the major influence on the fall in workplace-level consultative committees over the second half of the 1980s.

There was marked variation in the use of consultative committees in different parts of the economy, as Table 5A shows. They were reported by over half of managers in workplaces in Metals and Mineral Product manufacture, for example, but only in around one in ten workplaces in Textiles. In the service sector the incidence of committees ranged from around two thirds of workplaces in Central Government down to 6 per cent of workplaces in Construction.

Higher-level committees

In workplaces that are part of multi-establishment organizations consultative arrangements may take the form of committees at organizational levels above the workplace. We asked about such arrangements in both 1984 and 1990 and the results show little or no change between the two study periods. Overall, 43 per cent of managers in workplaces belonging to multi-establishment organizations reported such higher-level arrangements in 1990 compared with 45 per cent in 1984. Again, in very few cases these higher-level joint consultative committees were concerned with negotiation only (1 per cent in 1990, 3 per cent in 1984). However, more than three fifths in each survey – the majority of cases – were concerned with both consultation and negotiation, with the remainder being concerned with consultation only.

In 40 per cent of workplaces where a higher-level committee was reported there was also a joint consultative committee at the workplace itself, but this represented a fall from almost half of such workplaces in 1984. The drop could have resulted from an increase in the incidence of workplace-level representation on the higher-level committees that existed, as a substitute for committees at workplace level. But when we restricted the analysis to workplaces with higher-level committees dealing with consultation, the results showed that this was not the case. In 1990, 42 per cent of workplaces where a higher-level committee dealing with consultation was reported had workplace-level representation on that committee, indicating little or no change since 1984. Workplace-level representation on higher-level committees was much more common in private manufacturing, reported in three fifths (62 per cent) of cases, than in the publicly-owned or privately-owned service industries where it was reported in around two fifths of cases.

A broad measure of the incidence of consultative machinery available to employees at an individual workplace is whether it had either a workplace-level joint consultative committee or a higher-level consultative committee with representatives from that workplace. The proportions of workplaces with such arrangements are given in the lower half of Table 5.1 and show that there was also decline on this broader measure – from 41 per cent of all establishments in 1984 to 35 per cent in 1990. In terms of the overall proportion of employees in such workplaces, the fall was more significant – from 62 per cent of employees in 1984 to half of employees in 1990. The decline was concentrated in manufacturing and the difference between the public and private sectors identified in 1984 persisted. Three fifths of public sector workplaces had consultation arrangements on this broader definition, compared with a quarter of workplaces in both parts of the private sector.

The structure and make-up of workplace-level joint consultative committees

Our interest in formal consultation arrangements extended beyond simply whether or not they were reported in British workplaces in 1990. As in previous surveys we examined how many workplace-level committees there typically were, the types of employees who were represented on them and whether trade unions were involved in selecting representatives. As far as possible, we also explored the functions of committees: the kinds of issues they dealt with and the balance between consultation and negotiation in their activities. We turn first to the structure and make-up of committees.

Our previous surveys had shown that the proportion of establishments with consultative committees that had a single committee remained the same between 1980 and 1984 at around three quarters, but that there was some growth in the incidence of multiple committees. The proportion of establishments with four or more committees had increased from 4 per cent to 6 per cent over the 1980 to 1984 period. In 1990 it rose to 10 per cent. Thus, the trend towards more complex consultative arrangements continued, despite the decline in the incidence of committees overall.

The types of employees represented on principal joint consultative committees did not change between 1984 and 1990. Table 5.2 gives the results from all three surveys. We defined 'principal' and 'secondary' committees as the two most important according to the management respondent. In just over half (51 per cent) of cases with both manual and non-manual employees, worker representatives on principal committees were drawn from both the manual and the non-manual sections of the

**Table 5.2   Composition of principal and secondary consultative commit-
tees, 1980, 1984 and 1990**

Column Percentages

	Principal committee			Secondary committee		
	1980	1984	1990	1980	1984	1990
Committee has representatives of:						
Manual employees only	18	16[1]	16	26	16	13
Non-manual employees only	22	33	33	46	54	64
Both manual and						
non-manual employees	49	52	51	19	27	20
Not answered	11	–	1	9	3	2

Base: establishments where committee named in column heads was reported by
management respondent and there were manual and non-manual employees
present

Unweighted	*1030*	*1067*	*842*	*353*	*358*	*330*
Weighted	*671*	*683*	*472*	*149*	*152*	*169*

[1] See Note C.

workforce. In two thirds of the remainder only non-manual employees
were represented, identical to the results from the 1984 survey.

However, there were changes in the composition of secondary committees. The proportion which represented only manual employees halved
between the 1980 and 1990 surveys, whereas the proportion covering
only non-manual employees increased by some 40 per cent. The net
result was that by 1990 secondary committees were five times as likely
to represent only non-manual employees than only manual employees –
64 per cent as against 13 per cent. As with principal committees, there
was no change since 1980 in the proportion of secondary committees
covering both categories of employee. It was still the case that principal
committees were much more likely to represent both manual and non-
manual employees than secondary committees – 51 per cent compared
with 20 per cent.

We also explored the involvement of trade unions in consultative
arrangements through a question which asked, where there were union
members present, whether any of the employee representatives were
nominated by trade unions. An identical question had been included in
the 1980 and 1984 surveys. Overall, there was no change in the proportion of workplaces with union members where some of the employee
representatives were nominated by trade unions. In 1990, 36 per cent of

managers reported that all representatives on principal consultative committees were chosen by trade unions and a further 17 per cent said that some of them were. In 44 per cent of cases trade unions were not involved. Naturally, as before, union representation on committees was more common among workplaces with recognized unions. There was also little or no change in the pattern for secondary committees – in 1990 over half of managers (56 per cent) reported that representatives were not chosen by trade unions. Some 37 per cent said all representatives were chosen by unions and in just 5 per cent of cases some of them were.

In summary, then, trade unions were as involved in consultation arrangements in workplaces where union organization continued to be strong, but the fact that unionized workplaces were fewer in number in 1990 than before, meant that the involvement of the trade unions in consultation arrangements overall was smaller than previously.

The functions of joint consultative committees at workplace level
In addition to selecting representatives for consultative committees, trade unions' involvement in consultation arrangements can be evident from what committees do – the types of activity they engage in and the types of issue they address. All three of our surveys have pointed unequivocally to a degree of overlap between consultation and bargaining arrangements at establishments, a matter that had been widely discussed since the 1960s. Formal arrangements for consultation were more common in unionized than in non-union workplaces, for example. However, we also examined the linkages between consultation and bargaining activity within consultative committees through a more direct question. In 1984, just under a third of managers reported that the principal consultative committee at the establishment was concerned with both consultation and negotiation. The position in 1990 was very similar – 31 per cent of principal consultative committees and 27 per cent of secondary committees were also concerned with negotiation.[4] Consultative committees in private manufacturing and the public sector were twice as likely also to engage in bargaining (as well as consultation) as in private services. And, predictably, they more frequently bargained in workplaces where union organization was generally stronger.

The main issues discussed by workplace-level joint consultative committees changed between 1984 and 1990. In 1984 the four most important matters discussed by principal consultative committees during the year prior to interview were *production issues, employment issues, pay issues* and *employee involvement arrangements*. Production issues were still most frequently mentioned in 1990 (18 per cent of cases) – particularly in private manufacturing – and employment issues second most frequently (12 per cent), with a particular concentration in services. But employee involvement arrangements were rarely considered by committees in 1989–1990 (1 per cent of cases). This was nearer the 1980 picture than that for 1984 (10 per cent of cases). The fall since 1984 was most pronounced in manufacturing, from 16 per cent to just 1 per cent of workplaces. While this drop could be interpreted as indicating that such arrangements were increasingly becoming a matter for management to decide, an alternative view would be that by 1990 other channels of communication had developed through which such matters could be more appropriately addressed. We consider this further below.

The third most important issue in 1990 and up from virtually nothing to 9 per cent of workplaces was *government legislation or regulations*. This category included actual or prospective legislation or regulations and specific responses, such as employment legislation, the Education Reform Act, the White Paper on the National Health Service, local authority regulations and European Community Directives. As many of the proposed or actual legislation or regulations affected the public sector alone, it is unsurprising that most responses under this broad heading came from managers in public sector workplaces.

Next in terms of frequency of mention in 1990 were three issues that were each cited by 8 per cent of managers – *pay issues, health and safety* and *working practices*, the last of these increasing from just 1 per cent in 1984. Working practices were a more important preoccupation of committees in manufacturing than previously, up from 1 per cent to 6 per cent. Indeed, we show later that it was in the area of 'direct job-related' changes that employee involvement initiatives in manufacturing were concentrated. Health and safety issues were also more salient in manufacturing than previously, up from 6 per cent to 13 per cent.

How far and by what methods discussion in joint consultative committees was disseminated to the workforce was also the subject of specific questions in the worker representative interviews. Representatives of non-manual unions were more likely to report that they communicated the discussion of committees in 1990 than in 1984; among their manual counterparts there was little change. But there were changes in the means of communication used by both types of representative. Our question asked specifically about four channels: a separate meeting, orally informing people, circulating the minutes of committee meetings and communicating via a notice-board. Notice-boards were much less frequently reported than previously. Seven per cent of manual stewards reported using them (compared with 31 per cent in 1984) and just 4 per cent of non-manual representatives did so (20 per cent in 1984). The most frequent response from recognized manual stewards was that they orally informed their constituents, mentioned by 42 per cent, whereas in 1984 the most common method had been to circulate the minutes of meetings, indicating a marked shift by 1990 towards more direct methods.

Non-manual representatives in 1990 most frequently mentioned circulating the minutes (51 per cent).

In addition to the subjects discussed by workplace-level consultative committees, another aspect of their operation that may help to determine the importance attached to them is how often they meet. In fact, our results show no real change in the frequency with which principal committees of only non-manual employee representatives met – almost half (49 per cent) of managers reported that they met at least once a month in 1990 (46 per cent in 1984). However, exclusively manual committees were less likely to meet at least monthly than before (22 per cent as against 35 per cent) while those representing both manual and non-manual employees were more likely to meet at least once a month (46 per cent as against 35 per cent).

A crude measure of the importance attached to these committees by senior management is how often they themselves attend meetings. We have information on this from our 1980 and 1990 surveys. Results from both surveys were broadly similar, indicating that in the great majority of cases senior management attended most principal committees although, as before, fewer worker representatives reported senior management attendance.

In the most recent survey we sought a more direct measure of the influence of the principal consultative committee on management's decisions affecting the workforce, by asking both management and worker representatives to assess the influence of principal committees, using a four-point scale from 'very influential' to 'not at all influential'. In overall terms, eight out of ten managers described the principal committee as having some influence: a third rated it 'very influential' and a further 47 per cent as 'fairly influential' (Table 5.3). There was considerable common ground between managers and union representatives in that at least two thirds of either type of respondent described the committee as having some influence on management decision-making. However, there were also cases where managers and worker representatives held divergent views. This was particularly the case for non-manual representatives.

Arrangements for dealing with health and safety
Our questions about joint consultative committees in the WIRS series have always expressly excluded committees that deal with single issues, leaving health and safety representation, in particular, to be explored separately. In 1990, we asked managers two questions about these matters.[5] First, we asked which from a list of four phrases best described how health and safety matters were dealt with at the establishment. If other arrangements were mentioned that were not listed on our card, they too were recorded. Secondly, respondents at establishments with

Table 5.3   Influence of principal consultative committees on management's decisions affecting the workforce according to managers and worker representatives belonging to recognized trade unions, 1990

Column Percentages

	Managers[1]	Manual representatives	Managers[2]	Non-manual representatives
Committee is:				
Very influential	26	21[3]	29	18
Fairly influential	55	52	48	49
Not very influential	17	17	19	20
Not at all influential	2	8	3	9
Don't know/not answered	*	3	*	4

Base: all respondents who reported a principal consultative committee unless otherwise indicated

Unweighted	*379*	*379*	*382*	*382*
Weighted	*115*	*115*	*136*	*136*

[1] Managers where manual worker representatives belonging to recognized unions were interviewed.
[2] Managers where non-manual worker representatives belonging to recognized unions were interviewed.
[3] See Note C.

Table 5.4   Arrangements for dealing with health and safety, by broad sector, 1984 and 1990

Column Percentages

	All establishments		Private manufacturing		Private services		Public sector	
	1984	1990	1984	1990	1984	1990	1984	1990
Joint committee for health & safety	22	23	33	32	15	18²	23	25
Joint committee for health, safety & other matters	9	9	15	10	7	8	9	11
Workforce representatives, no committee	41	24	25	20	39	16	52	40
Management deals, consultation with employees	¹	5	..	3	..	5	..	5
Management deals, without consultation with employees	..	37	..	34	..	51	..	14
Management only, no consultation	22	..	22	..	34	..	10	..
Other answer	6	2	5	1	5	1	7	4
Don't know/not answered	*	*	*	*	—	—	*	*
Base: all establishments								
Unweighted	*2019*	*2061*	*592*	*630*	*597*	*799*	*830*	*632*
Weighted	*2000*	*2000*	*424*	*426*	*843*	*980*	*733*	*594*

¹ See Note J.
² See Note C.

union members who mentioned a health and safety committee of any sort (our question did not distinguish between statutory and non-statutory committees) were asked whether any of the employee representatives were chosen by the trade unions.

Results from the first question are given in Table 5.4 for each broad sector of the economy. These show that joint committees dealing solely or partly with health and safety matters were reported as frequently in 1990 as in 1984. Just under a quarter of managers in both surveys (23 per cent in 1990, 22 per cent in 1984) reported joint committees specifically for health and safety issues. These committees were still most commonly reported in private manufacturing (32 per cent) and least common in private services (18 per cent). Not surprisingly, given the statutory support for health and safety representation in unionized workplaces, committees were much more commonly found in workplaces with recognized unions than those without. This was also the case among establishments of similar size. Committees that partly dealt with health and safety were also as commonly reported as in 1984 – one tenth of managers said they had them in 1990. Only in manufacturing was there a fall since 1984, from 15 per cent to 10 per cent.

The big change in health and safety representation was a large decline in the incidence of health and safety representatives where there was no committee and a rise in the proportion of workplaces where managers dealt with health and safety issues without consultation. Workforce representatives (but no committee) were reported by only half as many managers in 1990 as in 1984 – 24 per cent compared with 41 per cent previously. The decline was particularly marked in services, among both publicly-owned and privately-owned workplaces. However, it affected both workplaces with recognized unions and those without, even among workplaces of similar size and suggests an increasing reluctance of individual employees to put themselves forward for representative roles in the late 1980s. This also seemed to explain some of the decline in the incidence of lay union representatives, reported in Chapter 4. More broadly, our results show that, by 1990, private sector workplaces were less than half as likely to have any form of health and safety representation – committees or representatives – if they were not unionized than if they were.

As a corollary to the drop in the number of workplaces with either representatives or committees for health and safety, the proportion of workplaces where management dealt with health and safety issues unilaterally, without consultation, rose dramatically. It increased across all three broad sectors of employment between our two surveys. Overall it increased from 22 per cent to 37 per cent and was still a more common feature of workplaces without recognized unions (57 per cent) than those where they were present (19 per cent). Even so, there were increases in both types of workplace since 1984. Save for the larger workplaces – employing 500 or more people – this change was evident when we compared workplaces of similar size.[6]

Results from our trading sector panel of workplaces confirm that managers dealt with health and safety issues without consultation much more commonly in 1990 than in 1984. In 93 trading sector workplaces management dealt with health and safety in this way in 1990 but had consulted employees in one way or another in 1984. This compared with 49 workplaces which changed in the opposite direction. The panel sample also confirmed that a fall in the number of employee health and safety representatives had occurred in the trading sector between 1984 and 1990. By 1990 such representatives had disappeared from 116 trading sector workplaces that had them in 1984, compared with 48 that acquired them over the 1984 to 1990 period.

In broad terms trade unions were as involved as previously in health and safety representation. Establishment-level health and safety committees included trade union representatives in around three quarters of cases (77 per cent) in both the 1984 and 1990 surveys with little variation by broad sector of employment. The proportion of workplaces where *some* representatives were chosen by unions actually increased – from 27 per cent to 36 per cent. However, there was a drop in the proportion of managers who reported that *all* the representatives were chosen by unions – from 48 per cent to 41 per cent.

So far we have considered consultative arrangements for health and safety in the absence of other data which might give clues as to the significance of health and safety issues within establishments. One of the more obvious indicators of this is the incidence of injuries of one kind or another. In 1990, for the first time in the WIRS series, we also collected rudimentary information on the incidence of 'major' injuries at our sampled establishments. Management respondents were shown a card on which were listed types of major injury.[7] We asked whether any employees had sustained any of the listed injuries in the 12 months prior to interview. In workplaces where they were reported we then asked how many employees had been affected. These results will enable an examination of the linkages between injury rates and the arrangements for dealing with health and safety matters that were in place.

Among all workplaces the overall injury rate – employees affected by our listed injuries per thousand employed – was 5.9,[8] but was higher in the service industries (6.2) than in manufacturing (5.3). The rate was well above the respective industry average in a number of sectors, such as Hotels, Catering and Repairs (21.0), Local Government (18.4), Transport (10.0), Construction (8.5), Timber, Furniture, Paper and Printing (7.9), Mechanical Engineering (7.7), Metal Goods (7.2) and Textiles

(6.3). The lowest rates of injury were in Banking (zero) and Leather, Footwear and Clothing (0.4).

The injury rate was higher in workplaces where management dealt with health and safety issues without consultation (6.6) than those where there was either a health and safety committee or employee representation (5.6). Results from the panel sample of trading sector workplaces are consistent with this pattern. These show that workplaces where managers did not consult in 1990 but had some other arrangement six years previously had an injury rate of 14 per thousand in 1990, compared with 7 per thousand for panel establishments as a whole. Naturally, no simple conclusions can be drawn from these findings. The actual linkages between injury rates and health and safety arrangements are likely to be very complex, not least because particular arrangements may either ultimately contribute to higher injury rates or be a direct, constructive response to them. There is much to be explored here in secondary analysis of the WIRS3 data.

Non-union representation

In addition to structures of representation involving trade unions, our first survey had explored the incidence of individual non-union representatives. It was possible that non-union representatives would become a more common feature of employee representation given the disappearance of any trade union presence in some workplaces. This did not happen. Analysis of data from our 1980 survey – pooled from four separate questions – revealed that such representatives were present in 11 per cent of workplaces overall.[9] This area of questioning was dropped from the 1984 survey but a single, broadly comparable question was asked of all managers in the 1990 survey. The results show that there were non-union representatives present in 8 per cent of workplaces in 1990. However, allowing the slight change in question wording and the possible multiple recording of such representatives from the several questions asked in 1980,[10] it is doubtful that the incidence of these representatives dropped over the decade.

As before, non-union representatives appeared to be concentrated in manufacturing industry in 1990, reported in 14 per cent of plants overall, and particularly commonly reported in parts of the engineering sector (Table 5A). They were reported in 3 per cent of public sector workplaces and 8 per cent of those in private services. The incidence of non-union representatives appeared to be unrelated to the number of employees on site, but was slightly higher in foreign-owned workplaces than their UK-owned counterparts. Non-union representatives were not restricted to non-union workplaces, as shown in some of the cells in Table 5A – such as Central Government.[11] However, it is true to say that non-union representatives were at least twice as common among workplaces with no recognized unions on site than their unionized counterparts: 10 per cent as against 5 per cent overall. And this pattern persisted when we examined establishments of similar size.

A second, related area that we explored in the 1980 and 1990 surveys was the incidence of committees of employees in establishments where there were no trade unions recognized. We asked the question separately, in relation to manual and then non-manual employees. There was little change over the 1980s. These committees were reported in 19 per cent of workplaces with no recognized trade unions in 1980 and 16 per cent in 1990. Again, in some cases committees of workers from one section of the workforce existed alongside formal bargaining machinery for the other section. This occurred in 2 or 3 per cent of cases. These committees of employees were reported in 9 per cent of all workplaces in 1990. In almost half of cases these non-union committees overlapped the joint consultative committees mentioned earlier and in a third of cases non-union committees for manual employees overlapped with their non-manual equivalents.

Communication with the workforce
So far we have focused largely on committees for consulting employees, but there are a number of other formal channels through which managements communicate with their employees, some of which we explored in our surveys. In the 1984 survey our management respondents were shown a card listing six specific methods, other than formal consultative committees, which they might use to communicate with or to consult employees. The results showed that a variety of channels were being used at any one time. In the light of this we were keen to include similar questions in the 1990 survey to assess developments since 1984. In fact, our pilot work for the third survey led us to expand the list of specified methods to seven and we slightly elaborated some of the 1984 items. Thus, in the 1990 survey, we asked management respondents whether they used any of the following methods to communicate or consult with their employees as a matter of policy:

Regular meetings among work-groups or teams at least once a month to discuss aspects of performance, such as 'quality circles' and other problem-solving groups
Regular meetings (at least once a month) between junior managers/supervisors and all the workers for whom they are responsible – sometimes known as 'briefing groups' or 'team briefing'
Regular meetings (at least once a year) between senior managers and all sections of the workforce (either altogether or section by section)
Systematic use of the management chain for communication with all employees

Suggestion schemes
Regular newsletters distributed to all levels of employee
Surveys or ballots of employees' views or opinions.

The first item on the list, referring to quality circles and other problem-solving groups, was not included in 1984. The second item had been included previously but without the explanatory phrase 'these are sometimes known as briefing groups or team briefing'. All remaining items were identical in both the 1984 and 1990 surveys. Interviewers were again instructed to record all methods identified or 'none of these' or to make a note of any other methods mentioned. Table 5.5 gives the results for each of the three broad sectors of employment, with those for 1984 alongside for comparison.

As expected, the most frequently mentioned method of communication of all those in the list was *systematic use of the management chain*, reported by 60 per cent of managers overall and with little variation by broad sector. Next most common were *regular meetings between junior managers or supervisors and all the workers for whom they are responsible*, mentioned by 48 per cent of managers, *regular meetings between senior managers and all sections of the workforce* and *regular newsletters distributed to all levels of employee* reported by 41 per cent of managers in each case. This rank-order of methods is identical to that found in 1984 and was unaffected by the addition of another item in the list used in 1990. While the same proportion of workplaces used the management chain in both our surveys the three other methods were more frequently mentioned in 1990 than in 1984, when each was reported by around a third of managers.

The considerable variation in use of these methods between broad sectors of the economy, seen in our 1984 results, is also evident in those for 1990. The new item we asked about – *regular meetings of work-groups* – was mentioned in 23 per cent of workplaces in private manufacturing but in around twice that number in the public sector (45 per cent) and a third of workplaces in private services. This item was fourth most frequently mentioned in private manufacturing plants and in fifth place among establishments in the service sector, regardless of ownership. *Suggestion schemes* and *surveys or ballots* were the least frequently mentioned in all three of our broad sectors, although there was still an increase overall in the incidence of each since 1984.

Table 5.5 also gives composite measures which show the proportion of workplaces with any of the communication methods we asked about. Overall, 90 per cent of establishments in 1990 used one or more of these methods – the figure was slightly lower in the private sector and slightly higher in the public sector. Including joint consultative committees increased the proportions by one percentage point, thereby indicating that

Table 5.5 Methods other than consultative committees used by management to communicate with or consult employees, by broad sector, 1984 and 1990

Percentages

	All establishments 1984	All establishments 1990	Private manufacturing 1984	Private manufacturing 1990	Private services 1984	Private services 1990	Public sector 1984	Public sector 1990
1 Regular meetings of workgroups	..[1]	35	..	23	..	33	..	45
2 Regular meetings of junior management	36	48	24	31	34	47	46	62
3 Regular meetings of senior management	34	41	37	38	33	40	33	46
4 Management chain	62	60	58	57	58	58	69	65
5 Suggestion scheme	25	28	15	14	25	31	31	31
6 Regular newsletters	34	41	24	22	33	44	41	52
7 Surveys or ballots	12	17	10	7	11	17	14	24
Other methods	8	13	8	11	8	13	8	16
None of these	12	9	17	14	15	11	7	4
Any of methods 1–7	..	90	..	85	..	88	..	96
Any of methods 1–7 or a joint consultative committee	..	91	..	86	..	89	..	97
1984 equivalent:								
Any of methods 2–7	86	86	80	81	83	85	92	91
Any of methods 2–7 or a joint consultative committee	87	87	81	81	84	86	94	92
Base: all establishments								
Unweighted	*2019*	*2061*	*592*	*630*	*597*	*799*	*830*	*632*
Weighted	*2000*	*2000*	*424*	*426*	*843*	*980*	*733*	*594*

[1] See Note J.

committees were associated with the incidence of other communication methods. The bottom two rows of Table 5.5 give the 1990 results that are directly comparable with those for 1984 – a measure of the incidence of any of the *six* communication methods asked about in our previous survey. These results show no change in the incidence of any of the six methods, with some 86 per cent of workplaces reporting at least one of the six in both 1984 and 1990.[12] However, more methods of communication were being used simultaneously in 1990 than previously: the mean number increased from 2.0 to 2.4 over the 1984 to 1990 period. There was a clear relationship between regular meetings of any sort and union presence even when we compared workplaces of similar size. Taken together, any of the three types of regular meetings were mentioned by 83 per cent of managers in the public sector, 71 per cent of those in the unionized part of the private sector and 62 per cent of those in non-union workplaces in the private sector.

So far we have reported the results on the various channels of communication between management and the workforce reported by our management respondents, but our surveys also provide data on the amount of information given by management and received by the workforce. Our question asked whether management at the establishment gave employees or their representatives information about a range of items before the implementation of any changes in them. There is, of course, the possibility that worker representatives may tend to understate the amount of information imparted while managers may overstate it. In this and other areas of possible divergent reporting our practice has been to ask both types of respondent identical questions, allowing us to assess the degree of overlap between them. The issues we focused on in 1990 were as follows:

Terms and conditions of employment
Safety and occupational health arrangements
Staffing and manpower plans
Major changes in working methods or work organization
Internal investment plans
The financial position of the establishment
The financial position of the whole organization (where part of larger organization).

With the exception of *safety and occupational health arrangements*, results on which were reported earlier, all the other items were asked in 1984. However, we also took the opportunity in 1990 to tighten the wording of one item, *internal investment plans*, which previously had had a rather broader interpretation (*investment plans*). We also asked a supplementary question in 1990 about the first four items on the list, con-

Table 5.6 **Information given to employees or worker representatives belonging to recognized unions, by management, 1984 and 1990, and by size of establishment, 1990**

Percentages

	All establishments		Size of establishment (1990)			
	1984	1990	25–99	100–499	500–999	1000+
Proportion of respondents reporting 'a lot of information' on:						
Terms and conditions of employment	66	62	60	68	79	78
Safety & occupational health arrangements	..	66	65	71	82	75
Staffing and manpower plans	40	33	33	31	33	36
Major changes in working methods or work organization	70	68	67	69	74	80
Internal investment plans	12	19	18	18	25	31
Financial position of establishment	30	28	27	32	38	49
Financial position of organization[1]	32	30	29	29	38	42
Proportion of respondents reporting consultation on:						
Terms and conditions of employment	58	55	54	61	71	70
Safety & occupational health arrangements	..	70	68	72	84	81
Staffing and manpower plans	50	46	46	45	50	61
Major changes in working methods or work organisation	73	73	73	72	82	83
Base: all establishments unless specified otherwise						
Unweighted	*2019*	*2061*	*704*	*717*	*262*	*378*
Weighted	*2000*	*2000*	*1560*	*388*	*34*	*17*

[1] Establishments that were part of multi-establishment organizations only.

cerning whether management *consults* with employees or their representatives about each of them.[13]

Table 5.6 gives the overall results from both the 1984 and 1990 surveys, with the 1990 results being given also in relation to establishment size. The results are based on the responses of managers and the upper part of the table gives proportions of establishments where managers reported that they imparted 'a lot' of information on the listed items. The lower part gives managers responses on whether they *consulted* on the narrower range of listed items.

The overall results show clearly that there were changes between our two surveys in the proportion of establishments where management reported giving a lot of information on three items. A smaller proportion of managers in 1990 than in 1984 reported that they gave a lot of information on *terms and conditions of employment* (62 per cent as against 66 per cent) and on *staffing and manpower plans* (33 per cent and 40 per cent respectively). Although the proportion who reported a lot of information on internal investment plans appeared to have increased, from 12 per cent to 19 per cent between the two surveys, this could have resulted from narrowing the scope of the question in 1990. On three items there was virtually no change: 68 per cent of managers reported that they gave a lot of information on *major changes in working methods and work organization*, 28 per cent gave the same response in relation to the *financial position of the establishment* and 30 per cent did so in relation to the *financial position of the organization as a whole*. The lower part of the table shows there was also no overall change in managers' reports of the incidence of consultation on the three items asked about in both surveys.

Managements in larger establishments in 1990 more commonly consulted or provided a lot of information on the listed items than those in smaller establishments. This was also clear from our 1984 results. On most items we could detect little or no change in the incidence of consulting or providing a lot of information about the listed items within each of the size-bands given in the table. However, there was one important exception – staffing and manpower plans. Table 5.6 shows there was relatively little difference in the incidence of providing a lot of information on this item within each size-band – but this marks a change since 1984 and reflects the fact that there was a decline in the proportion of managers overall who either consulted or gave a lot of information on this item.

The drop in the flow of information on this issue was greatest in the largest establishments. In 1984, 60 per cent of managers in establishments employing 1000 or more people reported that they gave a lot of information on staffing and manpower plans. By 1990 that figure had fallen to 36 per cent. The equivalent figures for establishments employing between 25 and 99 employees were 39 per cent in 1984 and 33 per cent in 1990. However, in addition to the general decline across establishments of all sizes, it was also clear that the drop was concentrated within the unionized sector. Managers in establishments with recognized unions were less likely to report giving a lot of information on staffing and manpower plans than previously (42 per cent as against 48 per cent), while the proportion of managers in establishments without recognized unions giving this answer remained unchanged at 23 per cent.

Results from our trading sector panel of workplaces confirmed that managements were much less likely than before to give to employees information on staffing and manpower plans. Indeed, there were 140 trading sector cases that gave some information on this item in 1984 but gave none in 1990 whereas there were 81 cases where management gave no information in 1984 but gave some information in 1990.

From our cross-sectional sample, unlike the picture for giving a lot of information, there was no comparable drop in the unionized sector in the incidence of consultation on staffing and manpower plans – almost six out of ten managers in workplaces with recognized unions said they consulted on this item in both the 1984 and 1990 surveys. And there was no change among workplaces with no recognized unions – a third of managers in each survey said that they consulted. But irrespective of union representation, the incidence of consultation on this item in the largest workplaces (1000 or more employees) fell from 72 per cent to 61 per cent over the period.

So far in our analysis of the various items on which managers inform or consult their workforce we have relied on the responses of managers alone. On this basis, as we saw above, consulting and informing was more common in union than in non-union workplaces and in larger than in smaller establishments. Results from union representatives confirmed that there was no change in the level of consulting or information-giving in union establishments between 1984 and 1990 (Table 5.7). So, some of the overall decline in the incidence of informing or consulting on the listed items must be due to the changing composition of workplaces. As relatively smaller, non-union workplaces formed a larger proportion of our sample in 1990 than in 1984, this was bound to be reflected in the lower overall figures.

The table shows the expected differences of perception between managers and union representatives. We remarked in our previous report that the biggest difference in reporting between managers and recognized worker representatives (particularly manual stewards) was in relation to consulting and informing about major changes in working methods or work organization, and this remained so in 1990.[14]

Table 5.7   **Information given to employees or worker representatives belonging to recognized trade unions by management, 1990**

Percentages

	Recognized manual representatives	Recognized non-manual representatives	Managers where representative interviewed	Managers at all establishments
Proportion of respondents reporting 'a lot of information' on:				
Terms and conditions of employment	54	54	69	62
Safety & occupational health arrangements	58	49	74	66
Staffing and manpower plans	30	29	41	33
Major changes in working methods or work organization	53	53	76	68
Internal investment plans	17	11	23	19
Financial position of establishment	24	28	33	28
Financial position of organization	25	26	28	23
Proportion of respondents reporting consultation on:				
Terms and conditions of employment	57	58	67	55
Safety & occupational health arrangements	70	67	81	70
Staffing and manpower plans	47	53	60	46
Major changes in working methods or work organization	65	60	81	73
Base: establishments with respondents named in column heads				
Unweighted	*726*	*670*	*1011*	*2061*
Weighted	*367*	*342*	*608*	*2000*

Information collected and disclosed by management

In the 1990 survey we extended our questioning about management–employee communication to explore the sort of information regularly collected, used and disseminated by management. Collecting information is clearly a crucial first step in any process of employee communication – information must be collected before it can be turned into a form suitable for dissemination. Interviewers showed management respondents a card on which were listed 11 items and asked the following question: 'Is information on any of these items collected and used by management, here or at a higher level, to review performance and policies on an annual or more frequent basis?' Those that answered positively were asked to indicate on which items information was collected and used. Interviewers then asked whether information on any of the listed items was given to employees or employee representatives on an annual or more frequent basis. The results from these two questions are shown in three pairs of columns in Table 5.8. The first pair gives results for all establishments in the 1990 sample and the second and third for, respectively, UK-owned and foreign-owned workplaces in the private sector.

Comparing the figures in the first pair of columns gives a broad indication of the differences between what managements as a whole collected and what they disclosed to their employees and employee representatives. For example, information was collected on the *number of resignations* in 52 per cent of workplaces, but information on that item was disclosed to the workforce in just 14 per cent of workplaces. This difference between information collected and disclosed was very similar for each of the 11 items we asked about. It was also the case that larger workplaces, those with recognized unions and those with higher union density were much more likely to both collect information on each of the 11 items and to disclose it to the workforce. Table 5A shows the incidence of workplaces that collected and disclosed information on any of the 11 items in a wide range of industries. In some sectors the differences between the incidence of collection and disclosure is relatively small, such as in Banking, Finance and Insurance, Local Government, and Posts and Telecommunications. In others the difference is much larger, such as in Vehicles and Transport Equipment.

There were some interesting findings in relation to equal opportunities issues. For example, workplaces with more than 10 per cent of employees from ethnic minorities were almost twice as likely to collect information on the ethnic mix of the workforce than those with less than 10 per cent, though the overall figures were still relatively small – 51 per cent and 28 per cent respectively. However, the proportions of workplaces where such information was disclosed were even smaller – 15 per cent and 8 per cent respectively. Similarly, information on the gender mix of the workforce was much more likely to be collected the higher was the concentration of

Table 5.8   Information a) collected and used by management and b) given by management to employees or worker representatives belonging to recognized trade unions, by ownership in the private sector, 1990

Percentages

	All establishments		UK-owned establishments		Foreign-owned establishments	
	collected	given	collected	given	collected	given
Number of resignations	52	14	45	11	60	7
Staff sickness/absence	75	24	72	23	80	29
Accidents/injuries	63	25	60	21	61	31
Occupational health	39	18	36	17	40	21
Labour productivity	48	20	54	21	62	32
Wage/salary costs	72	25	78	27	79	36
Training received	64	25	60	23	70	36
Skills/qualifications	54	15	55	15	50	28
Ethnic mix	32	10	22	5	22	8
Gender mix	33	11	26	7	27	2
Age mix	34	6	31	4	47	2
None of the above	8	44	9	48	9	5
Not answered	*	4	*	3	*	36
						4
Base: all establishments						
Unweighted	*2061*[1]	*2061*	*1162*	*1162*	*219*	*219*
Weighted	*2000*	*2000*	*1250*	*1250*	*137*	*137*

[1] See Note L.

female employees. But again the figures were relatively small. Some 43 per cent of workplaces where female employees made up over 70 per cent of the workforce collected information on the gender mix, compared with 21 per cent of workplaces where up to 30 per cent of the workforce was female. Again, the proportion of workplaces where this information was made known to the workforce was small – from 18 per cent of workplaces with 70 per cent or more female employees to just 5 per cent of workplaces with 30 per cent or fewer.

Turning again to Table 5.8, the overall results show that foreign-owned workplaces in Britain were more likely than their UK-owned counterparts to collect information on six of the 11 items and were as likely to collect information on a further four. Only on one item – 'skills and qualifications' – was this not so, and then only marginally. When we compared workplaces of similar size, some of these differences disappeared. However, in smaller workplaces (less than 100 people) and in larger workplaces (at least 1000), more foreign-owned than indigenous workplaces collected information on several items, no doubt partly due to the fact that they are, by definition, multi-national.

Foreign-owned workplaces were also on the whole more likely than their UK-owned counterparts to disclose information to the workforce: some 60 per cent of foreign-owned workplaces gave their employees information on at least one of the items we asked about, compared with around half of UK-owned workplaces. Again, among comparable large and smaller workplaces, those that were foreign-owned appeared to disclose more.[15]

Initiatives by management to increase employee involvement

The last question to managers in the section of questioning on consultation and communication in 1990 asked about new initiatives for increasing employee involvement taken in the three years prior to the survey. A similar question was also asked in our previous surveys, though in 1984 the recall period was four years rather than three. We asked a similar question of worker representatives in each survey. The question to managers was 'has management here made any changes in the last three years with the aim of increasing employees' involvement in the operation of the establishment?'. The equivalent question to worker representatives mentioned either 'manual' or 'non-manual' employees as appropriate. Respondents who answered positively were asked a supplementary, open question about the nature of the changes that had been made so that the full range of possible initiatives would be recorded.

Judging by the proportion of managers who reported introducing such initiatives in the three years prior to our survey in 1990, the level of activity in this area increased substantially since 1984. Newly-introduced arrangements for employee involvement were reported at just under half

(45 per cent) of all establishments in 1990 compared with 35 per cent in 1984. Given the reduced recall period in 1990, the increase from 35 to 45 per cent understates the growth of these initiatives. New initiatives were more frequently reported in the public sector than the private sector (55 per cent compared with 41 per cent). Within the private sector itself initiatives were more common in unionized than in non-unionized workplaces, 48 as against 36 per cent, a differential that persisted when we compared workplaces of similar size. In private manufacturing new initiatives were reported as frequently as before (32 per cent of workplaces). The growth of new developments in employee involvement was entirely in the service sector, regardless of ownership: around a third of establishments in both private services and the public sector had introduced initiatives in the 1980 to 1984 period. The equivalent figures for the 1987 to 1990 period were 45 per cent and 55 per cent respectively. Table 5A shows the variation in the incidence of newly-introduced employee involvement arrangements across all industries, ranging from three quarters of workplaces in Banking, Finance and Insurance to a fifth of workplaces in Food, Drink and Tobacco manufacture.

We expected that management respondents would report initiatives more frequently than worker representatives and this again proved to be the case. Although 48 per cent of managers in workplaces where union representatives were interviewed reported initiatives, around a third (31 per cent) of manual stewards and a third of non-manual representatives (35 per cent) did so (Table 5.9). Even so, we can be confident that there were more initiatives in the employee involvement area in the late 1980s than the early 1980s because the proportion of union representatives that mentioned new initiatives also increased significantly between the 1984 and 1990 surveys. Indeed, the proportion of non-manual representatives mentioning them doubled – from 18 per cent to 35 per cent – and the increase among manual stewards was similar (from 18 per cent to 31 per cent).

Having established the types of workplaces where new employee involvement initiatives were being reported, we can turn to the nature of the initiatives themselves. The full results from our open question are given in Table 5.10. The table shows a number of interesting features. First, the top portion gives the results on the incidence of structural initiatives, such as new committees or meetings: it is evident that there was an increased reporting of new joint meetings rather than formally constituted committees, particularly in the service industries. The rest of the table shows the incidence of 'non-structural' innovations. There were both increases and decreases in the extent of introduction of the various non-structural initiatives, depending on sector. For example, although the overall incidence of new initiatives on 'two-way communication' was unchanged – 13 per cent of all managers reported it in 1990

Table 5.9 Reporting of new employee involvement initiatives by managers and worker representatives belonging to recognized trade unions, by broad sector, 1990

Percentages

New employee involvement initiatives reported by:	All	Private manufacturing	Private services	Public sector	Unweighted	Weighted
Recognized manual worker representatives	31	32	26	32	726	367
Managers, where recognized manual representative interviewed	48	38	46	57	726	367
Recognized non-manual worker representatives	35	37	44	31	670	342
Managers where recognized non-manual worker representative interviewed	48	55	56	44	670	342
Managers where recognized manual or non-manual worker representative interviewed	48	39	50	50	1011	608
Managers at all establishments	45	32	45	55	2061	2000

Table 5.10 Recent changes made to increase employee involvement, as reported by managers, by broad sector, 1984 and 1990

Percentages

	All establishments		Private manufacturing		Private services		Public sector	
	1984[1]	1990[2]	1984	1990	1984	1990	1984	1990
Any initiative	**35**	**45**	**35**	**32**	**33**	**45**	**36**	**55**
New consultative committee	4	4	5	4	2	3	4	3
New health & safety committee	*	*	*	*	–	*	1	*
New joint meetings	5	9	6	5	4	9	6	13
Representative on top governing body	*	1	–	–	*	*	*	2
Any of above	**9**	**13**	**11**	**9**	**6**	**13**	**10**	**18**
Improved existing committee	1	1	1	1	2	*	1	1
More two-way communication	12	13	15	7	12	12	11	19
More information to employees	4	5	6	3	5	5	2	6
Participation scheme	1	*	1	*	1	1	1	*
Share scheme	*	*	1	*	*	1	1	–
Suggestion scheme	*	2	1	2	*	2	*	2
Autonomous work groups	2	2	1	1	2	*	4	4
Management training for participation	1	1	*	1	1	1	1	*
Quality of working life/job satisfaction	*	1	*	1	–	1	–	1
Quality circles	*	2	*	5	–	2	*	*

Table 5.10 continued

Percentages

	All establishments		Private manufacturing		Private services		Public sector	
	1984[1]	1990[2]	1984	1990	1984	1990	1984	1990
Involvement in technical change	*	*	*	*	*	*	—	*
Briefing/training groups	1	5	*	6	1	5	1	4
Delegation	3	6	1	2	4	8	3	6
Incentive scheme	1	3	*	1	1	5	1	2
Management reorganization	1	2	*	2	1	2	2	1
Any of above	**25**	**33**	**25**	**24**	**27**	**33**	**24**	**38**
Other answer	2	4	1	2	1	4	3	6
Don't know/not answered	1	*	1	—	*	—	2	*
Base: all establishments								
Unweighted	*2019*	*2061*	*592*	*630*	*597*	*799*	*830*	*632*
Weighted	*2000*	*2000*	*424*	*426*	*843*	*980*	*733*	*594*

[1] 1984: in the four years prior to interview.
[2] 1990: in the three years prior to interview.

– in manufacturing it was halved (from 15 per cent to 7 per cent) whereas in the public sector it doubled (from 11 per cent to 19 per cent). There was a similar pattern of results for 'more information given to employees'.

Although briefing groups and training groups were more frequently reported in all three sectors of employment, they grew from a very low base and occurred in just 5 per cent of all establishments in 1990. The incidence of delegation also increased, but again this was concentrated in the service sector. It was among 'work-group-related' initiatives – autonomous work-groups, job satisfaction programmes, involvement in technical change and, particularly, quality circles – that there was an increase among manufacturing plants. Again, however, new initiatives involving quality circles grew from a low base and were reported in 5 per cent of manufacturing plants in 1990.

Synopsis

The late 1980s saw a fall in the proportion of workplaces with joint consultative committees. However, there was no tendency towards abandoning committees, the change arose from the changing composition of workplaces. By 1990 there were fewer larger workplaces and fewer with recognized unions, where committees had been common. Where workplace-level consultative committees were in place, they were more often one of several committees on site.

Formal health and safety representation was as common, but there were more workplaces where management dealt with health and safety issues without consultation. Safety representatives (but no committee) were less often reported. Trade unions were as involved as before in formal arrangements for consultation and health and safety.

There was no change through the 1980s in the extent of non-union representation, with non-union representatives and committees reported as frequently at the end of the decade as at the beginning.

Managements were using a wide range of channels to communicate with their employees, including regular meetings of various types and regular newsletters. Most managements consulted and informed their workforce about a wide range of matters, although they were less likely to involve employees in decisions about staffing arrangements.

There was substantial growth since the mid-1980s in the overall reporting of a wide range of new initiatives for employee involvement, particularly in the service sector; they continued to be reported in a third of manufacturing workplaces.

Notes and references

1. The drop in private services, from 24 per cent to 19 per cent, could be due to sampling error.

2. Two thirds of those manual stewards who reported no joint consultative committee in 1990 said that a previous committee had last met since 1984. The equivalent figure for the five years to 1984 was 77 per cent. The unweighted bases were 95 in 1984 and 71 in 1990 – too small to be confident of any change in reporting. The pattern of responses among non-manual representatives was similar – 86 per cent in 1984 and 71 per cent in 1990, on even smaller bases (76 and 57). The small number of cases does not permit any more detailed analysis of these data. Regrettably, we had to drop this particular question from the 1990 management interview schedules to make space for new material.

3. Our analysis excludes those panel establishments that had dropped below 25 employees by 1990 and the few cases where there was some doubt as to the workplace in 1990 being the same as that in 1984.

4. As in 1984 there was a striking similarity between managers and worker representatives on this point, such that managers' responses could be used in our analysis – with the added advantage of their being a management respondent in all our sampled workplaces whereas worker representatives were interviewed in a sub-sample of them.

5. The refinements to the 1980 question-wording that were included in the 1984 survey were retained in the 1990 survey.

6. However, results from a later question which respondents may have interpreted as a broader definition of consultation indicate that, although consulting and providing a lot of information on *safety and occupational health arrangements* was less common in workplaces where managers had previously reported that they dealt with health and safety issues without consultation, some degree of consultation appeared to have taken place. This matter will need to be explored further.

7. The list of injuries, each sufficiently serious as to require at least some time off work for the employee(s) affected, was based on the Reporting of Injuries, Diseases and Dangerous Occurrences Regulations (RIDDOR) 1985. While it proved impractical in research terms to use the exact wording of RIDDOR, all the main types of injury listed in the regulations were covered by our survey question: *bone fracture; amputation; loss of sight – penetrating injury or burn to eye; loss of consciousness resulting from lack of oxygen; any injury (including burns) or loss of consciousness resulting from electric shock; acute illness or loss of consciousness resulting from either absorption of any noxious substance or possible exposure to an organism causing disease; or any other injury which resulted in immediate hospitalization for more than 24 hours.* Our interviewers did not refer to the regulations when they asked respondents the question.

8. The injury rates reported here differ from the statistics published in the Health and Safety Commission (HSC) *Annual Reports*, the latter being based on reports submitted by employers to relevant enforcement authorities, as required by RIDDOR. This is partly because RIDDOR is applicable across the whole of British industry, while our sample excludes coal mining and all establishments employing less than 25 employees. In addition, our question did not completely replicate the RIDDOR specification of injuries. Finally, our questions on injuries relied on managers' recall over the preceeding 12 months, although there may have been instances where our respondents referred to establishment records. A rather different matter concerns the possible under-reporting of injuries under RIDDOR, which led the HSC to commission a special health and safety supplement to the 1990 Labour Force Survey (LFS) (*HSE Annual Report, 1990–1991*). Initial analysis of these data (reflecting individual employees' accounts of any injuries affecting them in the 12 months prior to interview) showed marked differences from the RIDDOR figures. (Further analysis of the LFS supplement will appear in *Employment Gazette* in due course.)

9. This is the result of pooling the data from four separate questions. The question was asked separately in the sequence of questions asked in workplaces with recognized unions and, in similar form, in workplaces with no recognized unions.

10. This is similar to the multiple recording of representatives of recognized unions discussed in Chapter 4.

11. This may partly reflect some ambiguity in the survey question, leading some respondents to interpret it as a question about employee representatives of one kind or another whose union membership status was unrelated to the particular representative role. There may have been some confusion with employee representatives on consultative committees, for example.

12. Regrettably, Table 6.6 in our previous sourcebook contains an error. The figures in the row marked 'Any of the named methods' are five or six percentage points lower than is in fact the case. Correct figures are given in Table 5.5.

13. In the 1984 survey we asked whether management consulted employees or their representatives about all of the listed items (safety and occupational health was asked only in 1990). The questioning was restricted in 1990 to make room for other material.

14. N. Millward and M. Stevens (1986) *British Workplace Industrial Relations 1980– 1984: The DE/ESRC/PSI/ACAS Surveys*, Gower, Aldershot, p. 157.

15. Similar results emerge from other research. For example, see Advisory, Conciliation and Arbitration Service (1991) *Consultation and Communication: The 1990 ACAS Survey*, ACAS Occasional Paper 49.

Table 5A   Consultation arrangements and non-union representation, by industry, 1990

Percentages

	Joint consultative committees	Employee involvement initiative	Non-union representatives	Information collected	Information given to employees or representatives
All industries	**29**	**46**	**8**	**91**	**52**
All manufacturing	**23**	**32**	**14**	**91**	**51**
Metals & Mineral Products	51	44	26	89	79
Chemicals & Manufactured Fibres	(15)[1]	(23)	(11)	(96)	(94)
Metal Goods	(12)	(26)	(14)	(87)	(48)
Mechanical Engineering	18	30	13	88	43
Electrical & Instrument Engineering	15	37	24	91	39
Vehicles & Transport Equipment	38	49	5	100	37
Food, Drink & Tobacco	30	22	6	89	52
Textiles	(12)	(36)	(28)	(100)	(52)
Leather, Footwear & Clothing	(33)	(31)	(11)	(84)	(55)
Timber & Furniture, Paper & Printing	19	23	8	90	48
Rubber, Plastics & Other Manufacturing	(22)	(43)	(16)	(100)	(46)
All services	**30**	**49**	**6**	**91**	**52**
Energy & Water	40	61	1	99	79
Construction	6	38	1	84	35
Wholesale Distribution	17	28	10	92	60
Retail Distribution	24	58	9	98	56
Hotels, Catering, Repairs	26	39	11	96	47
Transport	23	40	6	85	35
Posts and Telecommunications	16	17	—	100	76
Banking, Finance, Insurance	17	73	12	100	75
Business Services	14	32	4	89	35
Central Government	67	43	9	94	58
Local Government	59	49	7	97	73
Higher Education	(55)	(32)	(10)	(64)	(43)
Other Education	40	61	2	81	49
Medical Services	45	51	3	86	49
Other Services	38	43	3	94	42

Base: all establishments (see Table 1A for bases and SIC codes)
[1] See Note B.

6 Procedures for Resolving Disputes

In this chapter we look at procedures for addressing and resolving disagreements between managers and employees and their trade unions. Such procedures play a key role in bringing fairness and consistency to employment relationships. In defining rules of discussion they provide avenues through which potential or actual conflicts over pay, conditions and working arrangements can be addressed positively and constructively by managements and workers. In providing opportunities for appeal against management decisions they require both employees and managers to consider what they are doing and why. We concentrate particularly on procedures for dealing with disciplinary and dismissal issues, individual grievances and health and safety. Given the close links which often exist between these matters and pay systems we look also at certain aspects of pay determination procedures, although our main discussion of these appears in Chapter 7. Procedural arrangements for all of these matters may of course link additionally with broader arrangements for consultation and exchange of information between managers and employees, an area where the scale and nature of developments has been hotly debated in recent years. We considered that broader area in Chapter 5.

By 1980, when we conducted our first survey, it was clear that written procedures for dealing with pay determination, discipline and dismissal and individual grievances had become much more widespread than in the past.[1] Our second survey showed evidence of further growth in coverage, fuelled in part by the growing importance of statutory protections against unfair dismissal, gender and race discrimination and other matters.

In approaching procedural arrangements in the 1990 survey we sought to explore two main issues. The first was whether, as we expected, there had been a still further extension of formal procedures across the economy. The second was to explore whether changes in procedural form and use could be detected. One interest here derived from the possibility, mentioned in other chapters, that the second half of the 1980s saw in larger organizations a growing devolution of decision-making on industrial relations matters to managers at establishment level. Associated with this was a suggestion that local managers were seeking to take greater control over their labour market decisions, with a consequent disinclination to involve outside third parties unless there was no alternative. If this were true we expected to find fewer references in procedures to fully external conciliation and arbitration.

The extent of procedures
In 1980 we distinguished three broad - and in some respects overlapping - areas in relation to which establishments might have formal procedures. These were disputes over *pay and conditions*; disputes over *discipline and dismissals other than redundancies*; and *individual grievances*. In both 1984 and 1990 we repeated our questions about these matters and added a fourth category of procedure related to *health and safety*. Table 6.1 shows the extent of each of these over the decade, as reported by managers.[2]

Given the already widespread – indeed in larger establishments almost universal – presence of procedures for these matters in 1984 it was not to be expected that major change would be evident in 1990. Nonetheless, with one surprising exception which we consider below, our expectation of growth and consolidation rather than decline was generally supported. Taking all establishments together, nearly all managers (94 per cent) reported that they had procedures covering at least one of the four areas, a similar figure to 1984. And as many as two thirds (62 per cent) reported that they had procedures covering all four. Within this overall picture the patterns of variation that we detected in 1984 also persisted. The presence of a multiplicity of procedures continued to be closely linked to size of establishment: 85 per cent of establishments with over 1000 employees had all four procedures in 1990, compared with 58 per cent of those with between 25 and 49 workers. It continued to be related to ownership, with 77 per cent of public sector establishments having four in 1990 compared with 56 per cent in the private sector, the figure falling to only 18 per cent among small, fully independent private sector firms.[3] And trade union recognition remained an important determinant: some 78 per cent of establishments where at least one trade union was recognized had all four in 1990, compared with 46 per cent of establishments where there was no recognition.

The extent of procedures for pay and conditions
Because of their strong connections with collective bargaining, formal procedures for pay and conditions have always been reported less often in our surveys than those for discipline and dismissals and other matters. Between 1980 and 1984 their coverage nonetheless increased in nearly every part of the economy. Overall 56 per cent of establishments in 1980 had such a procedure: in 1984 that proportion had increased to 68 per cent. While the increase was more marked in the public sector it was also substantial in private industry and commerce.

Table 6.1 Proportion of establishments with these main types of procedure, by sector, 1980, 1984 and 1990

Percentages

	All establishments			Private sector			Public sector		
	1980	1984	1990	1980	1984	1990	1980	1984	1990
Type of procedure:									
Pay and conditions	56	68	65	57	65	60	55	74	79
Discipline and dismissal	81	90	90	81	88	87	83	94	98
Individual grievances	77	88	87	74	84	83	83	96	96
Health and safety	..	89	87	..	85	83	..	95	95
Base: all establishments									
Unweighted	*2040*	*2019*	*2061*	*1330*	*1189*	*1429*	*710*	*830*	*632*
Weighted	*2000*	*2000*	*2000*	*1363*	*1267*	*1406*	*637*	*733*	*594*

We expected to see this pattern of growth continue. In fact, however, our respondents reported moves in two different directions. The period to 1990 did indeed see a further extension of pay and conditions procedures in the public sector, where four fifths (79 per cent) of establishments reported them, compared with three quarters (74 per cent) in 1984. This result is the more striking given the cessation, at the time of our survey, of all formal pay bargaining for school teachers in England and Wales. In the private sector, however, we observed decline rather than growth: overall three fifths of private sector establishments reported procedures of this type in 1990 compared with two thirds in 1984. Part of the explanation for this somewhat surprising difference may lie in the changing size composition of establishments – and particularly the fall in the number of large establishments – in the private sector in recent years. As in previous surveys we found a clear and positive relationship between number of workers in establishments and the presence of pay and conditions procedures. Overall eight out of ten private sector establishments with over 1000 employees had such procedures, while only 56 per cent with fewer than 100 did so. It was notable, too, that wholly independent small firms were much less likely to operate such procedures than others: only 37 per cent did so, compared with 73 per cent of private sector establishments which formed part of a larger organization. The point is reinforced when finer industry breakdowns are considered. As could be expected, relatively low proportions of establishments in Hotels and Catering (55 per cent), Food, Drink and Tobacco (49 per cent), Business Services (44 per cent) and Metal Goods (43 per cent) had pay and conditions procedures.

As Table 6.2 shows, however, these explanations cannot provide a full account of recent developments, as the decline in the incidence of procedures relating to terms and conditions in the higher end of the size range indicates. Another, more plausible, explanation lies in the changing pattern of trade union recognition which we described in Chapter 3. Table 6.3 shows that between 1980 and 1984 there was a very substantial increase in pay and conditions procedures in establishments where trade unions were recognized and that these procedures were even more common in such establishments in 1990. Overall, some 81 per cent of establishments with recognized trade unions had pay and conditions procedures in 1990. But as we showed earlier, unionized establishments made up a substantially smaller proportion of the total in 1990. Table 6.3 reveals further that the increase in pay and conditions procedures experienced in non-unionized establishments between 1980 and 1984 was not sustained in subsequent years. The overall effect of these two developments together probably accounts for the overall fall in pay and conditions procedures which we observed in the private sector. These tendencies were also clearly apparent in results from our panel of trad-

Table 6.2   Proportion of establishments with these main types of procedure, by size of establishment within sector, 1980, 1984 and 1990

Percentages

| | \multicolumn{12}{c}{Size of establishment} | | | | | | | | | | | |
| | 25–99 | | | 100–499 | | | 500–999 | | | 1000+ | | |
	1980	1984	1990	1980	1984	1990	1980	1984	1990	1980	1984	1990
Private sector:												
Type of procedure												
Pay & conditions	52	62	56	71	73	72	88	87	80	95	92	83
Discipline & dismissals	78	86	85	90	96	96	99	99	97	98	98	100
Individual grievance	70	81	79	90	94	96	98	100	99	99	98	100
Health & safety	..	83	80	..	91	94	..	98	97	..	97	96
Base: all private sector establishments												
Unweighted	*516*	*462*	*514*	*480*	*416*	*526*	*163*	*165*	*178*	*171*	*146*	*211*
Weighted	*1065*	*1001*	*1106*	*257*	*236*	*275*	*21*	*20*	*17*	*17*	*10*	*7*
Public sector:												
Type of procedure												
Pay & conditions	50	73	77	66	74	85	77	80	92	81	93	93
Discipline & dimissals	79	93	98	90	98	98	99	99	100	100	100	100
Individual grievance	80	95	96	91	97	97	97	97	99	99	100	100
Health & safety	..	94	95	..	99	95	..	96	98	..	100	96
Base: all public sector establishments												
Unweighted	*231*	*253*	*190*	*297*	*308*	*191*	*86*	*130*	*84*	*96*	*139*	*167*
Weighted	*447*	*532*	*454*	*164*	*169*	*113*	*18*	*20*	*17*	*9*	*13*	*10*

Table 6.3   Proportion of establishments with these main types of procedure, by union recognition, 1980, 1984 and 1990

Percentages

| | Recognized unions present | | | | | |
| | None | | | One or more | | |
	1980	1984	1990	1980	1984	1990
Type of procedure						
Pay and conditions	41	50	48	65	77	81
Discipline & dismissals	73	83	83	86	94	97
Individual grievances	64	77	78	85	94	94
Health & safety	..	79	79	..	94	94

Base: all establishments with pattern of recognition specified in column heads, as reported by managers

Unweighted	*465*	*426*	*644*	*1575*	*1593*	*1417*
Weighted	*722*	*673*	*943*	*1278*	*1327*	*1057*

Private sector only:

Type of procedure						
Pay & conditions	41	50	46	73	81	84
Discipline and dismissals	72	83	82	89	94	96
Individual grievances	63	77	77	86	91	93
Health & safety	..	79	77	..	91	93

Base: all private sector establishments with pattern of recognition specified in column heads, as reported by managers

Unweighted	*436*	*420*	*606*	*894*	*769*	*823*
Weighted	*684*	*663*	*868*	*678*	*604*	*538*

ing sector establishments. Those which maintained recognition between 1984 and 1990 were more likely to have procedures at the end of the decade, while the incidence of procedures among non-union establishments remained unchanged over the period.

The extent of disciplinary, grievance and health and safety procedures
Differences between the public and private sectors were less evident when we turned to other procedures, whose already high incidence was maintained and in certain areas extended between 1984 and 1990. Table 6.1 shows that while procedures for discipline and dismissal, individual grievances and health and safety remained somewhat more common in the public sector (where they had become nearly universal), they were

still reported in between 83 and 87 per cent of cases in the private sector. Once again their presence was positively related to numbers of employees although, as Table 6.2 shows, the incidence of these procedures had become almost the rule even in small establishments. As many as 85 per cent of managers in private sector establishments employing between 25 and 99 people reported the existence of formal disciplinary and dismissal procedures and only slightly fewer – some 79 and 80 per cent respectively – reported grievance and health and safety procedures. As before, however, smaller privately-owned independent firms were least likely to have procedures: 74 per cent of these had a disciplinary and dismissals procedure, 60 per cent an individual grievance procedure and 64 per cent a health and safety procedure.

Disciplinary procedures were least common in Construction and in Business Services, where 77 per cent and 74 per cent of managers, respectively, reported them. Grievance procedures were reported least often in Construction (70 per cent), Leather and Footwear (64 per cent), Textiles (59 per cent) and Metal Goods (48 per cent). Health and safety procedures were also least common in Business Services (61 per cent) and Metal Goods (60 per cent), and perhaps less common than might have been expected given their relatively high rates of reported injury,[4] in Construction (79 per cent) and Transport (78 per cent).

Trade union recognition and the presence of specialist personnel managers were again positively related to the presence of procedures. Managers in 97 per cent of establishments where at least one trade union was recognized operated a disciplinary and dismissals procedure, compared with 83 per cent of those without trade union recognition.

Broadly then, while the overall incidence of pay and conditions procedures in 1990 may have fallen slightly in the private sector when compared with 1984, largely reflecting changes in the extent of unionized parts of the private sector, procedures for other issues, always more common, spread to cover almost all larger establishments and the great majority of smaller ones. While there was some variation between sectors the main exception to this pattern remained the small, fully independent private sector firm with fewer than 200 employees, though even here there was evidence of growth. Overall we estimate that in 1990 some 14.5 million employees of the 15.6 million represented by WIRS were in establishments with formal disciplinary and dismissal procedures, some 14.2 million where there were individual grievance arrangements and nearly 14 million with health and safety procedures. Procedures for resolving disputes over pay and conditions were present in establishments employing some 11.4 million workers.

The characteristics and operation of disciplinary and dismissals procedures

Having established the extent to which procedures were present we asked more detailed questions about their form and operation. In previous surveys our detailed questions covered pay and conditions procedures and those for discipline and dismissal. On this occasion we also made more thorough enquiries about the use of individual grievance procedures, with a view to exploring how far they performed similar or different functions for the parties from the others. Unfortunately, within the space constraints of our questionnaire, it was not possible to extend our investigations to cover the operation of health and safety procedures.

The nature of disciplinary procedures

As in previous years we asked managers who reported that they had disciplinary and dismissals procedures whether or not these were substantially the same for all groups of employees, or whether they differed, for example between blue-collar and white-collar employees. We had observed in 1984 a trend towards uniformity in this area. That trend was consolidated. In 1990 more than nine in ten management respondents with disciplinary procedures reported uniform arrangements, as shown in Table 6.4; or to put it another way, some 84 per cent of all establishments in our sample were in this position compared with only 72 per cent in 1980. The change appears to have developed irrespective of the numbers employed on site, workforce composition, and trade union recognition, suggesting that it arose primarily from factors outside the immediate working environment, including unfair dismissal law and the growing role of industrial tribunals and the courts in examining employer practice.

A growing uniformity in disciplinary and dismissal procedures might be expected to follow in part from a greater tendency to write them down. Here too we had observed an increase in formality over the early 1980s and Table 6.4 shows that this continued: taking all establishments together, over nine out of ten disciplinary and dismissal procedures were in written form in 1990, almost completely so in the public sector and nearly completely so elsewhere. In all, we estimate that some 14 million employees worked in establishments where these procedures were in written form. Given the depth of their coverage it is not surprising that the positive associations we noted in 1980 and 1984 between written disciplinary procedures and size of establishment and trade union recognition were reduced, though they still remained. Indeed, the most significant change in the second half of the decade was the further spread of formality in smaller private sector establishments. In 1984 75 per cent of all such establishments with between 25 and 49 employees had written disciplinary and dismissals procedures: by 1990 that figure

Table 6.4 Characteristics of procedures for a) discipline and dismissal and b) pay and conditions, by sector, 1980, 1984 and 1990

Percentages

| | All establishments | | | | | | Private sector | | | | | | Public sector | | | | | |
| | Discipline & dismissal | | | Pay & conditions | | | Discipline & dismissal | | | Pay & conditions | | | Discipline & dismissal | | | Pay & conditions | | |
	1980	1984	1990	1980	1984	1990	1980	1984	1990	1980	1984	1990	1980	1984	1990	1980	1984	1990
Coverage																		
Similar for all workers	88	93	90	86	89	90	93	97	95	88	91	93	79	87	81	83	84	84
Different for different groups of workers	9	7	9	11	11	10	3	3	5	8	9	7	19	13	18	18	15	16
Not answered	3	—	1	3	—	—	4	—	—	4	—	1	1	—	2	—	—	—
Set out in a written document	89	94	93	93	87	90	91	85	90	91	83	87	98	99	98	98	98	97
Union representation																		
Employees covered represented by a trade union	65	69	71	70	74	71	51	50	45	58	58	52	94	99	95	96	99	100
Procedure agreed between management & trade union	59	62	65	65	70	65	44	42	41	52	53	51	90	94	87	92	95	90
Third-party intervention																		
Provision made	66	74	64	70	79	68	58	62	53	63	69	61	83	94	90	85	93	81
No provision made	29	25	36	25	21	31	37	38	47	32	31	39	13	6	10	8	5	17
No information	4	*	*	6	1	1	5	*	*	4	1	1	4	1	1	6	2	3
Base: establishments with procedure specified in column heads																		
Unweighted	*1829*	*1919*	*1979*	*1430*	*1154*	*1189*	*1188*	*1114*	*1346*	*949*	*898*	*1039*	*641*	*805*	*625*	*481*	*656*	*550*
Weighted	*1628*	*1808*	*1833*	*1127*	*1361*	*1338*	*1100*	*1117*	*1229*	*773*	*821*	*839*	*528*	*691*	*581*	*394*	*541*	*469*

had risen to 82 per cent. Even in small independent firms, which showed on every dimension the least tendency to have formalized employment relationships, written disciplinary and dismissal procedures existed in nearly three quarters of cases in 1990.

Trade union involvement in disciplinary and dismissal issues
Trade unions may be involved in dismissal and disciplinary processes in two main ways. The first is through representing or otherwise assisting individual members faced with a disciplinary investigation or sanction. To assess the potential for such assistance we asked whether the employees covered by the procedure were represented by trade unions. Overall managers in 71 per cent of establishments with dismissal and disciplinary procedures reported that this was the case, a similar figure to 1984, suggesting that trade unions continued to exercise an important role in this area. Where trade unions were recognized a potential role in disciplinary procedures was almost universal. Additionally, however, unions also exercised representational functions in a sizeable proportion of establishments where they were not formally recognized for pay bargaining purposes. No fewer than one in seven managers (15 per cent) who said they did not recognize trade unions for pay bargaining reported that trade union representatives played some part in resolving disciplinary and dismissal issues.[5]

A second main way in which trade unions may be involved in procedures is, of course, through discussing and agreeing their form with managers. In 1990, as in 1984, it was clear that disciplinary procedures had been agreed in 90 per cent of establishments where trade unions were recognized. This was true when we compared establishments of similar size, although once again small independent firms differed somewhat from others: only 79 per cent of small firms which recognized trade unions had agreed procedures. One small difference was that procedures were somewhat more likely to have been agreed with trade unions in newer establishments, that is those which had been conducting their main activity on the site for less than three years.[6]

The inclusion of third parties in procedures
Finally in considering the form of disciplinary and dismissals procedures we asked about the role of third-party intervention as a possible final stage. Third-party intervention may take a variety of forms. As in previous surveys we defined it in broad terms, to cover senior management in multi-establishment organizations outside the sampled establishment but within the same organization, as well as full-time trade union officers, employers' associations and a range of advisory bodies including ACAS. The results for all three surveys are given in the lower part of Table 6.4 and in Table 6.5.

Table 6.5 Provisions for third party intervention, 1980, 1984 and 1990

Percentages

	Discipline & dismissals			Pay & conditions		
	1980	1984	1990	1980	1984	1990
Person or organization specified within the procedure						
ACAS	29	18	15	35	27	31
Higher level management	39	60	64	27	51	48
Union official	7	24	11	7	24	15
Employers' association	8	4	4	10	8	7
Joint higher level management/ union officials	5	16	12	5	14	16
Joint employers' association/ union officials	6	9	7	10	11	12
Arbitrating body (not ACAS)	3	7	4	5	9	10
Other answers	5	16	7	5	13	3
No information	6	—	—	5	—	—

Base: establishments with any third-party provisions in procedures specified in column heads

Unweighted	*1253*	*1496*	*1237*	*1118*	*1329*	*1144*
Weighted	*1071*	*1341*	*1139*	*789*	*1069*	*867*

Results so far in this chapter have suggested a picture of stability and consolidation over the 1980s, rather than changes in direction. Matters were more complex here. Our surveys suggest that after significant growth there was a decline in the use of third parties during the latter part of the decade. By 1990 the proportion of establishments with third-party intervention written into their disciplinary procedures had fallen to 64 per cent, marginally below its 1980 figure and well below the 1984 figure of 74 per cent. In private sector establishments the proportion fell to the lowest level recorded in the survey series (53 per cent) and there was a much smaller but still notable fall in the public sector.

This overall pattern of declining provision for third-party intervention, however, concealed marked variations of detail. Between 1980 and 1984 there had been a substantial increase in the proportion of multi-establishment organizations which had provisions involving higher-level managers in disciplinary problems. While some two fifths (39 per cent) of procedures had included such provision in 1980, by 1984 the proportion had grown to three fifths (60 per cent). In 1990 further growth in such arrangements was reported, suggesting perhaps that managers in such organizations had become increasingly conscious that their approach to dismissals could be open to public scrutiny and that cases might, if mishandled, have damaging consequences not only for continuing management–employee relationships but for the employers' public standing.[7] The involvement of employers' associations was also maintained, notably in engineering where two fifths (39 per cent) of managers reported their use, and in Construction where the proportion was a third (32 per cent). In other respects, however, Table 6.5 shows that the earlier changes were reversed. Between 1980 and 1984, for example, there had been substantial increases in procedures which called for the involvement of full-time trade union officers and joint senior management–union bodies at the final stages of procedure. In 1990, arrangements of these kinds were substantially less common. Most notably the involvement of full-time officials was mentioned less than half as often as in 1984.

These changes were accompanied by a significant decline in mention of independent agencies and persons as a final stage in disciplinary and dismissals procedures. Most notably the reduction in frequency of mention of the Advisory, Conciliation and Arbitration Service, which we had observed between 1980 and 1984, continued through to 1990.[8] By then some 15 per cent of establishments with provision for third-party intervention in disciplinary procedures included reference in their procedure to ACAS as a final stage, compared with 18 per cent in 1984 and 29 per cent in 1980. With the exception of banking, where frequent use continued to be made of ACAS assistance, the fall was spread across the full range of industries and all categories of size, age, workforce composition and ownership of establishment.

Reference to ACAS can take two main forms, perhaps indicating different degrees of reliance on third-party assistance. Voluntary conciliation involves attempts by ACAS officials to bring parties together with a view to helping them reach agreement. By contrast, ACAS arbitration requires the parties to agree that an independent person appointed by ACAS should judge the merits and demerits of each side's position. Where the agreed terms of reference permit, this may entail varying the terms of a disciplinary sanction or dismissal. In 1990 only three fifths (60 per cent) of establishments which referred to ACAS in their disciplinary and dismissal procedures allowed for the possibility of both arbitration and conciliation, a substantial decrease from the four fifths (78 per cent) reported in 1980 and down on the two thirds (68 per cent) mentioned in 1984. A fifth (20 per cent) allowed only for conciliation (up from 9 per cent in 1980 and 11 per cent in 1984), and a tenth (9 per cent) for arbitration alone, a similar figure to earlier surveys. The private sector displayed a greater willingness to involve ACAS on either basis than the public sector, which showed particular reluctance to contemplate conciliation.

The use of disciplinary sanctions and dismissals in 1990
In addition to enquiring about the form of disciplinary procedures we asked managers about the use they had made of disciplinary measures and dismissals in their establishments and how their procedures had dealt with difficulties. In doing so we were aware of claims by many labour market analysts that growing competition in product markets had encouraged managements to become more selective in recruiting and retaining staff over the second half of the 1980s, and that disciplinary sanctions might be receiving correspondingly greater use.

We asked first whether a range of sanctions short of dismissal had been applied to any employee over the past year. We distinguished between three main kinds of sanctions, all indicating at least a possibility, as managers might see it, of serious misconduct or other inadequacy on the part of a worker.[9] These were: giving a formal written warning, which often indicates that further difficulties will lead to dismissal; suspension from work, with either full, reduced or no pay; and disciplinary deductions from pay such as fines for poor work or misconduct. Details of their reported use are set out in Table 6.6.

It was perhaps not surprising, given the apparent growth in uniformity in procedures described above, that the use of formal written warnings over the previous 12 months proved widespread. Overall some 58 per cent of managers reported issuing warnings, ranging from two fifths (39 per cent) in the public sector to two thirds (66 per cent) in private industry and commerce.

Within the private sector, however, there were substantial variations. Thus over four fifths of managers in Metals and Mineral Products and Metal Goods, Food, Drink and Tobacco, Rubber and Plastics and Wholesale Distribution reported giving at least one formal warning, compared, for example, with only a quarter (25 per cent) in Banking, Finance and Insurance. Formal written warnings were slightly less likely to arise where trade unions were recognized but relatively more common in establishments with large proportions of male workers, unskilled workers and full-time workers.

Suspension with full pay, widely recommended by advisory bodies where allegedly serious difficulties need to be investigated, had been used markedly less often, by about one in seven establishments (15 per cent), and suspension without pay (which is outside the strict terms of most employment contracts) by 7 per cent. Suspension with full pay was most frequently used in the public sector where 18 per cent of respondents reported it; suspension without pay most often in the private sector, where overall 9 per cent reported using it. Suspension with reduced pay was the rarest form of suspension: taking our sample as a whole only 1 per cent of establishments reported its use during the previous 12 months.

Table 6.6   **Disciplinary sanctions short of dismissal, by size of establishment and sector, 1990**

Percentages

| | All establishments | Number of employees in establishment | | | | Private sector | Public sector |
		25–99	100–499	500–999	1000+		
Formal written warning	58	54	56	88	87	66	39
Suspension with full pay	15	9	2	57	58	14	18
Suspension with reduced pay	1	1	2	14	10	1	2
Suspension without pay	7	5	13	26	37	9	5
Deduction from pay	6	6	6	13	15	7	6
Base: all establishments							
Unweighted	*2061*	*704*	*717*	*226*	*378*	*1429*	*632*
Weighted	*2000*	*1561*	*389*	*34*	*16*	*1406*	*594*

Our survey in 1990 was the first in which we asked about warnings and suspensions so we can make no estimates of changes in their use over time. In 1980, however, we did ask managers about disciplinary deductions from pay.[10] We asked then about three broad types of deductions: for bad work; for loss or damage to the employer's property; and for other disciplinary offences. Managers in about one in ten establishments (9 per cent) reported some use of deductions for these purposes in 1980, spread widely across industries and covering a broad range of occupations. Space did not allow us to repeat our questions in identical format, so that we cannot say with certainty that the 6 per cent of managers who reported using deductions in 1990 indicates a fall in the use of this sanction. As with 1980, however, we can report that deductions were used across a very wide range of industries and in nearly every kind of establishment in our sample.[11]

The incidence of sanctions

If substantial numbers of employers made use of sanctions short of dismissal, how often did they do so? We asked managers a broad question relating to all five types of sanctions. In most cases the number of employees against whom sanctions had been taken was small. Indeed, in two fifths of all establishments none of the five kinds of sanctions had been in use over the past year. Overall the mean number of 'sanctioned' employees was 3. Not surprisingly this number varied according to size of establishment. For example, establishments with between 25 and 49 employees had an average of 1.6 sanctioned employees over the year prior to interview, in those with 1000 and above 33 workers were affected. An additional measure, the number of sanctions per thousand employed, is shown in Table 6.7. This gives a very different picture, of a sanction rate markedly higher in smaller establishments than large ones. Establishments with fewer than 100 employees averaged no less than 38 sanctioned employees per thousand employed, while those with over 1000 workers only half that rate – 19 per thousand employed. Sanction rates, on this measure, were also markedly higher in private industry and commerce, where they averaged 39 per thousand employees, than in the public sector where the figure was just half this level, at 18.

Dismissals

After considering sanctions short of dismissal we went on to ask about the establishment's recent experience of dismissals themselves. Here we were able to repeat the questions we had asked in 1980 and 1984. In 1980 some two fifths (41 per cent) of managers reported that at least one employee had been dismissed during the previous 12 months for reasons other than redundancy.[12] In 1984, that proportion fell substantially to one third (31 per cent). In 1990 it rose again, to 43 per cent. The

Table 6.7 Disciplinary sanctions, dismissals and industrial tribunal claims per thousand employees, by size of establishment and sector, 1980, 1984 and 1990

| | All establishments | | | Size of establishment | | | | | | | | | | | | Private sector | | | Public sector | | |
| | | | | 25–99 | | | 100–499 | | | 500–999 | | | 1000+ | | | | | | | | |
	1980	1984	1990	1980	1984	1990	1980	1984	1990	1980	1984	1990	1980	1984	1990	1980	1984	1990	1980	1984	1990
Sanctions short of dismissal	::	::	32	::	::	38	::	::	31	::	::	27	::	::	19	::	::	39	::	::	18
Dismissals	14	9	15	19	15	29	::	8	16	7	5	10	4	3	7	18	14	20	::	3	5
Industrial tribunal claims	::	1.1	1.4	::	1.7	1.7	::	1.0	1.7	::	0.8	1.1	::	0.6	0.5	::	1.5	1.7	::	0.7	0.6
Base: all establishments																					
Unweighted	2040	2019	2061	747	715	704	777	724	720	249	295	262	267	285	378	1330	1189	1429	710	830	632
Weighted	2000	2000	2000	1512	1523	1651	421	405	389	39	40	34	26	23	16	1362	1267	1407	638	733	594

increase applied to all industries and to establishments of every kind. In the private sector it rose to 52 per cent (from 50 per cent in 1980 and 40 per cent in 1984) and in private manufacturing was as high as 62 per cent, compared with 55 per cent in 1980. Among small fully independent firms the proportion rose from 37 per cent in 1980 to 49 per cent in 1990. Even in the public sector, where the incidence of dismissals has traditionally been comparatively rare, 21 per cent of managers reported non-redundancy dismissals in their establishment during the past year, up from 15 per cent in 1984.

This picture of a wider use of dismissal at the end of the 1980s is reinforced when we look at the numbers of dismissals actually taking place. In 1984 managers in 4 per cent of all establishments said they had dismissed more than four employees for reasons unrelated to redundancy during the previous 12 months. By 1990 the figure had risen dramatically: managers in no fewer than 13 per cent of all establishments said that they were in this position.

Further evidence lies in the changes which took place in the rate of dismissal per thousand workers employed. For the economy as a whole that figure had been 14 in 1980 but only nine in 1984. In 1990 it rose to 15, though as in the past this global figure concealed wide variations. As Table 6.7 shows, dismissal rates were markedly higher in smaller than large establishments: establishments with between 25 and 49 employees dismissed 29 workers per thousand employed in 1990 (compared with 15 in 1984 and 25 in 1980) while those with 1000 or more dismissed an average of no more than 7. Fully independent single establishments also showed high dismissal rates in 1990, on average 26 workers per thousand employed. As in previous years there were substantial industry differences. For the private sector the rate was 20 per thousand, contrasting markedly with the public sector where it was no more than 5 per thousand and, if the nationalized industries are removed from the calculation, down to 4 per thousand.

We noted in Chapter 3 the possibility that dismissal rates might be substantially affected by trade union activity. It would not be surprising if they were. As we showed above, where trade unions were recognized for pay bargaining purposes they generally played a significant part in discussion about and the operation of disciplinary and dismissal procedures. We also showed that even where no recognition existed for collective bargaining purposes a sizeable minority of agreements allow for trade union representation for individual employees facing disciplinary action.

As in previous years we found a clear and positive relationship in this area: taking all establishments together, those with no union recognition dismissed some two and a half times as many workers employed per thousand as did those where trade unions were recognized. This relationship held true for both the private and public sectors. In private manufacturing, establishments with trade union recognition dismissed on average 16 workers per thousand employed, compared with 27 per thousand among establishments with no recognition. In private services the difference was no less pronounced: unionized establishments dismissed 13 per thousand employed, non-unionized some 25 per thousand.

On this point we noted in Chapter 3 the suggestions by some commentators, based on multivariate analysis of our earlier surveys, that trade unions might operate so as particularly to reduce dismissal rates in areas of high unemployment where alternative jobs for displaced workers would be difficult to find. Our results suggest that it is unlikely that any straightforward relationship of this kind was operating in 1990. Establishments operating in travel to work areas with less than 3 per cent unemployment, for example, dismissed on average no more and no fewer than those in areas where unemployment was as high as 11 per cent.[13] The suggestion is rather that the internal economy of the establishment may have been more significant at the end of the decade. Industrial and commercial establishments operating at somewhat or considerably below full capacity, for example, showed a clear tendency to dismiss employees more often than those working at full capacity; so did establishments where managers reported declines in labour productivity over the past three years. Interestingly, as in 1984, there were also clear indications that dismissal rates were significantly lower where 'non-standard' workers were present than elsewhere.[14] It appeared, too, that establishments employing substantial numbers of workers from ethnic minorities also had significantly higher dismissal rates than others.[15]

Disagreements over dismissal, if not resolved, may lead to applications to industrial tribunals for compensation and re-engagement. As in previous surveys we asked managers whether any employee or ex-employee had started an official industrial tribunal action in the past year. The question went wider than claims of unfair dismissal, to cover possible cases of sex and race discrimination and all other issues which can now form the subject of a complaint that the employee's statutory employment rights have been infringed.[16] Nine per cent of managers said that their establishment had faced such a challenge in the previous 12 months, including 13 per cent in private manufacturing and 8 per cent in private services. In line with their incidence of reported dismissals the proportion was much lower (5 per cent) in the public sector. In all but a handful of situations four or fewer cases had arisen. In 1984, 82 per cent of respondents reported that their cases had involved allegations of unfair dismissal. In 1990 that proportion fell to three out of four. A further 10 per cent involved allegations of race or sex discrimination, affecting all industries and types of establishment to some degree. The remainder, some one in seven cases, arose in other jurisdictions, including the Wages Act 1986.

The lower part of Table 6.7 shows the incidence of tribunal applications per thousand workers employed. Once again, according to this measure, difficulties over dismissal are seen to have arisen more commonly in smaller than large establishments. The figures ranged from 1.7 cases per thousand employed in establishments with fewer than 100 employees (including 1.6 per thousand in small independent companies) to 0.5 per thousand in the largest establishments. Unlike the situation with numbers of dismissals, however, there was no clear link between the presence of trade union recognition and the incidence of tribunal applications. Applications in areas where official unemployment rates were between 5 and 10 per cent, however, were as much as three times higher than those where unemployment stood at less than 3 per cent.

The adequacy of disciplinary and dismissal procedures
Finally, in considering disciplinary and dismissal procedures we asked two broad questions about how far respondents were satisfied with their operation. In our 1980 survey we were able to compare responses about satisfaction from both managers and worker representatives. We found that although management satisfaction was at a higher level, it generally followed the pattern of worker representative responses, both in terms of types of establishment and the length and complexity of procedures. In the light of these findings we confined our questions on this issue in 1984 to worker representatives and we followed the same course in 1990.[17]

Our first question asked whether there had been any occasion during the past year on which a disciplinary or dismissals issue had arisen which had not been dealt with through the formal procedure. In 1984 we found representatives reporting a fall since 1980 in the number of issues not being taken through procedure, a finding in line with our suggestion that the use of procedures was becoming more routinized within organizations. In 1990 there was further evidence of that trend: overall only 4 per cent of worker representatives reported that such a case had arisen, though with a greater incidence (8 per cent) in private manufacturing than elsewhere. In the public sector such situations were said almost never to have arisen. On this evidence it seems clear that the great bulk of disciplinary and dismissals issues were dealt with through formal procedures rather than on a more *ad hoc* basis which may be open to challenge. In this area it seems that once procedures had been adopted and formalized, they were widely followed by managers and employees.

Our second question was more openly evaluative, asking how satisfied representatives were in general with their procedures. Responses for 1990 are shown in Table 6.8. A clear pattern again emerges. Taking all relevant establishments nearly nine in ten worker representatives

Table 6.8   **Degree of satisfaction expressed by worker representatives at working of procedures, 1990**

Percentages

	All establishments	Private sector	Public sector
Type of procedure			
Disciplinary and dismissals			
Very or quite satisfied	87	86	88
Not very or not at all satisfied	13	14	12

Base: worker representatives belonging to recognized trade unions in establishments with disciplinary and dismissals procedures

Unweighted	*727*	*478*	*249*
Weighted	*354*	*215*	*139*

Pay and conditions			
Very or quite satisfied	78	83	73
Not very or not at all satisfied	21	17	26

Base: worker representatives belonging to recognized trade unions in establishments with pay procedures

Unweighted	*647*	*335*	*217*
Weighted	*287*	*189*	*119*

said that they were 'very' or 'quite' satisfied with the operation of disciplinary and dismissal procedures and only some 13 per cent that they were 'not very' or 'not at all' satisfied. These responses, more positive than those achieved in 1980 and 1984, were common to both private and public sector and to establishments in all size ranges.

Procedures for dealing with individual grievances

We reported above that nearly nine out of ten establishments in our sample in 1990 had a formal procedure for dealing with individual grievances. To ensure consistency with our earlier surveys we left it to respondents to define this term. We know from other inquiries, however, that grievance procedures may be used to deal with a wide range of issues, including some which can fall within the scope of disciplinary and pay procedures. For the 1990 survey we devised a small number of new questions aimed at exploring the issues which were actually dealt with under this heading.

We asked managers, first, whether any employees had actually raised matters through the individual grievance procedure during the past year. The responses suggest that procedures of this kind play a significant role in many workplaces. Overall more than a quarter (27 per cent) of managers in workplaces with individual grievance procedures said that they had been activated at least once in the past year. The figures ranged from a fifth (20 per cent) in establishments with between 25 and 49 employees to three quarters (73 per cent) in those with 1000 or more. Use in private industry and commerce, in 29 per cent of establishments, was somewhat

Table 6.9   Issues dealt with through grievance procedures, 1990

Percentages

	All establishments	Private sector	Public sector	Issues on which procedures considered ineffective
Pay, allowances and conditions	30	32	25	7
Equal pay	*	*	*	—
Job grading/ classification	9	7	14	6
Promotion/career development	7	7	7	1
Conditions of employment	4	4	5	7
Physical working conditions	13	15	6	—
Health and safety	5	5	3	—
Internal job transfers	4	2	9	—
Work allocation	3	2	6	*
Working practices/methods	4	5	2	*
Workload/pace of work	3	3	3	—
Performance/performance appraisal	11	11	10	27
Attendance/absence/ timekeeping	9	8	12	1
Disciplinary issues	27	32	12	4
Redundancy	2	3	1	—
Sexual harassment	2	1	4	5
Relations between employees	5	6	4	17
Relations with superiors	8	7	12	5
Personal property/damage/ theft	1	2	—	—
Other/Not answered	4	3	5	22

Base: all establishments where grievance procedures had been used

Unweighted	*899*	*604*	*295*	*115*
Weighted	*463*	*341*	*122*	*54*

higher than in the public sector where 21 per cent of managers reported it. Establishments employing substantial proportions of people from ethnic minorities also reported a higher than average use of grievance procedures.

We next asked about the issues which had been dealt with under the procedure. Table 6.9 summarizes the results. As expected it shows clearly that a good deal of complementarity and interchangeability arose between individual grievance procedures and those for dealing with disciplinary and pay issues. More than a quarter (27 per cent) of managers who had used their procedure in the past 12 months had done so in relation to a disciplinary matter. In addition there was substantial use in relation to problems of working time, relations with supervisors, sexual harassment by colleagues and theft or damage to property, all of which may constitute disciplinary offences. Slightly more managers (30 per cent) had also used them for resolving problems over pay and allowances. One finding of particular interest here was the widespread use of grievance procedures for resolving individual disagreements over work performance, performance appraisal and promotion and career development, particularly in establishments which operated performance-related pay systems. We return briefly to the operation of performance-related pay systems in Chapter 7 and deal more fully with them in our companion volume.

Finally, in exploring the use of individual grievance procedures we asked managers whether there were any issues for which their individual grievance procedure had proved ineffective. One in eight (12 per cent) considered that there were, covering a wide range of issues. Of these a quarter (27 per cent) again mentioned work performance and performance appraisals as areas of particular difficulty.

Procedures for resolving disputes over pay and conditions

We noted earlier the somewhat surprising finding that, by contrast with those for disciplinary matters and individual grievances where there had been a growth in coverage over the economy, procedures for resolving difficulties over pay and conditions had if anything become less common in private sector organizations over the second half of the 1980s. Much of the explanation for this, we suggested, lay in the declining incidence of union recognition which we observed in Chapter 3 and the declining involvement of union representatives in workplace bargaining which we described in Chapter 4.

As in our previous surveys we asked a range of questions designed to explore the characteristics of pay and conditions procedures. Given our more detailed discussion of pay determination machinery in Chapter 7 and the material we present in Chapter 8 on balloting about possible industrial action, we report the results here only relatively briefly.

Table 6.4 above showed that, like those for other issues, procedures for resolving pay and conditions generally took the same form for all workers in an establishment. This was true in 1990 in 93 per cent of private sector establishments and 84 per cent of those in the public sector. The tendency we noted in earlier surveys for a somewhat greater differentiation in private sector pay and conditions procedures than in disciplinary and grievance procedures, according to grade or occupational category of employees, seemed largely to have disappeared, no doubt reflecting changes in occupational structures within organizations and accompanying developments in trade union structures.

Similarly, as in previous years, pay and conditions procedures were widely set down in written agreements: overall some 90 per cent of establishments with such procedures had them in writing in 1990, with variations about this figure between the private sector and public sectors (87 per cent compared with 97 per cent) and between establishments with and without trade union recognition (96 per cent compared with 83 per cent).

A similar picture to earlier surveys was also apparent in the involvement of trade unions in pay and conditions procedures: where unions were recognized they were, not surprisingly, always involved in representing their members on such issues. As with other procedures, however, managers also reported a significant union involvement where no formal recognition had been agreed: nearly one in five (17 per cent) said non-recognized unions played a part in resolving disputes over pay and conditions even though they had been given no formal role in pay negotiations themselves.[18]

The adequacy of pay and conditions procedures
As with disciplinary and individual grievance procedures we asked our worker representative respondents two evaluative questions about the operation of pay and conditions procedures. As with the others it appears that pay and conditions procedures, once in place, were widely followed by the parties. Overall only 4 per cent of representatives reported that disputes had arisen over the past year which had not been dealt with through procedure, slightly more in the private manufacturing sector (8 per cent) than elsewhere, and very few (1 per cent) in the public sector.

Reported satisfaction with the working of pay and conditions procedures was also high, though, as in 1984, substantially less than for disciplinary and grievance arrangements. Overall, 78 per cent of manual representatives and 74 per cent of non-manual representatives reported being 'very' or 'quite' satisfied with the operation of their procedure, a small increase over 1984 but rather below the figure for 1980. In 1984 we observed rather greater dissatisfaction among public sector representatives than those in the private sector, linked, it appeared, to industrial action then under way in the public services. It was notable that this difference continued in 1990. As many as a quarter (26 per cent) of public sector representatives said that they were 'not very' or 'not at all' satisfied with their procedures for resolving pay disputes.

Final stages in pay and conditions procedures
As with procedures for disciplinary and dismissals issues we went on to ask about the form of final stages in pay and conditions procedures. These had attracted growing attention in the late 1980s, partly arising from the introduction of the new statutory requirements on industrial action balloting which we describe in Chapter 8. One obvious question here, given the broad-brush way in which such procedures have traditionally been drafted in Britain, is how far they actually included a clearly identifiable stage after which the parties were at liberty to consider industrial action.

Our question here had not been asked in previous surveys so we have no way of assessing the extent of any changes which may have occurred over time. The responses, however, suggest that the moves towards greater precision which we observed during the 1980s in the case of disciplinary and grievance procedures were not yet being carried over to pay disputes arrangements. Overall fewer than half (42 per cent) of managers reported that a specific stage of this kind was present in these procedures, with little variation across the private and public sectors and between establishments of different sizes. So far as pay determination was concerned it seemed that employers and trade unions continued to value flexibility in procedure rather than pre-determined formality. The 'failure to agree' remained for most a flexible option to be used as and when they pleased.

A second area of growing debate during the late 1980s had been the appropriateness of arbitration as a final stage in resolving disputes over pay, and the suggestion from some commentators that binding arbitration arrangements might be extended to cover new areas in both the private and public sectors. The discussion was fuelled in part by the development of a number of 'new style' agreements which included among their provisions arrangements for 'compulsory', 'straight choice' arbitration on pay as well as other matters. The development and operation of these arrangements and the lessons they suggest for the future development of employee relations in Britain are among the issues we consider in our companion volume. Here we report only a brief selection of our results.

As in our questions about disciplinary and dismissal procedures we began by defining third-party intervention in broad terms to cover the involvement not only of wholly independent bodies and individuals but, in multi-establishment organizations, of managers outside the particular workplace. Taking all such forms together, a picture once again emerged of some movement away from third-party intervention during the second part of the 1980s. As the lower part of Table 6.4 shows, overall 68 per cent of managers with pay and conditions procedures reported that these included provision for some kind of third-party intervention, compared with 79 per cent in 1984 and 70 per cent in 1980. There were falls in establishments in all sizes in both the public and private sectors, although as in previous surveys provision for reference to third parties remained more common in the former (81 per cent) than the latter (61 per cent).

As before, however, we found a rather different picture when we looked below these overall figures. We began this chapter by noting the possibility that the devolution of financial responsibilities which had been reported in many multi-establishment organizations during the 1980s might have led to a lessening of central management involvement in establishment industrial relations matters. We found, when considering disciplinary and dismissal procedures, that the reverse had occurred: if anything procedures in 1990 more often provided for the involvement of senior managers. Our results for pay procedures, while less dramatic, suggest a similar picture. As the right-hand side of Table 6.5 shows, inclusion of higher-level management continued at much the same level, 48 per cent, in 1990 as in 1984, as did provisions for involving employers' associations. The major changes, consistent again with our findings about discipline and dismissal, was in the involvement of union officials, down substantially from 24 per cent in 1984 to only 15 per cent in 1990.

The suggestion that in larger organizations a devolution of decision-making on industrial relations had taken place in the late 1980s is of particular interest where fully external third-party intervention is concerned. For if local managers were indeed assuming greater responsibilities for determining pay and conditions in their establishments one might expect them to show a growing disinclination to involve outsiders in resolving disputes.

Again, however, it turned out that reference to fully independent third-party intervention for pay issues remained at much the same level as in 1984. As then, managers reported that ACAS was referred to in a third (31 per cent) of pay and conditions procedures. One in ten establishments with such procedures also reported that they included provision for arbitration by an individual or body other than ACAS, again much the same as in 1984. Where ACAS was mentioned over half of procedures referred to the possibility of both conciliation and arbitration, with the bulk of the remainder allowing conciliation alone. Only one in 25 establishments where procedures envisaged the possibility of ACAS assistance in pay and conditions disputes allowed for arbitration alone.

Given the form of our questions and the fact that some establishments reported the possibility in their procedures of both ACAS and non-ACAS arbitration, there must be room for debate about the exact size of the total workforce whose pay and conditions procedures envisaged the

Table 6.10   Characteristics of arbitration arrangements on pay and conditions, by broad sector, 1990

Percentages

	All establishments	Private manufacturing	Private services	Public sector	Number of employees covered (millions)
Arbitrating body specified	38	38	43	27	1.0
Arbitrators decision					
final & binding	34	28	43	19	0.8
Straight choice	7	9	6	6	0.2
Base: establishments with provision for third-party intervention					
Unweighted	*373*	*127*	*143*	*216*	*373*
Weighted	*251*	*43*	*141*	*144*	*251*

possibility of arbitration in 1990. We estimate, on the basis of management responses, that a maximum of 3.5 of the 15.6 million workers covered by our survey were in scope of such provisions in 1990 and that the figure might have been as low as 2.6 million. Within private industry and commerce, procedures referring to possible ACAS involvement were to be found in most sectors and as often in foreign-owned as domestically-owned establishments, and in establishments of all ages.

As with disciplinary and dismissal issues pressure on space did not allow us to explore the extent of actual use of arbitration arrangements for resolving pay disputes.[19] We were, however, able to ask managers who had such procedures about the arrangements they had for resorting to arbitration. Table 6.10 summarizes the results. Again they suggest a continuing enthusiasm among managers for flexibility in pay procedures. Only two fifths of our respondents said, for example, that their procedure provided that the decision of an arbitrator must be final and binding on the parties. As many as another two fifths specifically denied that they were bound in this way.[20] A similar enthusiasm for flexibility arose in relation to the choice of arbitrator: rather less than half (44 per cent) of agreements specified the use of an already agreed individual or body, while a similar number (40 per cent) provided for the choice to be made only as the need arose. Even less enthusiasm was evident for straight-choice arbitration, which was envisaged by only 8 per cent of managers with procedures for arbitration. Unilateral reference, in which one party may require another to accept third-party involvement, was also reported very rarely, by only 2 per cent of those with arbitration arrangements.

Revisions to procedures

Given the scale and pace of statutory changes related to management–trade union relationships over the 1980s, we ended this section of our interviews by asking managers whether any of the four kinds of procedures discussed in this chapter had been revised since 1984 to limit the scope that trade unions had to strike or take other industrial action. Newer establishments were asked to consider changes since they had begun operating. Again we consider the results in depth in our companion volume and report them only briefly here. Overall, 5 per cent of establishments, or some one in ten (9 per cent) of establishments which recognized trade unions, said that they had introduced changes with this aim in mind, concentrated mainly in the public sector, where 13 per cent of managers reported they had taken such steps. Some one in twenty of the changes involved modifications to contracts of employment; some one in ten general restrictions on allowable industrial action; and perhaps most significantly a quarter related to new or revised balloting requirements and facilities. In two thirds of cases the changes were aimed not solely at strikes but at discouraging all forms of industrial action.

Synopsis

Results from our first survey, in 1980, suggested that the 1970s saw a massive spread of formal disciplinary and dismissal procedures across British industry and commerce. Our second and third inquiries showed that over the 1980s they became almost universal in all but the smallest workplaces. Procedures for resolving individual grievances were also widely introduced and health and safety procedures became commonplace. These arrangements were usually written down and where trade unions were recognized were almost always jointly agreed. They showed increasing precision and uniformity across all industries and types of establishment. Increasing standardization within multi-establishment organizations led to growing involvement of central management in dismissals and disciplinary appeals. On the whole, as the parties saw it, they worked well.

The reasons for this remarkable development in British industrial relations were various. One, perhaps, was the increasing incidence of non-redundancy dismissals over much of the economy which our latest survey reveals. But a key encouragement was undoubtedly the elaboration of individual employment law and the increasingly frequent public examination of employer practice undertaken by industrial tribunals when things went wrong.

Our surveys suggest that the 1980s saw changes, too, in the extent of procedures for resolving collective disputes over pay and conditions. But these procedures remained much more heavily tied than others to trade union recognition. The reduction in size of the most heavily unionized parts of the private sector over the decade led in consequence to some decline in 1990 in the numbers of establishments and workers they covered.

The form of pay procedures also changed, affected by developments in trade union structures, moves away from industry-wide bargaining towards enterprise and plant arrangements and moves by some employers to other simplifications of bargaining structure. In other respects, however, our evidence suggests that their character changed little over the 1980s. Contrary to the view expressed by some commentators, provision for central management involvement did not lessen in multi-establishment organizations. For the most part the language of procedures remained broad and general. The duties and obligations which agreements placed on the parties remained imprecise. Flexibility of form continued to be valued more highly by many managers and trade union officials than clarity and definiteness. And while third party intervention continued to be envisaged as a possibility in many procedures, it was seen for the most part more as an option the parties might consider than a binding obligation, and one whose form would be determined as and when the occasion demanded, rather than by detailed prior agreement.

Notes and references

1. The coverage of formal procedures for these matters in the 1960s and early 1970s is difficult to gauge. For discipline and dismissal the best source is perhaps the unpublished survey of 1100 establishments carried out by the Government Social Survey in 1969, which found only 8 per cent with formal disciplinary and dismissals procedures (S. Dawson (1971) *Disciplinary Practice and Procedures*, unpublished).

2. To ensure consistency with our earlier reports we concentrate mainly in this chapter on responses from management respondents, rather less on evidence from worker representatives.

3. In this chapter, as elsewhere, we define small fully independent private sector firms as single-establishment firms with fewer than 200 employees.

4. See Chapter 5.

5. We re-emphasize here that in all three surveys our definition of trade union recognition relates to recognition for pay bargaining purposes, thus excluding 'partial' recognition for representational and other purposes which may well have been present in some of these cases.

6. We shall be exploring this finding further in our companion volume.

7. The change contrasts interestingly, however, with the general trend towards plant autonomy in pay bargaining processes which we describe in Chapter 7.

8. A change consistent with ACAS's developing view that organizations were often better off not writing the Service into procedures in a routine way, lest they come to rely unduly on it to help them take difficult decisions. In relation to statutory employment rights issues ACAS is also required by statute to offer impartial conciliation assistance to parties involved in actual or prospective industrial tribunal claims. It did so on over 52,000 occasions in 1990 (see ACAS (1991) *Annual Report, 1990*, ACAS, London).

9. In defining these different kinds of sanctions we benefited from the ACAS Handbook (1988) *Discipline at Work*, ACAS, London.

10. Our focus in 1980 was on the operation of the Truck Acts which then regulated the practice of deductions for certain manual workers. Subsequently the law was changed by the Wages Act 1986 which provided different, arguably more limited, protections for a much broader range of workers.

11. In 1980 we noted a clear relationship between the use of disciplinary deductions and the presence, as managers saw it, of poor industrial relations in the establishment. In 1990 that relationship was not present.

12. The question remained unchanged during the three surveys. In 1980 it was immediately preceded in the interview by questions about redundancies. In 1984 and 1990 these were not asked at this point, perhaps emphasizing less prominently the differences between redundancies and other dismissals. It is possible also, given moves away from trade union based methods of management – employee relations that dismissals which were once seen as collective redundancies were increasingly seen by managements at the end of the decade as multiple individual dismissals. If true this might partly explain the substantial increases in dismissal rates between 1984 and 1990 which are noted below.

13. Only above this unemployment rate was there a significant fall in dismissal rates and caution is needed in interpreting this finding because of the small number of observations available at this end of the distribution.

14. We suggested in our report on the 1984 survey that the very 'flexibility' of labour utilization provided by a 'non-standard' workforce might operate so as to lessen the need for dismissal of 'core' employees. Since then a substantial body of work has appeared exploring the notion of 'flexibility', distinguishing for example between flex-

ibility in numbers of staff employed, in hours worked and in functions performed by staff (see, for example, C. Hakim (1990) 'Core and periphery in employers' workforce strategies: evidence from the 1987 ELUS survey', *Work. Employment and Society*, 4, 2, pp. 157–88). This particular issue has yet, however, to be explored in any depth.

15. This is one of a number of findings which suggest that employee relations may differ between establishments with and without substantial proportions of workers from ethnic minorities. Time has not allowed us to explore in detail how and why this should be so, and what significance it might have.

16. In 1990 there were no fewer than 22 jurisdictions which could form the basis of a complaint to an industrial tribunal.

17. To maintain comparability with 1980 and 1984 we report responses here of worker representatives from recognized trade unions, omitting those from the small number of other worker representatives interviewed in 1990.

18. Again this finding reflects our tight definition of recognition. In many of these situations some of the parties might have seen the situation as one of partial or informal recognition.

19. We know from other sources that this must have been small. ACAS, for example, arranged no more than 200 arbitrations in 1990, covering non-pay as well as pay issues; the Central Arbitration Committee only seven (see ACAS (1990) op. cit; Central Arbitration Committee (1991) *Annual Report for 1990*, CAC, London). Such evidence as is available of the use of straight choice arbitration in pay disputes suggests that hearings have never been common in Britain and in the three years to 1991 have been very rare (S. Milner (forthcoming 1992) *Final Offer Arbitration in the UK*, Department of Employment, Research Paper No 99, London.

20. Perhaps for this reason ACAS arranges arbitrations for parties only after it has received voluntary assurances from all sides involved that the decision of the arbitrator will be observed.

Table 6A   Extent of procedures and rate of dismissal per thousand employees, by industry, 1990

Percentages

	Pay & conditions	Procedures for		Health & safety	Rate of dismissal per '000 employees
		Discipline & dismissals	Individual grievances		
All industries	**65**	**90**	**88**	**89**	**15**
All manufacturing	**63**	**91**	**81**	**85**	**20**
Metals & Mineral Products	70	93	82	88	15
Chemicals & Manufactured Fibres	(43)¹	(87)	(100)	(95)	(8)
Metal Goods	(48)	(83)	(54)	(67)	(29)
Mechanical Engineering	65	86	79	92	15
Electrical & Instrument Engineering	61	100	97	83	23
Vehicles & Transport Equipment	87	89	89	89	6
Food, Drink & Tobacco	57	94	84	82	21
Textiles	(66)	(100)	(69)	(85)	(31)
Leather, Footwear & Clothing	(53)	(91)	(70)	(80)	(28)
Timber & Furniture, Paper & Printing	68	88	79	78	20
Rubber, Plastics & Other Manufacturing	(70)	(92)	(90)	(100)	(28)
All services	**68**	**92**	**90**	**89**	**13**
Energy & Water	95	100	100	94	9
Construction	57	79	73	80	17
Wholesale Distribution	58	92	83	87	19
Retail Distribution	68	95	93	95	22
Hotels, Catering, Repairs	57	88	86	89	46
Transport	68	89	82	82	19
Posts and Telecommunications	93	100	100	100	18
Banking, Finance, Insurance	90	95	100	97	4
Business Services	46	76	84	63	18
Central Government	79	100	95	95	2
Local Government	81	93	92	92	3
Higher Education	(40)	(60)	(60)	(73)	(3)
Other Education	62	97	95	92	2
Medical Services	86	100	91	92	5
Other Services	69	94	93	93	14

Base: all establishments (see Table 1A for bases and SIC codes)
¹ See Note B.

7 Pay Determination

In Chapter 3 we outlined some of the basic institutional structures of industrial relations in Britain and how the part played by trade unions had changed over the ten years covered by our surveys. We saw how the proportion of workplaces in which there were recognized trade unions had declined substantially in the latter half of the decade, suggesting a marked diminution in the role of collective bargaining in the determination of pay. Fewer establishments belonged to employers' associations, as we saw in Chapter 2, so that multi-employer bargaining could be expected to have diminished. But other developments would have suggested changes along these lines. Government policy, both through its dealings with its own employees and through persuasion and advocacy to other employers, encouraged a move away from national, multi-employer pay settlements towards more locally determined ones which were more sensitive to local labour markets and the circumstances of the employer. Systems of payment that bound employees into the financial destiny of their firm were encouraged by fiscal incentives. In parallel with this there was a pervasive advocacy of payment systems that reflect the performance of individual employees. These developments were seen as contributing to a more general goal of making the British labour market more responsive to economic circumstances and local conditions.

While the structures and processes of pay determination were the subject of much debate, the outcome of those processes – the levels of earnings received by employees – were of even greater interest. For employees, their income from employment constituted the economic reward for their work; for employers, employees' earnings represented a substantial element of their costs, in some cases the largest element. For the government, employees' earnings were the major precursor of consumer expenditure as well as an important determinant of employers' costs and hence the competitiveness and success of the economy. None of the main economic actors in the country could be indifferent to levels of pay and changes to those levels.

Against that backcloth we now undertake a more detailed examination of how pay is determined in the greater part of the British economy covered by our surveys – and of how the pattern of pay determination changed over the period. We begin by looking at the population of workplaces as a whole, using our separate questioning for manual and non-manual employees. Subsequently, we describe more detailed analysis for the three broad sectors of employment.

Pay determination – the overall pattern
To produce this general picture we use data from two pairs of questions in our interviews with managers, one pair relating to manual workers, the other to non-manual employees. In workplaces where there were recognized trade unions for manual employees we asked managers which was the most important of a number of levels of negotiations applying to the largest, or only, group of manual workers covered by collective bargaining when their most recent pay settlement was made.[1] The three 'levels' were multi-employer bargaining at national or regional level, single-employer bargaining, and plant or establishment bargaining.[2] We asked an identical question in relation to non-manual employees. The responses to these two questions are shown in the upper half of Table 7.1. Alternatively, where there were no recognized trade unions for manual workers and pay was therefore not determined by collective bargaining we asked a different question. Again referring to the most recent occasion, we asked where decisions were made about the level of pay. Responses to this question, and an equivalent one for non-manual workers, are given in the lower half of Table 7.1.

The first line in the table reproduces the changes in the overall extent of trade union recognition for collective bargaining, as already described in Chapter 3. Here we concentrate on the levels at which negotiations took place. As expected, the results show a substantial reduction of the extent to which there was multi-employer bargaining over rates of pay between 1984 and 1990; this more than reversed the increase between 1980 and 1984, which in our previous report we attributed to changes in the composition of our sample and to improved interviewing and coding in the 1984 survey.[3] In only a quarter of workplaces was multi-employer bargaining the main method of pay determination for manual workers in 1990; for non-manual employees the proportion was also a quarter. But multi-employer bargaining remained the predominant form of collective bargaining in the economy as a whole. Single-employer bargaining involving more than one site continued at very much the same extent as before, affecting around 15 per cent of establishments in respect of manual and non-manual employees alike. Establishment bargaining, the least prevalent level of collective bargaining, also stayed constant, affecting just over 5 per cent of workplaces regarding manual workers and just under 5 per cent for non-manual employees.

There were more marked changes in relation to the way pay was determined where there was no collective bargaining. Regarding manual

Table 7.1   Basis for most recent pay increase, all sectors, 1980, 1984 and 1990

Percentages

	Manual employees			Non-manual employees		
	1980	1984	1990	1980	1984	1990
Result of collective bargaining	55	62	48	47	54	43
Most important level:						
Multi-employer	32[1]	40	26	29	36	24
Single employer, multi-plant	12	13	13	11	13	15
Plant/establishment	9	7	6	4	4	3
Other answer	1	1	2	2	1	1
Not result of collective bargaining	44	38	52	53	46	57
Locus of decision about increase:						
Management at establishment	..[2]	20[3]	31	..	30	37
Management at higher level	..	11	15	..	15	17
National joint body	..	5	4	..	2	5
Wages Council	..	3	2	..	1	*
Not stated	..	1	*	..	*	*
Base: establishments with employees named in column heads						
Unweighted	*1899*	*1853*	*1831*	*2034*	*2010*	*2058*
Weighted	*1823*	*1749*	*1697*	*1988*	*1985*	*1992*

[1] See Note D.
[2] See Note J.
[3] See Note F.

workers, it became much more common for pay levels to be set by management at the workplace itself, the proportion rising from 20 per cent in 1984 to 31 per cent in 1990. For non-manual employees there was also an increase, but not so large (from 30 to 37 per cent). The second most common arrangement was determination by management at a higher level in the organization, which also showed modest increases. The two remaining categories remained uncommon. Determination by a statutory Wages Council continued to affect fewer than 5 per cent of establishments in our survey, the bulk of workplaces covered by the Wages Councils system being below our 25-employee threshold. Other national bodies, such as employers' associations, national negotiating bodies and public sector pay review bodies set rates of pay which management implemented in around 5 per cent of establishments – again little different from the figures in 1984.

These broad findings raise a number of questions which can more easily be addressed if we examine the three broad sectors of employment separately. By doing this in the sections that follow we shall see whether the overall pattern of change shown in Table 7.1 reflects similar movements in different parts of the economy or a variety of changes in pay determination procedures across and within them. We begin this analysis by looking at private manufacturing industry, introducing additional evidence from our survey questions as we do so.

Pay determination in private manufacturing
Table 7.2 shows data similar to those given in Table 7.1, but confined to establishments in private manufacturing industry. The first line of the table shows the familiar decline in the extent of collective bargaining for manual workers which we first discussed in Chapter 3. The next line shows a continuation of the decline in multi-employer bargaining that was evident between 1980 and 1984, with a further fall from 22 to 16 per cent of establishments with manual workers by 1990. This followed the decline in membership of employers' associations which we mentioned in Chapter 2. Indeed, establishments that were affiliated to an employers' association were just as likely to regard their national agreement as the most important influence on the pay of manual workers in 1990 as in 1984; it was just that so many fewer of them were members.

The other substantial change in the upper part of Table 7.2 is the fall in the extent to which non-manual employees had their pay determined by single-employer bargaining. But in general the upper half of the table indicates that the balance between bargaining levels for workplaces that had collective bargaining did not change dramatically between 1984 and 1990. Plant-level bargaining became the most important level for manual workers in rather more workplaces than either multi-employer or single-employer bargaining. For non-manual employees plant-level bargaining

Table 7.2   Basis for most recent pay increase in private manufacturing industry, 1980, 1984 and 1990

Percentages

	Manual employees			Non-manual employees		
	1980	1984	1990	1980	1984	1990
Result of collective bargaining	65	55	45	27	26	24
Most important level:						
Multi-employer	27[1]	22	16	5	5	7
Single-employer, multi-plant	10	11	8	8	9	5
Plant/establishment	26	21	19	13	11	9
Other answer	1	1	2	*	1	2
Not result of collective bargaining	35	45	55	73	74	76
Locus of decision about increase:						
Management at establishment	.[2]	33[3]	44	..	53	59
Management at higher level	..	10	9	..	21	17
National joint body	..	2	3	..	1	2
Wages Council	..	1	2	..	*	—
Not stated	..	*	1	..	*	*
Base: private manufacturing establishments with employees named in column heads						
Unweighted	*734*	*580*	*616*	*743*	*592*	*630*
Weighted	*498*	*412*	*417*	*503*	*424*	*426*

[1] See Note D.
[2] See Note J.
[3] See Note F.

remained the most common type of bargaining, although still affecting only about 10 per cent of workplaces.

There was more change in relation to managerially-determined pay. The proportion of workplaces where pay was determined at workplace level by management increased substantially for manual workers, from 33 per cent in 1984 to 44 per cent in 1990. Only a small part of this can be attributed to the fact that there were more independent workplaces in our manufacturing sample in 1990 than there were in 1984. The bulk of the change was because many more establishments that belonged to larger enterprises determined the pay of manual workers locally. For non-manual workers there was also a change in the same direction, but a smaller one. There was thus a general move away from decisions about pay being made at head offices or other managerial levels above the establishment, a change that is consonant with the picture of increased managerial autonomy which we outlined in Chapter 2. However, the characteristics of enterprises continued to have some influence on where pay was decided. When we looked at establishments that were part of a larger enterprise (roughly half of those in manufacturing without recognized unions) it appeared, for example, that pay was more likely to be determined at above-establishment level if the firm was vertically integrated, had several levels of management and was in a product market with many competitors.

So far our analysis has looked only at the proportions of workplaces using the different methods of pay determination. In our previous reports we showed that different methods predominated in different sizes of establishment and that looking at the proportion of employees in workplaces using the different methods gave a rather different picture from that obtained from looking at the proportion of establishments. In particular, plant-level bargaining was very much a feature of establishments with large numbers of manual workers, so that when we looked at the proportions of employees covered by the different methods plant-level bargaining was much more prevalent. This relationship persisted in the 1990 survey and is confirmed by comparing the 1990 results in Table 7.2 with those given in Table 7.3. For example, in Table 7.2 it can be seen that in 19 per cent of establishments plant bargaining for manual workers was most important, whereas Table 7.3 shows that 34 per cent of manual workers were in such establishments. A similar size effect for plant bargaining was apparent for non-manual employees, the corresponding figures being 9 per cent of establishments, but 24 per cent of non-manual employees. Enterprise-level bargaining was also more common in large plants, but the association was not so marked.

On the other hand, establishments where decisions about pay were made unilaterally by management tended to be smaller than those where it was agreed through collective bargaining. In consequence, the propor-

Table 7.3 **Basis for most recent pay increase in private manufacturing industry, 1984 and 1990 – employee analysis**

Percentages

	Manual employees		Non-manual employees	
	1984	1990	1984	1990
Result of collective bargaining	79	70	59	50
Most important level:				
Multi-employer	24[1]	19	8	6
Single-employer, multi-plant	19	15	19	17
Plant/establishment	35	34	31	24
Other answer	2	2	*	3
Not result of collective bargaining	21	30	41	50
Locus of decision about increase:				
Management at establishment	15[2]	25	32	41
Management at higher level	6	5	10	11
National body	2	1	1	1
Wages Council	*	1	*	—
Not stated	—	*	*	*

Base: employees named in column heads in private manufacturing establishments

[1] See Note D.
[2] See Note F.

tion of employees covered by such arrangements was smaller than the proportion of establishments in which they were found. Forty four per cent of manufacturing plants had wage-setting by local management for manual workers, whereas only 25 per cent of manual workers were employed in such plants.

Table 7.3 portrays, then, a rather different picture of pay determination arrangements in private manufacturing industry from that given in Table 7.2. But in terms of changes between 1984 and 1990 the story is very much the same. Fewer employees had their basic rates of pay primarily determined by multi-employer agreements with trade unions, enterprise bargaining declined a little, and plant-level bargaining declined slightly. Wage setting by management rose correspondingly, but only at plant level. The only point of real divergence between the two analyses arose in relation to non-manual employees. The employee-based analysis showed more marked changes for non-manual employees: for them plant-level bargaining declined (from 31 per cent in 1984 to 24 per cent in 1990) and plant-level determination by management increased (from 32 to 41 per cent). This may suggest that, particularly in larger establishments, pay for non-manual employees was less likely to be set by bargaining arrangements similar to those for manual workers at the same plant, but was more likely to be dealt with quite separately by management. Moreover, returning to an earlier point, the results do not show a movement from multi-employer to enterprise bargaining in manufacturing, but rather a change from multi-employer bargaining to no formal bargaining over rates of pay.

To explore further the picture of pay determination in manufacturing we now need to move away from the simplified sketch so far provided and fill out some of the detail, particularly on collective bargaining. For this we confine our discussion to establishments with recognized unions for manual workers, or for non-manual employees, as appropriate. There are several respects in which our discussion so far has been incomplete.

First, we obtained information only about the largest bargaining unit. As we saw in our discussion of bargaining structures in Chapter 3, a substantial minority of workplaces in manufacturing had more than one bargaining unit involved in separate negotiations about pay. It is reasonable to ask how typical were the arrangements for the largest group in such cases. Results from our first survey showed that pay bargaining levels for the second largest group were similar to the largest group. This led us to drop the questions for the second largest group in the second and third surveys. However, if the largest group now covered a much smaller proportion of employees, the results for it – although strictly comparable – could be less representative than previously of collective bargaining as a whole. This possibility can be assessed by looking at the data we collected in the 1984 and 1990 surveys on the proportion of employees covered by the largest negotiating group. In private manufacturing, the average in 1984 was 85 per cent for manual workers. That is to say, 85 per cent of manual workers in establishments with recognized manual unions were covered by the largest (or only) bargaining unit. In 1990 the comparable proportion was 83 per cent.[4] For non-manual employees the respective figures were 53 per cent and 51 per cent. Furthermore, even in establishments where there were several bargaining units it was still the case in 1990 that the majority of employees was covered by the largest one. We can, therefore, continue to regard our data on bargaining levels as representative of establishments' bargaining arrangements as a whole.

On the other hand, our data on bargaining arrangements for non-manual employees are clearly not a fair representation of how pay is determined for all non-manual employees in those establishments. This is because, in the main, the remainder of the non-manual workforce was not covered by collective bargaining at all, but had their pay settled without the agreement of trade unions or staff associations. In about a third of cases it was determined by management at a higher level in the enterprise, reflecting the likelihood that many of those affected were professional employees or managers themselves. But in the majority of cases for non-manual employees, and the great majority for manual workers, where employees were not covered by the collective bargaining arrangements at their workplace their pay was generally set by local management.[5]

The second respect in which our picture of bargaining levels has so far been incomplete is that we have only talked about what management thought was the *most important* level of bargaining in the most recent settlement. It is a feature of the British industrial relations system that the pay of an individual employee may be the subject of collective bargaining at more than one level. Frequently in manufacturing industry, until the early 1980s, national multi-employer agreements about basic rates of pay would be supplemented by additional amounts negotiated at a later stage on a company or individual plant basis. The extent to which this happened was revealed in our surveys by asking, prior to the question about the most important level, which of the levels already mentioned affected the pay of the group. Table 7.4 shows the results from these questions for manual and non-manual groups for the three surveys. From this it appears that the reduction in the amount of bargaining activity which we observed between 1980 and 1984 did not continue. The mean number of stages at which bargaining took place remained at its 1984 figure: 1.2 for manual groups and 1.1 for non-manual groups. Our panel sample showed similar stability between 1984 and 1990, the figures for both manual and non-manual employees matching those in the cross-sectional sample almost precisely.

In the minority of cases where multi-stage bargaining occurred, the most common combination was a multi-employer agreement supplemented by a plant-level agreement. Such was the case in 70 per cent of the establishments where manual workers were affected by multi-level bargaining. For non-manual groups the most common combination was multi-employer and enterprise bargaining, with multi-employer and plant also being reported.

These results, showing no change in the mean number of bargaining levels since 1984, allow us a firmer interpretation of the changes in the levels at which bargaining occurred. The fall in the extent of multi-employer bargaining between 1984 and 1990 apparent in Tables 7.2, 7.3 and 7.4, particularly for manual workers, came about from a move to other levels of bargaining (especially plant level) or, more commonly, to unilateral determination by management. It did not occur because fewer establishments supplemented national agreements with plant-level agreements.

Table 7.4   Levels of bargaining that influenced pay increases in private manufacturing industry, 1980, 1984 and 1990

	Manual employees			Non-manual employees		
	1980	1984	1990	1980	1984	1990
						Percentages
Multi-employer	61[1]	50	42	29	22	19
Single-employer, multi-plant	20	21	20	32	38	36
Plant/establishment	53	49	56	57	43	52
Other answer	2	2	—	3	5	—
Not stated	*	1	2	1	*	2
						Means
Average (where levels stated)	1.4	1.2	1.2	1.2	1.1	1.1
Base: private manufacturing establishments with recognized unions for employees named in column heads						
Unweighted	589	462	437	404	351	249
Weighted	322	228	184	134	109	47

[1] See Note E.

Table 7.4, confined to workplaces with recognized unions for the relevant category of employees, shows more clearly than the earlier tables the shift in the locus of bargaining away from multi-employer national agreements to establishment and to enterprise-level bargaining. Over the 1980s as a whole, there was a very substantial decline in the use of national, multi-employer negotiations for manual workers (from 61 to 42 per cent of workplaces with recognized manual unions) and a small increase in plant-level bargaining (from 53 to 56 per cent). For non-manual employees the changes were somewhat different and more diverse: again a decline in national agreements, but a small fall in plant-level bargaining and a rise in enterprise bargaining.

The decline in the influence of multi-employer, national agreements has, of course, been widely reported in the specialist media.[6] Less remarked on has been the role of foreign firms in this change. In our previous report we drew attention to the much less frequent participation of foreign-owned plants in multi-employer agreements, a finding confirmed by further analysis.[7] This association is still very much apparent in the 1990 results. When we add to this the fact that foreign-owned workplaces formed a greater proportion of all private manufacturing workplaces (especially larger ones), it is difficult to dismiss the suggestion that the increase in overseas-owned firms played a part in the decline in multi-employer bargaining.[8]

The third elaboration we wish to make of our picture of pay determination in manufacturing is to unravel what we have so far referred to as 'enterprise-level' or single-employer bargaining. Following the practice adopted in the 1985 Company Level Industrial Relations Survey[9] we distinguished in our 1990 questions between bargaining that covered 'this employer – all establishments' and 'this employer, but only some establishments'. Until now we have combined these two categories in reporting our 1990 results to make them comparable with the previous two surveys. In fact, the former category, 'this employer – all establishments' was the more frequently reported.[10] What we might call 'employer-wide' bargaining accounted for about two thirds of cases with single-employer (but multi-site) bargaining in relation to manual workers in manufacturing. With respect to non-manual employees the proportion was around four fifths.[11] This difference again reflects the greater tendency for pay to be determined locally for manual workers than for white-collar employees.

Pay determination in private service industries
The pattern of change in arrangements for determining pay in the private services sector of employment varied considerably from manufacturing. We begin again with the overall picture, as given in Table 7.5. Here the proportion of establishments with collective bargaining fell

Table 7.5   Basis for most recent pay increase in private services, 1980, 1984 and 1990

Percentages

	Manual employees			Non-manual employees		
	1980	1984	1990	1980	1984	1990
Result of collective bargaining	34	38	31	28	30	26
Most important level:						
Multi-employer	19[1]	20	11	12	11	5
Single-employer, multi-plant	10	12	16	10	15	19
Plant/establishment	3	4	4	2	3	1
Other answer	*	2	*	5	*	*
Not result of collective bargaining	66	62	69	72	70	73
Locus of decision about increase:						
Management at establishment	..[2]	30[3]	44	..	45	50
Management at higher level	..	21	21	..	24	24
National joint body	..	9	3	..	3	1
Wages Council	..	5	3	..	2	1
Not stated	..	1	—	..	1	*
Base: private services establishments with employees named in column heads						
Unweighted	*521*	*515*	*654*	*585*	*593*	*798*
Weighted	*733*	*689*	*780*	*854*	*836*	*977*

[1] See Note D.
[2] See Note J.
[3] See Note F.

only slightly over the 1980s as a whole, but the fall since 1984 was more marked. Multi-employer bargaining showed a substantial decline as the most important level affecting both manual and white-collar employees; the proportion of establishments reporting it fell from 20 per cent to 11 per cent between 1984 and 1990 for manual workers and from 11 to 5 per cent for non-manual employees. However, in contrast to the change in manufacturing, bargaining at single-employer, multi-site level increased substantially in private services. It affected nearly twice as many private services establishments in 1990 as it did in 1980. Establishment-level bargaining remained very rare in this sector. The equivalent analysis in terms of employees rather than establishments is given in Table 7.6. The pattern of change that it shows is very similar to that given in Table 7.5.

Where pay was not determined by collective bargaining the changes were like those in manufacturing. Pay was set by management at establishment level at more workplaces in 1990, particularly with respect to

Table 7.6   **Basis for most recent pay increase in private services, 1984 and 1990 – employee analysis**

Percentages

	Manual employees		Non-manual employees	
	1984	1990	1984	1990
Result of collective bargaining	53	42	40	38
Most important level:				
Multi-employer	26	13	16	6[1]
Single-employer, multi-plant	17	22	18	28
Plant/establishment	8	6	6	2
Other answer	2	1	*	1
Not result of collective				
bargaining	47	58	60	62
Locus of decision about increase:				
Management at establishment	15[2]	32	39	46
Management at higher level	22	22	20	18
National body	9	3	2	1
Wages Council	5	2	2	1
Not stated	*	—	*	*

Base: employees named in column heads in private services establishments

[1] See Note D.
[2] See Note F.

Table 7.7   Levels of bargaining that influenced pay increases in private service industries, 1980, 1984 and 1990

	Manual employees			Non-manual employees		
	1980	1984	1990	1980	1984	1990
						Percentages
Multi-employer	62[1]	58	41	46	37	18
Single employer, multi-plant	40	38	49	50	59	78
Plant/establishment	14	14	15	8	12	6
Other answer	7	2	—	11	2	—
Not stated	1	1	1	4	*	*
						Means
Average (where levels stated)	1.2	1.1	1.05	1.2	1.1	1.0
Base: private services establishments with recognized unions for employees named in column heads						
Unweighted	227	231	264	207	229	258
Weighted	253	260	219	236	247	213

[1] See Note E.

manual workers. Management at higher organizational levels was the locus of decision-making on pay in a minority of cases and the size of this minority did not change. These findings are mirrored in the employee analysis shown in Table 7.6.

In elaborating the picture of collectively bargained pay in private service industries we repeated the analyses described earlier for manufacturing. Our data about the largest bargaining unit were also representative of the large majority of manual workers in private services: in 1990, 77 per cent of manual workers were covered by the largest unit as were 72 per cent of non-manual employees, in establishments where they had recognized unions. These are, again, of the same order as the 1984 figures.[12] However, in contrast to the situation in manufacturing, employees excluded from the collective bargaining arrangements for other employees at their workplace had their pay set, in the main, by management higher in the organization. For the predominant non-manual employees this was so in about four fifths of cases; for manual employees it was so in about half.

Turning to the question of multiple levels of bargaining, Table 7.7 shows a reduction since 1984 in the number of levels of bargaining affecting both manual and non-manual workers' pay in private services. This continued the trend apparent since 1980. In fact, multi-stage bargaining, which characteristically involved multi-employer and subsequent company negotiations at the beginning of the decade, had virtually disappeared by 1990. This reflected the very sharp reduction in multi-employer bargaining which is evident from the top row of Table 7.7.

Single-employer bargaining, which had become the dominant form in private services, especially for the more numerous non-manual employees, was even more likely than in manufacturing to cover all establishments in a company. Thus 'enterprise-wide' settlements affected 94 per cent of workplaces with single-employer bargaining for manual workers; the corresponding figure for non-manual employees was 98 per cent.

Pay determination in the public sector

Throughout the 1980s the Government set its face against direct intervention in the determination of pay in the private sector. In the public sector things were different. Here the Government sought to influence both the level of pay settlements and the structures through which they were reached. We have already referred in Chapter 3 to a number of changes in the public sector that would inevitably affect the picture of pay determination in that sector in 1990. There was the dismantling of the collective bargaining machinery for settling the pay of nurses and midwives in the National Health Service and its replacement by a Pay Review Body. There was a similar move affecting teachers in state schools in England and Wales. Privatization removed many of the trading monopolies from the public sector altogether - and thus some of the largest workplaces with very high coverage of collective bargaining. And the contracting out of many services by local and central government could be expected to remove large numbers of employees from the scope of collective bargaining. How far was the basic picture of public sector pay determination changed by such developments? Tables 7.8 and 7.9 provide the answer.[13]

The establishment-level analysis of Table 7.8 indicates a very substantial drop in the extent of workplaces with collective bargaining, as already indicated in Chapter 3, for both manual and non-manual employees. Almost all of this fall was in multi-employer bargaining and was in the public services administered by local government. There was a corresponding increase in the proportion of establishments where pay was determined unilaterally by management at higher levels in the organization or by some external body. The large increase in this latter category in relation to non-manual employees, from 1 per cent in 1984

Table 7.8   Basis for most recent pay increase in the public sector, 1984 and 1990

Percentages

	Manual employees		Non-manual employees	
	1984	1990	1984	1990
Result of collective bargaining	91	78	98	84
Most important level:				
Multi-employer	72[1]	58	83	67
Single-employer, multi-plant	16	13	13	13
Plant/establishment	1	1	1	*
Other answer	3	5	2	3
Not result of collective bargaining	9	22	2	16
Locus of decision about increase:				
Management at establishment	1	1	*	*
Management at higher level	2	11	—	5
National body	3	7	1	11
Wages Council	2	*	—	—
Not stated	1	1	*	*

Base: public sector establishments with employees named in column heads
Unweighted	758	561	825	630
Weighted	648	500	726	590

[1] See Note D.

to 11 per cent in 1990, reflects the changed arrangements for determining the pay of teachers, nurses and midwives which we referred to above. The employee-based analysis of Table 7.9 indicates changes in the same direction but on a more limited scale. This is largely because the state school sector contains a large number of establishments with relatively few employees.

Both tables show that in early 1990 it remained the case that rates of pay were hardly ever settled at the level of the individual workplace in the public sector. Whether we look at manual or non-manual employees and at collectively determined pay or managerially determined pay, the findings are that 1 per cent or less of workplaces were involved and that 1 per cent or less of employees were affected. There is no indication in these results, then, of any delegation of pay determination to local levels in the public sector. The contrast between the public and private sectors in this respect still remained as striking as ever.[14]

When we elaborated our analysis of the public sector a number of notable differences between the public and private sectors emerged. The

Table 7.9   Basis for most recent pay increase in the public sector, 1984 and 1990 – employee analysis

Percentages

	Manual employees		Non-manual employees	
	1984	1990	1984	1990
Result of collective bargaining	98	92	99	90
Most important level:				
Multi-employer	74	72	87	76
Single-employer, multi-plant	20	17	11	12
Plant/establishment	2	1	1	*
Other answer	2	2	*	2
Not result of collective bargaining	2	7	1	9
Locus of decision about increase:				
Management at establishment	*	*	*	1
Management at higher level	*	3[1]	—	2
National body	1	3	1	6
Wages Council	1	*	—	—
Not stated	*	*	*	*

Base: employees named in column heads in public sector establishments

[1] See Note D.

predominance of national pay-setting arrangements was apparent whether we looked at the most important level of bargaining as seen by our management respondents (as given in Tables 7.8 and 7.9) or whether we took all the levels of negotiation that might affect a pay increase. But there had been changes in the extent of multiple-stage bargaining. For manual workers the mean number of stages fell from 1.14 to 1.04; but for non-manual employees the mean number rose from 1.07 to 1.17. It thus became common for white-collar employees in several parts of the public services sector of employment to have their pay partly determined by a national agreement and partly by a settlement confined to their own employer. On this basis, then, we can detect a move towards more local pay-setting arrangements for public service employees, although the contrast with the private sector remained strong.

The process of pay determination

So far in this chapter we have been looking at the basic structures through which pay is determined. Because our data are very largely obtained from respondents at establishment level, when our 1980 results were published they were suspected by some commentators of giving an exaggerated picture of the degree of autonomy of local management on pay matters. Such fears have been shown to have been largely unfounded by more recent research using data from respondents at different levels in the same organizations.[15] But clearly there are limits to the matters about which establishment managers can reasonably be asked and these have been recognized in the WIRS series.[16] Our questioning about the processes of pay bargaining has therefore generally been limited to cases where bargaining occurred at establishment level. In both 1984 and 1990 we asked managers two questions about whether they consulted managers higher in their organization about the most recent negotiations.[17] The questions were only asked in workplaces with recognized trade unions and where the manager reported the establishment as being the most important (or, in most cases, only) level of bargaining. The great majority of such cases were in private manufacturing industry. The two questions were whether they consulted management at a higher level in their organization before the start of the most recent negotiations and, secondly, whether they consulted at a higher level during the negotiations.

When we examined comparable results for the two surveys there appeared to have been no overall change in the extent of consultation with higher level management on pay negotiations. Before the start of negotiations about three fifths of managers in both surveys consulted with their superiors regarding manual pay negotiations. Regarding non-manual pay negotiations the proportion was about a half in both surveys. Consultations during negotiations with the trade unions were rather less common than consultations beforehand, but this was equally as true in 1990 as in 1984. On this measure, then, a move towards more local management autonomy is not evident.

In 1984, managements in foreign-owned workplaces appeared to behave differently from their British counterparts. They consulted with higher management more often prior to negotiations, but during negotiations they were less likely to consult up the line. In 1990 the pattern was different: foreign-owned plants more often consulted higher management both before and during negotiations than their British-owned counterparts. Whether this change in the pattern reflects a shift in the behaviour of long-established foreign-owned plants or results from the arrival of new ones with different practices is a question that could be addressed in further analysis of the WIRS data.

Consultations with their members by union negotiators
On the employee side of pay bargaining, union negotiators may also consult their constituents at various stages. We asked our trade union respondents whether there were consultations with members before the start of negotiations and, separately, before the final settlement was reached. Where there were, we asked how union members had ex-

Table 7.10 Consultations with union members by union negotiators prior to a final pay settlement, 1984 and 1990

Percentages

| | Largest manual bargaining unit | | Largest non-manual bargaining unit | |
	1984	1990	1984	1990
Any consultation with members	64	77	45	70
Method, if consulted:				
General feeling of meeting				
without a vote	19[1]	14	14	21
Show of hands at meeting	62	47	56	19
Voting slips/secret ballot at				
workplace or other meeting place	14	26	18	31
Postal ballot/secret postal ballot	5	14	12	33
Other answer	5	1	5	3
Base: worker representatives from recognized trade unions				
Unweighted	*894*	*716*	*946*	*663*
Weighted	*533*	*362*	*557*	*334*

[1] Base is establishments where consultations were reported.

pressed their views. Our questions about the initial consultation were limited to cases where bargaining took place at establishment level; the later questions covered all levels of bargaining. Our analysis is concentrated on the later questions because they give a broader picture of consultations with members about pay and because they relate to a more critical stage in most negotiations. Table 7.10 gives the overall results for 1984 and 1990.

There was a substantial increase in the extent of consultation by union negotiators between 1984 and 1990, particularly those negotiating on behalf of non-manual employees. By 1990 about three quarters of worker representatives reported such consultations: 70 per cent of non-manual representatives and 77 per cent of manual stewards. Increases were registered in all three broad sectors of employment, but consultation remained less common in the public sector than the private sector.

Changes in the method of consultation were also apparent. Informal methods (taking the general feeling of a meeting of members or asking them for a show of hands) became less common and gave ground to more formal and private methods (ballots at a meeting, at the workplace or through the post).[18] Informal methods remained the most common for manual workers (accounting for 61 per cent of cases); for non-manual employees, formal ballots were used in 64 per cent of cases and ousted informal methods as the most common.

The 1990 results showed a clear relationship between the amount and method of consultation and the most important level of bargaining (as reported by the trade union respondent). National, multi-employer bargaining entailed the least amount of consultation with ordinary union members. Plant-level bargaining involved consultation more often and was strongly associated with informal, face-to-face methods. These patterns are as might be expected in view of the different sizes of the bargaining units involved, as well as the practicalities of consulting in different situations.

Management consultations with employees when pay was not negotiated

Our third set of questions about the process of pay determination concerned employees whose pay was not negotiated by trade unions. We asked managers in these situations whether management alone decided on the level of pay or whether they discussed or consulted with employees or their representatives about it. These questions were asked if there were no recognized unions for manual (or non-manual) employees or if there were recognized unions but not all manual (or non-manual) employees were covered by the negotiations. The former cases were much more numerous, as we showed earlier in the chapter, and are the main focus of our attention here.

The extent of consultation about pay levels remained very much as it was in 1984.[19] The proportion of managers reporting consultations about manual workers' pay in 1990 was 23 per cent; for non-manual employees it was 19 per cent. There was interesting variation around these overall figures. Establishments were more likely to have had consultations if they were in manufacturing industry rather than private services (few were in the public sector because recognition was so widespread there) and if there were any union members present. Non-manual employees were particularly likely to have been consulted if manual workers had recognized unions. But the most striking difference was between establishments that had a consultative committee and those that did not. Those that did were twice as likely to consult employees or their representatives before deciding about increases in general rates of pay. And in the rare instances where the committee's representatives were chosen by trade unions it was almost always the case that there were discussions or consultations about pay increases.

The second type of situation where we asked if there were consultations about pay increases was where some (manual or non-manual) employees were covered by collectively bargained pay but others were not. These were much less common than those we referred to in the previous paragraph. But the influence of the unions can be seen to extend sometimes beyond those that they represent: about of a third of managers in establishments where pay was subject to collective bargaining for some workers but not for others said they discussed or consulted with employees or their representatives about general pay increases for employees not covered by the bargaining groups (compared with about a fifth where there were no recognized unions). Here, too, there was no change between 1984 and 1990.

Influences on the size of basic pay settlements
A further feature of the process of determining basic rates of pay that we included in our survey questions was the set of considerations taken into account by management negotiators or decision-makers. Our open-ended question was addressed to managers both in establishments where pay was determined by collective bargaining and in those where it was not.[20] The questions were asked separately for manual and non-manual employees: where there was bargaining the questions concerned the largest bargaining unit; where there was no bargaining it concerned all employees in the respective category in the establishment. We coded the questionnaire responses in up to three out of 21 separate categories, representing a rich variety of influences upon pay settlements. In the results given in Table 7.11, similar items have been grouped together under broad headings to give a clearer picture of general influences.

Table 7.11   Factors influencing the size of the most recent pay settlement according to managers, 1990

Percentages

	Manual employees			Non-manual employees		
	Private sector		Public sector	Private sector		Public sector
	Union[1]	Non-union[2]		Union	Non-union	
Cost of living	56[3]	47	50	57	47	44
Labour market:	29	39	13	40	30	25
Recruitment, retention	6	11	1	6	8	9
Economic performance:	36	36	12	38	35	9
Economic performance/ ability to pay	32	34	7	34	34	5
Productivity increases	5	3	5	6	2	4
Linked to other settlement	15	14	13	8	12	13
Other influences:	13[4]	29	32	17	39	41
Limits set by higher authority	3	1	15	5	2	15
Individual performance	2	23	4	4	32	4
Strike, threat/union bargaining power	2	*	6	2	1	13
Not stated	6	4	16	11	4	10
Unweighted	*701*	*511*	*433*	*507*	*859*	*565*
Weighted	*403*	*708*	*345*	*260*	*1075*	*464*

Base: establishments with employees named in column heads where most recent pay settlement determined at establishment or higher in the organization

[1] Establishments with recognized unions for employees named in column heads.
[2] Establishments with no recognized union for employees named in column heads.
[3] See Note E.
[4] See Note D.

The cost of living was by far the most frequently mentioned consideration in pay settlements. This was the case for both manual and non-manual employees, whether their pay was negotiated with trade unions or determined unilaterally by their employer. Around a half of all managers mentioned the cost of living. And for about a quarter of all managers it was the only influence upon the size of the settlement that they mentioned. As inflation was increasing – from around 7 per cent to nearly 10 per cent after several years at around 5 per cent[21] – this may appear unsurprising. On the other hand, the primacy of the cost of living persisted at the end of a decade during which both government and employers' associations had promoted the financial and market circumstances of enterprises and establishments as the appropriate basis for pay settlements.

In the private sector, besides the cost of living, three further considerations were widely mentioned. Labour market conditions were cited by managers in around a third of cases: some of them specifically mentioned recruitment or retention (between 6 and 11 per cent of cases, depending on the group concerned), but most of them gave a more general response referring to the labour market. Secondly, and just as commonly, respondents cited considerations about the employer's ability to pay. The majority of these responses either mentioned the commercial and financial performance of the establishment itself (or the company to which it belonged) or else, more generally, the employer's ability to pay. Also included with these responses in the table are some broader references to the national or external economic climate. A specific category for recent productivity increases was coded in around 5 per cent of private sector cases. A third major influence was the level of increase obtained in another pay settlement. In about one eighth of cases managers said that increases were geared to another settlement. Most of these referred to settlements outside the establishment in question.

A fourth factor was very largely confined to employees not covered by collective bargaining. For them individual performance was cited as a consideration influencing the level of their pay increase; something over a quarter of managers in establishments without recognized trade unions gave this response. Very few did so in unionized establishments. (We return to the question of individual performance-related pay later in the chapter.)

Several other considerations were mentioned in a small proportion of cases in the private sector. A few managers referred to limits set by head office management. A few mentioned the bargaining power of the trade unions or the threat of industrial action. In even fewer cases (not separately identified in the table, but included in 'other influences') there was mention of compensation for changes in the payment system, compensation for the loss of fringe benefits or other favourable conditions of employment and the general expectations of employees concerning increases in pay.

In the public sector the cost of living was still the most frequently cited consideration, but the balance of other influences was different. As most public sector workplaces did not trade commercially there were inevitably many fewer references to economic performance; but around one tenth of public sector managers cited ability to pay and about 5 per cent specifically mentioned recent improvements in productivity. Labour market considerations also featured prominently, particularly for non-manual employees; for them a quarter of managers mentioned general labour market considerations, including a tenth who cited the recruitment and retention of employees. The linking of pay increases to those obtained elsewhere was as common in the public sector as in the private sector, affecting around one eighth of establishments. But there were two distinct contrasts with the private sector. Managers in many more cases (15 per cent) mentioned the limits set by higher authorities, often explicity the Government or HM Treasury. And there was much more frequent mention of trade union power or the threat, or actual execution, of strikes or other industrial action.

This picture of the considerations taken into account by managers in pay settlements in 1990 can be compared with the picture derived from similar questions in our previous surveys. However, refinements to some of the categories used in coding the open-ended responses mean that it is not appropriate to compare the responses in full. For the categories which were left unchanged we are on firmer ground. We can be sure that the cost of living was cited by a much higher proportion of managers in 1990 than in 1984 in all of the six types of circumstance identified in Table 7.11; in broad terms the proportion rose from a third to half. We also have directly comparable results on the prevalence of links to other pay settlements. These were reported less frequently in non-union, private sector workplaces in 1990 than in 1984; in the other sectors there was no clear change. The performance of individual employees was more frequently cited as a factor in public sector workplaces than earlier, but there was no change in the private sector, whether unionized or not. For the other sets of considerations the comparisons are less secure, but they suggest a fall in the extent to which economic performance and conditions were regarded as salient and an increased influence of conditions in the labour market.

Variation in the influences upon basic pay settlements
Returning to the 1990 results, we explored a number of possible sources of variation in the pattern of influences on the size of pay settlements, but confined this analysis to workplaces where pay was determined locally and we had the most complete accounts from respondents.[22] As the

great majority of these were in the private sector we specifically restricted the analysis to that sector. We examined a number of economic characteristics of establishments, as well as our managers' reports of their recent performance, to try to isolate patterns of variation in the factors that were taken account of in collectively bargained pay settlements. But, as in our similar analysis of the 1984 survey results, it was difficult to identify clear patterns. We looked at the nature of the establishment's product market, its recent financial performance, its relative level of productivity and the change in productivity over recent years, its level of capacity utilization and its change or stability in the size of its workforce. Few of these registered clear patterns. But there was a suggestion that labour market considerations were more frequently taken into account during pay negotiations when recent financial performance was either very much better than similar firms in the same industry or when it was worse. There was also an indication that establishments that were operating at below full capacity were much less likely to take account of the rise in the cost of living and more likely to take into account labour market conditions and the firm's ability to pay. But such indications were not especially robust and do not give a strong impression that ability to pay and the state of the local labour market were the overwhelming considerations in determining the size of pay settlements. It seems likely that the cost of living – in the period of rising inflation in which our survey was conducted – was the starting point, if not the main consideration, in a great many pay settlements.

The outcomes of pay determination
We now move on from the structures and processes of pay determination to the outcomes. Clearly the most important outcome for employees is the actual level of pay. And for employers the level of pay may be a major element of costs – and hence competitiveness in the trading sector. But pay settlements, especially negotiated settlements, are often very complicated and may involve numerous other conditions of employment that make it extremely difficult to compare one settlement with another. They might involve changes in the normal hours of work, holidays or fringe benefits; they may be expected to run for a number of years or only one; they may contain indexation clauses; they may involve changes in working practices or job requirements. All these and many other matters would make it very difficult for our respondents to give us a single figure that would enable us to compare one settlement with another. Instead, our practice in the WIRS series has been to collect some basic information about the actual levels of pay at the time of the survey, levels which reflect the most recent settlement and all the preceding decisions about the pay of the employees in question.

Levels of pay

Our question aimed to find out the gross earnings of the typical employee in each of five occupational groups. Groups with less than five employees were excluded from the question in the 1990 survey (although not in the earlier ones). Because earnings might differ substantially for men and women (owing to different hours worked or other reasons) the question focused on whichever sex was the majority in the group. The typical (male or female) employee was defined as the one in the middle of a list, if employees were listed in order of their gross earnings. Respondents were asked which of a set of ranges of gross earnings on a card applied to this typical (median) employee.[23] The ranges were in increments of £1000 per year between £5000 and £10,000 per year and of £2000 per year at the upper and lower ends of the distribution. Table 7.12 shows the five groups about whom the question was asked, together with the proportion of establishments in the whole 1990 sample that employed five or more of them.

Although rather rudimentary, the WIRS information on the levels of pay for broad occupational groups has been extensively used by analysts of the two previous surveys and found to be robust and revealing.[24] Those analyses have largely focused on the pay of manual workers, generally explaining the pay of, say, semi-skilled manual workers by a statistical model containing a considerable number of explanatory and controlling factors (mostly related to the establishment). But as Table 7.12 makes clear, a similar approach to the 1990 survey data would have limited generality. Only a half of establishments employ any semi-skilled manual workers at all; only a third employ at least five of them. Our pay data for semi-skilled workers is therefore only present in, at most, a third of establishments. For unskilled manual workers it is present in nearly a half of the sample; for clerical and junior administrative employees just over half. All this makes it difficult to make broad general statements about the level of pay in a workplace.

The approach adopted in the following analysis overcomes this difficulty by taking the workplace as its focus (as opposed to particular groups within it). Within such a framework one can then establish whether any of the separate groups of employees in each workplace have typical pay above or below a certain threshold. The choice of a threshold is a matter of judgement, but there are two particular reasons for concentrating on the lower end of the distribution of pay. One is that the WIRS pay data are more complete for lower paid employees: the questions were not asked about technical, professional or managerial employees (partly because the greater heterogeneity of jobs and pay levels within these occupational groups makes it less appropriate to ask about the pay of typical employees). The second reason is that lower pay has been the subject of public discussion for much of the post-war period, including the last few years.

Table 7.12   **Prevalence of employees for whom gross earnings questions were asked, 1990**

Row percentages

	Proportion of establishments with			
	None	1 – 4	5 or more	Not stated
Type of employee				
Unskilled manual	28	20	48	4
Semi-skilled manual	47	16	34	4
Skilled manual	43	18	35	4
Clerical, administrative and secretarial	7	33	55	4
Supervisors, foremen	35	35	25	5
Any of above groups	..	..	96	—

Base: all establishments
Unweighted: 2061
Weighted: 2000

Our approach has been to classify a workplace as employing lower paid workers if any of the five groups of employees for whom pay levels were reported had hourly pay below a certain amount. This is especially appropriate when examining pay levels across the whole economy because it copes with the fact that the lowest paid workers in one establishment might, for example, be unskilled manual workers while in another they might be clerical or junior administrative employees. Our question about pay levels was asked wherever any of the five groups of employees had at least five workers; this amounted to 96 per cent of the sample, giving our results far greater generality than analyses which examine any one of the five groups. We also had to exclude cases where our pay questions were answered for none of the five groups of employees, even though at least one of the groups had the minimal number of employees required to be asked the question. This cut out a further 10 per cent. The combined result of these exclusions was to reduce our sample by 14 per cent.

Although the choice of a threshold for lower pay is arbitrary to a certain extent, our choice was made with regard to the overall distribution of earnings as depicted by the New Earning Survey. This showed that in April 1990, the lowest decile of hourly earnings[25] for all full-time employees was £3.27 per hour.[26] Our banded data on earnings and hours worked enabled us to approximate to this; in fact the chosen threshold was around £3.28 per hour, with variations between £3.22 and £3.31 per hour.[27] On this definition, 27 per cent of the sample of workplaces employed some lower paid employees.[28]

Table 7.13   Proportion of establishments with any lower paid employees in the private sector, 1990

Percentages

	Any lower paid employees	Unweighted base	Weighted base
All private sector	27	*1346*	*1306*
Manufacturing	22	*618*	*418*
Services	29	*728*	*888*
Number of employees at establishment			
25–99	28	*473*	*1021*
100–499	25	*501*	*261*
500–999	10	*169*	*17*
1000 or more	15	*203*	*7*
Percentage of workforce part-time			
41 or more	49	*165*	*191*
6–40	32	*338*	*447*
0–5	17	*832*	*662*
Percentage of workforce female			
71 or more	46	*174*	*221*
31–70	29	*453*	*444*
0–30	17	*563*	*561*
Ownership			
Independent establishment	30	*228*	*391*
Branch of larger organization	26	*1019*	*858*
Head office	13	*99*	*57*
UK owned	28	*1086*	*1160*
Foreign owned	13	*214*	*133*
Union representation			
No recognized union	32	*576*	*809*
1 or more recognized unions	19	*770*	*497*
Coverage where recognized unions			
1–49 per cent	32	*122*	*113*
50–79 per cent	26	*173*	*114*
80–99 per cent	13	*297*	*142*
100 per cent	9	*178*	*129*
Number of competitors			
None	27	*113*	*76*
1–5	22	*376*	*347*
More than 5	31	*590*	*702*
Capacity utilization			
Full	26	*465*	*414*
Somewhat below full	27	*434*	*339*
Considerably below full	24	*64*	*54*

Base: private sector establishments reporting typical pay and hours for at least one of five occupational groups

The private sector

Table 7.13 shows how the incidence of establishments with lower paid employees varied across the private sector of the economy. The overall figure was 27 per cent for the private sector, with manufacturing being lower than services at 22 per cent compared with 29 per cent. Detailed tabulations indicated that it was mostly unskilled and semi-skilled manual workers in manufacturing that were the lower paid groups; this was also true in the service sector, but less markedly so than in manufacturing. The manufacturing industries that had particularly high numbers of lower paying establishments (32 per cent or more) were: Textiles; Clothing; Food and Drink; and miscellaneous manufacturing. The notable service sector industries were Retailing; Hotels and Catering; Medical Services; and miscellaneous services. These are industries which other sources of information on pay also show to have substantial numbers of lower-paid, full-time employees. Table 7A at the end of this Chapter gives the detailed analysis by industry for the private and public sectors combined.

The next part of Table 7.13 shows the variation by size of workplace. There was a clear tendency for smaller establishments in the private sector to have some lower paid employees. The association with size is such that it is likely that they would be even more commonly found in the smaller establishments not covered by our survey – those with less than 25 employees. Indeed, most of the establishments covered by the current statutory minimum wage arrangements (Wages Councils) are below our size threshold.

The ownership characteristics of establishments also had quite clear influences on the incidence of workplaces with lower paid employees. Foreign-owned establishments had a lower incidence. Single independent establishments (small firms) had a higher incidence than establishments belonging to larger organizations; 30 per cent of them employed lower paid workers on our definition. Head offices of larger organizations were much less likely to contain such employees; only 13 per cent did so. This was particularly striking because our definition was not concerned with average pay or any other measure of the generality of pay levels, which we would expect to be higher in head offices because of the prevalence of senior managerial jobs. Clerical workers in head offices appeared to be substantially less likely to be lower paid than clerical workers elsewhere. Further analysis showed that this was only partly because head offices were disproportionately in the higher paying regions of the country. It seems possible that social mechanisms tending to compress pay differentials – and hence in this case raise the pay of the lower occupational groups – may also play some part in the explanation of this result.

The next part of the table shows how the incidence of workplaces with lower paid employees varied with two aspects of the composition of the workforce. Such employees were to be found much more frequently in establishments with a high proportion of part-time employees. Where more than 40 per cent of the workforce were part time, 49 per cent of workplaces had lower paid workers. By contrast, establishments with few part-time employees (5 per cent or less) were a third as likely to have lower paid employees. Since the great majority of our cases of lower pay concerned full-time employees, it seems clear that full-time employees were more likely to receive lower pay in establishments with many part-time workers. A high concentration of part-time workers would presumably also increase the likelihood of part-time workers receiving lower pay.

Most part-time employees are women and so it was hardly surprising that a similar pattern in the incidence of lower pay was apparent when we looked at the proportion of women in the establishment's workforce.[29] Establishments that had a predominantly female workforce (70 per cent or more) were nearly three times more likely to employ lower-paid workers than establishments with a predominantly male workforce.

Further analysis by gender of the three main groups of employees with lower pay showed that gender had a strong independent influence on the pattern. Of those establishments that employed five or more unskilled manual workers, 39 per cent were ones where most unskilled manual workers were female; but of the lower paying establishments 62 per cent had mostly female unskilled manual workers. For semi-skilled workers the differences were also marked: in 27 per cent of establishments employing them women were the majority; but in 50 per cent of lower-paying establishments they were the majority. For clerical workers the corresponding proportions were 92 per cent and 97 per cent. In part, then, lower pay is associated with a concentration of female employees in the broad occupational groups where lower pay most frequently occurs. But there appears to be an additional influence arising from the concentration of women within establishments.

These striking findings strongly suggest a need for further investigation. They could conceivably be an artifact of other relationships unaccounted for in our analysis. But it seems much more likely that the relationship between lower pay and the concentration of women in an establishment is substantial even when other influences are taken into account.[30] And it appears to arise from something in addition to the tendency for women to be concentrated in lower paying occupations. There is much to be explored here.

Continuing with our discussion of Table 7.13, another clear and independent source of variation on the extent of lower pay is the existence of trade union representation.[31] The presence of a recognized union at a workplace has been shown in all earlier statistical analyses of the WIRS pay data to be associated with higher typical pay levels, other factors held constant. Here in Table 7.13 we see a corollary of that relationship: 19 per cent of workplaces with recognized unions had lower paid employees compared with 32 per cent of those without recognized trade unions.

Within the unionized sector there was an even more striking and significant contrast. Where union negotiations covered less than half of the workforce, lower pay was still widespread: 32 per cent of such establishments had lower paid workers.[32] On the other hand, where union negotiations covered all workers only 9 per cent had any employees below our threshold of around £3.30 per hour.

It might have been the case that these findings on the relationship between lower pay and lower union coverage were an indirect result of a tendency for establishments with a high proportion of female employees to have lower union coverage. In fact there was no such tendency within the unionized part of the private sector. And when we examined both of these factors in relation to the incidence of workplaces with lower pay both of them appeared to exert strong independent effects.

Finally, Table 7.13 shows the incidence of lower pay in relation to an important characteristic of an establishment's product market, the number of its competitors. This is a very rough measure of the degree of competition the establishment faces. The table suggests that establishments that were in competitive markets were more likely to have lower paid employees than those that were not. Thus at least one product market characteristic seems to play a part in determining the pattern of pay.[33] Nevertheless in terms of magnitude the effect seems small in comparison with influences arising from the gender composition of the workforce and from trade union representation.

The public sector

Our examination of the incidence of lower paying establishments in the public sector was less extensive than that for the private sector, principally because there were fewer sources of variation to explore. There was so much less variation in the extent of trade union recognition and associated characteristics in the public sector that that part of the analysis would have been largely inappropriate; and the product market characteristics mentioned in the paragraph above were only relevant to a small proportion of the public sector. The extent of national pay scales across certain parts of the public sector also suggested there would be less variation to account for. However, those parts of the analysis that were relevant were repeated and are summarized in Table 7.14.

Twenty-seven per cent of establishments in the public sector employed lower-paid workers according to our definition, exactly matching

Table 7.14   Proportion of establishments with any lower paid employees in the public sector, 1990

Percentages

	Any lower paid employees	Unweighted base	Weighted base
All public sector	**27**	*552*	*423*
Number of employees at establishment			
25–99	24	*136*	*290*
100–499	32	*179*	*108*
500–999	41	*79*	*15*
1000 or more	35	*158*	*9*
Percentage of workforce part-time			
41 or more	33	*97*	*108*
6–40	29	*239*	*186*
0–5	18	*191*	*125*
Percentage of workforce female			
71 or more	32	*134*	*145*
31–70	23	*184*	*141*
0–30	17	*137*	*94*

Base: public sector establishments reporting typical pay and hours for at least one of five occupational groups

the proportion in the private sector. Unlike the private sector, however, the public sector had no tendency for smaller workplaces to be lower paying ones (Table 7.14).

The effects of workforce composition were a little less marked than in the private sector. Establishments with a high proportion of women were nearly twice as likely to employ lower paid manual or clerical workers as establishments with a low proportion of women (32 per cent compared with 17 per cent). It seems then that, despite the very widespread existence of collective bargaining machinery in the public sector, there remains a tendency for lower paid manual or clerical employees to be concentrated in public sector establishments with a large proportion of women.

The dispersion of pay
The strong positive association between the extent of trade union representation (collective bargaining coverage) and the absence of lower paid employees in an establishment suggests that trade unions may have the effect of compressing pay differentials between occupational groups.[34] Our data on pay levels are not especially suitable for addressing this

issue, but two new questions in the 1990 survey are. They were designed in combination to measure the dispersion of pay among full-time employees in an establishment. Management respondents were asked to ascertain the average gross earnings of full-time employees (including managers). They were then asked: a) approximately what proportion of full-time employees earned half that amount or less; and b) what proportion earned twice that amount or more. If, for example, average pay for full-time employees was £10,000 per annum the answer to a) would be the proportion that earned less than £5000 p.a. and the answer to b) would be the proportion that earned more than £20,000 p.a. Unsurprisingly, a larger than usual number of respondents found these questions difficult to answer. But for 81 per cent of the sample we do have responses to both questions and can compute a measure of the dispersion of earnings by adding together the proportions in questions a) and b).

Over the whole sample this measure of pay dispersion averaged 16 per cent. In about a quarter of cases the answer was zero, all full-time employees in those establishments having earnings that lay within the range from one half to twice the average. The average measure of dispersion (including the zero values) was lower in the more highly unionized public sector and within that sector there was little systematic variation that could not be accounted for by the spread of occupations within establishments. In the private sector, however, with its much greater variation in union representation, we were able to examine the possibility that extensive union representation was associated with less dispersion of pay. Table 7.15 confirms that there is indeed an association. Where there was no trade union recognition or where unions only covered less than half of the workforce, 19 per cent of employees had pay levels outside the range of a half to twice the average for their workplace. Where union coverage was between 80 to 99 per cent this figure was reduced to only 10 per cent. Surprisingly, the figure for workplaces with 100 per cent union coverage was a little higher at 13 per cent. (On further investigation, however, this proved due largely to the presence of recently privatized organizations which still had 100 per cent union coverage.) These results, and our earlier analysis of lower pay, cast a new light on the effects of trade unions on pay. The general unions' objectives of eliminating lower pay and reducing wage dispersion, it appears, were being achieved mostly in that minority of workplaces where unions represented the great majority of workers.

The joint regulation of issues other than pay

The scope of negotiations between managements and trade unions is not limited to pay. Hours of work and some other basic conditions of employment are inevitably either explicitly negotiated or implicitly agreed

Table 7.15   Pay dispersion of full-time employees in the private sector by collective bargaining coverage, 1990

Percentages

| | All establishments | Proportion of employees at establishment covered by collective bargaining | | | | |
		None	1–49 per cent	50–79 per cent	80–99 per cent	100 per cent
Proportion of full-time employees paid						
a) less than half average earnings	11	12[1]	13	10	7	9
b) more than twice average earnings	6	6	6	3	3	4
either a) or b)	17	19	19	14	10	13
Base: private sector establishments reporting valid answers on both a) and b)						
Unweighted	*1429*	*512*	*106*	*134*	*239*	*155*
Weighted	*1406*	*737*	*96*	*97*	*118*	*125*

[1] See Note D.

Table 7.16 Managers' accounts of the extent of joint regulation with the largest manual bargaining unit over specified non-pay issues, by broad sector, 1984 and 1990

Percentages

	All establishments 1984	1990	Private manufacturing 1984	1990	Private services 1984	1990	Nationalized industries 1984	1990	Public services 1984	1990
Negotiated at some level:										
Physical working conditions	78	76	75	76	69	69	87	94	82	80
Redeployment	62	57	63	64	43	43	85	68	66	60
Staffing levels	55	50	47	34	40	32	77	80	62	69
Size of redundancy pay	46	42	51	45	44	46	37	21	48	41
Recruitment	38	32	31	24	21	18	41	12	49	50
Reorganization of working hours	..	78	..	88	..	72	..	98	..	74
Negotiated at establishment level:										
Physical working conditions	39	42	64	58	33	42	63	72	24	28
Redeployment	33	32	55	50	27	26	69	35	19	26
Staffing levels	25	23	42	28	25	20	63	58	8	18
Size of redundancy pay	10	12	34	31	8	12	5	*	1	3
Recruitment	16	13	28	21	16	11	29	10	7	9
Reorganization of working hours	..	40	..	68	..	33	..	60	..	26
Base: establishments with one or more bargaining units for manual employees										
Unweighted	*1405*	*1134*	*462*	*437*	*231*	*264*	*191*	*71*	*521*	*362*
Weighted	*1077*	*748*	*228*	*184*	*260*	*219*	*103*	*41*	*486*	*303*

Table 7.17 **Managers' accounts of the extent of joint regulation with the largest non-manual bargaining unit over specified non-pay issues, by broad sector, 1984 and 1990**

Percentages

	All establishments		Private manufacturing		Private services		Nationalized industries		Public services	
	1984	1990	1984	1990	1984	1990	1984	1990	1984	1990
Negotiated at some level:										
Physical working conditions	76	78	60	66	69	70	81	88	81	82
Redeployment	61	62	61	64	44	52	80	63	65	66
Staffing levels	55	56	42	41	32	36	77	90	62	65
Size of redundancy pay	49	51	51	59	53	72	38	36	48	41
Recruitment	39	40	26	22	25	22	38	37	48	51
Reorganization of working hours	..	46	..	84	..	32	..	88	..	45
Negotiated at establishment level:										
Physical working conditions	30	34	48	43	18	32	50	46	27	33
Redeployment	26	30	51	43	18	22	52	26	20	33
Staffing levels	17	20	32	31	10	17	52	52	11	18
Size of redundancy pay	5	6	31	36	5	7	5	3	1	2
Recruitment	12	13	20	16	11	14	21	16	9	11
Reorganization of working hours	..	31	..	57	..	26	..	42	..	29
Base: establishments with one or more bargaining units for non-manual employees										
Unweighted	*1397*	*1072*	*351*	*249*	*229*	*258*	*195*	*75*	*623*	*490*
Weighted	*1069*	*724*	*109*	*47*	*247*	*213*	*105*	*40*	*608*	*423*

in each new pay settlement. A whole host of other matters may or may not be the subject of union–management negotiations. Throughout our survey series we have tried to explore in a crude way the overall scope of negotiation by asking management respondents whether each of a small number of issues were the subject of negotiation. Our results in 1980 showed surprisingly extensive negotiations on the issues we asked about. In 1984 the four issues that were covered by our repeat questions showed very substantial falls in the extent of negotiation, both in relation to manual workers and non-manual workers represented by recognized trade unions. Several observers took these results as indicative of an overall decline in the power of trade unions during the early 1980s. Tables 7.16 and 7.17 show the corresponding results for 1984 and 1990.

In broad terms, there was little change in the amount of reported negotiation over non-pay issues between 1984 and 1990.[35] Certainly the decline of the early 1980s was not continued. For manual workers the figures do suggest a slight decrease, largely confined to manufacturing and the nationalized industries. For non-manual employees no clear general change is apparent, although there are some indications of increasing activity in the private sector. It should be remembered, however, that our data here are only from workplaces with recognized trade unions[36] and, overall, the amount of union negotiating about the issues covered by our questions must have dropped severely because of the general decline in trade union recognition, detailed in Chapter 3.

In a further question on the selected issues, we asked – if the issue was negotiated with trade unions – at what level the negotiations took place. The extent to which such negotiations were at the workplace itself had also declined substantially between 1980 and 1984. Again, this was not repeated in the latter half of the decade. The lower half of Tables 7.16 and 7.17 shows no overall change in the extent of local negotiations affecting manual workers and a slight increase in relation to non-manual employees. The increase was confined to the services sector; elsewhere the change was probably a decrease. Broadly speaking the results show a small convergence between the different sectors of the economy: those sectors with relatively extensive local negotiations about non-pay issues (manufacturing and the nationalized industries) showed, if anything, a decrease; sectors with less extensive local negotiations (the service sectors) showed mostly increases.

The tables also show a clear stability in the relative frequency with which there were negotiations concerning the five issues asked about in both 1984 and 1990. Indeed, the rank order of the five issues remained the same, for manual and for non-manual employees, both in terms of whether the issue was negotiated at all and in terms of whether it was negotiated locally. Physical working conditions continued to be the most frequently negotiated of the issues we asked about; recruitment the least common. An additional issue asked about in 1990 – the reorganization of working hours – ranked highly in terms of the frequency with which it was negotiated. This was particularly the case for manual workers; in nearly 80 per cent of workplaces with recognized unions for manual workers managers reported that this issue was subject to joint regulation.

More detailed questioning on two other specific issues also showed no change since 1984 in the extent to which trade unions were involved in joint regulation with management. These issues were the introduction of new technology and the introduction of major changes in work organization or working practices, the focus of a specific module of questions in our 1984 survey and the separate volume of findings.[37] On these two issues we repeated a small number of questions in 1990, including those establishing whether any of these two types of change had been introduced at the workplace within the last three years. Where this was so and there were recognized trade unions for the relevant employees, managers were asked if the introduction of the change was, among other possibilities, 'negotiated with union representatives and dependent on their agreement'. In 1984, 8 per cent of managers reported that changes involving new technology were negotiated with manual workers' representatives; in 1990 the equivalent figure was 6 per cent. In respect of changes in work organization or working practices the corresponding figures were 24 per cent in 1984 and 27 per cent in 1990. Given that these types of change were reported in only about 10 per cent of workplaces or less (and our base numbers for comparisons are therefore rather small) there is no firm indication in these results of any increase or decrease in the amount of bargaining over new technology or working practices. The normal management practice on these issues, in cases where unions were recognized, continued to be consultation with union representatives that left management free to make the decisions.

Changes in the issues subject to joint regulation
Our final piece of evidence on the range of issues that were subject to joint regulation between management and unions comes from two new questions in the 1990 survey. One asked managers whether there were any issues currently negotiated with unions that were not negotiated three years previously. The other asked if there were issues negotiated previously but not currently. New bargaining issues with manual unions were reported by 11 per cent of managers; 8 per cent reported new issues bargained with non-manual unions. The public sector showed the highest incidence of new issues. Issues no longer negotiated were reported in 5 per cent of workplaces with recognized manual unions and 3 per cent with non-manual unions. Again most of the change was in the public sector.

The issues that became the subject of negotiation were fairly varied. They ranged from fringe benefits and 'single status' to payment systems, working practices, staffing levels, recruitment, performance appraisal and training. The most commonly mentioned were hours of work and holidays, fringe benefits (for non-manual employees in the private sector) and bonuses and payment systems. The issues no longer negotiated about showed a similar variety. The most common ones were manning levels and bonuses and payment systems.

Comparing responses from the two questions reinforces the general impression that the scope of bargaining did not change a great deal within the unionized sector of the economy as a whole. Issues that trade unions have aimed to raise as bargaining issues in recent years – such as equal opportunities and training – had clearly been conceded as a bargainable issue by very few managements in recent years. And in round terms over 90 per cent of workplaces with recognized unions bargained about the same range of issues as three years before. Perhaps the most significant change was on the question of employment numbers, where there was a clear preponderence of managers saying that they no longer negotiated these with unions over those saying that this was a new issue for negotiation. The number of cases was, however, quite small. But when we put this finding together with our results in Chapter 5 on the decline in consultation over staffing and manpower levels, it provided a firmer basis for concluding that there had been some reduction in the influence of trade unions over changes in employment levels. On the other hand, it could be argued that changes in staffing levels were less frequently on the bargaining agenda because fewer changes of this nature were being planned or carried out by management. In fact, this appeared not to be so. The proportion of establishments that had grown or contracted by more than 5 per cent in the previous 12 months was very similar in our 1990 survey to what it had been in 1984.

Systems of payment and control
Many of the changes in management philosophy and practice that occurred during the 1980s could be expected to have an impact on the means used by managers to monitor and maintain the level of effort and productivity of employees at the point of production and in other non-managerial positions. Our surveys contain a small number of questions that bear upon these issues, which are addressed more fully in our companion volume. Here our limited aim is to describe the changes over the period and comment briefly on the 1990 results.

Checking of starting and finishing times

One basic type of management control of workers' effort is to ensure that they are at the place of work at the times required. In 1980 we asked whether and how the starting and finishing times of manual workers and of non-manual workers were recorded at the workplace. An abbreviated question on similar lines was asked in 1990. Although the question in both surveys referred to 'clocking in' as one method of monitoring, the wording in relation to other methods was changed. There must be some doubts as to whether the two methods identified separately in 1980 covered the full range of 'other methods' asked about in 1990. The results, given in Table 7.18 are thus most dependable in relation to clocking in, shown in the top of the table.

The practice of requiring manual workers to clock in and out remained as extensive in 1990 as it was ten years earlier, with 34 per cent of establishments having this practice for the majority of manual workers. It remained at its most extensive in private manufacturing industry where 80 per cent of establishments reported it for the majority of manual workers. The public sector remained the least likely to use clocking in and out (7 per cent of establishments in 1990). However, for non-manual employees there appeared to have been a small increase in the practice, from 5 per cent of all establishments in 1980 to 8 per cent in 1990. All three broad sectors of employment showed an increase, although for private services it was marginal. The spread of 'flexitime' arrangements (often accompanied by electronic recording of start and finish times) may well account for some of this increased monitoring of the attendance of non-manual employees.[38] The clearest feature of Table 7.18, however, is the very marked difference between the treatment of manual and non-manual workers. Manual workers were very much more likely to have to clock in at the beginning and end of the working day.

Other methods of checking starting and finishing times (such as signing in or being checked in) appear to have increased between 1980 and 1990. The doubts arising from the change of question wording, mentioned above, must remain; but the fact that manufacturing industry showed virtually no change in the use of other methods of monitoring may add credence to the increases shown in the service sector. It seems clear, however, that other methods continue to be most widely used in the public sector and least commonly in manufacturing. As with clocking, these other methods of monitoring are more likely to be applied to manual workers than to non-manual employees.

In broad terms it seems likely that monitoring employee attendance became more extensive during the 1980s. The tighter monitoring of manual compared with non-manual employees remained very much in evidence, although the difference may have lessened a little.

Table 7.18 Methods of monitoring attendance at work, by broad sector, 1980 and 1990

Percentages

	All establishments		Private manufacturing		Private services		Public sector	
	1980	1990	1980	1990	1980	1990	1980	1990
Proportion of establishments where most employees were monitored by:								
Clocking in and out:								
manual	34	34	80	80	24	27	8	7
non-manual	5	8	8	13	4	6	4	8
Other method:[1]								
manual	25	34	6	8	25	37	43	53
non-manual	17	28	9	10	16	29	23	38
Not recorded[2]								
manual	41	30	14	10	52	35	49	37
non-manual	79	62	83	75	80	62	73	53

Bases: establishments with manual/non-manual employees

[1] In 1980, 'being checked in' or 'signing a book'.
[2] In 1980, 'none of these' (three specified methods).

Incentive pay

Another managerial device for monitoring and encouraging workers' effort is incentive payments. These vary from individual piecework, payment by results or merit pay through group bonuses to payments based on the profits of the enterprise as a whole, with numerous variants at each level.[39] The last of these was the subject of additional questioning, which we report on later. We begin our analysis of incentive pay by looking at responses to a general question about payment by results; by this we meant any method of payment where pay varies according to the amount done or its value, rather than just the number of hours worked. In 1984 we limited our questions to manual workers and to junior non-manual employees; in 1990 we asked them about all groups but excluded cases where there were fewer than five employees in the group in question. Table 7.19 shows the comparisons that are possible within these limitations.

For manual workers, the extent of payment by results (PBR) changed little between 1984 and 1990. The proportion of establishments where any manual workers were paid by results on an individual, group, establishment or organizational basis was 31 per cent in 1984; 32 per cent in 1990. There was a modest rise in manufacturing (where the proportion rose from 41 to 48 per cent); elsewhere there was probably a slight fall.

For junior non-manual employees there was some indication of an increase in the extent of PBR. Taking clerical, administrative and secretarial workers together with supervisors (the groups for which we have comparable data) the proportion of establishments where any of these employees had PBR rose from 16 per cent in 1984 to 19 per cent in 1990. The indications of an increase were clearest in private manufacturing and in the public sector.

It remained the case, therefore, that manual workers were substantially more likely than junior non-manual employees to operate under a system of payment by results, but the difference between the two groups had narrowed slightly.

Although the above comparisons are for payment by results of any type, our questions throughout the survey series have in fact distinguished between three types: those based on individual performance; group schemes; and ones based on the performance of the establishment or the whole organization. In 1990 we added a further question concerning merit pay – pay related to the assessment of an individual's performance. We thus sought to distinguish two types of individually-based incentive pay: individual PBR as traditionally applied to production workers (straight piecework, incentive bonuses and the like) where there was a mechanical relationship between the worker's pay and some relatively objective measure of output; and merit pay, which depended on a subjective judgement by a supervisor or manager of the individu-

Table 7.19 Extent of payment by results for selected groups, by broad sector, 1980, 1984 and 1990

Percentages

	All establishments		Private manufacturing		Private services		Public sector	
	1984	1990	1984	1990	1984	1990	1984	1990
Manual employees:								
Any PBR	31	32	41	48	30	28	25	21
Base: establishments with 5 or more unskilled, semi-skilled or skilled manual employees								
Unweighted	*1656*	*1688*	*556*	*607*	*443*	*584*	*667*	*497*
Weighted	*1526*	*1504*	*396*	*411*	*552*	*677*	*578*	*417*
Junior non-manual employees:								
Any PBR	16	19	16	19	21	22	9	12
Base: establishments with 5 or more clerical/administrative/secretarial employees or supervisors								
Unweighted	*1636*	*1770*	*528*	*576*	*480*	*664*	*628*	*530*
Weighted	*1248*	*1300*	*301*	*282*	*579*	*680*	*368*	*338*

Table 7.20　Types of incentive payment by occupational group, 1990

Percentages

	Any incentive pay	Individual PBR (a)	Merit pay (b)	Either (a) or (b)	Group PBR (c)	Establishment, organization bonus (d)	Either (c) or (d)	Un-weighted base	Weighted base
Any employees	52	27	34	45	12	6	17	2041	1970
Unskilled manual	28	12	10	19	10	4	13	1269	972
Semi-skilled manual	34	19	16	28	15	6	21	1018	691
Skilled manual	47	22	22	34	15	4	19	1133	722
Clerical/admin./secretarial	38	11	31	34	3	5	7	1603	1107
Supervisors	42	15	32	37	5	2	7	1155	525
Junior technical/professional	40	16	29	36	4	3	7	1157	672
Senior technical/professional	40	15	31	37	3	4	7	1097	616
Middle/senior managers	51	21	40	46	6	6	11	1343	722

Base: establishments with 5 or more employees in occupational group and reporting on payment methods al's performance. There must be some doubt that the results fully reflect this distinction and a suspicion, since it was asked about last, that merit pay has been under-reported.[40] For this reason the actual values given for merit pay in Table 7.20 should be treated with caution; the column headed 'Either individual PBR or merit pay' is likely to be more reliable.

Taking all employees together, 45 per cent of establishments had some employees with individual incentive pay – either individual PBR or merit pay. Amongst manual workers those with the highest skills were most likely to receive individual incentive pay. For unskilled and semi-skilled workers individual PBR was more common than merit pay; for skilled workers merit pay was at least as common as individual PBR. Manual workers on individual PBR were much less likely to have their hours of work monitored by having to clock in and out. Thus there is some support for the idea that individual PBR systems are used by management as an alternative to tight monitoring and supervision.

Amongst non-manual employees merit pay was much more common than individual PBR. In each of the five non-manual occupational groups that we distinguished in our questioning a third of establishments or more had some employees receiving merit pay. In many cases it is likely that most or all of the group was eligible for merit pay, but we did not ask such details.

Incentive pay based on the output of a group or of a whole establishment or organization was far less common than individual incentive pay (Table 7.20). Overall 17 per cent of establishments had some employees receiving either of these two types of payment. Group-based PBR was more common for manual workers than for non-manual employees.

Taking the three types of PBR and merit pay together, 52 per cent of establishments had some employees receiving at least one form of incentive pay. The proportion was substantially lower in the public sector (31 per cent) and highest in private manufacturing (66 per cent). It rose progressively with the size of workplaces so that almost all of the largest establishments had some employees on incentive pay. Management preferences presumably account for the fact that foreign-owned establishments were substantially more likely to have some employees on incentive pay than their British-owned counterparts in the private sector (76 per cent compared with 59 per cent). Trade unions also seem to have an impact. Overall, workplaces with recognized trade unions were less likely than non-union workplaces to have incentive pay (49 per cent compared with 54 per cent). But in the private sector alone and comparing workplaces of similar sizes the differences were also marked. Much of the overall difference appeared to arise from the tendency for merit pay in particular to be absent in unionized establishments. Indeed, in the few establishments where trade union density was at the highest level possible, merit pay was especially uncommon. It seems then that in Britain, as elsewhere, trade union as well as management policies on payment systems have a bearing on the actual extent of their use.[41]

Profit-related payments and employee share-ownership schemes
Payment systems that incorporate some broad notion of financial participation by employees in the economic success of their employing organization have been widely discussed in recent years. The government has encouraged the introduction of financial participation arrangements and provided support for certain types of scheme. The policy of the trade union movement changed through the decade from opposition to qualified support, although individual unions vary from outright dislike to clear endorsement. Our questions on such schemes in the 1990 survey distinguished five types of scheme: profit-related payments or bonuses (including those covered by the 1987 Finance Act); deferred profit-sharing schemes, where the profits are put in a trust fund which acquires shares in the employing company for employees (sometimes under the 1978 Finance Act); SAYE share-option schemes, where employees can buy their employer's shares from the proceeds of a Save As You Earn savings contract (sometimes under the 1980 Finance Act);[42] discretionary or executive share-option schemes, where selected employees have the option of buying shares at a previous market price (sometimes under the 1984 Finance Act); and other share-ownership schemes. The 1990 questions enable us to describe the extent of such schemes in ways that other sources cannot do because of the wide variety of establishment and organizational characteristics that we have in WIRS. Our specific questioning on the five types of scheme was certainly necessary; the schemes varied widely in their extent and their coverage of employees within workplaces.[43]

Direct profit-related payments or bonuses were certainly the most widespread type of financial participation arrangement. They were reported in 40 per cent of establishments in the trading sector of the economy. About a third of manufacturing workplaces had them; nearly a half of service sector establishments did so. Four characteristics distinguished establishments with profit-related payments or bonuses. Firstly, they were concentrated among larger organizations. Under a third of trading sector workplaces belonging to organizations with fewer than 200 employees had profit-related payments, compared with 70 per cent of those belonging to organizations with 50,000 to 100,000 employees. However, in the largest organizations with over 100,000 employees this type of scheme was not common, largely because of the prevalence of nationalized industries in that category of employer. Secondly, establishments with a high proportion of non-manual employees were much more likely to have profit-related payments. Thirdly, workplaces where recent financial performance was reported to be well above industry averages more commonly had this type of scheme.[44] Fourthly, establishments with recognized unions were slightly less likely to have them than establishments without recognized unions. This difference was small in aggregate (37 per cent for unionised workplaces, compared with 42 per cent for non-union ones), but very much more substantial when we compared workplaces belonging to organizations of similar sizes. The exception was organizations in the size range 10,000 to 100,000. In these cases, profit-related payments were more common where unions were recognized. This turned out to be a feature of the Banking, Insurance and Finance sector, where union policy is much more positive towards profit-related pay.[45]

Share-ownership schemes were covered by the last four items in the question, as given above. Their overall extent in the trading sector of the economy was: 9 per cent of establishments with employee share-ownership derived from deferred profits;[46] 24 per cent of establishments for SAYE schemes; 17 per cent for discretionary share option schemes; and 7 per cent for other types of share-ownership scheme. Altogether 32 per cent of establishments had one of the four types of employee share-ownership. And taking employee share-ownership and profit-sharing arrangements together, 55 per cent of trading sector workplaces had one of the five types of employee financial participation scheme.

Our limited questioning on the extent to which all employees were eligible for the different types of scheme enabled us to confirm that discretionary share-option schemes were indeed generally confined to small numbers of employees, typically less than 10 per cent of the workforce. The other four types of scheme had much higher proportions of the workforce who were eligible. We can be confident that discretionary schemes generally applied to senior staff. Therefore in considering schemes that might have some impact on the commitment or motivation of the workforce as a whole – as some of the other schemes are claimed to have – discretionary share-option schemes can reasonably be excluded. In our brief examination of the characteristics associated with the presence of schemes we looked at the existence of any of the four remaining types – what might be called broadly-based financial participation schemes.

Overall, 53 per cent of trading establishments had at least one of these broadly based schemes. Their incidence was, understandably, considerably lower in foreign-owned workplaces (38 per cent) and in workplaces that were not part of a larger organization. The size of the enterprise owning the establishment was a strong positive influence on the existence of schemes, although the very largest enterprises (those with over 100,000 UK employees) were less likely to have schemes than those in the second largest size category (50,000 to 100,000 employees). This largely reflects the fact that many of the very largest enterprises were nationalized industries and these rarely had any of the schemes. Another enterprise characteristic associated with the existence of schemes was the diversity of the enterprise's activities. Workplaces that were part of an enterprise consisting of a single business were half as likely to have schemes as those that were part of a conglomerate enterprise. Again this is likely to be partly a matter of size.

Generally, workplaces with a high proportion of non-manual employees were more likely to have financial participation schemes. But this was one of the few establishment characteristics that seemed to be associated with the existence of schemes. Since most schemes are probably company or enterprise wide this should come as no surprise. In view of this it was also unsurprising that the level of trade union organization at the workplace (however measured) had no obvious association with the presence or absence of schemes.[47]

The growth in profit-sharing arrangements

Despite the change to our survey question, there can be little doubt that there was a very substantial growth in profit-sharing arrangements between 1984 and 1990. The proportion of establishments in the industrial and commercial sector of the economy that had either cash-based or share-based profit-sharing rose from 18 to 43 per cent. Both manufacturing and service industries were affected, although services showed the faster rate of increase. There were increases in most but not all individual industries: those with the most dramatic rises were engineering, retail distribution and financial services. In Banking, Finance and Insurance 90 per cent of workplaces were covered by such arrangements by 1990. Retailing had them in 62 per cent of workplaces. By contrast, manufacturing establishments in the textile and clothing industries remained the least likely to have either of these types of scheme – only 11 per cent did so in 1990, little different from the figure in 1984. No doubt the preponderance of small firms in these industries has much to do with this; across the industrial and commercial sector as a whole small firms were very much less likely to have profit sharing arrangements, especially the broadly based ones.

The growth of profit-sharing arrangements was strongly confirmed by our panel sample. A third of establishments that were not covered by a scheme in 1984 were covered by one in 1990. Those adopting schemes outnumbered those abandoning them by a ratio of nearly six to one.

The growth of employee share-ownership

In assessing changes in the extent of employee share-ownership schemes we consider only the three types of scheme in our 1990 survey that are clearly comparable with the 'share-ownership or share-option schemes' we asked about in 1984. The growth of such schemes was less marked than for profit-sharing arrangements, but there was evidently growth here too. The proportion of trading sector establishments with such schemes rose from 23 per cent in 1984 to 32 per cent in 1990. In our panel sample, establishments gaining a scheme outnumbered those losing a scheme by three to one. The cross-sectional comparisons showed that manufacturing and service industries had roughly the same rate of increase, but by no means all of the individual industries within these two sectors had increases. Some appeared to have less of these types of employee share-ownership arrangement in 1990 than in 1984. The largest increases were registered by industries that had involved major privatizations. There were no increases among foreign-owned firms or in small firms, both of which continued to have very little employee share-ownership.

Eligibility for these employee share-ownership schemes fell a little within workplaces that had schemes. Where schemes existed the mean proportion of the workforce that was eligible for any of these types of share-ownership was 68 per cent in 1984; in 1990 it was 62 per cent. The median percentage fell from 79 to 70. Fewer establishments reported very high proportions, reflecting more extensive exemptions (for part-timers, those with short service records and the like) applying to many of the more recently introduced schemes. However, there are some doubts about the actual size of the fall because more respondents in 1990 were unable to give us an estimate of the proportion of employees covered by the schemes.[48] No doubt our elaboration of the question to identify the three types of scheme contributed to this. Even so it seems probable that the proportion fell slightly, partly because of the spread of discretionary or executive schemes. However, given that schemes were present in a considerably larger proportion of workplaces it is almost certainly the case that more employees were eligible for share-ownership schemes in 1990 than in 1984.

More significant than this perhaps is the fact that more employees actually participated in the schemes in 1990 than in 1984. The proportion of the workforce who participated in schemes, where they were available, rose from 22 per cent in 1984 to 34 per cent in 1990. This is the mean percentage in establishments with schemes. The median figure increased from 10 to 20 per cent.

The take-up rate of employee share-ownership schemes (again excluding those based on deferred profits) can be judged by comparing the percentage eligible with the percentage participating. Table 7.21 gives the two median percentages for cases where we have estimates for both proportions. The first row in the table covers any type of scheme; subsequent rows are for cases where only the specified scheme was present. From this we can see that the take-up rate was much higher

Table 7.21   Eligibility and participation in employee share-ownership schemes, 1990

Medians

	Percentage eligible	Percentage participating	*Unweighted base*	*Weighted base*
SAYE scheme **only**	80	20	*146*	*100*
Discretionary scheme **only**	9	8	*62*	*50*
Other scheme **only**	(80)	(15)	*21*	*29*
Any of the above schemes	70	20	*403*	*282*

Base: establishments having the types of scheme specified and providing estimates of eligibility and participation

(approaching 100 per cent) for the discretionary or executive schemes which have low eligibility. By contrast, for schemes where most of the workforce is eligible the take-up rate was about a quarter.

However, despite their relatively low take-up, the extensive availability of the broadly based schemes in 1990 makes it likely that there was a substantial increase over the period 1984 to 1990 in the proportion of employees in the industrial and commercial sector of the economy who owned shares or share options in their employing company. The higher proportion of workplaces with schemes and a higher rate of participation both contributed to this.

Whether the spread of profit-sharing and employee share-ownership had a discernable impact on economic performance or industrial relations in the enterprises concerned is an interesting and important question, to which we can only give a preliminary answer.[49] But our analysis did indicate that in workplaces with any of the broadly based financial participation arrangements (that is any of the five types of scheme excepting executive share options) financial performance was rather better although industrial relations less so than in establishments without such schemes.[50] These differences persisted when we carried out separate analysis of the unionized and non-union sectors, which differ markedly on both of these dimensions, as assessed by our management respondents. This is another area where more formal statistical analysis would be worthwhile.

Job evaluation
Job evaluation forms the basis of many pay structures because it is used to compare systematically the jobs within a workplace or an organization as a precursor to the setting of pay differentials. In our previous

Table 7.22 Distribution and nature of job evaluation, by broad sector, 1980, 1984 and 1990

	All establishments			Private manufacturing			Private services			Public sector		
	1980	1984	1990	1980	1984	1990	1980	1984	1990	1980	1984	1990
											Column percentages	
Whether formal job evaluation scheme present												
Yes	21¹	21	26	28	24	27	20	23	24	14	18	27
No	78	78	74	72	76	73	79	77	76	85	81	73
Not stated	*	*	*	*	*	*	1	*	*	*	*	*
Base: all establishments												
Unweighted	2040	2019	2061	743	592	630	587	597	799	710	830	632
Weighted	2000	2000	2000	503	424	426	859	843	980	637	733	594
											Percentages	
Number of schemes												
Two or more	22	34	29	31	48	32	15	35	24	21	22	34
											Column percentages	
Basis of largest scheme												
Points rating	46	46	45	45	34	43	45	45	45	50	56	46
Factor comparisons	9	7	15	8	6	7	10	4	12	8	12	24
Ranking	13	10	21	19	12	27	11	11	25	9	6	10
Grading	27	27	15	25	32	18	28	32	14	28	17	15
Other/not stated	5	10	4	3	15	5	5	9	4	5	9	6

Base: establishments with job evaluations schemes

¹ See Note C.

report we presented evidence suggesting a growth in the use of job evaluation: although the proportion of workplaces with any job evaluation had stayed constant at 21 per cent between 1980 and 1984, those workplaces that had schemes were more likely to have had more of them by 1984. This proliferation of schemes suggested a broadening of the overall coverage of job evaluation.

The changes since 1984 have been of a rather different nature (Table 7.22). The proportion of workplaces with any job evaluation rose from 21 to 26 per cent, suggesting an increase in overall coverage. On the other hand, fewer workplaces with schemes had more than one. This proportion fell from 34 to 29 per cent, but it remained higher than the 1980 figure of 22 per cent. Indeed, given that between 1980 and 1990 there was a rise both in the proportion of workplaces with any scheme and in the proportion of those with schemes that had two or more schemes, we can be fairly confident that the use of job evaluation grew somewhat over the ten year period. The distribution of job evaluation schemes within individual industrial sectors is shown in Table 7A.

Looking at the changes in the three broad sectors of the economy, the clearest indication is of an increase in the presence of schemes in the public sector. This was most apparent in medical and social services. There was also an increase in the use of multiple schemes in private services. Beyond these two changes there appears from our cross-sectional results to have been little change in the extent of the practice.

Our panel of trading sector workplaces shed further light on these matters. The overall results suggested a slight increase in the presence of job evaluation schemes; further examination revealed that the only sector to show a clear change towards the use of job evaluation was the nationalized industry sector as it existed in 1984. In fact, by 1990 much of this had been privatized; our panel data showed that job evaluation became more widely used both in the privatized portion and in the portion that remained under state ownership.

There was little change in the type of scheme most commonly used. Although we only have information on the basis of the largest scheme, where there was more than one in use, the fact that most workplaces had a single scheme makes this a good representation of schemes in general. Overall, points rating schemes accounted for 45 per cent of largest schemes in 1990, virtually the same proportion as in 1980. Factor comparisons, the other main analytical type of scheme, appeared to have become more popular, notably in the public sector. So there was a slight increase in the balance between analytical schemes and non-analytical schemes (grading and ranking). But in view of the incentives to adopt analytical schemes that are built into the law on equal opportunities it seems surprising that this growth has not been more substantial and widespread.

One reason for this might be that the weakening of trade union organization during the 1980s reduced the pressures on employers to introduce job evaluation – and particularly the analytical types of scheme – to justify pay differentials to employees and their representatives. Our analysis of the 1984 survey data had highlighted the much greater use of job evaluation in unionized establishments in the private sector. It was therefore of interest to see whether this strong association had persisted. Our analysis showed that indeed it had, although it was possibly not as strong. In 1990 we found that 38 per cent of private sector workplaces with recognized trade unions had job evaluation compared with only 17 per cent of non-union workplaces. The comparable figures in 1984 were 36 and 12 per cent. When we controlled for the size of establishments, another clear influence on the existence of job evaluation, the greater incidence of schemes in unionized workplaces was still very apparent.

This was also evident in our panel sample. Furthermore, when we looked at establishments in the panel sample that introduced job evaluation between 1984 and 1990, they were much more likely to have had recognized unions throughout the period than the panel sample as a whole. The introduction of job evaluation therefore seems to be associated with, although not confined to, workplaces with well-established trade unions. So it seems likely that job evaluation would have spread to more workplaces if the unionized part of the private sector had not shrunk. The lack of a significant spread in the practice appears to have occurred because influences such as the equal opportunities legislation that might have encouraged a spread were offset by trends in the opposite direction such as the decline in the size of workplaces and the reduction in trade union representation.[51]

Synopsis

Reflecting the significant falls in trade union representation and in the membership of employers' associations detailed in earlier chapters, there were important changes over the 1980s in the structures and processes used to determine periodic increases in basic rates of pay. There was a widespread decline in the extent to which basic rates were set by multi-employer negotiations with trade unions. Within the private sector there was also a decline in the extent to which multi-employer collective bargaining was accompanied by local bargains affecting the same group of employees. This reduction in the complexity of bargaining occurred in the early part of the decade in manufacturing, but throughout the decade in private service industries. Where basic rates of pay were not subject to collective bargaining, it was increasingly the case that local management, rather than head offices, took the decisions.

Processes as well as structures appeared to have altered. Where trade unions were involved in reaching an agreed settlement it was increasingly the case that they formally consulted their memberships during the course of the negotiations and used formal methods such as secret ballots to do so. An increase in formality was also apparent on the management side in that formal job evaluation schemes became more common as a way of establishing differentials in basic pay. However, collective influences declined to the extent that managers less commonly took account of other pay settlements and more commonly had regard to individual performance. But although labour market considerations and the commercial circumstances of employers were clearly important influences on the level of basic pay increases, the cost of living continued to be the most common and sometimes only factor that had a bearing on the matter.

Basic pay, however, was increasingly supplemented by other elements. It became more usual for non-manual employees to have some portion of their earnings dependent on their individual performance and there was a spread in the growth of profit sharing and employee share ownership.

Our analysis of the actual levels of earnings was aimed not at illuminating changes over time – other sources of information are better suited to that – but at certain features of the pattern of pay in 1990. It revealed, in a way that other sources cannot, a number of characteristics of establishments and their workforces that were associated with the employment of lower paid employees. Among these characteristics were the preponderance of women within the establishment's workforce and the absence of trade union representation, especially comprehensive union representation. Such findings raise questions for further analysis and issues for further debate in the complex area of pay determination.

Notes and references

1. In fact, our redesign of the 1990 questionnaire to take account of the possibility of unions having both manual and non-manual members entailed a further complication with respect to these results. Where there were recognized unions with manual members but none of those unions belonged to a negotiating group that consisted of predominantly manual unions, their pay was determined within a predominantly non-manual group of unions. In such cases whenever possible we have imputed the data about bargaining levels from the largest non-manual group. This affected about 1 per cent of workplaces with manual workers; the converse case affected about 0.5 per cent of workplaces with non-manual employees.

2. In fact in the 1990 survey single-employer bargaining was subdivided into two categories: single-employer involving all establishments; and single-employer, but only some establishments. The latter was rare and has been combined with the former for present purposes to give results comparable with the two previous surveys.

3. N. Millward and M. Stevens (1986) *British Workplace Industrial Relations 1980–1984: The DE/ESRC/PSI/ACAS Surveys*, Gower, Aldershot, pp. 62–4 and 225–8.

4. The calculation is complicated by the fact that some manual workers are covered by predominantly non-manual bargaining units, a possibility that was not allowed for in the

1984 questionnaires. Despite this we think it likely that the coverage of the largest unit is as high in 1990 as it was in 1984.

5. In about a quarter of cases involving manual workers not covered by the negotiating arrangements for other manuals at their establishment the management respondent reported that their pay was decided by an employers' association or national joint negotiating body. This appeared to be contradictory. All of these cases were small firms and half of them did not belong to an employers' association. Most of the respondents were general managers, rather than personnel or industrial relations specialists. We were inclined to interpret most of these responses as meaning that the management generally implemented the same pay increases as specified in their industry agreement even though they were not a party to the agreement.

6. See, for example, W. Brown and J. Walsh (1991) 'Pay determination in Britain in the 1980s; the anatomy of decentralisation', *Oxford Review of Economic Policy*, No. 1, pp. 44–59; Industrial Relations Review and Report, various issues.

7. A. L. Booth, (1989) 'The bargaining structure of British establishments', *British Journal of Industrial Relations*, July, pp. 225–34.

8. See W. Brown and J. Walsh (1991) op. cit. Interestingly, British-based multi-nationals are intermediate between foreign firms and purely domestic firms in their participation in multi-employer agreements. This suggests that there are influences on bargaining policy from both product-market competition and from foreign management culture.

9. P. Marginson, P. K. Edwards, R. Martin, J. Purcell and K. Sisson, (1988) *Beyond the Workplace: Managing Industrial Relations in the Multi-Establishment Enterprise*, Blackwell, Oxford.

10. It is worth noting that the term 'employer' used in this and other questions about collective bargaining is a more restricted concept than that of an 'enterprise'. In enterprises consisting of many companies, particularly conglomerate enterprises, it is unlikely that collective agreements apply across all establishments.

11. These proportions are quite similar to those reported by Marginson et al. (1988), op. cit.

12. The 1984 figures were 85 per cent for manuals and 65 per cent for non-manuals. See the caution in the earlier note in relation to manufacturing.

13. For a number of reasons, detailed in our earlier book, we have doubts about the accuracy of some of the public sector responses to our questions on pay determination in the 1980 survey; see N. Millward and M. Stevens (1986) op. cit., pp. 62–4 and 227. Our analysis therefore concentrates on the 1984 and 1990 results.

14. This is an area where there have been several recent moves in the public sector which are intended to increase the amount of decision-making at local level.

15. P. Marginson et al. (1988) op. cit., p. 235.

16. One additional question that we asked in the 1990 survey concerned the anticipated duration of the most recent negotiated settlement. In over 95 per cent of cases the answer was 12 months.

17. Naturally the questions were asked only in establishments that were part of a larger organization. In our analysis we have also excluded head offices and similar administrative centres.

18. Minor changes to question wording were made to these two pre-coded responses in 1990. The 1984 wording, 'voting slips' was changed to 'secret ballot at workplace or other meeting place'; 'postal ballot' in 1984 was altered to 'secret postal ballot'. 'Other answers' in 1990 accounted for 3 per cent of cases and were recoded from the written answers, but less than 0.5 per cent of cases were coded to 'non-secret ballot'; most fell

into the category, 'representatives ascertained members' views without a meeting or vote'. None of these minor technicalities detracts from our findings.

19. The findings in this paragraph concerning lack of change between 1984 and 1990 are strongly confirmed by the panel sample.

20. A similar question was asked in relation to employees not covered by collective bargaining in establishments where some employees were covered. The distribution of these responses was similar to that for establishments with collective bargaining except that very many more of them mentioned links to other pay settlements, particularly of groups within the same establishment.

21. As measured by the Retail Prices Index, the most commonly cited measure of inflation in pay negotiations. See Employment Gazette, December 1990.

22. As in the 1984 survey, the proportion of cases where we had no substantive answer was negligible where bargaining was at workplace level but rose to substantial levels where bargaining was at a higher level in the organization or on a multi-employer basis. It was also significant that the cost of living was the only factor mentioned in a much higher proportion of workplaces where bargaining was at a higher level.

23. Multiple responses were permitted to allow for the median being on the boundary of two ranges. They occurred in less than 1 per cent of cases where pay was reported, a much lower proportion than in 1984 when our pay levels question was less precisely worded. As in earlier surveys the card showed weekly amounts equivalent to the annual amounts mentioned in the text.

24. Much of the work is cited in: D. Blanchflower, A. Oswald and M. Garrett (1990) 'Insider power in wage determination', *Economica*, **57**, pp. 143–170; and M. B. Stewart (1991) 'Union Wage Differentials in the Face of Changes in the Economic and Legal Environment', *Economica*, **58**, pp. 155–72.

25. As far as we can tell, all secondary analysis of the 1984 WIRS pay data has used weekly pay (the 1980 survey did not collect typical hours); the results may therefore be substantially affected by overtime at premium rates. This possibility is greatly reduced in the current analysis by using hourly rates. The effect is also less important because our concentration on lower pay largely means that overtime earnings put pay even further above our threshold.

26. Department of Employment (1991) 'New Earnings Survey', HMSO, London, Section A, Table 26.2.

27. The threshold for lower pay was calculated using eight combinations of responses to the questions on typical pay levels and the hours required to earn that amount. As the pay data are banded and the hours data are to the nearest whole number the calculated amounts vary a little. Two examples will illustrate the point. One of the ranges of typical pay was from £6000 to £6999 per annum, or from £115 to £135 per week. If typical pay had been at the very top of this range and the employee had worked for 41 hours, his or her hourly rate (neglecting any overtime premium) would have been £3.29 per hour. Therefore, any group of employees for whom typical pay was between £115 and £135 per week and typical hours were 41 *or more* was classified as below the threshold. Similarly, workplaces where a group of employees had typical pay of £7000 to £7999 per annum (or up to £154 per week) and typical hours worked of 47 or more had employees earning £3.28 or less.

28. An estimate of 40 per cent of workplaces having lower paid workers was recently made by the Institute for Personnel Management on the basis of earnings data given in our report on the 1980 WIRS and uprated to 1990. That estimate included workplaces where the typical semi-skilled worker was part-time and, therefore, overstates the proportion based on equivalent hourly pay. (See Institute of Personnel Management (1992) *Minimum wage: an analysis of the issues*, Institute of Personnel Management, London, pp. 85–6.)

29. It should be noted that our calculation of the proportion of females in the workforce assumes that all part-time employees are women. An assumption was necessary because we did not collect separate numbers of women and men working part-time, although we did for those working full time. The September 1989 *Census of Employment* indicates that 83 per cent of part-time workers are women, when part-time is defined as working less than 31 hours per week.

30. Indeed, such a result could be inferred from our analysis of the 1980 WIRS earnings data in W. Daniel and N. Millward (1983) *Workplace Industrial Relations in Britain: The DE/PSI/SSRC Survey*, Gower, Aldershot, pp. 260–750, and from other analyses of those and the improved data in the 1984 survey.

31. Although the association between trade union representation and levels of pay has been the subject of much analysis, the relationship between union presence and the provision of fringe benefits has rarely been investigated. Preliminary findings on this matter suggest that the recognition of non-manual trade unions is associated with the provision of extra-statutory occupational pensions and that the recognition of manual and of non-manual trade unions are associated with the provision of extra-statutory sick pay, when other relevant factors are taken into account. A report of this PSI study, *Employers' Provision of Pensions and Sick Pay: Evidence from the 1990 WIRS* by B Casey, is forthcoming.

32. Further analysis would be needed to confirm that in workplaces with low union coverage it was the employees not covered that included the lower paid ones; but it can hardly be otherwise.

33. Earlier research that showed this in a number of industries was reported in C. Craig, J. Rubery, R. Tarling and F. Wilkinson (1982) *Labour Market Structure, Industrial Organisation and Low Pay*, Cambridge University Press, Cambridge.

34. The effect is well documented in the USA; see R. B., Freeman (1982), 'Union wage practices and wage dispersion within establishments', *Industrial and Labor Relations Review*, October, pp. 3–21. However, bargaining structure in the USA is less complex than in Britain, union coverage in unionized workplaces is higher and the results are therefore not directly transferable to the British situation.

35. These findings are confirmed by our analysis of the panel data.

36. Unfortunately, the complex structure of our questionnaires made it unworkable for us to ask about any negotiations there might be between unions and management in situations where unions were not recognized for pay negotiations but were for other matters. In the earlier surveys we were convinced that such circumstances were highly unusual. They do now exist in some parts of the public sector, but our data are not able to capture this.

37. W. W. Daniel (1987) *Workplace Industrial Relations and Technical Change*, Frances Pinter (Publishers) and the Policy Studies Institute, London.

38. Industrial Relations Services (1989) 'Flexible approaches to working hours', *Industrial Relations Review and Report No. 453*, December.

39. More detailed descriptions are given in B. Casey, et al., (1991) 'Payment systems: a look at current practice', *Employment Gazette*, August 1991, pp. 453–8.

40. The questions on merit pay all have very substantial numbers of cases coded as 'not answered'.

41. Similar relationships between union presence, size of establishment and the use of individual incentives have been observed in the United States. See C. Brown (1990) 'Firm's choice of method of pay', *Industrial and Labor Relations Review*, February (Special Issue), pp. 165–82.

42. Where these schemes are of the 1978 Finance Act variety, participation is open to most employees.

43. There appears to be little overlap between responses to these specific questions on profit-related pay or share-ownership and the question examined in the previous section on payment by results which related to the output of the establishment or organization. The most likely overlap was between profit-related pay and establishment or organizational PBR, but only 12 per cent of workplaces reporting the former also reported the latter.

44. A similar relationship was noted in the 1984 survey results but became insignificant when other factors were controlled for. See D. G. Blanchflower and A. J. Oswald (1988) 'Profit-related pay: prose discovered', *Economic Journal*, September, pp. 720–30.

45. The impact of unions on the incidence of profit sharing in 1984 was investigated in P. A. Gregg and S. J. Machin (1988) 'Unions and the incidence of performance linked pay schemes in Britain', *International Journal of Industrial Organization*, No. 6, pp. 91–107. That analysis, however, did not allow for the possibility that unions might have different policies on profit-related pay.

46. These schemes can for some purposes be regarded as a form of profit sharing; indeed, it is appropriate to do so when comparing the results from our 1990 survey questions with the less specific question in our 1984 survey. The relative rarity of share ownership based on deferred profits compared with SAYE share-option schemes *on the basis of the proportion of workplaces affected* should not be confused with the absolute numbers of schemes which for approved schemes are broadly similar.

47. Trade union recognition was weakly identified as being associated with the presence of profit-sharing schemes in multivariate analysis of the 1984 survey data. See D. Blanchflower and A. Oswald 'A picture of profit-sharing in Great Britain' London School of Economics, mimeo, 1987; P. Gregg and S. Machin (1988) op. cit. Both papers suggested that workplaces with stronger unions were less likely to have schemes than those with weak unions.

48. The proportion of cases where respondents were unable to estimate the proportion of the workforce eligible for a scheme rose from 10 per cent in 1984 to 26 per cent in 1990. In the latter year those with a single scheme were much more likely to give an estimate than those with multiple schemes.

49. Econometric analysis of the 1984 survey data failed to detect positive effects on financial performance, employment or investment; see D. Blanchflower (1991) 'The economic effects of profit-sharing in Great Britain' *International Journal of Manpower*, **12**, No. 1.

50. These evaluations were made by managers in response to single questions about financial performance and 'management-employee' relations.

51. The incidence of 'equal value' claims being made by individuals or their representatives within the year prior to our survey was ascertained from managers in workplaces where there was a job evaluation scheme covering both men and women. Responses indicated that some 4 per cent of workplaces with such schemes had been involved in a claim of this sort, amounting to 1 per cent of establishments in the survey. Private service industries accounted for most of the few cases that were reported.

Table 7A   Proportion of establishments with (a) any lower-paid employees and (b) job evaluation, by industry, 1990

Percentages

	Any lower paid employees	Job evaluation
All industries	**27**	**26**
All manufacturing	**22**	**27**
Metals & Mineral Products	9	44
Chemicals & Manufactured Fibres	(6)[1]	(35)
Metal Goods	(5)	(17)
Mechanical Engineering	10	14
Electrical & Instrument Engineering	25	22
Vehicles & Transport Equipment	5	65
Food, Drink & Tobacco	32	50
Textiles	(33)	(9)
Leather, Footwear & Clothing	(68)	(21)
Timber & Furniture, Paper & Printing	14	23
Rubber, Plastics & Other Manufacturing	(39)	(23)
All services	**28**	**25**
Energy & Water	5	79
Construction	24	8
Wholesale Distribution	25	31
Retail Distribution	32	22
Hotels, Catering, Repairs	65	15
Transport	16	25
Post and Telecommunications	9	29
Banking, Finance, Insurance	*	77
Business Services	23	15
Central Government	32	15
Local Government	19	23
Higher Education	(46)	(64)
Other Education	38	9
Medical Services	44	22
Other Services	32	33

Base: all establishments (see Table 1A for bases and SIC codes), but note that bases for first column are generally a little smaller than those given, for reasons stated in the text.

[1] See Note B.

8 Industrial Action

By its nature, industrial action is the most volatile feature of the industrial relations scene. Although industrial relations institutions tend to change relatively slowly, we know from our previous surveys that the incidence of strikes and other forms of industrial action varies quite markedly from year to year. And we know from other sources that the 1980s was characterized by large reductions in the incidence and intensity of strike action in most major Western countries as well as Britain.[1]

In Britain this period also saw the impact of marked changes in the legal framework governing the conduct of industrial action by trade unions. These included the requirement in the Trade Union Act 1984, further strengthened by the Employment Act 1988, for unions to hold properly conducted ballots before calling industrial action. These changes, together with evidence of the increasing readiness of employers to initiate legal redress against unlawful behaviour by unions,[2] suggested that trade unions in the late 1980s would be likely to become much more cautious about organizing industrial action than they had been earlier in the decade.[3]

Whether the current low level of industrial action will continue, and whether more overt forms of industrial action are being displaced by others, is a matter of some debate.[4] Our survey data allow us to explore some of the possibilities in this area, in the changing characteristics of industrial action and types of workplaces where it occurred.

There are two unique features of our information on industrial action which distinguish it from that provided by other sources. The first is that our unit of data collection and analysis is, of course, the individual workplace. Whereas the Employment Department's official figures for stoppages of work due to industrial disputes measure the total number of stoppages, the total number of workers involved and the total number of working days lost, our data refer to the proportion of workplaces affected. Clearly, a national but very short stoppage could in certain sectors nevertheless affect many workplaces – such as the half-day stoppage over national trade union membership at the Government Communications Head Quarters (GCHQ) recorded by the 1984 survey. Conversely, in other sectors a longer national stoppage may affect relatively few, but large, workplaces – as in the coal mining strike of 1984–1985.[5] In other words, the Workplace Industrial Relations Surveys and the Employment Department's official figures for stoppages of work measure different aspects of the same phenomenon.

The second unique feature of our survey is that information is collected on aspects of industrial action which is not available from any other source. This applies to not only all stoppages of less than a day[6] and those with political purposes (both of which are excluded from the ED series), but also the identification of particular forms of non-strike industrial action which employees engage in, the extent to which industrial action was 'official' and the extent and nature of picketing.

Although the focus of questioning has been at the collective level in the three surveys, in the 1990 survey we also included new questions covering other withdrawals from work such as labour turnover, absences and injuries. These data are reported in Chapters 5 and 9. However, we did not collect data on other forms of conflict behaviour such as sabotage or 'fiddling', since such phenomena may be more effectively researched using methods other than surveys.[7]

Changes in the extent and form of industrial action
Our measures of the extent of industrial action are based on survey questions which asked managers and worker representatives whether, in the year prior to interview, the sampled workplace had been affected by strike action of various durations or non-strike action of various forms. The 1990 survey typically covered the period from mid-1989 to mid-1990.[8] We expected to find the overall picture of decline in union organization since 1984, charted particularly in Chapters 3 and 4, feeding through into the level of industrial action experienced by our sampled workplaces.

The overall results for all three surveys are given in Table 8.1 and confirm the expected downward trend since 1984. Indeed, the fall was larger than the decline in recognition, detailed earlier, would have suggested. The overall extent of industrial action among either manual or non-manual employees fell by half between the 1984 and 1990 surveys from a quarter to 12 per cent of workplaces. The incidence of strike action also fell by half, from 19 per cent to 10 per cent of workplaces, but non-strike action declined even further, affecting 18 per cent of establishments in 1983–1984 but just 5 per cent in 1989–1990. The overall picture was much the same whether manual workers only or non-manual workers only were considered, as the top three rows of Table 8.2 show very clearly. Evidently, the overall decline in strike action was not offset by a rise in the overall incidence of non-strike collective action. Nor was there change in the rank order of various forms of non-strike action. Overtime bans and working to rule were still

Table 8.1 The extent to which establishments were affected by industrial action, as reported by any respondent,[1] 1980, 1984 and 1990

Percentages

	1980	1984	1990
Strike action	13	19	10
Non-strike action	16	18	5
Strike or non-strike action	22[2]	25	12
Strike action lasting:			
Less than 1 day	6	14	4
1 day or more	9	12	7
1 day but less than a week	..[3]	11	6
1 week or more	..	1	1
Non-strike action:			
Overtime bans/restriction	10	11	3
Work to rule	7	8	2
Blacking of work	5	3	1
Lock-out	1	*	—
Go-slow	1	*	*
Other pressure[4]	1	2	1
Base: all establishments			
Unweighted	*2040*	*2019*	*2061*
Weighted	*2000*	*2000*	*2000*

[1] The percentages represent those establishments where either the manager or the manual worker representative or the non-manual worker representative reported industrial action of the type specified.
[2] See Note F.
[3] See Note J.
[4] 'Work-ins', 'sit-ins', 'other action by employees' (1990 only) and 'other action' are included with the more general 'other pressure' category as so few cases were reported.

the most frequently used forms of non-strike action in 1989–1990, though affecting only 3 per cent and 2 per cent of workplaces respectively.

The decline in the extent of strike and non-strike action was widespread. Falls were evident in all types of workplace – manufacturing and services, publicly and privately owned, UK and foreign-owned, those with recognized unions, among all sizes of workplace and all levels of union density. Even so, the three broad sectors of employment showed very different trends in the extent of industrial action across the whole of the decade, and marked changes in the use of different forms of action.

In the private manufacturing sector there was a continuing drop in the level of industrial action over the whole of the decade, from almost a third of establishments being affected in 1979–1980 to just one in ten in

Table 8.2   The extent to which establishments were affected by industrial action among manual or non-manual employees, as reported by any respondent[1], 1980, 1984 and 1990

Percentages

	Manual			Non-manual		
	1980	1984	1990	1980	1984	1990
Strike action	11[2]	8	3	4	14	8
Non-strike action	10	8	3	8	12	2
Strike or non-strike action	16	13	5	11	18	9
Strike action lasting:						
Less than 1 day	4	5	2	2	10	3
1 day or more	7	5	2	3	9	6
1 day but less than a week	..[3]	5	1	..	9	5
1 week or more	..	1	*	..	*	1
Non-strike action:						
Overtime bans/restriction	7	6	2	5	6	1
Work to rule	4	2	1	4	6	1
Blacking of work	2	2	*	3	2	1
Lock-out	1	*	—	*	*	—
Go-slow	1	*	*	*	*	*
Other pressure[4]	1	1	1	1	2	*
Base: establishments with employees named in column heads						
Unweighted	*1899*	*1853*	*1831*	*2034*	*2010*	*2058*
Weighted	*1823*	*1749*	*1697*	*1981*	*1985*	*1992*

[1] The percentages represent those establishments where either the manager or the worker representative reported industrial action of the type specified.
[2] See Note F.
[3] See Note J.
[4] 'Work-ins', 'sit-ins', 'other action by employees' (1990 only) and 'other action' are included with the more general 'other pressure' category as so few cases were reported.

1989–1990. Both strike and non-strike action fell. But, non-strike forms of action were reported much more frequently than strikes among manufacturing establishments in 1990. This had been true in 1984, but not in 1980 when our survey had shown that they were equally common. The figures for the incidence of strikes in our three surveys were 22 per cent, 10 per cent and 4 per cent of manufacturing establishments respectively. For non-strike forms of action they were 21, 15 and 7 per cent. Of the ten groups of classes of manufacturing industry in Table 8A, Vehicles and Transport Equipment was still the sector most prone to industrial action. And only in this sector was strike action more commonly reported than non-strike action in 1989–1990 (14 per cent as against 8 per cent). Interestingly, this reversed the position in 1983–4 and was more akin to the picture in 1979–1980.

The proportion of private services establishments reporting any industrial action was roughly the same in our first two surveys – between 7 and 8 per cent. By 1990 this had fallen to 3 per cent of establishments. The proportion affected by strikes dropped slightly from 5 per cent to 2 per cent between the 1984 and 1990 surveys. And the figures for non-strike action were identical, indicating no change in the relative use of the two main forms of action in this sector. Table 8A indicates that the incidence of strikes was very similar to the incidence of non-strike action in many parts of the private services in 1990. This was true most notably in: Wholesale Distribution; Retail Distribution; Hotels, Catering, Repairs; Banking, Finance, Insurance; and Business Services reflecting a trend through the 1980s. The most marked fall in the incidence of both strike and non-strike action was in Banking, Finance, Insurance where both forms were reported at less than 0.5 per cent of workplaces in 1990 – in 1984 14 per cent had been affected by strikes and 6 per cent by non-strike action. Surprisingly, perhaps, there was a hint of a possible increase in strike action in Business Services although this only amounted to 6 per cent of workplaces being affected in 1990.

The incidence of industrial action remained much higher in the public sector, but even here we observed a substantial fall as the decade came to an end. This sector also showed greatest change through the 1980s. It was alone responsible for the overall increase in industrial action among our sampled establishments charted by the 1980 and 1984 surveys. Just over a third (35 per cent) of public sector establishments (excluding coal mining) were affected by some form of industrial action in 1979–1980 and by 1983–1984 that figure had increased to almost half (48 per cent). Our third survey shows that three out of ten establishments were affected by industrial action in 1989–1990. Strike action was reported in over a quarter of public sector workplaces in 1989–1990, compared with two fifths in 1983–1984 and 19 per cent in 1979–1980. Non-strike industrial action was reported in just 7 per cent of workplaces in 1990, barely a fifth of the 1984 level (of 34 per cent) and a quarter of that for 1980 (27 per cent). And whereas there was a preference for non-strike forms of action over strikes in 1979–1980 (particularly overtime bans and working to rule among non-manual employees) by 1983–1984 that had been reversed and by 1989–1990 strike action appeared as the predominant form of industrial action in the public sector. This was particularly so in Local Government, Central Government and Transport.

This overall picture, however, conceals dramatic falls in strike action between the 1984 and 1990 surveys in several parts of the public sector, notably Central Government (down from 61 per cent to 10 per cent of establishments) and schools and colleges (from 47 per cent to 24 per cent).[9] But strike action remained high and dropped little between our two surveys in Local Government (38 per cent in 1990, 41 per cent in 1984) and Higher Education (around two fifths in both surveys). For non-strike action the pattern was very similar, with the exception of Local Government, where some decline was evident.

Our previous surveys demonstrated a clear association between the incidence of industrial action and trade union strength. The same pattern emerged from our 1990 results. Industrial action was still more frequently reported in workplaces that were larger, had high union density, recognized trade unions (including multi-unionism) and were under public ownership. On a related matter, action was more common where our management respondents spent more of their time on industrial relations issues: from 4 per cent of those spending a tenth or less of their time on it through to a fifth of those who spent the great majority of their time on it. However, as unionized workplaces formed a smaller part of the economy in 1990 than in 1984, this may account for some of the overall decline in industrial action since the mid-1980s. In addition to the drop in union membership, the weakening of local union organization in each of the three broad sectors of employment, detailed in Chapter 4, may explain some of the changed balance between different forms of action. For example, insofar as local paid union officials and lay union representatives are particularly necessary to organize and sustain strike action, their continuing presence in the public sector (especially in Local Government) may play a part in explaining the continuing, relatively high level of industrial action there.

However, the widespread decline in the incidence of industrial action across such a variety of workplaces suggests that other developments outside the immediate working environment, such as broader economic factors[10] and changes in relevant law could also have been important influences. The impact of these developments may be seen in the changing characteristics of industrial action, which was the subject of detailed questioning of our worker representative respondents. We can put those results in context using information available for the whole of our sample on a particular characteristic of strike action – it's duration – as measured by our 1984 and 1990 surveys.

The duration of strike action

We asked both managers and worker representatives whether the establishment had been affected by strike action lasting less than one day or one shift; at least one day but less than one week; and one week or more. Our data show clear differences in behaviour between 1984 and 1990. Table 8.1 shows that the most dramatic fall was in the incidence of very short strikes – those lasting less than a single day or a single shift. Overall, these short strikes were reported in just 4 per cent of workplaces in 1990, compared with 14 per cent six years previously. Manual and non-manual workers were similarly involved (Table 8.2). Some of this dramatic change is explained by the widespread occurrence of very short stoppages in the public sector in 1984 in protest at the Government's refusal to allow national union membership at GCHQ – short strikes occurred in 28 per cent of public sector establishments in 1983–1984 compared with just 8 per cent in 1989–1990. Within this total, however, there was notably little change in Transport, which includes the rail and underground sectors that were particularly affected by short, unofficial strikes during 1989. In the private sector the downward trend was more consistent. In 1990 short strikes were reported in just 2 per cent of workplaces in manufacturing industry and 2 per cent of workplaces in services – compared with 7 and 4 per cent of establishments in 1984.

There was a similar pattern of decline in the reporting of longer strikes – those lasting one day or more – in both parts of the private sector. In private services such strikes were almost non-existent in 1989–1990 and they were reported in just 2 per cent of private manufacturing plants. However, in the public sector the drop was very much smaller. A fifth of public sector workplaces reported these longer strikes in 1990 (compared with just over a quarter in 1984), virtually all of them lasting between one day and one week in length. Again, however, there were differences within the public sector. Among Local Government workplaces the incidence of strikes of one day or more increased, from 19 per cent to 31 per cent, whereas among schools and colleges there was a sharp decline, from 35 per cent to 12 per cent. It was notable, however, that there was a detectable increase in the incidence of even longer strikes in these two sectors. In 1990 strikes lasting a week or more were reported in 3 per cent of Local Government workplaces and 2 per cent of schools and colleges; in both cases they had been virtually non-existent six years earlier. Full details of the incidence of strikes of various durations in 1989–1990 are given in Table 8B. The net result of these changes is that although strikes of all durations were reported less frequently in 1990 than in 1984, longer strikes (those lasting one day or more) formed a larger proportion of those that were reported (Table 8.1). In this sense the picture of strike action in the public sector in 1989–1990 was similar to that in 1979–1980.

Strike duration is only one of the characteristics of industrial action that we explored in our survey series. Other aspects were covered in our interviews with worker representatives and it is to this material that we now turn.

The characteristics of the most recent industrial action

As on previous occasions, our detailed questioning was directed at the most recent strike of one day or more and the most recent non-strike action.[11] Workplaces that had experienced both forms of action were asked the same sequence of questions about each. It is fair to say that, once again, our survey results reflect the concentration of industrial action in the public sector. In 1989–1990, 71 per cent of recent strikes of one day or more involving manual workers and fully 97 per cent of those involving non-manual employees were in public sector workplaces. Non-strike action among non-manuals was slightly more dispersed, but even here over eight out of ten cases were in the public sector. Only among workplaces with non-strike action among manual workers was there a different pattern. A third of these cases were in the public sector, 58 per cent were in private manufacturing plants and 8 per cent were in private services.

The reasons given for industrial action

In line with our previous surveys, we asked worker representatives what they thought were the main reasons for the most recent strike and the most recent non-strike action at their establishments. Using the same coding frame as that used by the Employment Department's statisticians for classifying the causes of stoppages due to industrial disputes, we allowed multi-coding of the answers we received using the nine broad categories of cause.

In 1984 we were struck by the very large proportion of respondents who gave reasons for industrial action that could not be coded to any of the Department's categories of cause. The reason given by our worker representative respondents in 1984 for almost half of recent manual strikes and a fifth of recent non-manual strikes had to be classified to the 'miscellaneous' category. Further analysis of the distribution of these 'miscellaneous' reasons revealed that our coding frame would need to be expanded to encompass three additional substantive codes.[12] These covered disputes in protest at the government's privatization plans, other protests against government plans, such as the abolition of the Metropolitan County authorities, and action in sympathy with workers in dispute elsewhere, such as miners and nurses. These particular categories of cause fall outside the scope of the Employment Department's classification, although the disputes in question may have been coded to one or more of the other categories of cause in that series.[13] Since our previous book was published we have undertaken the additional coding work and can now report the revised results for the 1984 survey incorporating the additional categories. Naturally, we also incorporated the revisions to our 1984 coding scheme into the frame used for the 1990 survey and these results are reported below.

As the cost of living was an important factor in pay negotiations in the year prior to our survey (see Chapter 7), reflecting the increasing rate of inflation at the time, we expected this to show up also in cases where the parties had failed to agree a settlement, which resulted in industrial action. This was so. Pay was by far the single most important reason given for striking throughout the 1980s. Indeed, the importance of pay over other issues increased substantially since our last survey – during 1989–1990, almost nine out of ten cases of strike action among non-manual workers arose from a dispute over pay (Table 8.3). Respondents in two thirds of workplaces affected by strike action among manual workers also gave pay as the chief reason for that action, double the proportion who gave this answer in 1984. It is notable that in 1990 no non-manual representatives and just 1 per cent of manual stewards reported 'extra wage and fringe benefits' as the main reason for strike action in 1990. For manuals this indicates a sharp fall since our previous surveys. Rather, it was disputes about the major part of the pay packet – wage rates and earnings – that gave rise to the bulk of recent strike action among our sampled workplaces in 1989–1990. Of course, the exceptionally high level of stoppages generated by the GCHQ dispute in 1983–1984 partly explains the smaller proportion of disputes due to pay matters during that year.

Table 8.4 gives a similar picture for non-strike action, at least among manual workers. By contrast, non-manual representatives reported pay as the main reason for non-strike action only half as frequently in 1990 as six years previously (29 per cent as against 56 per cent) and in 1990 'extra wage and fringe benefits' hardly figured at all. In other words, our data show that where strike action was used it was increasingly seen as the most appropriate strategy in disputes over pay involving non-manual workers in 1990, the great majority of which were in the public sector. Manual workers were still more inclined than non-manual workers to use both strike and non-strike sanctions to win pay increases. Irrespective of the forms of action used, however, these results suggest that in 1989–1990 trade unions were concentrating their efforts in their more traditional areas of bargaining activity.

Table 8.3   **Reasons given by worker representatives for most recent strike action, 1980, 1984 and 1990**

Percentages

| | Most recent strike of one day or more | | | | | |
| | Manual | | | Non-manual | | |
	1980	1984	1990	1980	1984	1990
Pay: wage rates and earnings	59[1]	32[2]	66	61	54	87
Pay: extra wage and fringe benefits	12	7	1	1	2	—
Duration and pattern of working hours	20	8	9	2	3	6
Redundancy issues	3	16	*	12	7	2
Trade union matters	6	10	2	2	19	1
Working conditions and supervision	2	4	3	*	6	5
Manning and work allocation	6	15	6	9	10	7
Dismissal and other disciplinary measures	6	2	5	3	1	1
Against privatization	.[3]	16	—	:	3	1
Against government (other than privatization)	:	11	—	:	5	1
Sympathy action	:	8	5	:	8	4
Miscellaneous reasons	6	2	*	6	2	3
Not answered	7	*	6	12	3	7

Base: worker representatives belonging to recognized trade unions reporting recent strike action of one day or more

Unweighted	*185*	*152*	*68*	*70*	*143*	*129*
Weighted	*77*	*51*	*31*	*26*	*115*	*77*

[1] See Note E.
[2] Figures for 1984 differ slightly from those previously published due to recoding of other answers.
[3] See Note J.

Table 8.4 Reasons given by worker representatives for most recent non-strike action, 1980, 1984 and 1990

Percentages

| | Most recent non-strike action | | | | | |
| | Manual | | | Non-manual | | |
	1980	1984	1990	1980	1984	1990
Pay: wage rates and earnings	41[1]	39[2]	58	56	56	29
Pay: extra wage and fringe benefits	4	8	4	5	4	*
Duration and pattern of working hours	20	12	4	6	3	3
Redundancy issues	5	10	1	8	8	*
Trade union matters	6	4	1	5	2	*
Working conditions and supervision	3	7	9	1	2	8
Manning and work allocation	21	13	17	22	15	36
Dismissal and other disciplinary measures	1	1	1	*	*	2
Against privatization	.[3]	5	—	:	1	—
Against government (other than privatization)	:	5	*	:	1	*
Sympathy action	:	4	1	:	3	*
Miscellaneous reasons	7	*	2	5	9	3
Not answered	7	9	5	4	6	21
Base: worker representatives belonging to recognized trade unions reporting recent non-strike action						
Unweighted	*212*	*237*	*163*	*207*	*233*	*118*
Weighted	*96*	*91*	*52*	*102*	*151*	*37*

[1] See Note E.
[2] Figures for 1984 differ slightly from those previously published due to recoding of other answers.
[3] See Note J.

This is reinforced by the results on the other main reasons for industrial action given in the two tables. In 1990 redundancy issues and trade union matters were much less likely to be mentioned as the reasons for any form of industrial action among any section of the workforce than in previous surveys. Less than 0.5 per cent of cases of recent manual strike action in 1989–1990 related to redundancy and just 2 per cent of cases of recent non-manual strike action; the equivalent figures in 1984 were 16 and 7 per cent respectively. Similarly, just 1 per cent of recent manual non-strike action in 1989–1990 and less than 0.5 per cent of recent non-strike action among white-collar employees arose over redundancy issues (compared with, respectively, 10 and 8 per cent in 1983–1984).

As fewer workplaces overall made any redundancies in 1989–1990 compared with six years earlier (see Chapter 9) it comes as no surprise that the issue was less likely to give rise to industrial action. In addition, however, given losses in local membership, trade unions in 1989–1990 may have been less likely than previously to believe that industrial action was a viable strategy for preventing plant closure and redundancy. The example of large-scale industrial action which nevertheless failed to prevent job-losses, such as the 1984–1985 coal mining strike, may have no doubt contributed to that view.[14] For similar reasons, it is perhaps unsurprising that action over 'trade union matters', such as recognition, union facilities and disciplining of worker representatives, also declined since our last survey.

We might have expected disputes over working hours to figure more prominently in our results given, for example, the campaign during 1989–1990 within the engineering industry for a reduction in the working week. Set against that, however, is the selective nature of that campaign, in which a small number of key workplaces were targeted for action by unions, with members in other workplaces providing financial support for the relevant strikers but not taking strike action themselves. Our data show that the proportion of manual stewards giving working hours as the reason for striking actually declined between 1984 and 1990, although there was little or no change in the extent of non-strike action by manual workers over this issue. The more pronounced impact of this dispute on working days lost, as measured by the Employment Department's series,[15] is explained by the fact that the small number of workplaces targeted for action by the engineering unions employed a relatively large number of people.

By contrast, manning and work allocation issues figured much more prominently than previously as reasons for non-strike action among non-manual workers. Over a third (36 per cent) of non-manual representatives gave this reason for non-strike action in 1990, compared with just 15 per cent six years earlier. In fact, this issue was the single most important reason given for non-strike action among non-manual employees – very largely in the public sector – in 1989–1990. This may reflect a shift of tactics by public sector unions, from strike to non-strike action over this issue, or the effect on our results of an increase in the proportion of workplaces with unions which were more likely to opt for non-strike action over this issue. The increased impact of Local Government workplaces in our figures for industrial action in the public sector could also be part of the explanation.[16]

As in 1984, dismissal and disciplinary issues did not figure very highly as the main reason for any form of action among any section of the workforce. This is perhaps unsurprising given the continuing high proportion of workplaces with formal procedures for dealing with disputes in this area that we described in Chapter 6. While the increase in dismissals over the period (also reported in Chapter 6) might have been a focus for collective conflict in 1989–1990, this does not appear to have happened.

Tables 8.3 and 8.4 also show that industrial action 'against the government', such as against actual or proposed privatizations, was largely a mid-1980s phenomenon, concerning manual workers in particular. In 1984, 27 per cent of manual stewards reported strike action against government proposals (16 per cent over privatization and 11 per cent over other proposals), whereas in 1990 none gave this answer. The pattern among non-manuals was probably similar, although some action over these issues was still detectable in the 1990 results. Our figures for the proportion of non-manual representatives reporting strike action over privatization fell from 3 per cent to 1 per cent and those for strike action over other government proposals fell from 5 per cent to 1 per cent. The pattern of change was similar for non-strike action, though in 1984 non-strike action over these issues was reported only a third as frequently as strike action.

'Sympathy' action (where employees in one workplace take action in support of those in another) also declined in importance, particularly involving non-strike action. Some 8 per cent of worker representatives (manual or non-manual) reported strike action in sympathy with other workers in 1984, with 3 to 4 per cent reporting non-strike action undertaken for a similar reason. The equivalent 1990 figures were half those for 1984.[17]

The duration, continuity and locality of recent action
It was clear from previous surveys that non-strike sanctions were typically employed for much longer periods than strikes. Strike action typically lasted a day or less in 1984 and non-strike forms were often employed for considerably more than a week. In our previous book we suggested that trade unions may have been increasingly resorting to 'cut price' strike action in preference to either strikes of longer duration or

non-strike forms of action. One possible reason for this was that potentially longer but unlawfully organized strikes were increasingly being terminated at an early stage because employers sought and obtained court injunctions.[18]

The period since our last survey, however, has seen the impact of further changes in statute which restrict the circumstances in which unions can lawfully organize such action. In particular, the Trade Union Act 1984 and the Employment Act 1988 provide that unions retain immunity from civil law proceedings only if they hold properly conducted ballots before calling for industrial action. In 1988 union members were also given protection against being disciplined by their union for failing to support or participate in industrial action. Taken together, such legislative developments are likely to have deterred trade unions at local level from attempting to use the 'short, sharp strike' as might otherwise have happened.

Our more detailed 1990 results from worker representatives for the duration of recent action are given in Table 8.5. They confirm that non-strike action still lasted longer than strikes – at least in respect of action involving manual workers. While a majority of recent manual strikes in 1989–1990 lasted just a single day, a clear majority of recent manual non-strike sanctions lasted at least six days. It is notable, however, that the difference was much less clear cut for industrial action involving non-manual employees. Just less than half (45 per cent) of recent non-manual strikes in 1989–1990 lasted at least six days, whereas just over half (56 per cent) of cases of non-strike action did so. This confirms the results from our management respondents reported earlier and marks a change since our last survey, when very few cases of non-manual strike action were reported as having lasted more than a single day. As we noted earlier, in addition to any possible deterrent effect of legislation in this area, part of the reason for the change is the disproportionate effect on the 1984 survey of the very short strikes in the public sector about national union membership at GCHQ. Comparing the 1984 and 1990 results, the proportion of cases of recent non-manual strike action lasting a single day declined by two thirds, from 91 per cent to 30 per cent.

Another aspect of the change, however, is that some two thirds of cases of recent non-manual strikes reported in 1990 were conducted intermittently rather than over consecutive working days. Intermittent action was a factor in a major dispute during 1989–1990 in Local Government, where one-day and two-day strikes took place over several weeks over pay and bargaining arrangements. It is worth noting, however, that this tactic of organizing intermittent days of industrial action was a feature of the 1979–1980 disputes within the steel and engineering sectors that were recorded by our 1980 survey. On that occasion, as

Table 8.5 Reports by worker representatives of recent industrial action in relation to duration and whether on consecutive or intermittent days, 1980, 1984 and 1990

Percentages

	Manual			Non-manual		
	1980	1984	1990	1980	1984	1990
Strike action:						
Duration in working days						
1	31	59	55	67	91	30
1–3	47[1]	77	75	77	95	51
4–5	10	4	3	1	3	3
6 or more	42	17	21	10	2	45
Other answers[2]	*	2	*	12	—	*
Consecutive or intermittent days[3]						
Consecutive	46	80	(57)[4]	(64)	(92)	31
Intermittent	54	20	(40)	(36)	(2)	67
Not answered	—	—	(2)	—	(6)	2
Base: worker representatives belonging to recognized trade unions reporting recent strikes of one day or more						
Unweighted	*185*	*152*	*68*	*70*	*143*	*129*
Weighted	*77*	*51*	*31*	*26*	*115*	*77*
Non-strike action:						
Duration in working days						
1–3	24	21	20	9	12	6
4–5	8	6	9	6	3	11
6 or more	57	48	65	56	44	56
Other answers	11	25	—	29	41	—
Consecutive or intermittent days						
Consecutive	95	92	89	90	96	71
Intermittent	4	5	6	7	2	7
Not answered	*	3	1	3	2	1
Base: worker representatives belonging to recognized trade unions reporting recent non-strike action						
Unweighted	*212*	*237*	*163*	*207*	*233*	*118*
Weighted	*96*	*91*	*52*	*102*	*151*	*37*

[1] See Note C.
[2] Includes cases where either no information was available or the action was still in progress.
[3] Base for action over consecutive or intermittent days is relevant action lasting two days or more.
[4] See Note B.

Table 8.5 shows, it was manual workers who employed the tactic. The adoption of these tactics by unions representing non-manual workers in the public rather than the private sector of the economy may be a development of some significance.

Although two fifths of manual strikes in 1989–1990 were conducted over intermittent days, whereas a fifth were intermittent in 1983–1984, it might have been expected that such strikes would form a larger proportion of all strikes given the campaign for a shorter working week within the engineering industry. Here again, however, the union strategy of targeting key workplaces made for an effective strike without widespread impact on the overall figures.

There was little overall change in the duration and continuity of non-strike forms of action. In 1989–1990, the mean duration of manual non-strike action (mostly overtime bans or working to rule) was 71 days compared with 109 days for non-strike action among white-collar staff. As in previous surveys, the bulk of non-strike action was conducted over consecutive days.

Our surveys also allow us to assess the extensiveness of reported industrial action. We defined industrial action as local if only our sampled establishment was involved in the action. We found in our previous surveys that there was a change in the pattern of local action between the 1980 and 1984 surveys. In 1984, as compared with 1980, both strike and non-strike action involving manual workers more frequently involved only the sampled establishment, whereas non-manual strike action was less likely to be local than previously. Our questions were repeated in 1990 and the results suggest little change in the overall pattern since 1984. Table 8.6 gives the results. Manual strikes were local in a third of cases, whereas non-manual strikes were rarely so (5 per cent of cases in the 1990 survey). With its more centralized bargaining arrangements, the disproportionate impact of the public sector on the results for non-manual strike action partly explains the more widespread action there. Non-strike action among manual workers was twice as likely to be local than strike action, being reported in two thirds of cases. By contrast, non-strike action among white-collar employees was reported in just 16 per cent of cases.

Incidence of first-time action

Another indicator of the character of industrial action, included in WIRS since its inception, is a question asking whether the particular sections of the workforce[19] involved in industrial action in the period covered by the survey were taking action for the first time. In fact, both our previous surveys showed that, in the great majority of cases, those involved in industrial action had some previous experience of it. There were changes since 1984. Table 8.6 shows that in a larger proportion of cases,

Table 8.6   Extent to which recent industrial action was local and where employees were taking action for the first time, 1980, 1984 and 1990

Percentages

	Manual			Non-manual		
	1980	1984	1990	1980	1984	1990
Strike action						
Local	17	32	34	21	1	5
First-time	34	30	48	38	31	47
Base: worker representatives belonging to recognized trade unions reporting recent strikes of one day or more						
Unweighted	*185*	*152*	*68*	*70*	*143*	*129*
Weighted	*77*	*51*	*31*	*26*	*115*	*77*
Non-strike action						
Local	47	61	68	9	10	16
First-time	50	18	42	38	24	34
Base: worker representatives belonging to recognized trade unions reporting recent non-strike action						
Unweighted	*212*	*237*	*163*	*207*	*233*	*118*
Weighted	*96*	*91*	*52*	*102*	*151*	*37*

sections of the workforce which had not previously taken industrial action did so in 1989–1990. The increases since the 1984 survey in the incidence of first-time strike action among non-manual employees and first-time non-strike action among manual workers, are particularly marked. In almost half of cases of non-manual strike action in 1989–1990, the sections concerned were taking action for the first time. This compares with 31 per cent of cases reported in 1984. The proportion of cases of manual non-strike action that were novel for the sections involved increased from 18 per cent in the 1984 survey to 42 per cent in 1990.[20] So while the overall extent of industrial action declined across the 1984 to 1990 period, the composition of the workforce taking action also changed, resulting in an increase in the proportion of employees with experience of industrial action.[21]

When we looked at the particular sections of the non-manual workforce involved in strike action in 1989–1990, a difference from our previous survey was that a larger proportion of respondents said all sections of the non-manual workforce were involved and, consequently, a smaller proportion said just one section was involved. Clerical workers were twice as frequently mentioned in 1990 (41 per cent) as in 1984 (23 per cent), with technical and professional workers mentioned less than half as frequently (a fifth compared with half). Both findings are consistent with the shift in the location of public sector strike action from Central Government towards Local Government.

The predominance of pay as the principal reason for action in 1989–1990 may go some way towards explaining why particular sections of the workforce who had not taken action previously did so in that year. Another factor may be that in some disputes in 1989–1990 fundamental procedural issues relating to proposed changes in bargaining machinery and moves to new bargaining levels were under debate (e.g. Local Government). But the degree of official endorsement or authorization by trade unions themselves may also be important. These issues we consider below.

The extent of recent industrial action made official

A novel feature of our 1984 survey was the information we collected from worker representatives about whether the most recent form of industrial action was *'made official by the union at any stage'*. This was an important innovation as there had been no data published on this matter from any source since 1981.[22] The form of questioning used allowed us to capture cases where unions had given official backing to industrial action at various stages of a dispute.

At the time of our survey the law required unions to ballot their members before organizing industrial action *only* if the call to take action was one for which the union was responsible in law (and such responsibility was generally confined to acts of national union leaders or employed officials). However, during the development work for our third survey the Government published a Green Paper containing proposals for legislation to make trade unions potentially responsible for certain acts of their lay representatives (including calls for industrial action).[23] The proposals subsequently became part of the Employment Act 1990 which came into effect in January 1991, *after* fieldwork for the 1990 survey. In these circumstances, therefore, the inclusion of the previous question in a survey just prior to a change in the law will help to form a benchmark from which to assess the impact of the changes in the law on the balance between 'official' as opposed to 'unofficial' action.

Perhaps it is worth re-emphasizing, however, that our figures relate only to industrial action given official union backing in workplaces with recognized unions where a senior worker representative was present on site. As such, our data will understate the overall extent of such action in the economy as a whole. Also, the fact that we limited our questioning

Table 8.7 **The extent to which establishments were affected by recent industrial action that was made official, 1984 and 1990**

Percentages

| | Manual | | Non-manual | |
	1984	1990	1984	1990
Strike action				
Made official	61	65	98[1]	94
Remained unofficial	38	34	2	4
Status not reported	*	1	*	2

Base: worker representatives belonging to recognized trade unions reporting recent strike action of one day or more
| *Unweighted* | *152* | *68* | *140* | *126* |
| *Weighted* | *51* | *31* | *115* | *75* |

Non-strike action				
Made official	38	28	90	59
Remained unofficial	54	69	8	26
Status not reported	8	3	2	15

Base: worker representatives belonging to recognized trade unions reporting recent non-strike action
| *Unweighted* | *237* | *163* | *233* | *118* |
| *Weighted* | *91* | *52* | *151* | *37* |

[1] See Note C.

on recent strikes to those of at least one day in length obviously means that shorter strikes were excluded. Very short strikes are most likely to be unofficial given their spontaneity.[24]

Results on the extent to which each main form of recent industrial action was made official are given in Table 8.7. The consistency with which strike action received official backing between the two surveys, regardless of the section of the workforce involved, is notable. Two thirds of cases of manual strike action in 1989–1990 and well over nine out of ten cases of non-manual strike action were made official.

Of equal interest, however, is the increase over the same period in the proportion of cases of non-strike action that remained unofficial. A quarter of cases of non-strike action involving white-collar employees remained unofficial in 1989–1990 compared with just 8 per cent in 1983–1984. However, manual non-strike action was still much more likely than its white-collar equivalent to remain unofficial. This was so in some seven out of ten cases in the 1990 survey, marking an increase since the 1984 survey, which found just over half (54 per cent) remaining unofficial. In 1989–1990, as previously, the great majority of cases of recent industrial action by manual workers in the private manufacturing sector remained unofficial. The drift of these results was confirmed by some additional questions asked of managers in our 1990 survey, designed to assess the overall extent of official action in our sample as a whole.[25]

We explored the timing of official union backing further in the 1990 survey by inserting a supplementary question which asked those who had reported official strike and non-strike action whether the action was '*made official by the union before the workforce here began the action, at the same time, or afterwards?*' Our results show that in the great majority of cases strike action was authorized by the relevant union *before* the strike had actually begun at our sampled workplaces. Ninety-two per cent of manual stewards and 95 per cent of non-manual representatives who had reported official strikes gave this answer, with a further 5 per cent in each case reporting that official backing was given at the same time as the action began. Unfortunately, the absence of a similar question from our 1984 survey means we cannot tell whether this marks a change from previous practice.

Responses on the timing of official union backing for *non-strike* action were more mixed, however, perhaps reflecting their relative spontaneity. Smaller proportions of worker representatives who reported official non-strike action said official union authorization was given prior to the start of the action (72 per cent manual, 81 per cent non-manual). In a fifth of cases of official non-strike action among manual workers and a tenth of cases involving non-manual employees, union authorization was given at the same time the action began. In 6 per cent of manual cases and 8 per cent of non-manual cases the action was officially endorsed by the relevant union after it had begun. Even in cases of official non-strike action, therefore, it was rare for unions to endorse the action after it had begun.

Consultations with members before initiating and calling-off recent industrial action

Official union backing may increase the legitimacy of industrial action for union members as potential participants, whether or not they vote in favour of it. Those who vote against action in a ballot, for example, may be either pursuaded by the general will or be reluctant to be seen to ignore it, while the more agnostic may await the outcome of the ballot to help decide their orientation. Either way, successful ballots or other votes in favour may result in individuals or sections of a workforce taking action who might not otherwise have done so. If the incidence of balloting before industrial action is increasing, therefore, it may partly explain the apparently increased willingness of some union members to take action for the first time, reported earlier.

One of the aims of the legal changes in the area of industrial action has been to require trade unions to seek a formal mandate from their members prior to calling for or otherwise organizing industrial action. Indeed, the Government has argued that the Trade Union Act 1984 and subsequent legislation have amounted to one of the most significant reforms of industrial relations law since 1979.[26] However, we saw in Chapter 4 how, in areas where they were still free to choose, trade unions tended to opt for less formal methods of consulting their members than balloting (although there were moves towards more formal consultations on pay offers, as shown in Chapter 7). How far this was true in one of the key areas now governed extensively by statute was explored through additional questioning in our 1990 survey.

At the end of the sequence of questions about the characteristics of recent action, we asked our worker representative respondents several broad questions concerning the nature of their consultations with members about the action.[27] Our intention was to measure the extent of consultation about decisions both to take and to call off the action. However, our form of questioning may well have been interpreted by some of our respondents to also include consultation on actual offers made in negotiations, which was the subject of specific questioning in the pay section of our questionnaires.[28] Bearing this caveat in mind, the overall results are given in Table 8.8. We look first at the extent of consultation prior to organizing and calling off the various forms of action, before moving on to consider the particular methods of consultation used in each case.

The first row of Table 8.8 shows that regardless of the form of industrial action under consideration at least three quarters of worker

Table 8.8   Consultation on industrial action, 1990

	Manual		Non-manual	
	Strike action	Non-strike action	Strike action	Non-strike action
				Percentages
Consultation before start of industrial action:				
Members consulted	74	74	87	76
Don't know/not answered	1	4	2	15
Base: worker representatives belonging to recognized trade unions reporting industrial action named in column heads				
Unweighted	*68*	*163*	*129*	*118*
Weighted	*31*	*52*	*77*	*37*
			Column percentages	
Frequency of consultation:				
Once	31	21	26	20[1]
More than once	69	79	74	76
Don't know/not answered	—	—	—	3
				Percentages
Method of consultation:				
Ascertained views without a vote	*[2]	5	—	1
General feeling of meeting	5	8	6	17
Show of hands at meeting	24	72	23	39
Secret workplace ballot	29	12	22	27
Secret postal ballot	35	2	59	12
Other answer	3	—	—	—
Don't know/not answered	6	—	—	—

Base: worker representatives belonging to recognized trade unions reporting consultation with members before industrial action named in column heads began

Unweighted	*55*	*124*	*115*	*90*
Weighted	*23*	*38*	*67*	*29*

Consultation before industrial action called off:

Members consulted	50	47	62	35
Action not called off	*	13	*	20
Don't know/not answered	9	6	6	17

Base: worker representatives belonging to recognized trade unions reporting industrial action named in column heads

Unweighted	*68*	*163*	*129*	*118*
Weighted	*31*	*52*	*77*	*37*

Table 8.8 continued

	Manual		Non-manual	
	Strike action	Non-strike action	Strike action	Non-strike action
	Column percentages			
Frequency of consultation:				
Once	33	52	38	40
More than once	67	46	62	60
Don't know/not answered	—	2	—	*
				Percentages
Method of consultation:				
Ascertained views without a vote	(-)[3]	3	*	2
General feeling of meeting	(14)	16	8	38
Show of hands at meeting	(30)	73	48	33
Secret workplace ballot	(56)	7	17	21
Secret postal ballot	(1)	—	20	8
Other answer	(—)	1	*	—
Don't know/not answered	(1)	*	7	*

Base: worker representatives belonging to recognized trade unions reporting consultation with members before industrial action named in column heads was called off

Unweighted	*42*	*92*	*76*	*61*
Weighted	*16*	*25*	*48*	*13*

[1] See Note C.
[2] See Note E.
[3] See Note B.

representatives (either manual or non-manual) reported that union members at the establishment had been consulted before action began. In the case of strike action among non-manual employees the figure rose to almost nine out of ten. At the same time, while consultation prior to the start of industrial action was clearly the rule in 1989–1990, in around a quarter of cases union members had not been consulted prior to the start of the action.

Although the emphasis of the legislation in this area has been on consulting union members prior to the official authorization of industrial action, we were also interested in the extent to which unions sought members' views prior to calling it off.[29] A notable feature of the results in Table 8.8, however, is the much higher non-response to the question about consultation prior to calling off industrial action compared with that in relation to its initiation. Part of the explanation for this may be the relative importance attached to each event by those concerned. In the absence of any legal pressure to do otherwise, unions with no tradition of consulting members directly on offers made by employers during a dispute are unlikely to opt for it. Excluding the higher non-response, together with those cases where industrial action was still in progress at the time of our fieldwork, the incidence of consultation prior to calling off industrial action was clearly much lower than that prior to organizing it. Around half of manual stewards reported that members had been consulted prior to either strike or non-strike action being called off. The same proportion of non-manual representatives gave this answer in relation to non-strike action. But, again, non-manual representatives were the most likely to consult about calling off strike action, with almost two thirds giving this answer.

Regardless of whether industrial action was being organized or was drawing to a close, Table 8.8 suggests that in the great majority of cases union members involved in industrial action were consulted on more than one occasion. The only exception here was in relation to calling off non-strike action by manual workers, with respondents dividing fairly equally between those reporting once-only consultation and consultation on more than one occasion. Unions may consult members on more than one occasion during a dispute to reconfirm support for the action – such as its intensity, coverage, form and duration, for example. But some of those reporting multiple consultations may have been referring, in addition, to seeking views about employers' offers at various stages of the negotiations.

But it was in relation to the method of consultation used by trade unions that there were some interesting differences in our results. If we look at consultation prior to industrial action first of all, the prevalence of balloting methods in relation to strike action is particularly clear. Almost two thirds of manual stewards and four fifths of non-manual representatives mentioned pre-strike ballots of one kind or another.[30] Postal ballots were only slightly more commonly reported by manual stewards than were workplace ballots, whereas three times as many non-manual representatives reported postal compared with workplace ballots. With this exception, however, methods of pre-strike consultation between manual and non-manual unions were remarkably similar. Less normal methods of consultation, such as a 'show of hands' and taking the 'general feeling of a meeting', were as commonly reported by each type of respondent. Around a quarter reported a show of hands and a twentieth reported assessing the general feeling of a meeting.

There was rather less similarity between manual and non-manual unions in relation to methods of assessing members' views prior to non-strike forms of action. Although the law requires balloting prior to either official strike action or official 'action short of a strike', our results show that ballots were used relatively rarely in cases of non-strike action – a show of hands was by far the single most common method reported by both manual and non-manual representatives. Almost three quarters (72 per cent) of manual stewards and two fifths (39 per cent) of non-manual representatives reported it. Just 14 per cent of manual stewards reported some sort of balloting procedure compared with two fifths of non-manual representatives and the majority in each case were workplace rather than postal ballots. There was also a marked preference for workplace rather than postal ballots prior to non-strike action by white-collar workers. Indeed workplace ballots and, surprisingly perhaps, the general feeling of a meeting were reported as the method of consultation twice as frequently by non-manual than manual representatives in relation to non-strike action.

The bottom section of Table 8.8 gives results on the method of consultation prior to calling off industrial action. Again there were differences between manual and non-manual unions but most notably with the methods used by each type of union prior to the start of any industrial action, such as the virtual absence of postal balloting from the methods used by manual stewards and its much less frequent occurrence in the responses of non-manual representatives (whether calling off strike or non-strike action was involved). Manual unions favoured workplace balloting, a show of hands and the general feeling of a meeting for calling off strikes whereas non-manual unions, perhaps surprisingly, favoured a show of hands over other methods. Almost half (48 per cent) of non-manual representatives gave this answer, compared with a fifth in each case reporting workplace and postal ballots.

The preference for more informal methods of consultation was even more marked in relation to calling off non-strike action. Balloting was virtually absent from the methods used by manual unions whereas a show of hands was reported by 73 per cent and the general feeling of a meeting by 16 per cent. Fully 71 per cent of non-manual representatives reported either a show of hands or the general feeling of a meeting, dividing equally between the two. Although a fifth of white-collar representatives still mentioned workplace ballots, just 8 per cent mentioned postal ballots.

In those cases where worker representatives had mentioned that some form of balloting procedure had been used before either organizing or calling off industrial action, we asked several supplementary questions about aspects of the balloting procedure. For example, we asked what proportion of the membership at the establishment who were entitled to vote had actually voted in the ballot; whether the unions who organized the ballot had received any assistance from management for the conduct of the ballot; and whether the unions had used the services of any external balloting agency.[31] In fact, the number of cases of strike and non-strike ballots among manual workers was too small for a full analysis in these terms and as balloting was relatively infrequently used for non-strike action involving white-collar employees, we report below only the main results for white-collar strikes.

In over 80 per cent of cases of pre-strike ballots of white-collar union members, at least 60 per cent of the local electorate were reported to have voted in the ballot. In three fifths of cases at least 80 per cent had voted and in a further quarter of cases between 60 and 79 per cent did so. When we asked whether the unions had encountered any difficulties in conducting the ballot, only one in ten of our respondents reported any sort of difficulty. A quarter said they had received some assistance from management for the conduct of the ballot.[32] Two fifths mentioned that the services of an external agency, such as the Electoral Reform Society or Unity Security Ballot Services had been used in connection with a ballot.

Strike pay

In 1990, we asked worker representatives (for the first time) whether the union members on strike at the establishment received any payments from the union itself during the dispute. The issue had become topical as a result of the tactical use of strike action and strike pay during the dispute in the engineering industry over hours of work. The results from this new question show that almost a fifth of manual stewards and a third of non-manual representatives reported that at least some members on strike at the sampled establishment had received strike pay during 1989–1990; there appeared to be little variation in the incidence of strike pay by broad sector of employment.

To gain some idea of the amount of strike pay we asked a supplementary question concerning the value of the payments for the average striker, as a proportion of the total earnings lost as a result of being on strike. The number of manual stewards who were asked the question is too small to draw reliable conclusions. However, there was a sufficient number of non-manual representatives and the results show that the average non-manual member received around two thirds of earnings through strike pay from the union.

Picketing and secondary blacking

Finally, we turn to the results on picketing and secondary blacking. Our previous surveys charted a decline of around half between 1980 and 1984 in the extent to which establishments were picketed, despite an increase in the extent of strike action over the same period. Part of the decline was explained by the much shorter duration of strike action in

Table 8.9   The extent to which establishments with strikes were affected by primary picketing,[1] by size of establishment, 1990

Percentages

	All establishments	Size of establishment			
		25–99	100–499	500–999	1000 or more
Primary picketing in year prior to survey in:					
1980	29	21	37	31	45
1984	15	10	22	25	30
1990	33	21	45	61	59

Base: establishments where any respondent reported strike action
[1] The percentages represent those establishments where any of the three main respondents reported primary picketing as a proportion of those establishments where any respondent reported a strike.

1983–1984 than in 1979–1980 which may have obviated the need for extensive picketing. Allowing for the decline in the extent to which establishments were affected by strike action between 1983–1984 and 1989–1990, we might have expected our 1990 survey results to show a similar decline in the extent of picketing. However, there was no such result. Indeed, there were similar proportions of establishments picketed in both 1983–1984 and 1989–1990 (6 per cent and 7 per cent respectively).[33] As previously, the 1990 results show a strong relationship between picketing and establishment size and, as might be expected, the great bulk of picketed establishments were in those sectors affected by strike action, particularly in Local Government, Central Government and Transport (Table 8A).

The decline in strike action, coupled with the lack of change in the incidence of picketing across our two most recent surveys, suggest that strikes were more likely to be accompanied by picketing in 1989–1990 than in 1983–1984. This certainly proved to be true when we looked at the relationship between strike action and 'primary' picketing – picketing in relation to a dispute at the picketed establishment. As in 1984, primary picketing was more common the larger the establishment affected; nonetheless, as Table 8.9 shows, strikes at all sizes of establishment were around twice as likely to be accompanied by primary picketing in 1989–1990 than in 1983–1984. This pattern applied irrespective of the length of the stoppage; those lasting between one day and a week were accompanied by primary picketing in 40 per cent of cases, compared with 20 per cent in 1984. Strike action of a week or more was accompanied by primary picketing in almost three fifths of cases in 1989–1990 compared with just under half in the earlier survey. In overall terms the incidence of primary picketing changed little through the 1980s, with 4 per cent of establishments overall being affected in 1989–1990 (5 per cent in 1979–1980).

Tables 8A and 8B point to the linkage between strike duration and picketing.[34] The low level of picketing in the Posts and Telecommunications sector relative to strike action (4 per cent as against 29 per cent), for example, is explained to a large extent by the preponderance of very short strikes there (28 per cent of establishments). In Local Government, by contrast, picketing and strike action were as frequently reported (38 per cent and 37 per cent), with most strike action in the sector lasting longer than a single day (34 per cent).

Characteristics of primary picketing
In line with our previous practice, detailed questions on the characteristics of picketing related to the most recent instance of picketing. We asked about the number of pickets and the number of gates picketed, the organizers of the picket and its effectiveness. We also asked about the proportion of pickets who were employed at the establishment. Again we use the responses of managers alone when reporting this material on the characteristics of picketing, as there was a management respondent at all our sampled establishments, while worker representatives were interviewed in only a sub-sample of them. We deal, first, with primary picketing.

Our results show that the average maximum number of primary pickets at our sampled establishments in 1990 was nine and the typical (median) number was five, excluding those who could not answer the question.[35] This represents a fall compared with the 1980 survey results when the equivalent numbers were 15 and ten.[36] Consequently, as Table 8.10 shows, the proportion of establishments where primary picketing activities involved 6 or fewer pickets increased over the decade and those with more than 6 decreased. Mass picketing (101 or more pickets) was still very rare by 1989–1990, with less than 1 per cent of establishments being affected. But of course these are overall figures covering cases where picketing was spread over several entrances whereas in most cases in the 1990 survey and previous surveys a single entrance was picketed. When we restricted the analysis to only those cases with a single picketed entrance the typical (median) maximum number of pickets was 4 in 1989–1990; it had been 6 in 1979–1980.[37]

There was little overall change since the 1980 survey in the extent to which managers reported that all primary pickets were employed at the

Table 8.10 Characteristics of primary picketing, 1980, 1984 and 1990

	1980	1984	1990
Maximum number of pickets			*Percentages*
1–6	46	45	58
7–20	36	40	17
21–100	16	14	7
101 or more	1	1	*
Not answered	—	*	—
Not known	—	—	18
Number of gates picketed			*Column percentages*
1	77	71	66
2	13	15	15
3+	10	14	11
Not known	—	—	8
Organizers of picketing			
Stewards: same employer,			*Percentages*
various establishments	71	94	73
Stewards at establishment	69	93	67
Stewards: same employer,			
other establishments	3	7	20
Stewards: other employer	*	2	*
Any paid union official	21	6	24
Employees themselves	8	2	16
Other answer	—	—	1
No information	2	—	1
Effects of picketing			
Establishment's or contractors' employees	36	30	21
Establishment's employees	23	21	13
Contractors' employees	17	18	12
Goods/services received or sent	53	53	51
Goods/services received	42	50	42
Goods/services sent	47	41	31
Any of above effects	**59**	**59**	**54**
Visitors to establishment	..[1]	6	34
Not answered	*	—	—

Base: establishments with primary picketing in previous year, as reported by managers
Unweighted	*124*	*66*	*142*
Weighted	*54*	*26*	*56*

[1] See Note J.

picketed establishment – around two thirds of managers gave this answer in 1990. Just 2 per cent (5 per cent in 1980) said less than half were employed there, but a further 12 per cent in 1990 said none of the primary pickets were their employees. Results given in Table 8.10 on the organizers of picketing shed further light on these 'external' pickets.

In general terms the distribution apparent from the 1990 survey is similar to that from the 1980 survey. However, although establishment-based lay representatives were still the most frequent organizers of primary picketing in 1989–1990, two other groups were also more important than previously, employees themselves (doubling since 1980), and lay representatives working for the same employer but from different establishments (increasing from 3 per cent to 20 per cent). The latter is consistent with the likely effect on our results that the relatively increased incidence of public sector strikes of more than a day would have; the consistent importance of establishment-based stewards should come as no surprise, given the maintenance of local steward organization in the public sector discussed in Chapter 4.

Effects of primary picketing
In overall terms primary picketing appears to have been as effective in 1989-1990 as in 1979–1980, at least in terms of the categories of effect we asked about (Table 8.10). In the 1990 survey just over half (54 per cent) of managers mentioned some restriction on the movement of people, goods or services by primary picketing (59 per cent in 1980). However, within this broadly similar figure there was a slight decline in the overall effectiveness of primary picketing in terms of preventing the movement of the establishment's or contractors' employees. Just over a fifth (21 per cent) of managers mentioned this in 1990, compared with 36 per cent ten years previously.

Our results show a dramatic increase in the proportion of managers mentioning a restriction on the movement of visitors to the establishment since our last survey in 1984, though this may partly reflect the fact that establishments picketed in 1989–1990 tended routinely to have more visitors than those so affected in 1983–1984. Again, this may be explained by the shift in industrial action from Central Government to Local Government in the two surveys.

It is worth emphasizing again here that our results only allow us to quantify the instances where picketing had some effect on the movement of goods, services or people. It would have taken a good deal more questioning than our resources allowed to be able to specify the magnitude of those effects within establishments – whether 10 per cent or 90 per cent of employees were prevented from entering or leaving on the last occasion of picketing. Neither can we specify the effect of picketing on the actual outcome of disputes.

Secondary picketing

We now turn briefly to 'secondary' picketing, which is defined in the WIRS series as picketing *not* in connection with a dispute at the picketed establishment.[38] In contrast to the picture for primary picketing given above, there was a decline in the incidence of secondary picketing between 1979–1980 and 1989–1990, from 7 per cent to 4 per cent of all establishments. Three quarters of cases of secondary picketing were in Division 9 of the *Standard Industrial Classification* – Other Services – so it is unsurprising that establishments in Local Government, Central Government and the finer category of 'Other Services' were particularly

Table 8.11   Comparison of primary and secondary picketing characteristics, as reported by managers, 1980 and 1990

	Primary picketing		Secondary picketing	
	1980	1990	1980	1990
Maximum number of pickets				*Numbers*
Median	10	5	8	5
Average	15	9	10	10
Organizers of picketing				*Percentages*
Stewards of same employer, various establishments	71[1]	73	34	68
Stewards at establishment	69[2]	67	27	38
Stewards of same employer, other establishments	3	20	9	45
Stewards of another employer	*	*	2	5
Any paid union official	21	24	43	34
Employees themselves	8	16	3	16
No information	2	1	16	4
Effects of picketing				
Employees entering or leaving	36	21	25	13
Goods or services in or out	53	51	53	21
Any effect	**59[3]**	**54**	**63**	**27**

Base: establishments where manager reported picketing of the type specified in column heads

Unweighted	*124*	*142*	*158*	*108*
Weighted	*54*	*56*	*93*	*53*

[1] See Note D.
[2] See Note E.
[3] See Note F.

affected (respectively 19 per cent, 14 per cent and 12 per cent of establishments).

Table 8.11 gives an overview of the main results on the characteristics of secondary picketing for both the 1980 and 1990 surveys, with the results for primary picketing given alongside for comparison. The table shows the number of primary and secondary pickets was similar in 1990, the average was ten and the median was five. But this means that secondary picket numbers fell by a smaller amount than primary picket numbers since the 1980 survey.[39]

The changes in the organization of secondary picketing are similar to those for primary picketing and appear to reflect the relative concentration of industrial action in the public sector in 1989–1990. In particular, lay union representatives from the same employer, but different establishments, were much more likely to organize secondary picketing in 1989–1990 than previously. In contrast to primary picketing, there was a large drop in the effectiveness of secondary picketing, with 27 per cent of managers reporting some effect in 1990 (less than half the proportion in 1980, 63 per cent). This consolidates the decline between 1980 and 1984 and reflects a fall on both main types of effect we asked about – employees entering or leaving, and goods and services in or out. The decline in the effectiveness of secondary picketing in preventing the movement of goods and services was particularly marked.

An additional type of picketing that our data enable us to throw light on is what we previously called 'external secondary picketing'. This refers to cases where none of the pickets were employees of the establishment, and the picketing was not in connection with a dispute at the picketed establishment. In 1989–1990 just 1 per cent of all establish-

Table 8.12   The extent to which establishments were affected by picketing of the type specified in the previous year, as reported by any respondent, 1980, 1984 and 1990

Percentages

	1980	1984	1990
Any picketing	11	6	7
Primary picketing	5	3	4
Secondary picketing	7	4	4
External secondary picketing	4	2	1
Base: all establishments			
Unweighted	*2040*	*2019*	*2061*
Weighted	*2000*	*2000*	*2000*

ments were affected by this form of secondary picketing. In 1984 it was reported in 2 per cent of establishments and, in 1980, in 4 per cent. By way of summary, these and the other results on the extent of all forms of picketing, for all three surveys, are given in Table 8.12.

Secondary blacking
Table 8.1 referred to earlier in the chapter contains the overall results on the varieties of non-strike industrial action undertaken at our sampled establishments in the year prior to interview. Included in the range of types of non-strike action was 'blacking' of work, and the results showed that just 1 per cent of establishments were affected by such blackings in 1989–1990. Such actions involve outlawing work, equipment or production processes at the sampled establishment. However, at the end of the sequence of questions about picketing, we asked a rather different question designed to find out whether, in addition to such blacking in relation to local issues, there was specifically any blacking of goods or services at the sampled establishment that was in connection with an industrial dispute elsewhere. Taking the 1980 and 1984 surveys, the incidence of this form of 'secondary blacking' fell slightly, from 4 per cent to 3 per cent of establishments. In line with the pattern for the other forms of action considered in this chapter, managers at just 1 per cent of establishments reported experience of such action in 1989–1990, with half of all cases occurring in private services.

Synopsis
There was a very substantial and widespread fall in the extent of industrial action in the second half of the 1980s, much more than the decline in trade union recognition might have suggested likely. It was not just strike action that was affected. All forms of non-strike action moved in the same downward direction. Some forms of pressure, such as secondary blacking and secondary picketing almost disappeared. While overtime bans were almost as common as strikes at the start of the decade, by 1990 they were less than a third as common, affecting just 3 per cent of workplaces. Contrary to what has sometimes been assumed, non-strike forms of action were not being substituted for strikes.

Primary picketing, by contrast, was as common as before, reflecting the fact that the strikes that were undertaken were more likely to be picketed in 1990 than previously. This was partly because longer strikes formed a larger share of the total number in 1990 than before. They were also concentrated in the public sector of the economy, where the local union organization necessary to mount and sustain strike action remained strong. In the great majority of cases, strikes had official union backing. A high proportion of employees took action for the first time in 1989–1990.

Prior to strikes and other action being undertaken in 1989–1990 it was the norm for unions to consult their members. The use of ballots prior to the start of industrial action was widespread, although postal ballots were used twice as commonly by white-collar unions than by their blue-collar counterparts. Prior to calling industrial action off, informal methods of consulting members were most often used.

Pay remained the principal reason that galvanized unions and employees to take strike action in 1990. The most common reason for non-strike action among white-collar workers in the public sector was in relation to manning and work allocation issues.

Notes and references

1. D. Bird (1991) 'International comparisons of industrial disputes in 1989 and 1990', *Employment Gazette*, 99, 12, pp. 653–8.

2. E.g. see S. Evans (1987) 'The use of injunctions in industrial disputes, May 1984–April 1987', *British Journal of Industrial Relations*, 25, pp. 419–35.

3. W. Brown and S. Wadhwani (1990) 'The economic effects of industrial relations legislation since 1979', *National Institute Economic Review*, February, pp. 57–70.

4. P. K. Edwards (1991) 'Industrial conflict: a review of recent research', Paper presented at the *Conference of the British Universities Industrial Relations Association*, June.

5. Although coal mining was excluded from all three of our surveys, our figures for industrial action in 1983–1984 will reflect the indirect effects of the 1984–1985 dispute within the industry. More generally, the exclusion of coal mining will very slightly understate the extent of *workplaces* affected by industrial action in each survey period. The exclusion of the figures for working days lost due to stoppages of work in coal mining would have a much more pronounced effect on the Employment Department's national series.

6. The Employment Department's series does include stoppages of less than one day where the aggregate number of working days lost exceeds 100.

7. P. K. Edwards and C. Whitson (1989) 'Industrial discipline, the control of attendance and the subordination of labour: towards an integrated analysis', *Work, Employment and Society*, 3, 1–28.

8. As in 1984, the 1990 questioning was restricted to establishments with five or more manual workers, or five or more non-manual workers. The first survey showed industrial action to be extremely rare in workplaces below this threshold. We established in the previous sourcebooks that taking the combined responses of managers and worker representatives provides the best possible measure of the overall extent of industrial action. This covers the situations where one type of respondent reports action where the other does not. Where possible, we have retained this measure in the material presented below. However, to make the analysis from all three surveys comparable, the small number of representatives of non-recognized unions have been excluded from the 1980 and 1990 figures presented here. Due to limitations of questionnaire space in 1990, as in 1984, the more detailed questioning about the characteristics of industrial action was asked only of worker representatives. These data are reported later in the chapter.

9. Strikes almost disappeared from Energy and Water (from 36 per cent to just 1 per cent of establishments), but of course by 1990 the water industry was no longer part of the public sector.

10. The negative relationship between aggregate unemployment and strikes has been widely discussed. Our 1990 results indicate that, if anything, strike incidence (the

proportion of workplaces affected) in the private sector increased as the rate of *local* unemployment *increased.*

11. In our 1984 survey we omitted the detailed questioning in our interviews with managers about their most recent experience of industrial action, retaining it in our interviews with worker representatives. We did the same in 1990, which, in the context of decline in the extent of industrial action since the 1984 survey, means that the scope for detailed analysis of the 1990 material is limited due to the smaller number of relevant cases. However, the shift towards strikes of a day or more since 1984 means that the 1990 results are more likely than previously to be representative of all strikes in 1989–1990.

12. N. Millward and M. Stevens (1986) *British Workplace Industrial Relations 1980–84: The DE/ESRC/PSI/ACAS Surveys*, Gower, Aldershot, p. 295 (Note 8).

13. For example, where disputes over privatization involved possible redundancies and changes to working practices, the dispute will have been coded to those categories by the Employment Department's statisticians. Disputes involving sympathy action with workers elsewhere are classified to the main strike cause in the ED series.

14. Data from ACAS on conciliation cases during 1991 suggest that subsequent to our survey the level of conflict over redundancy matters may have increased.

15. In the 12 months to July 1990, 11 per cent of strikers were in dispute over the duration and pattern of working hours (generally the engineering dispute) and these accounted for 30 per cent of total days lost during the 12 month period yet only 6 per cent of the total stoppages (D. Bird (1991) 'Industrial Stoppages in 1990', *Employment Gazette*, **99**, 7, pp. 379–90).

16. Unfortunately there are no panel data to adjudicate here, because, first, the panel sample was restricted to the trading sector only and hence excluded much of the public sector and, secondly, worker representatives were not interviewed in panel workplaces.

17. It should be emphasized that this definition of 'sympathy' action is different from the definition of 'secondary' action in the law. Respondents who reported sympathy action in our surveys could have been referring to action by workers at the sampled establishment in sympathy with workers at another establishment *of the same employer*, which would not have been secondary action.

18. S. Evans (1987) op. cit.

19. We defined 'sections' as in the *Basic Workforce Data Sheet*: unskilled manuals, semi-skilled manuals, skilled manuals, clerical/administrative/secretarial, supervisors, junior technical and professional, senior technical and professional, middle/senior managers.

20. The changes in our results for manual strike action and non-manual non-strike action are not statistically significant.

21. This increase in the experience of individuals taking industrial action for the first time in the year to 1990 is confirmed by recent results from the British Social Attitudes Survey series. These show a sharp increase in the proportion of employee respondents in the public sector who said they had *ever* been on strike. See J. Dibden and N. Millward (1991) 'Trade union membership: development and prospects', *Policy Studies*, **12**, 4 pp. 4–19.

22. Details of stoppages of work known to be official ceased to be published by the Employment Department in 1981 because at that time they were liable to a margin of error for various reasons, including the fact that a strike might become official some time after it was recorded by the Department. (See *Hansard* (1985) House of Lords written answer, 26th March, col. 1018.) As we show below, however, in the year to mid-1990, there were very few instances where strike action was made official subsequent to it beginning.

23. Cm 821 (1989) *Unofficial Action and the Law*, London, HMSO.

24. Cm 821 (1989) *Ibid.*

25. Managers at almost half (48 per cent) of workplaces affected by strikes involving manual workers in 1989–1990 reported that they had been made official on at least one occasion. The incidence of official non-strike action among manual workers was reported in 30 per cent of workplaces. In all, nine out of ten managers who reported strike action among white-collar employees confirmed that it had been official on at least one occasion. The same was true of non-strike action.

26. Cm 1602 (1991) *Industrial Relations in the 1990s: Proposals for further reform of industrial relations and trade union law*, HMSO, London.

27. Naturally, as our questions were only asked where industrial action had either taken place or was in progress they did not cover ballots and other consultations that resulted in a vote in favour of action that did not subsequently take place.

28. Our questions were as follows: 'During the period before the start of the recent (strike/other) action did the union consult its members here before the action began?'; 'In the period before the most recent strike/other action was called off did the union consult its members here before the strike/other action was called off?' It is possible that some respondents who answered positively could have been referring to consultations about an offer made in the negotiations rather than the more specific issue of whether or not to take or call off the industrial action itself. On the former, see Chapter 7.

29. There is no statutory obligation on a trade union to consult its members before withdrawing authorization or endorsement of industrial action.

30. Expenditure by the Certification Officer on refunds of ballot costs totalled £2.6m in 1990, almost double the 1989 total (*Annual Report of the Certification Officer*, 1991).

31. An additional question asked whether the majority of voters at the sampled establishment voted either in favour or against starting/continuing the action. Unfortunately, a misplaced filter in the printed questionnaires meant that not all the appropriate respondents were asked the question. However, the limited results we do have indicate that in the large majority of cases the voters at our sampled establishments did indeed vote either to take or cease industrial action.

32. We could not unambiguously allocate all cases of pre-strike balloting to either 'postal' or 'workplace' forms. This was because respondents who reported consulting the membership more than once but did *not* report the use of a ballot on the last occasion of consultation were asked whether a ballot had been used on *any* occasion. Respondents who answered positively to this question were then also asked the more detailed questions about ballots, allowing that we did not then know the precise form of balloting that had been used. Thus, the proportion reporting management assistance is likely to have been higher in cases where workplace ballots were reported, for example, given the statutory obligation for employers to make premises available for such ballots in certain circumstances. Indeed, this was the case when we restricted the analysis to cases where the membership was consulted by workplace ballot on the last or only occasion they were consulted. In addition, however, our form of questioning was fairly broad and respondents who did not report management assistance may have assumed, for example, that management approval to conduct the ballot in work time fell outside the scope of the question.

33. For similar reasons to those given above for industrial action, we again used the combined responses from both managers and representatives of recognized unions to assess the extent of picketing.

34. Both 'primary' and 'secondary' picketing are reflected in the figures in Table 8B.

35. It is worth noting that the level of non-response to the questions about the number of pickets taking part and the number of gates picketed increased substantially between 1984 and 1990. In 1990 almost a fifth of managers simply could not say how many

pickets there were and almost a tenth did not know how many gates had been picketed. Virtually all these cases were in the public sector and there was obviously some relation between non-response to the two questions. In almost half of cases managers answered 'don't know' to both questions.

36. We concentrate on reporting changes in the characteristics of 'primary' picketing between the 1980 and the 1990 surveys due to the larger number of relevant cases in each of these surveys. Results for all three surveys are given in tables for completeness.

37. The statutory Code of Practice recommends that in general the number of pickets at any entrance should not exceed six (Employment Department *Code of Practice: Picketing*, HMSO, London).

38. This differs from the statutory definition. Unlawful secondary picketing is picketing other than at the pickets' own place of work. In WIRS, therefore, some of that picketing which we define as 'secondary' could have been in relation to a dispute at another establishment of the same employer and would have been lawful if it had taken place at the pickets' own place of work. This is most likely to have occurred in the public sector, where disputes were concentrated in 1989–1990.

39. Although the cases where respondents could not answer the question were excluded from these calculations, it is again notable that non-response to the question about the number of 'secondary' pickets (17 per cent) was fairly high in 1990 compared with previous years.

Table 8A   Proportion of establishments affected by industrial action, as reported by any respondent, by industry, 1990

Percentages

	Either manual or non-manual workers involved in		
	Strike action	Non-strike action	Picketing
All industries	**10**	**5**	**7**
All manufacturing	**4**	**7**	**2**
Metals & Mineral Products	4	8	1
Chemicals & Manufactured Fibres	(6)[1]	(4)	(2)
Metal Goods	(2)	(7)	(—)
Mechanical Engineering	6	6	2
Electrical & Instrument Engineering	2	11	1
Vehicles & Transport Equipment	14	8	5
Food, Drink & Tobacco	3	6	1
Textiles	(5)	(5)	(4)
Leather, Footwear & Clothing	(3)	(5)	(2)
Timber & Furniture, Paper & Printing	3	9	1
Rubber, Plastics & Other Manufacturing	(2)	(3)	(2)
All services	**11**	**4**	**8**
Energy & Water	1	2	4
Construction	6	2	7
Wholesale Distribution	3	3	1
Retail Distribution	*	*	1
Hotels, Catering, Repairs	*	2	1
Transport	10	1	9
Posts and Telecommunications	29	28	4
Banking, Finance, Insurance	*	*	*
Business Services	6	4	7
Central Government	10	1	15
Local Government	38	12	37
Higher Education	(45)	(52)	(14)
Other Education	24	2	4
Medical Services	5	4	6
Other Services	17	7	19

Base: all establishments (see Table 1A for bases and SIC codes)
[1] See Note B.

Table 8B Proportion of establishments affected by strike action of various durations, as reported by any respondent, by industry, 1990

Percentages

	Strike action lasting		
	Less than one day/ one shift	One day but less than one week	One week or more
All industries	4	6	1
All manufacturing	2	2	*
Metals & Mineral Products	2	2	*
Chemicals & Manufactured Fibres	(3)[1]	(3)	(—)
Metal Goods	(2)	(2)	(—)
Mechanical Engineering	5	1	*
Electrical & Instrument Engineering	1	*	1
Vehicles & Transport Equipment	4	9	2
Food, Drink & Tobacco	—	2	—
Textiles	(—)	(5)	(—)
Leather, Footwear & Clothing	(2)	(1)	(—)
Timber & Furniture, Paper & Printing	3	*	*
Rubber, Plastics & Other Manufacturing	(—)	(2)	(—)
All services	4	7	1
Energy & Water	1	*	*
Construction	1	6	—
Wholesale Distribution	3	*	—
Retail Distribution	*	*	—
Hotels, Catering, Repairs	*	*	—
Transport	1	9	*
Posts and Telecommunications	25	4	—
Banking, Finance, Insurance	*	—	—
Business Services	*	4	1
Central Government	6	4	—
Local Government	7	31	3
Higher Education	(38)	(7)	(—)
Other Education	11	12	2
Medical Services	4	2	1
Other Services	1	15	2

Base: all establishments (see Table 1A for bases and SIC codes)
[1] See Note B.

9 Employment and Working Practices

Staffing and work allocation were much debated during the 1980s, not only because difficulties over them sometimes led to industrial action, but for much broader reasons. Indeed it is no exaggeration to say that the 1980s saw an explosion of interest in the contribution which increased 'flexibility' in employment practice might make both to organizational effectiveness and performance and to increased opportunities and rewards for employees.

One issue here was numerical flexibility: it was argued that competitive pressures were increasingly encouraging employers to take measures to increase or reduce the size of their workforce more rapidly than before, so as to take quick account of seasonal and other fluctuations in demands for the goods and services they provided. A greater use of temporary workers, sub-contractors, workers on fixed-term contracts and homeworkers was thought to follow. Related to this, it was argued, were two other forms of flexibility. The first was in hours of work, notably moves to increased part-time employment, shift working and more variable shift patterns. The second was in moves towards increased functional flexibility, with the development of broader occupational definitions and the removal of demarcations between skilled and unskilled, blue-collar and white-collar employees. Some observers saw these developments as rapid and wide-ranging; others were less sure. Some saw them as benefiting employers at the expense of labour: others suggested that employees, too, were more and more seeking variety in their jobs and the hours they worked. The increasing role of women in the labour force was thought by many to reinforce such developments.[1]

The WIRS series contains a good deal of systematic information on employers' employment and working practices in the 1980s, which will continue to inform these discussions. The surveys collected information about employers' recruitment activity, workforce reductions and the incidence of various types of so-called 'non-standard' employees. The particular advantage of including these questions in WIRS comes from being able to combine them with the wealth of other information from the survey about the industrial relations characteristics and economic performance of workplaces.[2]

In the 1990 survey we went further than in previous surveys. Just as employers can reduce their demand for labour in an establishment either temporarily or permanently, employees themselves can reduce the supply of labour on a temporary or permanent basis, through absences and resignations. We included questions on these topics for the first time in 1990. Secondly, we incorporated into the main management interviews several questions concerning the scope that existed for managements to organize work as they wished and changes that had been introduced to increase the flexibility of labour. We had explored this subject in a limited way with production managers in larger manufacturing plants as part of the 1984 survey, particularly in relation to the introduction of new technology.[3] Thirdly, we also included new questions on employers' use of subcontracting, which was becoming a more common feature of discussions about flexible working practices including possible linkages with the growth of self-employment.

These areas formed the key additions to our core questioning about employment and working practices in the 1990 survey. In the first half of this chapter we report results on employers' recruitment practices, the incidence and management of workforce reductions and the rate of resignations and absences. The second half describes results on the way working practices were organized within establishments. Our companion volume will consider in much greater depth the association between different forms of employment and working practices and the so-called 'new' industrial relations arrangements that existed, including results from several new questions about the 'harmonization' of employment conditions between manual and non-manual occupations.[4]

Additions to the workforce
As employment in the economy as a whole was growing at the time of the 1990 survey we expected this to be reflected in the decisions of managers to expand their own workforces at that time. Certainly, it was clear from results presented in Chapter 2 that recruitment activity was a more time-consuming activity for our managers in 1990 than before. Our questioning about additions to the workforce focused on the incidence and type of *external* recruitment undertaken at our sampled workplaces in the year prior to interview. As expected, the proportion of managers reporting that they had taken on at least one new employee increased from 85 per cent to 89 per cent of workplaces between 1984 and 1990, as the two surveys were conducted at different points in the economic cycle. And the 1990 results show that recruitment activity was again widespread, affecting workplaces in all industries.

These results are, of course, a fairly crude indicator of the buoyancy of the labour market in 1990 because we did not also ask in each survey about the numbers of employees recruited. We could identify establish-

Table 9.1   **Level of jobs filled by external recruitment, 1984 and 1990**

Percentages

	Unskilled manual		Semi-skilled manual		Skilled manual		Clerical, secretarial administrative		Supervisors or foremen		Junior technical or professional		Senior technical or professional		Middle or senior management	
	1984	1990	1984	1990	1984	1990	1984	1990	1984	1990	1984	1990	1984	1990	1984	1990
All establishments	44	54	41	48	36	49	46	52	13	20	45	51	29	35	20	26
Base: establishments with any types of employees named in column heads which recruited these types of employees in the 12 months prior to interview																
Unweighted	*1665*	*1508*	*1344*	*1231*	*1470*	*1317*	*1959*	*1872*	*1609*	*1518*	*1392*	*1378*	*1418*	*1398*	*1893*	*1848*
Weighted	*1491*	*1387*	*1114*	*1005*	*1218*	*1076*	*1874*	*1771*	*1297*	*1216*	*1110*	*1060*	*1177*	*1110*	*1776*	*1735*
Private manufacturing	47[1]	57	49	55	44	54	43	49	15	19	44	40	24	32	24	28
Private services	48	55	38	48	40	51	51	57	12	22	44	53	31	33	19	27
Public sector	40	49	36	34	22	34	42	46	14	19	46	56	31	40	20	21

[1] Bases for the subcategories in the variable were calculated in the same way as for the total but have been excluded from this table for presentational reasons.

ments that had grown during the year prior to interview using data from the *Basic Workforce Data Sheet*. Naturally enough, those that had grown on these measures were more likely to report taking on new employees. But in our interviews with managers we did also ask about the types of employees recruited, as we had done in the 1984 survey. Then, generally speaking, recruitment activity was concentrated among the lower skill or occupational grades, as Table 9.1 shows. The same was also true in 1990. Even so, the table also shows that larger proportions of workplaces than previously were recruiting among each group of employees that we asked about. There was little variation in this across the three broad sectors of employment, suggesting that all types of workplace were more frequently recruiting all types of employee than previously. It was still the case, however, that recruitment activity was least common among supervisors, senior professionals and middle or senior management, probably indicating the continuing predominance of internal promotions and transfers for filling these types of post.

In the broad, there was little difference in 1990 in the level of staff taken on according to the level of unionization, but workplaces with no recognized unions were slightly more likely to have recruited among three of the eight types of employee we asked about: semi-skilled manuals, skilled manuals and middle or senior management.

Reductions in the workforce
The expansion of employment in the economy during 1989–1990 also led us to expect to find fewer workplaces shedding employees than at the time of the 1984 survey. There was likely to be more emphasis on the retention of existing employees, in addition to recruiting more from outside, to meet the growing demand. This proved to be the case. We again asked our main management respondents whether they had reduced numbers of employees in any section or sections of the workforce in the 12 months prior to interview. The broad picture was that the decline in reporting of reductions between 1980 and 1984 continued to 1990. Table 9.2 gives the results. Workforce reductions were reported in a third of establishments in 1990, compared with two fifths in 1984 and 45 per cent in 1980. Results from the earlier surveys very clearly reflect the large 'shake-out' in manufacturing industry in the early 1980s – certainly there was no change in the sector between 1984 and 1990, with two fifths of establishments having made some reductions in each case. The decline in the incidence of labour-shedding since 1984, however, occurred largely in the public sector, from half to a third of workplaces, with only a slight drop in private services, from 32 per cent to 28 per cent.

Although workforce reductions remained most common in larger establishments, there are obviously more opportunities with larger num-

Table 9.2 Establishments making workforce reductions and methods used, by broad sector, 1984 and 1990

Percentages

	All establishments		Private manufacturing		Private services		Public sector	
	1984	1990	1984	1990	1984	1990	1984	1990
Reductions in any section or sections of the workforce in last year	41	32	41	39	32	28	52	34
Base: all establishments								
Unweighted	*2019*	*2061*	*592*	*630*	*597*	*799*	*830*	*632*
Weighted	*2000*	*2000*	*424*	*426*	*843*	*980*	*733*	*594*
Methods used to reduce a section or sections of the workforce								
Natural wastage	70[1]	67	67	64	64	68	76	70
Redeployment within workplace	38	45	44	53	40	42	33	40
Early retirement	35	26	38	20	23	18	42	41
Voluntary redundancies	20	21	37	26	16	16	14	23
Compulsory redundancies	25	30	52	52	34	35	6	4
Other methods	13	7	7	7	11	11	18	11
None	..[2]	9	..	10	..	..	..	5
Base: establishments making workforce reductions in last year								
Unweighted	*1073*	*917*	*335*	*314*	*249*	*305*	*489*	*298*
Weighted	*824*	*639*	*174*	*168*	*268*	*270*	*382*	*202*

[1] See Note E.
[2] See Note J.

bers of employees, they were mentioned less frequently than before among workplaces of all sizes. Table 9A gives the results on the incidence of labour-shedding for all industries: Textiles was particularly affected (62 per cent), with Higher Education least affected of any (15 per cent).

The assumption must be that employers reduce their workforce when the establishment's or organization's economic position worsens, which may occur in some sectors even when the economy as a whole is expanding. In fact, our results from the 1990 survey allow us to examine the linkage between job-loss and the performance of individual establishments directly. We introduced two new questions which sought managers' assessments of labour productivity at the sampled workplace, first, relative to the period three years prior to interview and, secondly, relative to the prevailing average level of productivity within the industry in which the establishment operated. Using results from these questions, and a previous question on the trend in the establishment's output, it was clear that among workplaces where productivity was higher on either of our measures, workforce reductions were more than twice as common where output was stable or falling than where it was rising.

In 1990 there was little difference in reporting workforce reductions among union and non-union workplaces – around a third in both cases. Only in larger workplaces, with 500 or more employees, was the incidence more pronounced where unions were recognized. We show later that attempts by managements in the late 1980s to change working practices were more commonly reported in larger, unionized workplaces – reducing the size of the workforce could be one consequence of such changes. The broad picture had been very different in 1984 when workforce reductions were reported in just under a third (30 per cent) of establishments with no recognized trade union present compared with almost half (47 per cent) of those with one or more recognized trade unions, a pattern that persisted when we compared establishments of similar sizes. Again, this probably reflects the more severe contraction in employment during the early 1980s among larger unionized workplaces.

Reasons for workforce reductions
The reasons most commonly given in 1990 for workforce reductions were similar to those given in 1984. For example, *lack of demand* (37 per cent in 1990, 35 per cent in 1984) and *reorganized working methods* (37 per cent and 36 per cent respectively) were most common. In third place was *improved competitiveness or efficiency or cost reduction* – mentioned slightly more frequently than before (29 per cent, 1990; 24 per cent, 1984). In 1990, 18 per cent of managers mentioned *cash limits*, a large fall since 1984 (29 per cent), partly reflecting the decreased inci-

dence of workforce reductions in the public sector over the period. One in ten managers mentioned *automation* in both surveys. Additionally, in 1990, 7 per cent of managers identified *staff shortages* as a main reason for workforce reductions.[5]

This broad picture was much the same for the private sector alone, although a lack of demand remained predominant in manufacturing (53 per cent of cases in 1990) and reorganized working methods took over from a lack of demand as the most common reason mentioned in private services (42 per cent), probably reflecting staff changes as a result of privatization. Staff shortages were more commonly mentioned by private sector managers than those in the public sector (9 per cent as against 5 per cent), especially among foreign-owned workplaces (20 per cent) rather than their UK-owned counterparts (8 per cent).

In the public sector, not surprisingly, cash limits were still the main reason for workforce reductions, but were less likely to be mentioned in 1990 (34 per cent) than in 1984 (45 per cent). The one reason which was more often mentioned by managers in the public sector in 1990 than in 1984 was improved efficiency or competitiveness or cost reduction, up from 17 per cent to 24 per cent. The impact of automation was less often reported, declining from 14 per cent in 1984 to just 3 per cent in 1990. It was notable, however, that sub-contracting was mentioned by 5 per cent of public sector managers, a matter we return to later in this chapter.

Methods of reducing the workforce
Given that workplaces in 1990 were more reluctant to lose existing employees than they had been in 1984, we wondered whether this would be reflected in the number and nature of the methods they used to make workforce reductions. Questioning on this topic has been included in all three of our surveys and the results show little overall change in the frequency with which the main methods were reported. Table 9.2 gives the results. As before, it was common for more than one method to be used in the same establishment: typically, two methods were used in 1990. The fall in the average number of methods used in manufacturing industry – from 2.5 to 2.2 – reflects the relative severity of the rationalization of the early 1980s. Elsewhere there was very little change.

Natural wastage remained the predominant method used, mentioned in over two thirds of cases, as in 1984. Over two fifths (45 per cent) of managers mentioned redeployment, a slight increase in both private manufacturing and the public sector, suggesting that some employers were aiming to make better use of their existing employees rather than lose them altogether. A fifth of managers in 1990 mentioned voluntary redundancy, an increase in the public sector and a drop in private manufacturing since 1984. Three out of ten managers mentioned compulsory redundancy, a slight increase from 1984 and suggesting that, for some employers, losing rather than redeploying employees was thought to be necessary. Only early retirement was less frequently mentioned than previously, down from a third to a quarter of cases and virtually all of this drop in the manufacturing sector. The scope for using this method in the late 1980s was presumably much smaller than it had been earlier in the decade.

Compulsory redundancies were still much more commonly reported in private manufacturing plants than elsewhere in 1990, reported by managers in half of cases. This compares with a third of cases in private services and just 4 per cent in the public sector. To put these results in broader perspective, we looked at the incidence of enforced redundancy in the sample as a whole, regardless of whether any workforce reductions had been made. Table 9A gives the 1990 results on this basis for all industries. In many parts of manufacturing at least a fifth of workplaces experienced compulsory redundancy in 1990; in Textiles it was two fifths. In the service industries compulsory redundancy was most commonly reported in Transport (17 per cent), Construction (14 per cent), and Business Services (13 per cent). Notably, compulsory redundancies were hardly ever reported in Central Government or Posts and Telecommunications, where unions remained strong.

More generally, with the exception of compulsory redundancy, all the methods of reducing the workforce referred to above were more commonly reported in larger establishments and where trade unions were recognized. This had been true in 1984. When we compared establishments of similar size, those without recognized trade unions much more commonly made compulsory redundancies than those where they were present. Overall, compulsory redundancies were reported in 46 per cent of workplaces without recognized unions that had made workforce reductions, compared with 17 per cent where recognized trade unions were present. The figures were very similar for the private sector alone, as just 1 per cent of all public sector establishments had compulsory redundancies in 1990. Among workplaces where trade unions were recognized compulsory redundancies were associated with lower levels of trade union membership. This suggests that enforced redundancies were more commonly reported where the scope for opposition to them from unions was limited, which is unsurprising given trade unions' traditionally strong resistance to enforced redundancies.

Where trade unions are unsuccessful in resisting compulsory redundancy, they have often pressed managements to agree to select employees to be made redundant on the basis of their length of service: 'last in – first out'. It is an issue we have explored in the WIRS series. In fact, our survey question in 1990 was a broad one, asking managers to indicate whether they had used any of a number of bases for selecting employees.[6] Half of managers who reported compulsory redundancies – the largest proportion – said the reason was that specific jobs had been abolished, thus rendering the job holders redundant. This was more commonly mentioned in union workplaces (55 per cent) than non-union workplaces (39 per cent), even when we compared establishments of similar sizes. Perhaps surprisingly, given that unions had become less prevalent by 1990, the incidence of 'last in – first out' as the basis for selection was as common in 1990 as it had been before – around half of all cases (47 per cent and 46 per cent in 1990 and 1984 respectively). Three out of ten managers (29 per cent) mentioned an employee's level of skills or qualifications; among larger workplaces this was more commonly related to recognition. The performance record of employees was mentioned by managers in a quarter (23 per cent) of cases and an employee's disciplinary or attendance record by 19 per cent.

It is notable, and perhaps surprising, that the incidence of 'last in – first out' increased in private manufacturing between 1984 and 1990 from half to three fifths. In private services there was decline from half to a third, suggesting that unions in manufacturing were successfully negotiating their preferred method, which accounts for the stability of 'last in – first out' among all establishments.[7] Table 9A gives the 1990 results for all industries and indicates that 'last in – first out' was a feature of manufacturing industry, but was also commonly practised in Construction and Transport. There were some changes in relation to unionization, however. In 1984 there was a relatively small difference in its use between union and non-union workplaces (52 per cent and 42 per cent of cases respectively). But by 1990, length of service as a criterion for selection was much more clearly a feature of union establishments, reported in 70 per cent of workplaces with recognized trade unions that had made enforced reductions but in only 35 per cent of those without, a pattern that persisted when we compared establishments of similar sizes. Length of service is obviously the criterion for selection that is least relevant to management's concern to balance the mix of labour inputs. Clearly, the most recently recruited employees may be the most skilled or able workers. It is more clearly a 'collectively' determined basis for selection, in terms of notions of fairness, and it is significant, though expected, that it should be more commonly practised in unionized rather than non-union workplaces in 1990.

Temporary reductions
Short of complete plant closure, enforced redundancy is the more extreme option open to employers to reduce their workforces. It is often a last resort because there may be additional, long-term costs associated with it if their activities subsequently expand – such as the permanent loss of skilled workers to competitors. Sometimes employers attempt

temporarily to reduce the amount and cost of labour while still retaining their employees, in the hope that economic prospects will eventually improve sufficiently to allow resumption of normal working. Questions on these temporary arrangements have been included in all our surveys. We asked our management respondents on each occasion whether, in the 12 months prior to interview, they had used any of the following arrangements: *short-time working*; *temporary lay-offs*; a *reduction in the number of shifts worked*; or *any other work-sharing arrangement*.

The pattern of results was broadly similar in each of our surveys. Overall, managers in 9 per cent of establishments in 1990 reported that some form of temporary reduction in labour had occurred at the establishment in the previous 12 months. In 1984, 7 per cent of managers reported such an arrangement; in 1980, 8 per cent did so. It is notable, however, that the incidence of these temporary working arrangements did not fall between 1984 and 1990, even though the incidence of permanent workforce reductions did so. That such temporary reductions should form a larger share of all workforce reductions in 1990 compared with 1984 (a quarter compared with a sixth) is also consistent with the view that not only were employers recruiting more heavily at the time, they were also keen to retain existing employees rather than lose them permanently.

These temporary arrangements were twice as frequently reported in private manufacturing as in either private services or the public sector. However, though the proportions remained small, there was a greater increase between 1984 and 1990 in the service sector as a whole than in manufacturing. Naturally, temporary reductions were more commonly reported in establishments that were performing relatively poorly. The presence of recognized trade unions or the level of trade union membership at an establishment appeared to be unrelated to the incidence of these temporary reductions.

Respondents were again asked about the type of arrangement that had been temporarily in place, with answers being multi-coded.[8] For the sample as a whole, results in 1990 were similar to those in 1984. Three per cent or fewer managers reported each of the three specific types of arrangements we asked about: short-time working; temporary lay-offs; a reduction in the number of shifts worked; any other work-sharing arrangement.

Resignations
So far in this chapter we have considered labour turnover only insofar as it results from the decisions of employers to re-shape their labour requirements – through redundancies, early retirement and so forth. However, another important component of labour turnover is one which employers can usually only react to. This is when employees leave of

their own accord. This we examined in a question new to the 1990 survey which sought information from managers about the number of employees who had resigned or left the establishment in the 12 months prior to interview. In overall terms, nine out of ten managers (92 per cent) reported that one or more permanent employees had resigned or left in the year prior to interview, with little variation by broad sector of employment.

It would be hardly meaningful to compare the raw numbers of resignations across establishments of widely different sizes. More meaningful are comparisons which standardize for the size of the workforce, such as the percentage 'quit-rate'. Our analysis concentrates on that measure, and overall, 14 per cent of employees resigned from our sampled workplaces between 1989 and 1990.[9] Establishments in private services were well above average, with a resignation rate of 19 per cent, those in private manufacturing recorded 12 per cent and those in the public sector 10 per cent. Table 9A gives details of resignation rates by industry. The table reflects the fact that high quit-rates were a feature of certain industries. For example, they were very much more than twice the service sector average of 15 per cent in Hotels, Catering and Repairs, where 38 per cent of employees left over the year, and exactly twice the average in Retail Distribution.

Our data allow us to move beyond analysis at the aggregate industry level, however, to examine the rate of resignations in relation to a variety of characteristics thought to influence the willingness of individuals to stay or leave their existing employer. These include, for example, the characteristics of the workforce, the incidence of employee involvement and financial participation arrangements, and the condition of the local labour market. Our analysis can only begin to explore the wealth of information that the survey datasets contain.

Our initial analyses of both public and private sector cases indicated that quit-rates were higher in workplaces with higher concentrations of part-time employees, female employees and employees from ethnic minorities. But, there was little or no difference among workplaces which used temporary workers, freelance workers or homeworkers, 15 per cent as against 17 per cent. There was also little overall difference in quit-rates in relation to the presence of joint consultative committees at workplace level, new employee involvement initiatives, and/or the presence of share schemes. However, eligibility of all manual or all non-manual employees for profit-related pay arrangements seemed to be associated with lower quit-rates – 14 per cent as against 20 per cent in each case.

There were differences in relation to the presence of recognized unions, however, irrespective of the presence of the various employee involvement arrangements. In fact, workplaces with each type of arrangement but no recognized unions had twice the resignation rate of their equivalents with recognized unions. In addition to being more likely to experience enforced redundancy, then, employees from non-union workplaces were also more likely to leave of their own accord than their counterparts in union workplaces, in part reflecting the less well-developed internal labour markets in such places. The overall rate of resignations was 11 per cent among establishments with one or more recognized unions and 20 per cent in establishments with no recognized unions. For the private sector alone the figures were 20 per cent and 12 per cent, a differential which persisted when we compared establishments of similar sizes. Among establishments with 100 per cent union density just 8 per cent of employees resigned between 1989 and 1990, around half the national average.

The propensity of individuals voluntarily to leave their existing jobs is likely to be partly dependent on the availability of jobs elsewhere. When we looked at local unemployment rates as indicators of the availability of jobs, our results seemed to confirm that possibility. The resignation rate was 17 per cent where unemployment in the relevant *Travel To Work Area* was below 3 per cent and fell to 9 per cent where unemployment was 11 per cent or more.

Absences
Resignations reflect relatively permanent changes in the supply of labour, but reductions in the total hours worked by employees at an establishment can also arise for other reasons. One of these is industrial action, examined previously: another is by individual employees temporarily being absent from work. Apart from annual leave and attendance on training courses, absences may arise from sickness or for a number of other reasons. It would be unreasonable in a survey such as ours to ask managers about absences attributable to these varied reasons. However, a question new to the 1990 survey asked managers about the proportion of employees at their establishment who *were away sick or absent* for the most recent period for which figures were available. The length of the reporting period was also recorded,[10] and these data enable us to relate absence rates to other characteristics of establishments in a way which is not possible from traditional survey sources based on individual employees. Our analysis concentrates on the pattern of weekly absence, the patterns for other reporting periods being broadly similar.[11]

Some four fifths (79 per cent) of workplaces where weekly absence returns were reported had between 1 and 9 per cent of employees recorded as absent, and half had between 1 and 4 per cent of staff recorded as absent. These proportions were similar across each broad sector of employment. At the other end of the scale, 10 per cent of establishments had no absences at all in the week prior to interview – more commonly in private services (16 per cent) than in private manufacturing (6 per cent) or the public sector (3 per cent).

We examined the median weekly absence rate in relation to a variety of workplace characteristics. In some respects the broad results were similar to those presented above for resignations. The median weekly absence rate was slightly higher in workplaces with high concentrations of females and high concentrations of employees from ethnic minorities, but there was no variation in relation to the proportion of employees working part-time.

Weekly absence rates were slightly higher in workplaces with recognized trade unions than those without and among establishments with some union members compared with those with no members. Interestingly, when we conducted a similar form of analysis to that reported above for resignations, our results pointed in the opposite direction. We found that irrespective of the presence of employee involvement mechanisms of various types – joint consultative committees, new employee involvement initiatives and share schemes, for example – absence rates were slightly lower in workplaces without recognized unions than in those where they were present. The rate of resignations had been higher. In other words our results indicate that non-union workplaces had higher quit-rates and lower absence rates than union workplaces.

Working practices

So far in this chapter we have described our results on the movement of employees into and out of the workplace, on a temporary and permanent basis. We now focus on the management of labour resources within the workplace. The extent to which management can readily deploy employees to different tasks and types of work is often seen as an indicator of 'flexibility' in the workplace. And the incidence of changes in working practices that reduce job demarcations is an important indicator of the success of management's efforts to achieve greater flexibility among the workforce.

Management's freedom to organize work

We first examined the constraints which managements faced in organizing work as they wished as part of our interviews with production managers in our 1984 survey. However, this gave an incomplete picture because production managers were not interviewed in all our sampled establishments. In the 1990 survey we included this topic as part of the main management interview to obtain a nationwide picture. Naturally, the change of respondent meant that we lost comparability with our previous survey, but this was more than made up by the breadth of coverage in 1990. Our analysis, therefore, focuses on only the 1990 results.

We first asked a rather general question as follows: 'In practice, is management here able to organize work as it wishes among non-managerial employees or are there limits to the way it can organize work?' Managers who mentioned that there were limits were then asked about the type of constraints they faced. Overall, managers in a third (32 per cent) of all workplaces reported that there were limits to the way they organized work. There were marked differences in response between sectors. In the public sector, managers in over half of establishments reported limits, compared with only a quarter of private sector establishments. But managers in the service sector (public and private) were almost twice as likely to report limits as their counterparts in manufacturing (36 per cent and 20 per cent) respectively. Table 9B shows that the reporting of limits to management freedom in manufacturing industry ranged from as low as 7 per cent in Metal Goods to 45 per cent in Metals and Mineral Products. The range was even greater in the service sector, from 9 per cent in Higher Education to 63 per cent in Local Government.

Managers were more likely to mention limits to their freedom to organize work at establishments with recognized unions (46 per cent) than those without (17 per cent), a pattern that persisted when we compared establishments of similar sizes. And the more complex was local union organization, the more frequently managers mentioned constraints. In workplaces where there were no union members, for example, only 15 per cent of managers reported constraints, whereas in establishments with 100 per cent density, the proportion was 60 per cent. Similarly, among establishments with only one recognized trade union, 37 per cent of managers reported constraints; the comparable proportion where there were five or more trade unions recognized was 63 per cent.

The impetus to make changes to working practices in the 1980s came in part from a belief that the constraints managers faced in organizing work contributed to relatively poor economic performance. Following this, we might expect establishments where managers reported limits to their freedom to organize work to have been in poorer economic shape than those where managers were free to organize work as they wished. But, our results show that this was not always the case. In fact, some 44 per cent of managers who reported limits to their freedom also said that their establishment was operating at full capacity, compared with 29 per cent of those who were free to organize as they wished. Similarly, the trend in output over the year prior to interview was rising in 45 per cent of workplaces where managers reported limits to their freedom compared with 39 per cent of those who were free to organize work.

The expected negative effect of limits on management freedom to organize work did not surface in relation to the financial performance of the establishment. This was reported to be better than average by 49 per cent of managers operating within some constraints and by 42 per cent of those with no such constraints. Further, improved labour productivity was reported by 84 per cent of managers with constraints but by three fifths of those who said they were free to organize work as they wished, perhaps reflecting more scope for recent improvements among the types of workplaces with constraints.

In sum, then, our initial analysis suggested that the linkage between management's expressed freedom to organize work and the performance of the establishment was far from clear. It was not the case that establishments where there were constraints on management were poorer performers. There is much to be explored here in further analysis of the WIRS data. However, we examined the issue further through a question asking about the nature of the constraints management faced. Our main management respondents were shown a card and asked whether any of the following categories of constraint listed, or any other, affected them.

Opposition from groups of ordinary union members
Opposition from groups of workers who are *not* union members
Opposition from shop stewards or representatives
Formal agreements with trade union(s)
Lack of skills amongst the workforce
Lack of suitable premises or equipment
Lack of management expertise
Other reasons

Table 9.3 gives details of the specific responses and a number of summary measures constructed from them. It is clear that by far the most common single constraint mentioned concerned formal agreements with trade unions, reported by 14 per cent of managers overall (and by 26 per cent of managers in workplaces with recognized unions). The second most frequently mentioned constraint was a lack of skills among the workforce at the establishment, reported by 9 per cent of managers overall.

Looking at the summary measures in the table, some 16 per cent of managers overall mentioned some form of union constraint, 13 per cent felt constraints were related to some non-union issue affecting employees and 8 per cent mentioned some form of management-related constraint.

It is clear from Table 9.3 that these summary measures (and most specific types of constraint) were more frequently reported by managers in the public sector, where unions remained strong. The significance of union agreements in limiting the freedom of public sector managers is particularly clear. But other categories of constraint that affected man-

Table 9.3   **Constraints on managers' ability to organize work among non-managerial employees, by broad sector and trade union recognition, 1990**

Percentages

	All establish-ments	Private manu-facturing	Private services	Public sector	Any recognized unions	No recognized unions
Type of constraint						
Formal agreements with trade unions	14	8	9	25	26	—
Opposition from stewards or representatives	5	7	3	7	10	—
Opposition from ordinary union members	5	6	3	9	10	*
Any union constraint	**16**	**10**	**10**	**29**	**30**	*
Availability of staff	2	*	2	4	3	2
Lack of skills amongst workforce	9	7	9	12	14	4
Opposition from employees who are not union members	3	4	2	3	4	1
Agreement of supervisors	*	—	*	*	*	—
Any workforce-related constraint	**13**	**8**	**13**	**17**	**19**	**6**
Lack of suitable premises or equipment	6	4	4	10	9	2
Lack of management expertise	3	4	2	4	4	2
Any management-related constraint	**8**	**6**	**5**	**13**	**11**	**3**
Any workplace-related constraint	**24**	**18**	**19**	**37**	**38**	**9**

Table 9.3 continued

Percentages

	All establish-ments	Private manu-facturing	Private services	Public sector	Any recognized unions	No recognized unions
Limits from higher management	3	*	2	8	4	3
External coordination requirements	3	*	3	4	3	2
Restrictions from professional body	1	*	1	1	1	1
Any external constraint	**7**	**1**	**6**	**12**	**7**	**6**
Any constraint	**32**	**20**	**26**	**51**	**47**	**15**
Don't know/ not answered	1	1	*	2	*	2
Base: all establishments						
Unweighted	*2061*	*630*	*799*	*632*	*1417*	*644*
Weighted	*2000*	*426*	*980*	*594*	*1058*	*952*

agers in the public sector especially included a lack of suitable premises and equipment and limits from higher-level management. The largest difference between the public and private sectors concerned union-related factors, reflecting in part the difference in unionization between the two sectors. However, in light of the expected finding that trade union related constraints were most frequently reported in establishments with recognized unions than those without (47 per cent against 15 per cent), we examined the unionized and non-unionized sectors in terms of our non-union related summary measures of 'any workforce-related constraint' and 'any management-related constraint'. Again, constraints were more frequently mentioned in unionized than non-unionized places. The one non-union summary measure on which there was little or no difference between unionized and non-unionized establishments was 'any external constraint' (7 per cent and 6 per cent respectively).

Changes in working practices
Against the background of the increased interest in flexibility issues in the 1980s, we attempted to discover the extent to which managers were actually taking initiatives expressly designed to increase the flexibility

of working at their workplace. We asked our main management respondents the following question: 'During the last three years has management introduced any changes in working practices that have reduced
job demarcation or increased the flexibility of working at this establishment?' Where such changes were reported we asked which sections of
the workforce had been affected.

Overall, managers in over a third (36 per cent) of all workplaces in
our sample reported that changes to working practices had been made.
This was reflected across the three broad sectors of employment, but
there were noticeable differences between certain industries, as Table
9B shows. In manufacturing, changes to working practices were most
frequently reported in Chemicals and Manufactured Fibres (52 per cent)
and Leather, Footwear and Clothing (51 per cent) and least frequently
reported in Vehicles and Transport Equipment (20 per cent). In the
service sector the range was between three fifths in Banking, Insurance
and Finance and in Posts and Telecommunications down to 15 per cent
in Construction.

We were interested to examine possible linkages between changes in
working practices and the extent to which managements were free to
organize work as they wished. For example, if changes to increase
flexible working had been made over the three years prior to interview
yet managers were still reporting limits to their freedom then it would
indicate continuing difficulties for management. Conversely, if no changes
had been made and managers were free to organize work, it would
indicate that management appeared to be satisfied with the current state
of affairs. The other two possible outcomes suggest that, on the one
hand, management had achieved some flexibility through initiating
changes and, on the other, a possible requirement for management action to ameliorate currently perceived limits to their freedom. There is a
slight difficulty in that our question on changes to working practices
was in relation to the three years prior to interview, whereas the degree
of freedom managers said they had related to the position in 1990. This
should be borne in mind in what follows.

Our results indicate that among workplaces that had introduced changes
in working practices a slight majority of managers reported that they
were free to organize work as they wished – 57 per cent. This suggests
that in some two fifths of cases changes had been made but there were
still limits to management freedom. Among workplaces that had *not* made
changes, a larger proportion of managers appeared to be satisfied with
the prevailing state of affairs, as 73 per cent said they were free to
organize work. This leaves managers in a quarter of workplaces where
no changes to working practices had been made experiencing some
difficulties.

Managers in unionized workplaces where changes had been made were more than twice as likely to report constraints than their non-union counterparts, though this partly reflects our question in that union related constraints do not apply in non-union situations. Bearing in mind the oft-declared benefits from changes to working practices, some relationship with improvements in productivity might be expected. In fact, there was a notable difference when we looked at changes in levels of productivity over three years, the same reporting period as our question on changes to working practices. Improvements in labour productivity were reported in 72 per cent of establishments which had changed working practices compared with 56 per cent of those where no changes had taken place.

Managers who reported changes to working practices were asked which of seven types of workers[12] were affected. Given that any one change might affect more than one group of workers, and that more than one change may have occurred, interviewers were briefed to probe for more than one answer. Our results presented here concentrate on changes affecting broad categories of employee: any manuals; any non-manuals; and all non-managerial employees.

In all establishments where changes to working practices were made, these affected manual employees and non-manual employees in equal measure (57 per cent and 58 per cent respectively). Manual workers were much more frequently affected by change in private manufacturing (82 per cent) than either private services (49 per cent) or the public sector (50 per cent). For non-manuals, the reverse was the case: 64 per cent in private services, 61 per cent in the public sector and 44 per cent in private manufacturing. Changes affecting all non-managerial employees were reported in 8 per cent of establishments.[13] The most widespread changes had taken place in private services, where one in ten managers reported changes affecting all non-managerial employees, compared with 7 per cent in private manufacturing and 5 per cent in the public sector.

For non-manual employees, changes were much more frequently reported in establishments with no recognized non-manual trade unions than in unionized places (66 per cent and 52 per cent respectively). The reverse was true for manual employees, with 69 per cent of workplaces with recognized manual trade unions having changed working practices compared with 62 per cent of places where no manual unions were recognized. Changes affecting all non-managerial employees were made in one in ten establishments with any recognized trade unions but in only 3 per cent of places where they were not present.

Shiftworking

Shiftworking does not usually figure prominently in discussions about flexible working arrangements, partly because it tends to be undertaken by full-time, permanent employees rather than those on 'non-standard' employment contracts. Even so, shiftworking accounts for a significant component of the variation in working time in Britain.[14] For the employer, shiftwork certainly extends the hours of a 'normal' working day, allowing maximum use of equipment, or the hours of potential contact with customers, while minimizing costs associated with starting and stopping of production or opening and closing of establishments. And some employees clearly prefer the non-standard working hours offered by working at night or in the early evening. Obviously, shiftworking is largely related to technological and economic factors beyond our area of interest, but our results can throw some light on the incidence of shiftwork in relation to industrial relations characteristics, other indicators of flexible working and the performance of workplaces.

In fact, there was no overall change in the incidence of shiftworking since our first survey in 1980: 37 per cent of establishments operated some kind of shift system in each of our three surveys. The 1990 survey showed that it was still more common in larger establishments, though there appeared to have been some decline, since 1984, among the very large establishments. Shiftwork remained as common among workplaces in each of the three broad sectors of employment, more frequently so in both private manufacturing (42 per cent) and the public sector (44 per cent) than in private services (31 per cent). Table 9B gives 1990 results on shiftworking by industry and shows the expected high incidence in certain sectors, such as: Medical Services; Hotels, Catering, Repairs; Food, Drink and Tobacco; and Metals and Mineral Products.

The presence of recognized trade unions was still associated with shiftworking. In 1990, three fifths of establishments with some form of shift system had recognized trade unions, compared with 49 per cent of those without. In 1984 the figures were 73 per cent and 63 per cent respectively. The fall reflects the drop in the overall incidence of recognition since our last survey, reported in Chapter 3. In 1990, taking the private sector alone, there was little difference in the presence of recognized unions between establishments which worked shifts and those that did not – 42 per cent and 36 per cent respectively.

Given the underlying economic rationale behind shiftworking, we might expect to find it associated with more positive indicators of economic performance. Our data suggested, however, that this was not necessarily the case. In 1990, there was little or no difference between establishments with shiftworking and those without in terms of levels of output, capacity utilization or financial performance. That is, establishments with no shiftworking were as likely to be working at maximum capacity, to have rising output, or report above average financial performance as those operating shifts. Only in terms of labour productivity was there a hint of any difference. Two fifths of establishments with shiftworking had productivity higher than the industry average, compared with a third of those without it, according to the assessments of our management respondents.

Our surveys also allow us to look more directly at shiftworking and other aspects of flexible working. In particular, we examined the incidence of shiftworking in relation to the questions reported earlier concerning changes in working practices designed to increase flexibility and on management's ability to organize work freely. Our broad results showed that changes in working practices were more commonly reported in shiftworking establishments than in those without shiftworking – two fifths compared with a third. But there was no overall difference between shift and non-shift workplaces in relation to managers' freedom to organize work – in both types of establishment around two thirds of managers said they were able to organize work as they wished.

'Non-standard' employment
Another way that managements may have attempted to ensure that labour inputs are more responsive to product market conditions is through a wider use of 'non-standard' forms of employment relationship – such as part-time working, freelance working, homeworking and subcontracting – and a decline in use of permanent, full-time employment. Certainly the number of male, full-time jobs has been in secular decline for 40 years. In discussions about a flexible workforce, the incidence of other forms of employment has probably received most attention. The increase in part-time employment in the 1980s is clear from a variety of statistical sources.[15] And, as we saw in Chapter 1, our surveys showed a similar pattern – 18 per cent of all WIRS employees were working part-time in 1990, compared with 16 per cent in 1984 and 14 per cent in 1980. We concentrate here on so-called 'non-standard' employment; a later section examines the incidence of subcontracting.

In 1990, we asked about employees on short (less than 12 months) fixed-term contracts, freelance workers and homeworkers and outworkers.[16] Overall, managers in some 37 per cent of establishments reported any of these forms of employment, little or no change since 1984. Nor was there any change in the overall incidence of the three categories of worker we asked about. In 1990 employees on short fixed-term contracts were reported in 21 per cent of workplaces, freelancers in 16 per cent and homeworkers/outworkers in 5 per cent.[17]

Although the overall picture remained broadly unchanged, Table 9.4 shows that any changes that did take place occurred in the public sector. The table indicates that over half of public sector workplaces employed

Table 9.4   **Presence of non-standard workers, by broad sector, 1984 and 1990**

Percentages

	All establishments		Private manufacturing		Private services		Public sector	
	1984	1990	1984	1990	1984	1990	1984	1990
Any non-standard workers	**35**	**37**	**39**	**38**	**29**	**28**	**39**	**51**
Short, fixed-term contracts	19	22	11	9	11	12	35	45
Freelancers	14	16	21	20	19	17	6	10
Homeworkers/outworkers	4	5	12	13	3	3	*	1
Base: all establishments								
Unweighted	*2019*	*2061*	*592*	*630*	*597*	*799*	*830*	*632*
Weighted	*2000*	*2000*	*424*	*426*	*843*	*980*	*733*	*594*

some employees on non-standard contracts in 1990, up from 39 per cent in 1984. Most of this change was due to an increase, from 35 per cent to 45 per cent, in the use of employees on short fixed-term contracts, underlining the fact that such workers were still concentrated in the public sector. Although there was a slight rise among public sector workplaces in the incidence of freelance workers, their use remained largely a feature of the private sector.

Table 9C gives results for each category of employee by industry. It shows that the incidence of employees on short, fixed-term contracts was particularly high in public sector services such as education and health. Freelance workers were reported twice as frequently as the industry average in Mechanical Engineering, Construction, Business Services and Higher Education. Homeworking was still a feature of the clothing industry, though its incidence was above average in Rubber, Plastics and Other Manufacturing, and Medical Services.

Our surveys do not provide information on the levels of union membership among non-standard workers themselves, although evidence from other sources suggests that they are less likely to be members. However we can look at the prevalence of these workers in relation to unionization of the 'core' workforce at the establishment. As in 1984, employees on short, fixed-term contracts were more frequently reported in workplaces with recognized unions than in those without, 28 per cent as against 15 per cent, reflecting their public sector concentration. This pattern persisted when we compared workplaces of similar sizes. Freelancers and homeworkers, by contrast, were more frequently reported in non-union workplaces. In the private sector, freelancers were twice as commonly reported in non-union workplaces as in those with recognized unions – 22 per cent as against 11 per cent. Again, this pattern persisted when we compared workplaces of similar sizes. Homeworkers or outworkers were reported in 8 per cent of private sector establishments with no recognition and 3 per cent of those where trade unions were recognized.

Subcontracting

We turn, finally, to our results on subcontracting. The use of subcontracting became an industrial relations issue of some prominence in the 1980s. Some argued that employers were increasingly subcontracting a number of services, and even some parts of the manufacturing process, to avoid the costs and restrictions in unionized workplaces. In the public sector the Government encouraged subcontracting both directly within its own departments and by legislation and other means in the health service and services administered by local government. Indeed, we saw earlier in this chapter that 5 per cent of public sector managers mentioned subcontracting as the reason for reducing the employee numbers in sections of their workforce. Such moves were usually resisted by the relevant unions – in comprehensively unionized workplaces subcontracting represents a loss of potential membership to the unions and, *inter alia*, a possible union-avoidance practice for management.

We had no questions on the practice in our 1984 survey so we cannot document the change in the use of subcontracting since then, but it seems likely that the practice did increase in the years prior to 1990. In fact, 38 per cent of our financial manager respondents reported that the value of subcontracted services as a proportion of total costs had increased since 1987. Only 8 per cent reported that it had decreased.

Our survey questions aimed to explore the incidence of what might be described as 'complete' and 'partial' subcontracting of work. Complete subcontracting occurs when services are provided by a different organization, partial subcontracting is when services are conducted outside the workplace but elsewhere in the same organization.[18] We concentrate here on 'complete' subcontracting.[19] The services we asked about were: *cleaning of buildings and premises; security; catering; building maintenance; printing and photocopying; pay roll;* and *transport of documents and goods.*

Our results are given in Table 9.5. The top three most frequently mentioned services that were completely contracted out to another organization were: building maintenance (46 per cent); cleaning of buildings and premises (41 per cent); and transport of documents/goods (30 per cent). The next most frequently mentioned services were all reported in about a fifth of workplaces: security (21 per cent); printing and photocopying (18 per cent); and catering (17 per cent). In all, 72 per cent of all establishments had one or more of these services carried out by workers from another employer.

Establishments that were part of more complex organizations were more likely than independent establishments to contract out fully the cleaning of buildings and premises, and catering. Independent workplaces more frequently contracted out a broader range of services, particularly building maintenance, printing and photocopying and pay-roll matters. Not surprisingly, workplaces that were part of more complex organizations drew on other workplaces in their organization for pay-roll matters.

Complete subcontracting of any of the seven services was as commonly reported by private sector workplaces that recognized unions as their equivalents which did not – some 80 per cent in each case. Just over half of public sector managers reported any complete subcontracting. Table 9B gives results for the incidence of complete subcontracting by industry, showing that its incidence was widespread. Among Central Government workplaces it was almost universal, whereas in Construction the incidence was, predictably, lowest (44 per cent).[20]

Table 9.5 The incidence of complete and partial subcontracting of specified services, 1990

Percentages

| | Complete subcontracting | | | Partial subcontracting | Complete or partial |
	All establishments	Single independent	Part of multi-establishment organization	Part of multi-establishment organization	Part of multi-establishment organization
Cleaning of buildings and premises	41	25	45	7	52
Security	21	17	22	6	28
Catering	17	9	19	8	27
Building maintenance	46	54	44	23	67
Printing and photocopying	18	30	15	13	28
Pay roll	8	15	7	42	49
Transport of documents and goods	30	33	29	21	50
Base: all establishments					
Unweighted	*2061*	*253*	*1808*	*1808*	*1808*
Weighted	*2000*	*418*	*1582*	*1582*	*1582*

Finally we looked at complete subcontracting in relation to coverage of collective bargaining. In the private sector there was little difference: 82 per cent of workplaces that were comprehensively unionized subcontracted some services and 81 per cent of those with coverage of between 1 and 99 per cent did so. But our results for public sector establishments were more revealing. We saw earlier that subcontracting was mentioned by 5 per cent of public sector managers as a reason for making workforce reductions during the year prior to interview in 1990. When we analysed our results on complete subcontracting in relation to the coverage of collective bargaining, a clear pattern emerged. The incidence of subcontracting was highest in public sector workplaces that were comprehensively covered. Some 60 per cent of public sector workplaces where all employees were covered by collective bargaining subcontracted at least one of the services we asked about. Where coverage was between 1 and 99 per cent or less, subcontracting was mentioned in just over half (53 per cent) of workplaces. Given that subcontracting became an issue of some prominence in the public sector during the late 1980s, these results suggest that the public sector unions were less successful in resisting the spread of subcontracting in the most highly-unionized workplaces.

Synopsis
The general expansion of employment in the economy as a whole at the time of the 1990 survey was reflected in increased reporting of recruitment activity and a drop in workforce reductions since the mid-1980s. Increased use of redeployment and the fact that temporary reductions formed a larger share of all reductions in 1990 suggested that employers were more keen than before to retain their existing workers.

In 1984, reductions had been more commonly reported in unionized than in non-union establishments, reflecting the contraction of traditional industries, but by 1990 they were as common in both. Lack of product demand and the reorganization of working methods were still the main reasons for reductions. Where compulsory redundancies were made, selection on the basis of length of service was as common as before, despite the drop in union presence, reflecting an increased usage in the unionized parts of the private manufacturing sector.

Preliminary results from new survey questions on the incidence of absences and resignations showed that non-union workplaces in the private sector had higher quit-rates and lower absence rates than their counterparts in the union sector.

In 1990, limits to managements' freedom to organize work were reported in a third of workplaces. Constraints of various kinds were more common in union rather than non-union workplaces. Changes to working practices to increase flexible working in the 1987–1990 period were reported in a third of workplaces. Improvements in labour productivity were more frequently reported in establishments which had changed working practices than in those which had not.

Increases throughout the 1980s in part-time working were confirmed by WIRS, but there was little overall change in employers' use of various forms of 'non-standard' employment over the second half of the 1980s. But it was clear that the use of subcontracting increased, particularly in the most highly unionized parts of the public sector.

Notes and references

1. For different views see, for example, J. Atkinson (1984) *Managing for uncertainty: some emerging UK work patterns*, Institute of Manpower Studies, Brighton, A. Pollert (1988) 'The flexible firm: fixation or fact', *Work, Employment and Society* **2** (3), pp. 281–316; C. Hakim (1990) 'Core and periphery in employers' workforce strategies: evidence from the 1987 ELUS survey', *Work, Employment and Society*, **4** (2), pp. 157–88.

2. In 1987, a follow-up survey of WIRS2 establishments focused on employers' labour use strategies. See D. Wood and D. Smith (1989) *Employers' labour use strategies: first report on the 1987 survey*, Research Paper 63, Department of Employment; L. C. Hunter and J. MacInnes (1991) *Employers' Labour Use Strategies – Case Studies*, Research Paper 87, Department of Employment. In 1991 a follow-up survey of WIRS3 establishments explored the area of employment practices in greater depth. Analysis of the Employers' Manpower and Skills Practices Survey (EMSPS) is now in progress and results will be available in due course. The combined WIRS3/EMSPS dataset will form a most powerful source of information on industrial relations and employment practices for some years to come.

3. W. W. Daniel (1987) *Workplace Industrial Relations and Technical Change*, Frances Pinter (Publishers) and the Policy Studies Institute, London.

4. In workplaces which had five or more manual employees *and* five or more non-manual employees we asked about the availability of four types of non-cash benefits: *occupational pension schemes, sick-pay over and above statutory requirements, free or subsidized food or meals* and *a standard working week of less than 36 hours*. Initial analysis showed that pensions and preferential sick-pay arrangements were available in 86 per cent and 75 per cent of cases respectively. Subsidized meals were mentioned in 47 per cent of cases and a working week of less than 36 hours in three out of ten. In around two thirds of cases where each benefit was mentioned it was available to all groups of employees. And where one group had more favourable treatment, it generally applied to white-collar workers, especially, middle and senior management. A fuller analysis of these results will appear in W. W. Daniel and N. Millward (1993) *The New Industrial Relations?*, Policy Studies Institute, London. A report by B. Casey, *Employers' Provision of Pensions and Sick Pay*, is also forthcoming (see also Note 30 in Chapter 7).

5. *Staff shortages* was a new code in 1990, introduced at the coding stage following analysis of the 'other answers' category. It covered cases where, for example, a lack of skilled workers meant a reduced requirement for other employees.

6. There were, in fact, two questions in 1984. The first asked if selection was based on the principle of 'last in – first out' (LIFO) *or* some other method. The subsequent question, put *only* to those who had said 'other method', asked about these other methods. The format was changed in 1990. The two 1984 questions were collapsed into one, thus allowing respondents to indicate whether there were methods of selection *in addition* to LIFO. While the 1990 and 1984 data therefore are not strictly comparable in all respects, it is still possible to assess changes in the extent of LIFO as a basis for selection for compulsory redundancy. Compared with 1984, the 1990 results would tend to inflate the

proportion of responses indicating bases other than LIFO. Respondents were shown a card with the list of methods and asked which applied in their establishments, all of which were coded.

7. There were too few cases of compulsory redundancy in the public sector to allow further analysis.

8. In 1984 our question distinguished between short-time working with and without government subsidies. In 1990 no such distinction was necessary as the relevant scheme had been withdrawn.

9. Just 4 per cent of respondents could not provide an exact number of employees.

10. Around a third (34 per cent) of establishments had a reporting period of a week, a further third (32 per cent) had a month, while 13 per cent had some other period. A fifth of respondents (21 per cent) were coded as not answered.

11. Nine out of ten (89 per cent) of managers gave an estimate of the proportion of employees away sick or absent. Of these, nine out of ten (89 per cent) also provided details of the period covered by the estimate. And in over two fifths (43 per cent) of these, the accounting period was one week, in a further two fifths (41 per cent) it was one month, and in the remainder it was some other period, such as quarterly or half-yearly.

12. The groups were: unskilled manual; semi-skilled manual; skilled manual; clerical, administrative and secretarial; supervisors and foremen; junior technical/professional; and senior technical/professional. There was also an 'all sections' category.

13. Of course, managers who reported changes affecting all non-managerial employees could be referring to a series of changes over the three year reporting period, each of which might have affected different sections of the workforce.

14. For a discussion of this see A. Wareing (1992) 'Working arrangements and patterns of working time in Britain', *Employment Gazette*, **100**, 2, March, pp. 88–100.

15. For example, see M. Naylor and E. Purdie (1992) 'Results of the 1991 Labour Force Survey', *Employment Gazette*, 100, 4, pp. 153–72.

16. In 1984, we also asked about temporary workers from private employment agencies. These questions were omitted from the 1990 survey.

17. The incidence of homeworking is much higher among workplaces below the WIRS threshold of 25 employees. (See C. Hakim (1987) *Home-based work in Britain*, Research Paper No. 60, Employment Department, London.)

18. Our management respondents were shown a card listing seven services and asked whether any of them were carried out 'mainly by people who are *not* employees of this establishment'. Managers in workplaces that were part of multi-establishment organizations who had mentioned any of the listed services were then asked whether the service was carried out for them by another part of their own organization.

19. In a few cases respondents told us that the service was partly provided from outside the organization and partly from inside the organization. However, these cases made up less than 0.5 per cent of cases for four of the services considered, 1 per cent for a further two services and 3 per cent of cases (18 weighted cases in all) of 'printing and photocopying'. We have excluded these few cases from the results presented.

20. Our question referred to completed buildings, whereas often the sampled establishment in the construction industry was, by definition, still being constructed.

Table 9A   Details of workforce reductions and rates of resignation, by industry, 1990

	Workforce reductions	Compulsory redundancy	Last in/first out basis for redundancy	Resignations (per cent of employees)
All industries	**32**	**10**	**4**	**14**
All manufacturing	**39**	**21**	**12**	**12**
Metal & Mineral Products	48	28	28	7
Chemicals & Manufactured Fibres	(35)[1]	(9)	(3)	(10)
Metal Goods	(20)	(15)	(10)	(12)
Mechanical Engineering	24	16	7	9
Electrical & Instrument Engineering	49	27	4	14
Vehicles & Transport Equipment	44	20	3	7
Food, Drink & Tobacco	40	7	2	15
Textiles	(62)	(40)	(33)	(13)
Leather, Footwear & Clothing	(43)	(22)	(11)	(19)
Timber & Furniture, Paper & Printing	46	23	17	11
Rubber, Plastics & Other Manufacturing	(31)	(20)	(20)	(14)
All services	**30**	**7**	**2**	**15**
Energy & Water	47	4	—	8
Construction	27	14	12	13
Wholesale Distribution	36	11	3	11
Retail Distribution	36	8	*	30
Hotels, Catering, Repairs	24	7	—	38
Transport	39	17	9	10
Posts and Telecommunications	16	*	*	9
Banking, Finance, Insurance	9	3	—	14
Business Services	18	13	1	16
Central Government	32	*	—	12
Local Government	44	4	3	9
Higher Education	(15)	(10)	(—)	(11)
Other Education	37	2	1	9
Medical Services	24	2	1	16
Other Services	27	4	3	16

Base: all establishments (see Table 1A for bases and SIC codes)
[1] See Note B.

Table 9B   The incidence of a) limits to the way management organizes work, b) changes to working practices, c) shiftworking and, d) subcontracting, by industry, 1990

	Limits to way management organizes work	Changes made to working practices	Any shiftworking	Any complete subcontracting
All industries	**32**	**36**	**37**	**72**
All manufacturing	**20**	**39**	**42**	**85**
Metals & Mineral Products	45	48	72	68
Chemicals & Manufactured Fibres	(19)[1]	(52)	(50)	(90)
Metal Goods	(7)	(28)	(28)	(96)
Mechanical Engineering	19	31	28	93
Electrical & Instrument Engineering	21	41	28	87
Vehicles & Transport Equipment	26	20	28	63
Food, Drink & Tobacco	17	33	58	90
Textiles	(16)	(43)	(67)	(95)
Leather, Footwear & Clothing	(11)	(51)	(12)	(64)
Timber & Furniture, Paper & Printing	19	36	45	88
Rubber, Plastics & Other Manufacturing	(20)	(56)	(73)	(94)
All services	**36**	**36**	**36**	**69**
Energy & Water	51	46	38	83
Construction	22	15	14	44
Wholesale Distribution	21	33	26	92
Retail Distribution	27	38	29	85
Hotels, Catering, Repairs	15	20	72	67
Transport	17	26	46	70
Posts and Telecommunications	58	57	53	77
Banking, Finance, Insurance	59	58	7	88
Business Services	13	30	16	86
Central Government	29	29	31	98
Local Government	63	46	36	75
Higher Education	(9)	(52)	(29)	(84)
Other Education	53	31	23	43
Medical Services	56	44	83	60
Other Services	36	42	63	51

Base: all establishments (see Table 1A for bases and SIC codes)
[1] See Note B.

Table 9C   Employment of non-standard employees, by industry, 1990

	Any non-standard employees	Any employees with short fixed-term contracts	Any freelance workers	Any homeworkers/ outworkers
All industries	**37**	**22**	**16**	**5**
All manufacturing	**38**	**9**	**19**	**13**
Metals & Mineral Products	11	5	9	1
Chemicals & Manufactured Fibres	(23)[1]	(18)	(7)	(1)
Metal Goods	(12)	(10)	(5)	(1)
Mechanical Engineering	50	9	37	6
Electrical & Instrument Engineering	42	7	20	18
Vehicles & Transport Equipment	27	4	22	3
Food, Drink & Tobacco	45	23	26	1
Textiles	(12)	(4)	(4)	(4)
Leather, Footwear & Clothing	(60)	(8)	(9)	(40)
Timber & Furniture, Paper & Printing	42	7	23	18
Rubber, Plastics & Other Manufacturing	(50)	(13)	(18)	(25)
All services	**37**	**25**	**14**	**2**
Energy & Water	28	28	1	—
Construction	37	7	30	3
Wholesale Distribution	14	6	4	5
Retail Distribution	24	15	8	4
Hotels, Catering, Repairs	21	10	11	—
Transport	26	12	9	7
Posts and Telecommunications	22	13	9	*
Banking, Finance, Insurance	14	8	6	*
Business Services	46	17	35	4
Central Government	15	13	5	2
Local Government	32	25	12	1
Higher Education	(94)	(31)	(73)	(1)
Other Education	72	67	11	1
Medical Services	70	43	27	12
Other Services	41	31	17	6

Base all establishments (see Table 1A for bases and SIC codes)
[1] See Note B.

10 Conclusions

The 1970s and 1980s saw growing concern in Britain about many areas of social and economic life. With that concern came increasing questioning across all parts of society and within all shades of political opinion about the operation of long-established institutions. Nowhere was that questioning more vigorous and more challenging than in the field of employee relations. The wide variety of management, trade union and tripartite institutions which had been developed in previous decades came under scrutiny. Critics argued that many of these institutions no longer met the needs of a fast-changing economy, more exposed to international competition. They were said, in some cases, to be engendering rather than reducing or containing destructive conflict. They inhibited adaptation. A changing workforce, it was claimed, was bringing new needs and demands to employment which required new styles of management and new constructive ways of working together. The traditional institutions of industrial relations should, some suggested, be consigned to history or at the very least made more flexible and open. Calls for reform became the rule.

Despite widespread agreement on the need for change there was much less accord on what precisely should be done – whether by governments, managers or workers and their trade unions. Nor was there agreement on the best methods of achieving necessary changes. In particular there was widespread debate about the role of the law and the courts, a part of the fabric of society which until recently had had little relevance for most people to the pressing concerns of day-to-day employment relationships.

All this ensured that almost every aspect of employment relationships in Britain received greater attention from commentators and students of social behaviour during the 1980s than ever before. The growing body of scholarly and popular writers in the field found it easy to disagree, not only on the desirable outcomes but also on the very nature of the system they were wanting to change.

It was to provide a factual underpinning to these debates that the survey series reported in this book was conceived. Large-scale, rigorously designed surveys, coupled with modern computing, have transformed our capacity to describe, analyse and understand many areas of social and economic life. In the field of industrial relations, the Workplace Industrial Relations Surveys of 1980, 1984 and 1990 provide a unique and rich source of data on which to draw.

In previous chapters of this book we have given an initial overview of results in each of the main topic areas covered by the series. That overview has concentrated on comparisons between all three of the surveys or the two most recent ones. To have done otherwise would have been to ignore the enormous advantage of having a series. We have supplemented those comparisons over time with a brief account of most of the new questions included in the 1990 interviews. This was partly to alert other analysts and researchers to the potential of the new material, but also to add further, recent evidence to the perspectives that commentators, practitioners, researchers and policy-makers can bring to their interpretation of our main findings and their understanding of contemporary industrial relations.

Our aim in this concluding chapter is to address a number of broader themes and issues to which the material presented in earlier chapters is particularly relevant. Four over-arching conclusions can be stated before we enter more detailed discussion.

The first is that, contrary to what some have claimed, there were major changes in employee relations during the 1980s. Perhaps the most important of these were the decline in the representation of workers by trade unions and the decline in the coverage of collective bargaining, particularly in the private sector. Indeed, so great were the changes that it is not unreasonable to conclude that the traditional, distinctive 'system' of British industrial relations no longer characterized the economy as a whole. But, secondly, in workplaces where trade union representation and collective bargaining persisted, surprisingly little altered. That is to say, change occurred more because the proportion of workplaces operating the British 'system' of industrial relations declined so markedly, rather than because there was uniform decline in trade union representation and collective bargaining across all sectors and types of workplace.

Thirdly, no new pattern of employee representation emerged to replace trade union representation. There was no sign of a new form of industrial relations system to replace the old. Indeed, where new forms were adopted they were more commonly a complement for trade union representation, rather than as a substitute filling a gap left by its decline. Fourthly, an important but neglected influence upon the pattern and types of change in industrial relations was major structural change in the economy, both in the types of workplaces that it included and in the types of employees that worked in them.

The institutions of industrial relations

Up to 1980, relations between employers and employees in Britain were readily characterized as a system of collective representation designed to contain conflict. Voluntary collective bargaining between employers, employers' associations and trade unions was the central feature of the system. Collective bargaining encompassed a wide range of issues and worked through largely voluntary procedures with infrequent recourse to external bodies. The style of negotiations was adversarial, reflecting the historical development of the institutions involved, as in many other areas of political, legal and economic activity in Britain. This picture of the 'system of industrial relations in Britain' applied to large parts of manufacturing industry and the whole of the public sector. To a lesser extent it applied to large employers in private services. In most respects the picture was still a reasonable portrayal in 1984. But by 1990 there had been such widespread and marked changes in both management and trade union arrangements as to require substantial revision to the traditional characterization of the British 'system' of industrial relations.

One of the most marked changes was on the employers' side, where multi-employer representation in collective bargaining diminished substantially. The proportion of workplaces that were affiliated to an employers' association halved between 1980 and 1990, until only one in eight were members. Multi-employer bargaining with trade unions over rates of pay became less common, particularly in the second half of the decade, even within the smaller portion of the economy where any form of collective bargaining remained. Formal procedures for resolving difficulties in pay settlements in the private sector became less common after 1984 and fewer of those procedures contained a role for employers' associations in the final stages. In addition, as a source of advice on a range of matters, employers' associations were much less frequently used in 1990 than ten years earlier. Whereas they were the most commonly cited body external to the workplace in 1980, in 1990 they were one of the least commonly used bodies for advice. In short, employers' associations were a far less important part of the institutional structure of industrial relations in 1990 than they were a decade or more earlier.

A reduced role for employers' associations does not, of course, necessarily mean that collective bargaining became any less common. Collective bargaining is still 'collective' when one party to the negotiations is a single entity, such as a single employer, as long as the other party to the negotiations represents a collective entity. Trade unions (and some staff associations) fill this role on the employees' side of the negotiating table. Thus our principal indicator of the existence of collective bargaining is the recognition of trade unions by management for negotiating periodic revisions to basic pay. The fact that fewer workplaces had recognized unions in 1990 than in 1980 was our strongest evidence of the decline in collective bargaining as an institution. The fall was stark, substantial and incontrovertible.

Nor was this all, for the decline in collective bargaining was not simply a matter of its reduced extent among the population of workplaces. Within workplaces where trade unions were recognized by management fewer employees were covered by negotiations. In consequence, the proportion of employees covered by collective bargaining declined more markedly than the proportion of workplaces which retained a negotiating structure. By 1990 only just over half of employees in our sample were covered by collective bargaining, much lower than earlier in the decade. In the economy as a whole (including the very small workplaces excluded from our surveys) the proportion must have been well under half.

A further indication of the weakening of trade unions in collective bargaining came from our questions about the extent to which workplaces with recognized unions had representatives on site. The proportion that did so fell throughout the 1980s. Moreover, representatives were less likely to be appointed by competitive elections and more likely to emerge as the only person willing to take on the role.

At the same time, in places where unions were still represented, many features of local trade union organization remained much the same. Within the strongly unionized sector,[1] full-time lay representatives were rare, but no more so than previously. However, they were less often the blue-collar convenors of manufacturing industry than the white-collar public sector equivalents by 1990. Representatives had, on average, much the same number of members to deal with. Joint shop stewards' committees were as common in 1990 among workplaces with multiple unions as they had been ten years earlier. Training for union representatives was still generally done in employers' time. Facilities provided by management were no less common – and some were more so. Furthermore, union membership generally held up in workplaces where unions were recognized.

To summarize, the structures of collective bargaining remained in many respects similar in character to those at the start of the 1980s, but they were present in fewer workplaces and affected fewer employees. We will go on later in the chapter to discuss both the origins of these changes and the question of what replaced collective bargaining in those parts of the economy where it lost ground. But first we turn to the question of what issues remained within the scope of collective bargaining.

Unquestionably, pay and the basic conditions of employment (such as hours of work) remained the primary focus of joint regulation between managements and trade unions. Pay also remained the issue that most commonly gave rise to strikes and other industrial action. Indeed, from the worker representatives' point of view, pay was more commonly the issue in dispute in 1990 than in 1980, albeit that industrial action was far less common than before. In 1990, as in earlier years, managers also saw pay as the most important employee relations issue that they had to deal with, as the results in Table 10.1 amply testify.[2] Pay levels were the most important issue during the last three years in the view of 25 per cent of managers in 1990, nearly 30 per cent of those who gave a view on which issues were most important. No other issue was mentioned with anywhere near the same frequency. Issues strongly associated with pay, such as hours of work, job grading and fringe benefits, also featured prominently in their list of concerns. Pay dominated the issues of concern to managers in workplaces where unions were recognized and equally in workplaces where there were no unions.

If pay continued to come first on the collective bargaining agenda and in the concerns of both management and trade unions, what other issues were commonly subject to joint regulation? Our evidence showed that matters such as physical working conditions, staffing levels and redeployment within the workplace were frequently negotiated between management and recognized unions. Other matters such as recruitment, redundancy pay, the introduction of new technology and major changes in work organization or working methods were negotiated in some workplaces, but by no means the majority of those with recognized unions. Moreover, where we were able to compare the scope of bargaining between one survey and another the indications were that its scope had declined within the unionized sector. Broadly speaking, fewer issues were subject to joint regulation in 1990 than in 1980, although most of the change appears to have occurred in the early part of the decade. Given the contraction of the unionized sector, the reduction in bargaining activity, overall, has been substantial.

Issues which came into greater prominence in the latter part of the decade and which the trade unions at national level often sought to put on the agenda – such as equal opportunities and training – did not appear to have become part of established collective bargaining at employer or workplace level. Employment levels and closely-related issues were the ones that management most commonly succeeded in removing from the bargaining agenda. There were very few cases where pay increases and workforce reductions were agreed in the same set of negotiations.[3] So there is little evidence of any spontaneous move on the part of those actually involved in bargaining to negotiate the kind of comprehensive collective employment agreements that exist in some other industrialized economies.

Given the decline in the extent and the scope of collective bargaining, a central question for the economy and for industrial relations is whether the trade unions retained as much influence as they previously had on the issue at the centre of collective bargaining – the level of pay. The complex statistical investigation required to answer this question precisely lies outside the scope of this volume. Analyses carried out by other authors on the 1980 and 1984 survey data suggested there had been no reduction in the wage premium resulting from union bargaining.[4] Our own analysis of the data on pay levels in the 1990 survey, while adopting a different approach, strongly suggested that trade unions continued to have a significant impact on pay levels, particularly on the pay of the lower paid and in workplaces where collective bargaining covered all or nearly all workers. But, of course, the number of such workplaces had declined.

Other trade union functions at the workplace
Besides their continuing but diminished role in collective bargaining, what other functions were trade unions performing at the workplace? Their second best option, if they cannot secure negotiating rights, is to aim at least to be consulted by management on issues of collective concern to employees. In fact our first survey demonstrated that formal committees for consultation on a broad range of workplace issues were much more common in workplaces with recognized unions than in those without them. This remained true in 1990. Indeed, the fact that fewer workplaces had consultative committees seemed to be largely because fewer workplaces had a significant union presence. But in situations where there were consultative committees and unions were recognized it remained common for the union or unions to select all or some of the employee representatives on the committee. Even so, it appeared that union representatives were being consulted less often and being given less information than before on a number of issues.

On issues of health and safety there were two significant changes in the private sector regarding employee representation. More workplaces with recognized unions had a specific health and safety committee in 1990 than in 1984, but among workplaces with no such committee, fewer had individual representatives for these matters. On balance it appeared that health and safety representation maintained its strength in the unionized sector, while it clearly declined in the non-union sector. By 1990 workplaces in the private sector were less than half as likely to have any form of health and safety representation if they were not unionized. Again, the declining proportion of workplaces with recognized unions added further to the reduction in employee representation on these issues in the economy as a whole.

We mentioned earlier the much-reduced role of employers' associations in procedures for dealing with collective disputes over pay and conditions of employment. Naturally trade unions retained their role in such procedures where they were recognized. But another important and indeed more widespread trade union activity is to take part in the resolution of grievances and disputes about disciplinary matters. Here there was no sign of any diminution of the role of the unions. In 1990 more establishments with recognized unions had formal grievance procedures and more had formal disciplinary and dismissal procedures than had done so a decade earlier; indeed, such procedures were almost universal in the unionized sector in 1990. Unions almost always, as before, had a role in formulating such procedures jointly with management. And any tendency for disciplinary matters to be dealt with by management outside the agreed formal procedure was less apparent at the end of the decade than at the beginning. More satisfaction with the operation of disciplinary procedures was registered by worker representatives. Dismissal rates remained much lower in the unionized sector, perhaps the clearest indication of a continuing role for trade unions in limiting management's scope for unilateral action and in trying to ensure fairness of treatment for employees.

Decentralization
Much comment on the changes in management and industrial relations during the 1980s was concerned with the issue of decentralization. The emphasis on deregulation and market mechanisms in much of government policy and in debates about management and business policy suggested that many issues within the field of employee relations, particularly pay, would be increasingly dealt with at local levels, even within the workplace itself. We have already seen that on the employers' side there was a move away from collective, largely national, institutional arrangements. What other signs of moves towards local decision-making did we find?

Still for the moment staying with the issue of pay, the clearest indication of a move towards local decision-making in the unionized sector would have been an increase in the extent of plant bargaining. In fact, there was no increase of this kind in the unionized sector; nor was there any reduction in the extent to which managers involved in plant-level negotiations consulted their colleagues or superiors at head office or other higher levels in the enterprise. Rather than lead to more plant-level negotiations, the move away from multi-employer negotiations was accompanied by an increase in negotiating structures at enterprise or company level.

It was in fact in the non-union sector that the increasing autonomy of local managements on pay matters was evident. However, even here the change was not especially marked. In proportionate terms there was a slight increase in local determination; but, in the main, the reason why more establishments had pay determined by local managements in 1990 than in 1984 was because fewer establishments had collective bargaining.

Another indication of a general move towards local autonomy in industrial relations matters might be that fewer enterprises had appropriate specialists on their boards of directors.[5] Our results did suggest that, in the trading sector of the economy, a small change in this direction had occurred. Fewer establishments that belonged to larger enterprises came under boards with members who specialized in personnel or industrial relations matters. This could well be a response to the broad pattern of change that we have already described.

Sources of change

In our discussion of the substantial changes in industrial relations structures and practices so far, there has been little mention of what lay behind the changes that we observed. This was deliberate, as the causes of any individual change are rarely simple. However, it is appropriate at this point to mention the main sources of change that appear to have had a broad impact on the range of features of workplace industrial relations to which we have given attention in the WIRS series.

The changing population of workplaces

We start by discussing compositional effects, that is changes deriving from the developments in the structure of the economy and the patterns of employment within and between different types of workplace. We begin here for three reasons. First, compositional effects have been largely ignored in many discussions of the influences on the changing pattern of industrial relations in Britain. Secondly, a large part of the changes that we found between 1980 and 1984 did seem to arise from the changing composition of the population of workplaces, particularly the fall in the numbers of large, highly unionized manufacturing plants that occurred during the recession of the early 1980s. Thirdly, changes in the structure of the economy are particularly enduring and mostly irreversible. One cannot readily imagine, for example, that Britain – against the trend of history in the developed world – would ever again see a rising proportion of its workforce in manual occupations in large-scale, heavy manufacturing industry. So what was affected by the changing composition of workplaces over the decade up to 1990?

There can be little doubt that some of the decline in trade union membership and representation arose from compositional change. The decline of heavy manufacturing industries with their concentrations of male manual workers, the tendency towards smaller workplaces, the steady rise of the service sector, the contraction of the public sector, the rising proportion of overseas-owned workplaces, the increase in part-time employment – all these changes worked against trade union membership. The falls in membership, particularly in cases where membership density was already low, accounted for part of the drop in the proportion of workplaces with recognized trade unions. And this accounted for some of the decline in many features of the institutional structure of industrial relations that were in place at the start of the 1980s: fewer employees covered by collective bargaining, fewer shop stewards, fewer closed shops, fewer joint consultative committees and fewer strikes. Changes in the composition of workplaces, in our view, accounted for much of the change in these matters. However, other influences were also evidently at work.

The changed legal environment

Most obvious was a fast changing legal environment. The 1980s saw a remarkable volume of statutory change affecting different aspects of employment relationships and an unprecedented involvement of tribunals and courts in the resolution of employment-related disputes.

Here, two connected but contrasting developments were to be observed. The first was a substantial elaboration of the already sizeable body of statute law, put in place in the 1960s and 1970s by successive governments, which provided rights and protections for individual workers against unreasonable behaviour by their employers. By 1990 complex and wide-ranging arrangements covered many aspects of recruitment practice, disciplinary and grievance handling as well as dismissal. Industrial tribunals, responsible for public adjudication between the parties in cases where conciliated agreements could not be reached, were deciding disputes under more than 25 jurisdictions and dealing with over 30,000 cases each year.

How precisely these jurisdictions operated and how well they met the needs and demands of the parties concerned are questions which have received a good deal of attention in recent years and have been much debated. What is clear, however, is the very substantial encouragement they gave in a broader way to the development of formal industrial relations procedures. By 1990 formal disciplinary and dismissal procedures had become universal in all but the smallest employments. Written procedures for resolving individual grievances had been very widely introduced. In 1990, when personnel managers sought advice from outside their organization they were very much more likely to turn to the legal profession, or to state agencies such as ACAS, than they were at the beginning of the decade. So far as these matters were concerned, it was clear that the law had come to exercise a more significant role than ever before in the day-to-day conduct of employment relationships.

Changes in employment law in the 1980s were not, of course, confined to the regulation of individual relationships. Over the course of the decade successive Conservative governments engaged in a substantial and radical programme of reforms to the law which regulated the collective relationships between managements and trade unions. The legislation which, since 1976, had provided a means for trade unions to use the law to gain recognition from unwilling employers was repealed. The government also made other legal changes which impacted on the extent of trade union recognition. The abolition of the negotiating machinery for teachers in state schools in England and Wales removed large numbers of public sector employees from the scope of collective bargaining over pay.

Another part of the legal changes with an obvious implication for union membership and its concomitants was a progressive restriction on closed shop arrangements. Our results confirmed that over the 1980s there was a dramatic decline of the closed shop as an institution. At the same time it appeared that organizations which had abandoned closed shops during the period generally experienced only small falls in trade union membership. Many of the characteristics of those workplaces and their employees that had engendered high membership under a closed shop arrangement continued to do so without that institutional support.

However, the issue upon which the law had its clearest impact was the conduct of industrial disputes. Although industrial conflict is a more volatile phenomenon than most covered by our survey series, there can be little doubt that some of the decline in the extent of industrial action during the course of the 1980s was a consequence of the legal changes. The changes to the statutory definition of a trade dispute, the requirements for balloting, the financial penalties that could be imposed on trade unions inducing unlawful industrial action, the limits of lawful picketing – all these and other changes made it more difficult for the trade unions to mount and sustain effective industrial action. Some would argue that other influences were more important than the legal changes. There were many developments in the economic environment which tipped the balance of power in the direction of management and away from trade unions. Higher unemployment and fears about job security must have been important factors here. The much publicized failure of major campaigns of industrial action in coal-mining, printing and publishing and certain other sectors in the mid 1980s was thought by some to have had an important influence in demonstrating the very severe difficulties which trade unions could sometimes face from managements determined to introduce new working practices and new terms and conditions.

Whatever the relative importance of these and other factors, however, there can be no doubt that the incidence of industrial action fell very substantially during the decade. Our data showed that industrial action still affected a significant minority of establishments in the year up to mid-1990 and in the public sector the proportion was as high as it had been ten years earlier. Nonetheless some forms of pressure, including secondary blacking and secondary picketing, both of which had been expressly targeted by the legal restrictions, almost disappeared. Other forms of non-strike action such as overtime bans also showed a marked decline.

If we cannot yet be clear about the precise effect which changes in the law had on the extent of strike action, we can be more certain about their consequences for the way that action was organized and conducted. Here there were again dramatic changes. Most obviously in 1990 trade unions contemplating the possibility of industrial action were very much more likely to undertake formal ballots of their members than before. Indeed, there was noticeably more consultation of all kinds between officials and their members when difficulties arose in negotiations. While these changes had rarely, in 1990, been incorporated into the formal wording of procedure agreements, there can be no doubt that trade union behaviour had altered. Here again, formality and standardization of arrangements were becoming the rule.

Other government action
Direct changes to industrial relations and employment law are by no means the government's only method of influencing events in the field. Two other main sources of influence that we have commented upon when interpreting our results are the policy of privatization and the actions of the government as an employer. The latter can have both direct and indirect impacts on our concerns.

Over the decade the policy of privatization achieved a major switch from public to private ownership of commercial monopolies with large numbers of highly-unionized employees. As public corporations, most of these organizations had had a statutory obligation to recognize trade unions and consult employees through various mechanisms; management policy had positively encouraged and supported trade union membership. As private sector enterprises, their managements were released from these obligations and changes in policy and practice were widely expected. Regarding trade union negotiating rights we saw virtually no evidence from our panel sample that these had been comprehensively withdrawn from privatized workplaces. Less extensive changes than wholesale de-recognition may well have occurred, but this is one of the many areas where more detailed analysis has yet to be done on the data.

Another manifestation of the government's policy of reducing the size of the public sector was a series of directives to local authorities and health authorities concerning the contracting out of services such as cleaning, maintenance, transport and security. Such a policy was viewed with alarm by public sector trade unions since it threatened substantial job losses and the transfer of many jobs to private contractors who it was thought would be less disposed to trade union representation. Among the issues of concern to management that are briefly reported in Table

Table 10.1   **Most important recent[1] employee relations[2] issues as reported by managers, 1980, 1984 and 1990**

Percentages and rank order within year

	1980		1984		1990	
	%	rank	%	rank	%	rank
Pay levels[3]	30	1	27	1	25	1
Hours of work	5	3	8	2	7	2
Employee consultation	7	2	2	9	7	3
Job grading	2	11	1	17	6	4
Morale	4	5	1	28	5	5
Working methods	1	16	2	7	5	6
New technology	2	15	3	6	4	7
Relocation of establishment	1	17	2	13	4	8
Recruitment, retention	1	22	1	19	3	9
Demand for products, services	5	4	7	3	3	10
Productivity, efficiency	3	8	5	4	3	11
Physical working conditions	3	6	2	11	3	12
Job security	3	7	2	10	3	15
Fringe benefits	2	12	2	8	3	16
Safety	3	9	2	14	2	20
Payment systems	2	10	2	12	1	21
Strikes, industrial action	2	13	3	5	1	27
No important issues	25		29		17	
Base: all establishments						
Unweighted	*2040*		*2019*		*2061*	
Weighted	*2000*		*2000*		*2000*	

[1] 1980 and 1990: last three years; 1984: last four years

[2] 1980 – 'industrial relations issues'
    1984, 1990 – 'employee relations issues'

[3] Issues included are those in the top ten of any of the three surveys. The order in the table reflects the 1990 ranking. Number of issues separately coded: 62 in 1980, 63 in 1984, 70 in 1990.

10.1, 'privatisation or the hiving-off of services' was the second most important issue according to public sector managers in the three years up to 1990,[6] although it was only rarely mentioned as an issue for consultation. Only 'pay levels' eclipsed it as the employee relations issue of most widespread concern to public sector managers.

The government's approach to industrial relations was also apparent from changes in its own behaviour as an employer. One strand of this was the transfer of work to semi-independent agencies, a variant of 'privatization'. This issue rated highly among those of concern to managers in the central government part of our sample. It was the fourth most frequently mentioned issue of concern to them, whereas the one of highest rank in local government was the contracting-out of services.

A more direct manifestation of the government's approach to industrial relations as an employer was its withdrawal of trade union recognition and banning of individual trade union membership among staff at the Government Communications Headquarters (GCHQ) which precipitated the widespread industrial action in the civil service recorded in our 1984 survey. While the immediate significance of that change affected a very small number of workplaces, it suggested to the trade unions that the traditional strong endorsement of trade union membership for civil servants might not endure. In fact, our survey results confirmed this – the proportion of workplaces in central government where managers said that management strongly recommended trade union membership for all employees halved between 1984 and 1990.

A third respect in which the government's behaviour as an employer appeared from our results to have changed was in its use of performance-based reward systems. By 1990 most central government establishments had employees with an element of their pay determined by individual performance or their manager's assessment of it.[7] This is both an indication of the tendency towards individual-centred employee relations practices and the inability of trade unions to resist such developments.

The management of employee relations

In discussing the influences behind the changing picture of workplace industrial relations over the decade, we have so far focused on three types of influence: the changing composition of workplaces; the changing legal environment; and the influence of government policy. Clearly the second and third of these influences have their effect through changes in the actual behaviour of managements, trade unions and employees at the place of work. But some important aspects of management's specific role in the area remain to be addressed.

A much discussed issue in this regard has been whether the declining importance and complexity of traditional industrial relations structures has led to a down-grading of personnel management in its broad sense. It appeared from our evidence that this had not happened. Workplaces were as likely to have a specialist manager dealing with personnel, industrial relations or employee relations matters in 1990 as in earlier years. These managers were no less likely to have relevant professional qualifications and they were just as likely to have support staff. Other managers from different functional specialisms were more likely to say that the personnel function was increasingly influential and important, rather than the reverse. Our questioning on the actual activities and responsibilities of personnel specialists – and their sources of advice and assistance – led us to the conclusion that it was the increased salience of employment law that accounted for much of this change in the early part of the decade. In the more recent period the more marked tendency was for managers to be giving more attention to systems of pay and associated matters, and instituting closer monitoring of hours of work – tendencies that could hardly be attributed to the law. Indeed, it could be argued that they were a response to the increasing competition that was evident in parts of the economy and the moves that this engendered in management to improve efficiency.

Debate on the desirability of and appropriate methods for involving employees in the broad purposes of their employers continued throughout the 1980s, following the late 1970s discussions of the Bullock Report and in response to proposals from the European Community. Management initiatives aimed at increasing employees' involvement at work were made with rising frequency throughout the 1980s. The types of initiative continued to show considerable variety, ranging from new consultative meetings or committees to quality circles, briefing groups and increasing the flow of information to and from employees. Where trade unions were recognized we found that consultative and other arrangements were generally supplementing collective bargaining arrangements rather than replacing or supplanting them. Although infrequently mentioned by our respondents in this context, profit-sharing and employee share-ownership also spread, largely in the wake of tax incentives.

Management initiatives designed to reduce the extent and complexity of trade union representation were also apparent towards the end of the decade. Apart from the public sector, which we mentioned earlier, wholesale de-recognition of trade unions rose from extreme rarity in the early 1980s to a more substantial phenomenon in the private sector. Often, however, such cases appeared to be where support for union representation had become weak.

On the complexity of union representation there was also a discernible change. Some of this is unquestionably attributable to mergers or amalgamations of trade unions, but there was also evidence of successful – and unsuccessful – initiatives by management to reduce the complexity of bargaining structures. Both multiple unions and multiple bargaining groups became less common. But there was no evidence of any widespread move towards 'single-table bargaining' where both manual and non-manual unions negotiated jointly.

'Union-free' employee relations

Many of the developments in industrial relations that occurred during the course of the 1980s led a number of commentators to suggest that Britain was moving towards a situation where the institutional structures and formal practices and procedures that have been a central concern of our survey series would be confined to the public sector and a small portion of traditional manufacturing industry. In this scenario, the majority of workplaces in the private sector of the economy would be 'union-free' and characterized by quite different employee relations practices. Indeed, 'industrial relations' would be replaced by 'employee relations' and even, some argued, 'human resource management'. In the remainder of this chapter we aim to sketch out what this implies, using relevant results from our 1990 survey. Our focus is on private sector establishments without recognized trade unions.[8] The comparisons, often only implied, are with private sector, unionized workplaces.

Of course, many of the differences can in some senses be explained by the smaller size of the typical non-union workplace and the fact that more of them were independent, rather than part of a larger enterprise. But our purpose here is not to explain the differences in employee relations between the two types of workplace, but rather simply to say what these differences are. From our sketch of employee relations in the non-union sector, the reader may infer what the general picture in the private sector would move towards if the trend away from union representation in the private sector was to continue.

Employee relations were generally seen by managers as good or very good in the non-union sector, rather better than in the union sector.[9] Strikes were almost unheard of and other indicators of dissatisfaction, such as absenteeism, were evidently no worse. Labour turnover, on the other hand, was high. Perhaps as a consequence, many managers thought morale was one of the most important employee relations issues at their workplace. Safety was also more commonly an issue of concern to management, perhaps reflecting the higher rate of injuries at work or the lack of employee representatives with whom to discuss health and safety issues. However, the employee relations issues of most concern to managers were levels of pay and hours of work – just as they were to managers in the union sector.

Without the constraint of union negotiations, pay levels were set unilaterally by management, generally managers at the workplace. In a minority of cases management at head office or some other level in the enterprise took responsibility for setting levels of pay for a group of workplaces. Only in rare cases was pay set by statutory minima. However, managements in around a fifth of non-union workplaces claimed to consult employees or their representatives about pay increases. Labour market and commercial and financial considerations dominated managements' thinking on the size of pay settlements to a much greater degree than in the unionized sector. Pay was more a matter of individual performance, with formal job evaluation being rare. Again reflecting the lack of union influence, differentials between the highest and lowest earners in non-union workplaces tended to be relatively wide. Lower-paid employees were more common.

Managers generally felt unconstrained in the way they organized work. Opposition from employees to changes in working methods was rare and the lack of skills which managers in unionized workplaces often cited as a problem was also rare. Greater use of freelance and temporary contract workers was another aspect of the greater flexibility of labour in the non-union sector. Workforce reductions were no more common, but they were much more likely to be achieved by compulsory redundancies than by less painful methods such as natural wastage. Dismissals (other than those arising from redundancy) were common, nearly twice as frequent per employee as in the union sector. Claims to industrial tribunals for unfair dismissal and other alleged mistreatment were no less common, despite employees lacking the trade union support for pursuing such claims.

In a sizeable minority (a quarter) of workplaces, employee relations were conducted on such informal lines that there was no procedure for employees to use if they had a grievance. In a similar proportion there was no procedure for employees to raise health and safety issues. About a fifth had no formal procedure for dealing with disciplinary matters and possible dismissal. Moreover, despite the more informal relations between managers and employees, disciplinary sanctions such as deductions from pay and written warnings were no less common than in the union sector.

Informality also characterized the general flow of information and advice between managers and employees. On a wide range of matters that could be expected to be of interest to employees our results showed that managers in the non-union sector were much less likely to collect information on a regular basis to review performance or policies. They were also far less likely to disseminate such information to employees or their representatives. Even on a matter of such broad interest as the financial position of their workplace, as many as a half of managements gave their employees no regular information at all.

Methods of communication reflected the greater informality. Managements in non-union workplaces were considerably less likely to use each of the main methods of communication covered by our questioning. A third of them used regular meetings between supervisors and all the employees they supervised. A similar number used an annual or more frequent meeting between senior managers and all sections of the workforce. Only half systematically used the management chain to communicate to all employees. Only a fifth had a consultative committee or similar body for consulting employees on general matters. Yet consultation with employees was one of the most important employee relations issues according to managers in the non-union sector, as important as in the union sector where the formalized methods and structures for consulting and informing employees were so much more common.

All this suggests that employee relations in non-union, industrial and commercial workplaces had relatively few formal mechanisms through which employees could contribute to the operation of their workplace in a broader context than that of their specific job. Nor were they as likely to have opportunities to air grievances or to resolve problems in ways that were systematic and designed to ensure fairness of treatment. Broadly speaking, no alternative models of employee representation – let alone a single alternative model – had emerged as a substitute for trade union representation. Some would argue that such a development would be unnecessary and undesirable and that initiatives in this area should be the responsibility of management. Others argue that such a development is desirable and would only come about by legal requirement.

No doubt the many findings of relevance to this and related issues that we have included in this volume will contribute to this continuing debate. Further analysis of our survey data can add to these discussions, not only about desirable ends and effective policies to achieve them, but also about explanations for the changes that have occurred. We hope to make a further substantial contribution to those debates about the nature and impact of Britain's emerging patterns of industrial relations in our forthcoming companion volume.

Notes and references

1. We use the term 'strongly unionized' here as a shorthand for having recognized trade unions and a senior lay representative on site.

2. Worker representatives were not asked the question about the most important recent issue at their workplace in 1990, but they were in 1980 and 1984. On both occasions *pay levels* was the issue most frequently mentioned by both manual and non-manual representatives.

3. The result from this new question in 1990 was that 3 per cent of managers in workplaces with recognized manual unions reported that their most recent pay settlement contained an explicit agreement about workforce reductions. The proportion with regard to non-manual unions was identical.

4. M. B. Stewart (1991) 'Union wage differentials in the face of changes in the economic and legal environment', *Economica*, **58**, pp. 155–72.

5. An indication of this (more direct than our workplace-based measures) will be available when the results from the University of Warwick's second Company Level Industrial Relations Survey are published.

6. 'Privatization or hiving off of services' does not appear in Table 10.1 because that table includes the whole of the private sector, where it was almost never cited. Over the sample as a whole it was the thirteenth most commonly mentioned issue.

7. We lack directly comparable data from the earlier surveys but have little doubt that this proportion increased over the decade.

8. This over-simplifies the contrasts slightly, because there are a few workplaces where unions have members and may even have a representational role.

9. Similar differences are evident from individual employees' evaluations, as recorded by the British Social Attitudes Surveys.

Technical Appendix[1]

This appendix describes the design and execution of the 1990 survey, making comparisons with previous surveys where appropriate. Fuller technical details of the 1980 and 1984 surveys were included as appendices to our earlier reports.[2] The bulk of the material relates to the main, cross-sectional sample; a later section deals with the panel sample of workplaces interviewed in both 1984 and 1990.

The sampling frame and the sample

The sample design for the 1990 main survey broadly followed that developed for previous surveys. The sampling frame was the Employment Department's 1987 *Census of Employment*; for the 1984 survey it was the census conducted in 1981; and for the 1980 survey it was the census conducted in 1977. As in previous surveys, all census units recorded as having 24 or fewer employees were excluded, as were units falling within Agriculture, Forestry and Fishing (Division 0) of the *Standard Industrial Classification* (1980). Otherwise all sectors of civil employment in England, Scotland and Wales were included in the sampling universe – public and private sector, manufacturing and service industries. In 1990, as in previous surveys, larger units (on the basis of number of employees) were oversampled.

A census unit is in most cases a number of employees working at the same address who are paid from the same location by the same employer. The requirement of the survey design was for a sample or establishments, that is of individual places of employment at a single address and covering all the employees of the identified employer at that address. In general there is a sufficient degree of correspondence between census units and establishments for the census to serve as a viable sampling frame for the survey series. However, some census units have been found to refer to more than one establishment and in others to just part of an establishment. In later paragraphs we describe the procedures developed in 1980, and refined in 1984 and 1990, for dealing with these difficulties.

At the time of the design of the 1990 sample, the 1987 *Census of Employment* file contained just over 142,000 units with 25 or more employees, slightly more than the 135,000 in the 1981 census used for the

1984 survey. From this file a stratified random sample totalling 3572 units was drawn; in 1984 the figure was 3640 units and in 1980 the figure was 3994 units. The selected sample was smaller in 1990 for two reasons. First, the number of establishments at which interviews were required was 1870, as against 2000 in the first survey. Secondly, as none of the 'reserve pool' of nearly 500 units had been used in 1984 and the 1984 experience gave a good guide to the extent of out-of-scope and non-responding addresses, the size of the reserve pool in 1990 could be reduced. In the event none of the 357 units selected for the 1990 reserve pool was used.

The selection of units from the census involved an initial division of the file into seven files, each containing units within a size range: 25 to 49 employees, 50 to 99 employees, and so on. Within each of the seven files the census units were then re-ordered by: the proportion of male employees, within the proportion of full-time employees, within the *Activities* of the *Standard Industrial Classification (SIC)*. Differential sampling fractions were applied to the six lower size bands, the seventh (top) band having the same sampling fraction as the sixth band. From the re-ordered lists, samples were selected by marking off at intervals from a randomly selected starting point, the list being treated as circular. The numbers of census units, sampling fractions and subsample sizes are given in Table A.1, with the figures for 1984 and 1980 alongside for comparison.

The range of sampling fractions employed has been progressively increased during the course of the series. Partly this was because the number of large units in the population has declined and we still wanted to have sufficient large establishments in our achieved sample to permit comparisons between establishments of different sizes. It also reflected an increased emphasis on estimates focusing on employees rather than establishments. Analysis or the 1980 results had shown that employee estimates could be improved with little loss of accuracy on establishment estimates if the sample contained more large, and fewer small, units.

Besides the withdrawal of the 10 per cent of addresses for the reserve pool, the sample selected in 1990 was also reduced by a further 209 addresses from SIC Classes 91, 93 and 95. This innovation was made because analysis of the previous surveys had demonstrated that there was less variation within these easily identifiable parts of the public sector on most of the matters of interest in the surveys. It seemed advisable, therefore, to spread the survey resources that could be saved by undersampling these sectors over the remaining sectors of the population. The result of these two types of withdrawal from the selected sample – the reserve pool and the undersampling of Classes 91, 93 and 95 – was to bring the number of units in the initial sample down to 3006.

Table A.1 Sampling fractions and numbers of census units drawn for the selected main samples, 1980, 1984 and 1990

Year of survey	1980	1984	1990	1980	1984	1990	1980	1984	1990
Year of census (sampling frame)	1977	1981	1987	1977	1981	1987	1977	1981	1987
	Number of census units			Sampling fractions			Sample selected		
Number of employees recorded at census unit:									
25–49	66959	70000	74956	79	92	100	849	760	748
50–99	33881	33288	35215	42.5	51	56	799	650	623
100–199	18340	17625	18178	26	28	32	700	620	569
200–499	10649	9880	9921	15	16	19	699	600	513
500–999	3098	2796	2693	6	6	6	499	500	450
1000–1999	1332*	1169	960	5.5	3.3	2	249	360	485
2000+	571*	484	360	3	3.3	2	199	150	184
Total	134825	135242	142283	33.7	37	40	3994	3640	3572

* Estimated subdivision

There were several other minor types of withdrawal from the initial sample prior to its issue for fieldwork. Together these accounted for 135 cases. The most numerous were 'aggregate returns'. In these cases our preliminary scanning of the sample suggested that the census data unit was for a group of employees that could not possibly be employed at a single address, but were from several establishments of the same employer. Generally such cases arose in local authority employment and might, for example, include all the teachers in a Local Education Authority district. In each of the 47 such cases the employer was asked in a letter from the Employment Department research team to provide a breakdown by establishment of the employees covered by the sampled census unit. A response was received in 27 cases, while the remaining 20 employers had not replied by the end of July 1990, despite several follow-up letters and telephone calls.[3] Twelve of the 27 employers who responded did provide lists of establishments with numbers of employees so that resampling could be carried out according to the basic design. This generated 12 units which were added to the sample. A further 12 of the employers who responded indicated that they were unwilling or unable to provide the required information. In the remaining three cases it was agreed that the census return referred entirely to peripatetic or part-time employees who could not be allocated for our purposes to individual addresses. These three cases were withdrawn, along with 18 similar cases identified during the scanning of the sample.

Barring the above exceptions, census units consisted of employees of the same employer at a single address. However, the census unit did not necessarily include all employees of that employer at the address. Other census units relating to the same employer at the same address would also have had a chance of selection if they contained 25 or more employees. If they appeared in the sample it was necessary to delete all but one of the census units relating to the *multiply-sampled establishment* and apply an appropriate individual weight to the remaining unit if it led to a successful interview. There were 15 deletions from the sample arising from the identification of such cases.

In 1984, all addresses in the deep coal-mining industry had been withdrawn from the sample prior to fieldwork, owing to the industry-wide dispute current at the time. In 1990 the deep coal-mining industry was again excluded so that the industrial coverage of the three surveys in the series would be identical.

The remaining withdrawals prior to fieldwork were:

10 units where the address was too incomplete to pass to interviewers;

5 units which duplicated units retained in the sample;

6 units classified as extreme geographical outliers;

2 units interviewed during the course of pilot work.

Thus the issued sample amounted to 3006 addresses.

Questionnaire development and fieldwork

Development work for the 1990 survey began in November 1988 following a conference organized by the ESRC to discuss the uses made of the two earlier surveys and possible changes if there were a third.[4] Subsequently, users of the 1980 or 1984 data, plus a number of other academics in the fields or industrial relations, industrial sociology and labour economics, were canvassed for their suggestions for the design and content of the proposed third survey.[5] In March 1989 the Steering Committee representing the four sponsoring bodies met to begin discussions of its general design and method of conduct. Detailed consideration of questionnaire items took place in the months leading up to the pilot survey in late September and early October 1989.

Pilot work

The pilot survey was carried out in 54 establishments, 42 of which were selected from the list of addresses where interviews had been carried out in 1984. The remaining 12 were in workplaces less than three years old, identified by interviewers by observation in their locality. The main objectives of the pilot were to test the content and length of the draft questionnaires and the feasibility of interviewing a financial manager (a new type of respondent for the WIRS series). Because there were many suggested new questions for the main management questionnaire, some of the core questions from previous surveys were not repeated for some sections of the workforce even though they would be in the main survey; the time saved by doing this was subsequently allowed for in the redesign before the main fieldwork. The pilot survey included 29 interviews with manual and non-manual worker representatives and 15 financial managers; the numbers of these were fewer than desirable but were all that were practical within the short period allowed for the pilot survey.

The main outcome of the pilot work was a drastic redesign of the main management questionnaire, principally aimed at reducing the length of the longest interviews. This redesign had two main elements. First, the parallel questioning on union membership and recognition for manual employees and for non-manual employees was combined into a single section, as detailed in our discussion of the results in Chapter 3. Secondly, many or the background and performance questions which had been asked of both the main management respondent and the financial manager respondent in the pilot were retained in the financial manager questionnaire but only asked in the main management interview if a financial manager interview was not anticipated. This substantially reduced the length of the main management interviews but introduced complications for the analysis, as we mention in Chapter 1. A further reduction was achieved by reducing still further the number of questions asked of worker representatives and the main management respondent. The final trimming of the questionnaires excluded new questions which had not worked well or were considered or lesser interest or value.

Main survey fieldwork
The initial approach to employers to gain access for survey interviews was carried out by the research team at the Employment Department, using methods which had been devised at the start of the WIRS series and subsequently refined. An essential preliminary to this was to recognize that different approaches were necessary for different parts of the sample.[6] To begin with a list was compiled of organizations which, from previous experience – or knowledge of how centralized their management structure was – were thought to require a head-office approach. The list included all large central government departments, a few of the large metropolitan local authorities, all police authorities, most state-owned (nationalized) industries – or recently-privatized ones – and a number of large companies in the private sector, notably in financial services and retailing. The sample list produced from the *Census of Employment* was then scanned to pull out all addresses where the employer's name corresponded to one of these large employers. These addresses comprised what was called 'Wave 2' of the sample, the remainder – those needing a direct approach to the establishment – being processed initially as 'Wave 1'. In broad terms 'Wave 2' comprised a sixth of the main sample and involved head-office approaches to over 100 organizations. These were made by the Employment Department research team (sometimes with supporting correspondence from PSI). 'Wave 2' access sometimes entailed lengthy negotiations. In a fifth of the organizations contacted subsequent discussions were required at divisional or area levels before approval to approach establishments was given. Once that approval had been given to the Employment Department, subsequent dealings with the organizations were handled by the SCPR research team.

The target was always to obtain permission for an interview with the prescribed role-holder within the establishment. Failing this, some cases were dealt with by collecting some information at head office and the remainder locally; generally the head-office information was about matters that were factual and uniform across all establishments, but some of these head-office, partial interviews collected information that was specific to each sampled address. As a last resort, if neither of the previous two approaches could be agreed, a purely head office (or regional office) interview was conducted covering all the organization's establishments in the sample. Naturally this necessitated some questions being not answered, either because the higher-level respondent did not know the answer or because the question was only applicable to an establishment-level respondent. Figures for the location of main management interviews are given in a later section.

The remainder of the sample, 'Wave 1', received a direct approach by letter from the Employment Department on behalf or the four sponsoring organizations. This described the purposes of the survey, set out in detail the procedures for preserving the anonymity of respondents, referred to the published outputs of the earlier surveys and informed the recipient of the forthcoming request for an interview from SCPR.

Interviewing for the main survey was carried out by 147 interviewers, of whom 46 had interviewed before on the WIRS series. Almost all of the 147 attended one of the two-day briefing conferences on the survey, the remaining nine being briefed individually by SCPR research and field staff later in the fieldwork period. The briefing conferences were each conducted in January 1990, by a member of the SCPR research team jointly with a researcher from either the Employment Department, or the Policy Studies Institute, or ACAS. They involved a full description of the survey design, the definition of establishments in doubtful cases, contact procedures, the selection of respondents and a complete dummy run of the questionnaires. Written interviewers' instructions amounted to some 50 pages.

Fieldwork began by interviewers making telephone contact with each sampled establishment, identifying the main management respondent and establishing that he or she had received the initial approach letter from the Employment Department. After any further explanations about the nature and purpose or the survey and obtaining the respondent's agreement to be interviewed, the interviewer sent a letter of confirmation – together with a small pre-interview questionnaire about numbers of employees, called the *Basic Workforce Data Sheet (BWDS)*. Over 90 per cent of these were completed before or at the start of the interview, mostly by the respondent or an assistant; the remainder were completed later and returned to SCPR separately. In the latter cases the basic totals had been agreed with the respondent at the start of the interview.

Interviewing started in late January, shortly after the main interviewer briefings, and continued until September 1990, with the bulk of interviews taking place in February to July. The median date for the main management interviews was late March, compared with May for the 1984 survey and June for the 1980 survey. For financial managers the median was mid-April 1990, with nearly 80 per cent of interviews being held at a later date than the main management interview. For manual worker representatives, the median date was also mid-April; for non-manual representatives it was the beginning of May. In both cases just over 80 per cent or interviews were held on a later visit than the main management interview. The timing of interviews largely reflected the release of establishment addresses to interviewers, with 'Wave 2' addresses being later than 'Wave 1'. Large organizations earmarked for initial approaches to head offices thus featured in the later stages of fieldwork, with nationalized industries in particular being towards the tail end.

Interview lengths were similar to those on previous surveys. The main management interview lasted a mean of 99 minutes, with a median length of 93 minutes. The primary determinant of length was the complexity of trade union representation: in establishments with five or more recognized trade unions the mean length of the main management interview was nearly 120 minutes; in unionized establishments as a whole it was 108 minutes; and in establishments with no recognized unions it was 80 minutes. The supplementary interviews were almost always much shorter. Those with financial managers lasted a mean of 36 minutes; those with manual and non-manual worker representatives' lasted 45 and 46 minutes on average respectively. The latter average lengths were very similar to those for previous surveys.

As before, fieldwork quality control consisted of two distinct procedures, one applying to every interviewer and the other applying to every completed set of questionnaires. The first of these procedures consisted of a full clerical check on the first questionnaires of each interviewer; any errors or substantial omissions were documented and reported back to the interviewer for amendment, sometimes by further reference to the respondent by telephone. These early work checks covered 240 questionnaire sets, nearly 10 per cent of the achieved sample (both main and panel). The second procedure, the 'structure check', was applied to all completed questionnaire sets sent in by interviews. It consisted of transcribing a number of the fundamental items or information from the questionnaire on to a form so that the research team could assess the basic internal consistency of the set of interviews and confirm that the correct establishment had been interviewed about. Queries arising from this procedure were resolved by reference back to interviewers or their supervisors.

Further quality control measures involved a postal check on a 20 per cent random sub-sample of establishments after the fieldwork period was over. The letters of thanks and short forms for comments about the interview were sent to 875 respondents at 473 establishments; replies were received from 90 per cent of establishments and 76 per cent of interviewees. Nearly half of the forms returned were without comment (much the same as in earlier surveys). The majority of comments about the main management questionnaire were critical of its length, its inapplicability to the particular circumstances of the respondent's establishment or the difficulty of some of the questions. Such comments reflected the difficulty of designing a standardized questionnaire for use across a vast range of types of work organization and were similar to those given on previous surveys.

Overall response

The outcome of the sampling, initial approach and fieldwork operations in 1990 may be judged from the summary statistics in Table A.2, which also contains the equivalent 1980 and 1984 figures. (The 135 addresses withdrawn prior to issue have already been discussed in an earlier section.) Ineligible or out-of-scope addresses, as before, fell into three main groups: those which were found to have closed down between the taking of the census in September 1987 and interviewing in early 1990, of which there were 143; those which were found to have fewer than 25 employees, of which there were 179; and those which were found to be vacant or demolished premises or where the establishment had moved, leaving no trace of its new whereabouts, of which there were 74. In broad proportionate terms these three main groups were similar in size to previous occasions.

Non-productive addresses also fell into three main groups: those for which a refusal was received at the Employment Department in response to the original letter, of which there were only 36 cases; those for which a refusal was received by the SCPR interviewer or at SCPR offices, of which there were 334; and those at which no effective contact was made (40 cases) or at which questionnaires were completed but could not be

Table A.2 **Summary of fieldwork response for main samples, 1980, 1984 and 1990**

Numbers

| | Addresses | | |
	1980	1984	1990
Initial sample (less reserve)	3307	3154	3006[1]
Resampled units[2]	25	55	17
Total sample	3332	3209	3023
Less:			
Withdrawn at sampling stage	205	135	135
Ineligible/out-of-scope	376	449	396
Non-productive addresses	686	606	431
Interviews achieved	2040	2019	2061

[1] Excludes 210 units deleted to achieve under-sampling of SIC Classes 91, 93 and 95.
[2] Units resampled from aggregate census returns, including five generated during fieldwork in 1990.

used (21 cases). These were also very similar to previous occasions except for the number of refusals arising from the initial letter. The very large fall from 220 in 1984 to 36 in 1990 in the number of direct refusals to the Department was partly the result of an alteration to the text of the approach letter. Recent legislation governing the use of *Census of Employment* returns for government-sponsored research had made it possible to advise sampled employers directly that they would be contacted by interviewers, rather than request a response to the Employment Department first. Other factors that may have contributed to the reduced number of refusals were: the endorsement of the survey by senior officials of the Confederation of British Industry and the Trades Union Congress; and the reputation of the WIRS series among those with a serious interest in industrial relations research or practice.

The overall response rate, judged by the completion of at least a satisfactory management interview and Basic Workforce Data Sheet, was 82.7 per cent. This is some six percentage points higher than that achieved in 1984 and eight points higher than in 1980.

The response rate was analysed by region, industrial activity and establishment size. In regional terms there was a little more variation than before, with the Midlands being lowest at 77 per cent and Wales, East Anglia and Northern England being highest at 88 per cent. Every one of the 11 regions registered an improvement in the response rate compared with 1984, markedly so in the cases of Wales, Yorkshire and Humberside, and Scotland.

The range of response rates for different industrial sectors was again rather greater than for regions. In 1990 it varied from 73 per cent for Construction to 88 per cent for SIC Division 2 (Extraction; Metal, Mineral and Chemical Manufacture). Six out of the nine SIC Divisions registered an improvement compared with 1984 and there was less variation between industrial sectors than in the earlier surveys.

The pattern of response in relation to size of unit[7] was similar to previous surveys, the response rate generally increasing with size. It ranged from 75 per cent among units with 25 to 49 employees to 87 per cent among units with 1000 to 1999 employees. The range of response rates by size was similar to that for 1984, which was a little higher than in 1980.

Our discussion of the response so far has been based upon the achievement of a successful interview with a main management respondent (plus a completed *Basic Workforce Data Sheet*). As mentioned earlier, not all of these interviews were with a manager who was based at the sampled establishment. In fact, 1697 (82 per cent) of them were, compared with 90 per cent in 1984. Of the remainder, 134 cases were at the organization's head office, 136 were at an intermediate regional or divisional office, and 94 were split between two or more sites. Apart from the 94 multi-site interviews, there were two or more respondents for the main management interview in an additional 131 cases.

Response among worker representatives and financial managers
The selection of additional respondents depended upon circumstances identified during the course of the main management interview, as discussed earlier. Of the 2061 productive cases, 1831 employed manual workers and, of these, 1134 were identified as having recognized unions covering manual workers. However, 205 of these had no union representative on site, leaving 929 cases where an interview with a manual union representative was required. Interviews were obtained in 726 cases, a response rate of 78 per cent, a little lower than in 1984 (79 per cent) and 1980 (84 per cent). Corresponding figures for non-manual representatives are also shown in Table A.3.

As in previous surveys, the major reason for failing to obtain an interview with a worker representative was the refusal to grant permis-

Table A.3 **The selection and achievement of interviews with union representatives, 1990**

Numbers

	Manual	Non-manual
None of these employees present	230	3
No union members among these employees	474	709
No recognized unions for these members	121	119
No negotiating group consisting of unions predominantly representing these employees	102	158
Appropriate negotiating group, but no representative on site	205	228
Union representative present and:		
interview achieved	726	670
interview required but not achieved	203	174
Total	2061	2061

sion by management, usually at the workplace. Half the missing interviews were due to this, very similar to the proportions for previous
surveys. The next most common reason was that the representative was
never available, accounting for just over a fifth of cases. Some of these,
perhaps most, could well have been tacit refusals; explicit refusals by
the representatives themselves accounted for no more than 4 per cent of
missing interviews. In several cases trade union officials contacted the
Trades Union Congress or the Employment Department for clarification
of the objectives and methods of the survey. There were no recorded
cases of refusal by the trade union to which the representative belonged.

If we take the two categories, 'refusal by representative' and 'never
available' as our measure of union representatives' unwillingness to be
interviewed, this element of non-response among manual representatives decreased from 38 per cent in 1984 to 25 per cent in 1990. The
decrease among non-manual representatives was similar, from 41 per
cent in 1984 to 24 per cent in 1990. It may be that trade union opposition
to government policy on industrial relations, which contributed to the
increase in refusals by union representatives in our 1984 survey compared
with 1980, had abated somewhat by 1990.

A further requirement of the 1990 survey design, not featured in
either of its predecessors, was an interview with worker representatives
in situations where manual/non-manual employees were present but not
represented by recognized trade unions. The existence of such representatives was ascertained in the main management interview when
respondents were asked if there was a committee of manual/non-manual
representatives which discussed with management matters affecting
manual/non-manual workers. A further question asked if there was a
senior worker representative on site. In 41 establishments such a representative was reported in respect of manual workers; in 66 cases there
was an equivalent representative for non-manual workers. Interviews
were achieved in 63 per cent and 67 per cent of these cases respectively.
As with union representatives, refusal by management was the most
common reason for an interview not taking place.

The additional interview with a financial manager, another innovation
in the 1990 survey, also depended on information gained during the
course of the main management interview. As with the 1984 selection of
works managers, the requirement for a financial manager interview
depended on establishing that the main management interview was with
a specialist in industrial, employee or staff relations or in personnel.
This was achieved by ascertaining that the words 'personnel', 'human
or manpower resources' or 'industrial, employee or staff relations' occurred in the main management respondent's job title and also that they
did not have responsibility for financial management at the establishment. Financial manager interviews were only required in industrial and

commercial establishments, of which there were 1510 in the achieved sample. At 667 of them the main management respondent was a personnel specialist in the terms described above, but in 66 of these there was no identifiable financial manager at the establishment. Of the remaining 601 establishments, financial managers were successfully interviewed in 454 cases, a response rate or 76 per cent.

The most common reason for the absence of a financial manager interview was a refusal by the main management respondent to effect an introduction to an appropriate person. There were 101 such cases. However, in 83 of these the main respondent agreed to answer the abbreviated set of equivalent questions in the main management interview schedule (which had been skipped because they were a specialist). The second most common reason for lack of a financial manager interview was refusal by the potential respondent (24 cases). In 18 of these the abbreviated set of equivalent questions was answered by the main management respondent.

The dataset contains a further 35 financial manager interviews in cases where they were not strictly required, the main management respondent not being a specialist as defined in the questionnaire. Strictly, this is a matter of interviewer error, but it may also reflect the situation at the establishment The research team examined these questionnaires during the coding and editing stages and decided to include them in the dataset, taking into account the element of arbitrariness in the definition of the circumstances in which these interviews were required.

Coding and editing of the data

Coding and editing of the completed questionnaires was carried out between February 1990 and January 1991. It was done by a small team of experienced clerical workers, most of whom had worked on the earlier surveys. There was also substantial involvement by research team members from the Employment Department, the Policy Studies Institute and SCPR.

Particular attention was paid to the *Basic Workforce Data Sheets (BWDS)*. Obscurities or inconsistencies in their completion were the most common reasons for referring back to interviewers, but only major problems were dealt with in this way. In less substantial cases the research team were able to modify the *BWDS* figures on the basis of information contained in the body of the questionnaires or to rectify inconsistencies. Internal inconsistencies in the 35 numeric fields on the *BWDS* concerning current numbers of employees were noted in 509 of the 2061 cases in the main sample. In 202 cases the errors were minor, involving a discrepancy of 10 per cent or less between subtotals; such discrepancies were left. More sizeable – those involving more than 10 per cent of a subtotal or at least 25 employees – were examined by the research team and resolved wherever possible. Altogether 307 such cases were found, and in 302 of these the problems were resolved so that no inconsistencies remained. In 33 cases there were inconsistencies which could not be resolved and these were left unamended. All these cases with initial discrepancies at the coding stage, whether resolved or not, are identified in the dataset with appropriate codes. Analysis of these codes using many characteristics of the establishment and several concerning details of the interview and respondent has failed to show any significant correlations and it appears that the sources of the initial errors are randomly distributed in the sample.

Computer editing of the data was carried out in two stages. The first edit program consisted of a rigorous check of ranges and filters and questionnaire structure. Inspection of the questionnaires and any corrections required at this stage were carried out by the coding team. The second edit program comprised a number of logic checks, checks on extreme values and on relatively complex relationships between different sections of the questionnaires. Inspection of the questionnaires and any corrections to the data at this stage were carried out by the research team. In 21 cases the questionnaire sets were rejected as too incomplete, obscure or internally inconsistent to be usable.

When all of this editing work was complete the achieved sample was compared with the population from which it was drawn (the 1987 *Census of Employment*) and, subsequently, to the 1989 census results and extrapolations up to March 1990. These comparisons helped determine the final details of the weighting scheme to be used in the analysis. The complete data file incorporating the initial weighting scheme was handed over by SCPR to the Employment Department in January 1991. The final form of the second weighting scheme was held back until the 1989 census results became available in March 1991 and was incorporated into the final version of the dataset delivered to the Department on 8 May 1991. Further detailed work on the file was also done by SCPR in order to provide an anonymized version for the ESRC Data Archive. This was sent to the Archive in September 1991 and made available to researchers from the beginning of February 1992 under conditions specified by the WIRS Steering Committee.

Weighting of the data
All of the results presented in the main text of this report, unless otherwise stated, have been adjusted by weighting factors derived from two separate stages of calculation. The first stage compensated for the inequalities of selection that were introduced by the differential sampling of census units according to their number of employees. This first stage of weighting is imperative, otherwise the results from each size stratum simply cannot be added together to provide a meaningful aggregate. The

second, and additional, stage of weighting was applied in order to adjust for the observed under-representation of small establishments in the distribution resulting from the first stage. Details of the two stages are discussed in turn.

Where the sampled census units corresponded precisely to an establishment (83 per cent of cases), the first stage of weighting involved applying a stratum weight corresponding to the inverse of the probability of selection of census units in that size stratum. There were 12 such stratum weights in the 1990 survey: 6 for SIC Classes 91, 93 and 95, which were undersampled for reasons given earlier; and 6 for the other SIC Classes. In the remaining cases an individual weight was calculated, reflecting the fact that establishments comprising more than one census unit had increased probabilities of selection. Such cases were identified using the same procedure as that used in 1984. This entailed the Employment Department members of the research team listing all census units in the same postcode as all those in the achieved sample and then combing the lists for any instances of units of the same employer with the same postcode as those in the achieved sample. This procedure revealed 345 such multiple-census-unit establishments among the achieved sample, compared with 300 in 1984.

The second stage of weighting compensates for the fact that the achieved sample includes too few small establishments. This is because establishments which closed down or shrank to less than 25 employees between the census in September 1987 and fieldwork in early 1990 are not offset by their opposites – those that grew to at least 25 employees, or were set up after September 1987 and employed at least 25 employees, by early 1990. Further details are given elsewhere.[8] The additional factors derived from the second stage of weighting are incorporated into a single set of weights, representing both stages, which are referred to as the second weighting scheme. It is this that we have applied throughout this report and strongly recommend other analysts of the data to use also.

The size match between the sample, applying the second weighting scheme, and the adjusted population is given in Table A.4.

The 1984–1990 trading sector panel sample

Besides the main cross-sectional survey which has been discussed in this appendix so far, the 1990 WIRS contained a 'panel' sample consisting of establishments which had been included in the 1984 survey. The idea of including a panel in the design had emerged early in the life of the WIRS series and an experimental panel sample of 235 cases that had been interviewed in 1980 was included in the 1984 survey. In practical fieldwork terms the experiment had raised few difficulties and the analysis contained in our report on the 1984 results gave some indications of

Table A.4 Comparison, by employment size, of sample after second weighting and estimated population, 1990

	Estimated population		Survey sample after second weighting	
	Employees (thousands)	Employees per unit	Employees (thousands)	Employees per unit
Total	15303	101.3	15423	102.1
Size of unit (employees)				
25–49	2725	34.0	2896	36.2
50–99	2605	69.0	2618	69.3
100–199	2624	137.3	2634	137.8
200–499	3065	300.1	3072	300.8
500–999	1770	679.7	1782	684.2
1000–1999	1263	1349.4	1277	1364.3
2000 or more	1251	3353.9	1146	3070.7

how a panel sample could augment or modify interpretations of changes apparent from comparing the 1980 and 1984 cross-sectional samples. However, very few users of the 1984 data made use of the panel sample and this was held to be because of its small size and the computational difficulties of setting it up. The report of some methodological work,[9] commissioned by the Employment Department, recommended an enlarged panel sample in any future surveys in the WIRS series; discussions with experienced analysts of the WIRS data during the development stage of the 1990 survey elicited strong support for this. Because of budget limitations it was subsequently agreed that it should be confined in scope to the industrial and commercial sectors of the economy – the 'trading sector' – with a target sample of between 375 and 400 cases.

The 1984 main sample contained 1385 trading sector establishments from which to draw the sample for 1990 panel interviews. It was anticipated that a considerable proportion of those in the smallest size band (25 to 49 employees) would have closed down in the intervening six years and so all cases in this size band were included. All the largest establishments were also retained because there were relatively few of them to begin with. For the remainder a sampling fraction of six in ten was used. Prior to this, 48 cases where the management respondent in 1984 had not agreed to be re-contacted were withdrawn. A random sample of three in ten cases was then withdrawn to leave 704 cases in the panel sample issued to interviewers.

Interviews were achieved at 541 of the 704 establishments selected. Four cases were subsequently rejected, either because of incompleteness or because there were doubts about the 1990 interviews covering the same establishment as the 1984 interview had covered. The panel dataset thus contains 537 cases.

Unproductive cases included: 2 that had been used for pilot work; 87 which had closed down or were untraceable; 54 which refused an interview; 12 where interviewers failed to make contact; and a further 12 which were unproductive for some other reason (including the 4 rejected at the editing stage). The response rate of 87 per cent was much higher than anticipated and accounts for the achieved sample being considerably larger than planned.

In virtually every respect panel sample cases were treated in the same way as main sample cases. There were three significant exceptions. First, the scope of the panel included cases which by 1990 had fewer than 25 employees; these may need to be excluded from some analyses when comparisons are being made between the panel results and change between the 1984 and 1990 main samples. Secondly, interviews with worker representatives were excluded, largely because it would be difficult to ascertain that the bargaining unit used for selecting the worker representative respondent in 1990 was the same unit as the one which had formed the basis for selecting the worker representative in 1984. This consideration did not apply to financial managers, who were being asked questions about the whole establishment or its superordinate enterprise, and interviews with them were included in the 1990 panel fieldwork. The requirement for a financial manager interview (specified as in the main sample) arose in 239 establishments in the panel sample. In 35 of these no suitable respondent could be identified. Interviews were achieved in 157 of the remaining 204, a response rate of 77 per cent. A further 11 financial manager interviews were conducted in cases where they were not strictly required, making a total of 168 financial manager interviews included in the panel dataset.

The third respect in which the panel was treated differently from the main sample was in an extra phase of editing. This entailed matching up the 1984 and 1990 questionnaires and extracting from them a number of critical variables to confirm that it was indeed the same establishment that had been interviewed about on the two occasions. It also involved a number of logic checks between data from the two surveys. This process culminated in the rejection of four cases, mentioned earlier, and the application of seven possible codes indicating important apparent discrepancies between the two surveys. The two most important ones indicate that the establishment appears to have been defined more widely in 1990 than in 1984, or *vice versa*; 28 cases were given one or other of these codes and these cases have been excluded from all the analysis reported in this book.

In contrast to the experimental panel sample in the 1984 survey, the 1990 panel dataset contains no 'chance repeats', that is cases which occurred by chance in both the 1984 and 1990 main samples and which were subsequently identified as being the same establishment. Although such cases no doubt existed, no attempt was made to identify them because to do so had proved expensive on the previous occasion and analysis of the weights in the 1984 panel sample had shown that such cases added little to the effective sample size for statistical purposes. The panel dataset does, however, contain cases that also appear in the main sample dataset. There are 48 of these.

Weighting for the panel dataset involved two stages. The first compensated for the different probabilities applied in the selection of the sample (and any differences in response rate) so that the profile of productive interviews matched, in terms of size bands, the profile of the 1984 trading sector less those that had subsequently closed down. The second stage involved multiplying these weights by the weights already applicable to each case in the final 1984 weighting scheme. The weights resulting from this process were then scaled to an arbitrary base of 500.

Table A.5   **Sampling errors and design factors for a selection of 1990 survey variables[1]**

	Sampling error	Design factor
	(per cent)	
Manual union members present	1.6	1.4
Manual unions recognized	1.5	1.3
All manual employees in closed shop	0.6	1.5
Industrial action by manual employees	0.5	0.9
Non-manual union members present	1.2	1.1
Non-manual unions recognized	1.2	1.1
Industrial action by non-manual employees	0.9	1.4
Formal procedures for disputes over pay and conditions	1.2	1.1
Job evaluation scheme present	1.2	1.2
Proportion of manual employees in establishments recognizing manual trade unions	1.6	1.4
Proportion of employees in establishments with joint consultative committee	0.9	0.9
Proportion of employees in establishments with formal procedure for discipline and dismissals	0.7	1.5

[1] Source: main management respondents.

Sampling errors

Sampling errors for the 1990 main cross-sectional sample are generally larger than for a simple random sample of equivalent size. Sampling errors were calculated for a number of variables in the survey and are shown in Table A.5. The table also gives the 'design factor' which is the ratio of the sampling error for the complex design to the sampling error for a simple random sample of equal size. The sampling errors for the 1990 survey are similar to those for previous surveys for the same variables and for practical purposes a design factor of 1.25 has again been assumed throughout this report. These sampling errors need to be doubled to produce 95 per cent confidence limits.

Notes and references

1. The material on the 1990 survey contained in this appendix is largely based upon the more detailed WIRS3 technical report: C. Airey, N. Tremlett and R. Hamilton (1992) *Workplace Industrial Relations Survey (1990) Technical Report (Main and Panel Samples)*, Social and Community Planning Research, London. Colm O'Muircheartaigh of the Joint Centre for Survey Methods provided advice on the design of the sample and the weighting.

2. For the 1984 survey see N. Millward and M. Stevens (1986) *British Workplace Industrial Relations 1980–1984: The DE/ESRC/PSI/ACAS Surveys*, Gower, Aldershot, pp. 319–33. For the 1980 survey see W. W. Daniel and N. Millward (1983) *Workplace Industrial Relations in Britain: The DE/PSI/SSRC Survey*, Gower, Aldershot, pp, 321–33. Complete technical reports are available from the ESRC Data Archive.

3. The low response to this attempted resampling of aggregate returns, compared with previous surveys, appeared to derive from the local authorities' simultaneous difficulties with the administration of the community charge and local elections and, in some cases, antipathy towards central government.

4. A review of analysis carried out by users of the 1980 and 1984 WIRS data, presented at the conference, was subsequently published: N. Millward (1990) 'Descriptive and analytic uses of the Workplace Industrial Relations Surveys', *ESRC Data Archive Bulletin*, Spring, pp. 2–10. Other papers presented to the conference were mostly revised for publication and have been referred to in the relevant substantive chapters of this book.

5. Further suggestions were received at the Labor Studies Summer Institute of the National Bureau of Economic Research, Boston, Massachussetts, July 1989 and during the course of the development of the Australian WIRS in mid 1989.

6. Some of the material in this section was originally published in N. Millward, (1991) 'Sampling establishments for social survey research', *The Statistician*, **40**, 2, pp. 145–52.

7. All the analysis of response rates is, or course, in relation to the characteristics of the census units selected, not the establishment actually interviewed about. For region and industry the correspondence between the distribution by census units and by establishments is almost total, but in relation to size the differences are not trivial. The degree of correspondence between census units and establishments was discussed in an earlier section. Size is also likely to have changed between the census date and the survey interview.

8. C. Airey, N. Tremlett and R. Hamilton (1992), op. cit.

9. D. Lievesley (1988) 'The use of panel studies in the Workplace Industrial Relations Survey programme', Social and Community Planning Research, mimeo.

Index